CUSTOMER SATISFACTION MEASUREMENT AND MANAGEMENT

USING THE VOICE OF THE CUSTOMER

By

EARL NAUMANN

KATHLEEN GIEL

of Naumann and Associates Consultants
Boise, Idaho

THOMSON EXECUTIVE PRESS

A Division of South-Western College Publishing

Customer Satisfaction Measurement and Management
Earl Naumann and Kathleen Giel

Library of Congress Cataloging-in-Publication Data

Naumann, Earl
    Customer satisfaction measurement and management using the voice
of the customer / by Earl Naumann, Kathleen Giel.
       p.   cm.
    Includes index.
    ISBN 0-87389-427-8
    1. Customer satisfaction—Evaluation.   2. Customer service—
management.   I. Giel, Kathleen.   II. Title.
    HP5415.5.N328   1995
    658.8'12—dc20   94-43419
                                                                        CIP

10 9 8 7 6 5 4 3

ISBN 0-87389-427-8

ASQ Mission: To facilitate continuous improvement and increase customer satisfaction
by identifying, communicating, and promoting the use of quality principles, concepts, and
technologies; and thereby be recognized throughout the world as the leading authority on,
and champion for, quality.

Attention: Schools and Corporations
ASQ Quality Press books, videotapes, audiotapes, and software are available at quantity
discounts with bulk purchases for business, educational, or instructional use. For information, please contact ASQ Quality Press at 800-248-1946, or write to ASQ Quality Press,
P.O. Box 3005, Milwaukee, WI 53201-3005.

For a free copy of the ASQ Quality Press Publications Catalog, including ASQ membership
information, call 800-248-1946.

Printed in the United States of America

 Printed on acid-free paper

American Society for Quality

Quality Press
611 East Wisconsin Avenue
Milwaukee, Wisconsin 53202

PREFACE

A management revolution is sweeping across businesses worldwide, causing a fundamental shift in traditional practices. This paradigm shift is not yet complete; certainly, additional new ideas and other innovations will spring forth from fertile minds around the world. Certain aspects of the shift, however, are becoming apparent.

The major shift consists of organizations' becoming more customer driven. Driving the voice of the customer into every corner of the business is an expressed goal of most of the innovative firms.

The result is so-called customer-driven quality or a customer-focused organization. Customer-driven quality requires that organizations focus on core competencies—those areas where a firm has distinct competence in creating customer value. Customer value is a key driver of continuous improvement and process reengineering. Customer-driven core competencies are central to learning organizations. Analysis of value-creating activities guides downsizing, delayering, and outsourcing. The customer is clearly a central, if not *the* central element of the paradigm shift.

Becoming customer driven is significantly different from becoming market driven. Market driven means identifying market growth, market attractiveness, and target markets. Market driven is concerned with share, and marketing matrices about dogs, pigs, and cows. Unfortunately, most of these concepts are now far less relevant than 15 or 20 years ago, when they were developed.

Being customer driven means using the customer to drive continuous improvement, organizational reinvention, and radical redesign. Customer driven means appointing the customer to be the judge of a firm's value-added processes. The ultimate measure of customer-driven performance is made by customer satisfaction measurement.

The firms that achieve high levels of customer satisfaction are generally very customer driven. Such firms view every customer as a cherished asset. They strive for 100% customer satisfaction and 100% customer retention. And they strive to develop long-term, partnership relationships and alliances with their customers.

But as with any reasonably new field of study, customer satisfaction measurement, or CSM, is still in a formative stage. CSM is both an art and a science. But the field is maturing enough so that its cutting-edge, state-of-the-art business practices can be captured and described in this book.

The book grew out of the differently perceived needs of each author. Earl Naumann has taught a customer satisfaction measurement courses for four years. There has been no suitable book to use with such courses and seminars, and much of the material consists of an expansion of workshop materials. Kathleen Giel has been director of CSM at a Fortune 500 company for nearly four years. During that time, she took CSM from concept to deployment, to continuous improvement and development of customer satisfaction management. There were few resources to guide the process, so she gathered information from many sources; her experiences at her company and her learnings from peers at other companies constitute her contribution to this book.

The book is intended to be comprehensive enough to appeal to a broad audience. Managers in firms just beginning the move toward a customer-driven strategy should find the book full of ideas, guidelines, and examples. Managers in firms with well-developed CSM programs should find value in the treatment of such cutting-edge issues as internal customers, soft CSM, using the data, and gain sharing. Both authors had searched for a book like this for years; the book finally evolved out of their needs and desire to contribute to the paradigm shift.

This book is organized into three parts. The first part (Chapters 1–4) deals with issues that must be addressed before implementing a CSM program. The second part (Chapters 5–11) deals with issues involved with the design and implementation of a CSM program. The third part (Chapters 12–20) deals with the managerial use of CSM data.

Part one is relevant for all managers interested in any aspect of CSM. The topics discussed have significant strategic implications.

The second part is particularly suited for those involved in the design and use of the data. The issues discussed are the more technical research considerations that need to be addressed to develop a world class CSM program.

The third part of the book is also relevant for all managers, particularly those in innovative firms. The topics are those that are critical to effectively using the CSM data. Accordingly, the topics are largely best in class CSM practices.

The authors hope this book saves you from the mistakes many have made. They also hope it will expedite your endeavors to become customer driven and to learn how to harness the voice of the customer so that your business, no matter what its size, becomes more successful in meeting your goals. There's no need to reinvent the wheel when a guide can be used to develop your own formula for success. After reading this book, you will be able to hit the ground running!

ACKNOWLEDGMENTS

Many business professionals contributed to the developmental process of this book. We especially wish to thank and acknowledge Dean Bolon, Roger Burns, Greg Diehl, George Harad, Hollis Hohense, Ray Kordupleski, Doug Park, Dick Parrish, Jackie Pauls, Dave Pittman, Richard Wargo, Jim Waugh, Maura Burke Weiner, Meg Willet, and Pam Zych. We are particularly grateful for the support and enthusiasm of the individuals from Thomson Executive Press/South-Western Publishing who made this book possible—Jim Sitlington, Harold Utley, and Holly Terry—as well as Margaret Trejo from Trejo Production. We also wish to thank Sue Ellis and Mel McLenna for their enthusiasm, technical expertise, and sense of humor during the manuscript production. Finally, we wish to thank Bailey for an unrelenting faith in the process.

CONTENTS

CHAPTER 1:
INTRODUCTION: COMMITMENT TO CUSTOMER SATISFACTION   1

Rapid Technological Change   1
Increasing Global Competition   2
Demanding Customers   3
Customer Value   5
Management Challenges   5
What to Do   6
How to Improve   7
Sources of Innovation   8
Corporate Culture   8
The New Culture   10
A Customer Satisfaction Measurement Program   12
The CSM Process   13
Chapter Summary   15
Eastman Chemical Company   16

CHAPTER 2:
OBJECTIVES AND HYPOTHESES   19

General Issues   20
Why Are We Doing This?   20
Who Will Use the Data?   21

The Most Common CSM Objectives 22
To Get Close to the Customer 22
Measure Continuous Improvement 24
To Achieve Customer-Driven Improvement 24
To Measure Competitive Strengths and Weaknesses 25
To Link CSM Data to Internal Systems 26
Research Hypotheses 28
Implicit Hypotheses 29
CSM is Two-Way Communication 30
Chapter Summary 31
Ceridian Corporation 32

**CHAPTER 3:
RESEARCH DESIGN 35**

Factors Influencing Research Design 36
Objectives 36
Reliability 36
Validity 37
Bias 38
Meaningfulness 39
Precision 39
Comparing the Research Alternatives 40
Costs 40
Staffing Characteristics 43
Implementation Time 44
Data Quality 44
Anonymity/Confidentiality 48
Chapter Summary 49
NCR Corporation 50

**CHAPTER 4:
SELECTING CONSULTANTS 53**

Why Start with a Consultant? 54
How to Find a Consultant 55
Evaluating the Consultant 55
CSM Expertise 56
Industry Expertise 56
Project Management Skills 57
Contract and Payment Schedule 59

Interpersonal Skills   62
Commitment to Total Quality and CSM   63
Willingness to Assist in Transition to an In-House Process   63
Reference Checks   64
Chapter Summary   65
Relentless Corporation   66

CHAPTER 5:
IDENTIFYING THE ATTRIBUTES   69

Internal Sources   69
Warranties and Guarantees   69
Customer Service Records   70
Customer Contact Personnel   70
Managers   70
External Sources   71
Depth Interviews   71
The Interviewer   72
The Respondent   73
The Depth-Interviewing Process   74
Background Research   74
Conducting the Interview   78
Analysis and Summary Report   79
Depth Interview Summary   80
Focus Groups   80
Advantages   81
Disadvantages   81
Planning   82
Objectives   82
Moderator   83
Participants   84
Facilities   84
Conducting the Focus Group   85
Analysis   86
Summary   86
Reducing the Attribute List   86
Managers   87
Focus Groups   88
Reducing the List Statistically   88
Chapter Summary   90

GTE Corporation   91
Investors Diversified Services   92

CHAPTER 6:
BASIC ISSUES IN QUESTIONNAIRE DESIGN   93

Communication Model   93
Basic Issues in Questionnaire Design   96
Attitudes   96
Volatility   97
Bias   98
Validity   99
Meaningfulness   104
Awareness and Salience   105
Reliability   110
Some Basic Guidelines   111
Keep It Simple   111
Be Specific   112
Make the Tasks Manageable   112
A Questionnaire Is a Funnel   113
No Opinion/Don't Know   114
The CSM Questionnaire   115
Chapter Summary   116
Deere & Company   117

CHAPTER 7:
DESIGNING MAIL QUESTIONNAIRES   119

Cover Letter   119
Introduction   123
Directions   126
The First Questions   127
Measuring Importance   128
Interval Scaling   128
Rank Ordering   132
Forced Allocation   133
Statistical Analysis   135
Performance Ratings   136
Overall Ratings   137
Good–Bad Ratings   137
Satisfied–Dissatisfied Ratings   140

Expectations Measures   141
Open-Ended Questions   145
Surveys by Diskette   145
Chapter Summary   146
Graniterock   147

CHAPTER 8:
DESIGNING TELEPHONE QUESTIONNAIRES

Telephone Interview as Social Interaction   149
   The Respondent   150
   The Interviewer   152
   The Interview Situation   153
   The Topic   153
Most Common Errors in Telephone Questionnaires   154
The Questionnaire   154
   General Guidelines   154
   Introduction   157
   Directions   160
   First Questions   162
   Question Structure   162
   Question-writing Guidelines   163
   Open Questions   165
   Types of Open Questions   166
   Closed Questions   168
Chapter Summary   172
Computer-Assisted Telephone Surveys   174

CHAPTER 9:
PRETESTING THE CSM PROGRAM   175

What Is a Pretest?   175
Managerial Issues   176
   Budget Constraints   176
   Time Constraints   177
   Declared versus Undeclared Pretests   178
Conducting the Pretest   180
   Sample   180
   Questionnaire   182
   Data Analysis   187
   Internal Customers   188

Chapter Summary   189
Intercept Research   190

CHAPTER 10:
DESIGNING A SAMPLING PROGRAM   191

A Census or a Sample?   192
Conducting a Census   192
  Defining the Term *Customer*   192
  Costs   193
  Time Considerations   194
  Census Summary   195
Using a Sample   195
  Define the Customer   195
  Develop a Customer List   196
  Select the Sampling Procedure   197
  Determine the Desired Sample Size   203
  Identify Specific Customers to Be Contacted   209
  Collecting the Data   210
  Types of Nonsampling Error   210
Chapter Summary   213
The Praxis Institute   214

CHAPTER 11:
ANALYZING THE DATA   215

Components of a CSM Model   216
  Business Performance   217
  Overall Customer Satisfaction   218
  Summary Characteristics   220
  Specific Attributes   221
  Critical Activities   222
Building a CSM Model   223
  Identifying the Key Attributes and Processes   224
  Factor Analysis   224
  Multiple Regression   225
  Canonical Correlation   228
  Multivariate Summary   230
Tracking Analysis   230
  Cross-Tabulations   230

Frequency Distribution   231
Means and Standard Deviations   232
Derived Importance   234
Verbatim Comments   235
Motivational Issues   237
Chapter Summary   238
SPSS   240

CHAPTER 12:
USING THE DATA FOR PROCESS IMPROVEMENT   241

Communicating Your CSM Results   241
Critical Processes Ultimately Drive Customer Satisfaction   246
Defining a Corporate Metric   246
Linking CSM to Corporate Financial Performance   248
Communicating CSM Results to Customers   251
Key Corporate Performance Measures   252
Getting Employees to Use the Data   254
Intrinsic Rewards   255
Information Sharing   256
Suggestion Programs   258
Group Discussions   259
Task Forces   260
Cross-Functional Teams   260
Autonomous Work Groups   261
Chapter Summary   263
L-S Electro-Galvanizing Company   264

CHAPTER 13;
LINKING CSM DATA AND COMPENSATION   265

Recognition Programs   266
An IBM Example   269
Recognition Summary   269
Financial Rewards   270
Profit Sharing   272
Gain Sharing   273
Involvement   275
Organization Strategy and Culture   276
Technology   277

Competition   277
Size   278
Unions   278
Benefits of Gain Sharing   278
Implementing Gain Sharing   279
Gain-sharing Task Force   281
Designation of the Group   281
Developing the Formula   283
Baseline   285
Share   286
Payout Frequence   287
Payout Method   287
Deficit Reserve   288
Adjustment Mechanism   289
Payout Cap   290
Chapter Summary   290
Harris Corp.   291
First Interstate Bank   294
Motorola's Team Competition   295

CHAPTER 14:
BENCHMARKING

Internal Benchmarking   297
Competitive Benchmarking   300
Key Competitor Benchmark   300
Industry Average Benchmark   308
Best-In-Class Benchmarking   310
Planning Phase   312
Analysis Phase   315
Integration Phase   315
Action Phase   316
International Benchmarking Clearinghouse   318
Benchmarking Etiquette   318
Chapter Summary   319
Toronto Stock Exchange   322

CHAPTER 15:
SOFT CSM   323

Objectives of Personal Contact   323
Types of Customer Contact   325
   Proactive Customer Contact   325
Planning for Customer Contact   329
   Customer Selection   329
   Customer Analysis   330
   Setting the Agenda   331
   Issues Affecting the Customer Interview   331
   Flexibility   332
   Respondent Motivation   332
   Time Considerations   333
   Ethical Issues   333
Conducting the Customer Interview   334
   Summary Report   334
Chapter Summary   337
Intuit, Inc.   338

CHAPTER 16:
MULTINATIONAL ISSUES   339

General Issues   340
   Research Quality   341
   Cultural Diversity   341
   Unit of Analysis   343
   Who Conducts the Research?   343
   Research Infrastructure   345
   Costs   345
Specific Considerations   346
   Objectives   346
   Identification of the Attributes   347
   Questionnaire Design   348
   Pretesting   351
   Sampling   351
   Benchmarking   354

Data Analysis   354
Soft CSM   358
Chapter Summary   359
Moore Corp.   360

CHAPTER 17:
CSM FOR INTERNAL CUSTOMERS   363

Unique Characteristics of Internal Customers   364
Internal Customer Satisfaction Measurement   366
   A Process for Soliciting Internal Customer Satisfaction   366
   Employee Satisfaction versus Internal Customer Satisfaction   373
Chapter Summary   375
Corning   378

CHAPTER 18:
COMPLAINT HANDLING   381

Encourage Complaints!   383
Characteristics of a Good Complaint System   390
   Easy Access   390
   Fast Responses   391
   No Hassles   393
   Empowered Employees   394
   Employee Staffing and Training   395
   Customer Databases   397
   Organization Commitment   399
Chapter Summary   399
Diamond Shamrock   400

CHAPTER 19:
CSM FOR THE SMALL BUSINESS   403

   Step One: Get Help!   404
   Step Two: Define the Objectives   405
   Step Three: Identify the Customers   406
   Step Four: Identify the Attributes   407
   Step Five: Develop the Questionnaire   409
   Step Six: Pretest the Questionnaire   410
   Step Seven: Select Sampling Procedures   411
   Step Eight: Gather the Data   412

Step Nine: Analyze the Data   414
Step Ten: Use the Data   415
Step Eleven: Improve the CSM Program   417
Chapter Summary   418
Durham College   419

CHAPTER 20:
FUTURE DIRECTIONS   421

American Customer Satisfaction Index   423
Customer-Driven Core Competencies   424
Customer-Driven Learning   425
Alliances and Partnerships   426
Customer-Driven Reengineering   427
High-Involvement Teams   428
Chapter Summary   428

APPENDIX   431

Customer Satisfaction Measurement Survey, Intercept
Research Corporation   433
Graniterock Mail Survey   443

INDEX   449

1

Introduction: Commitment to Customer Satisfaction

"Total customer satisfaction" is becoming the dominant goal for many innovative businesses. Firms like Motorola and Xerox were among the first to adopt the "100% customer satisfaction" goal. For these firms, and for many other recent followers, customer focus was the outcome of a maturing quality movement. For other firms, like L. L. Bean and Nordstrom's, the customer focus was part of a founder's vision, a business application of the "Do unto others as you would have them do unto you" biblical rule. To understand how to achieve this emerging corporate goal of total customer satisfaction, we must first understand why strategic acceptance of the concept has been so widespread. Three basic changes are taking place in industrialized economies that are leading to a focus on the achievement of customer satisfaction. Developing strategies to proactively address these changes greatly enhances the probability of a firm's survival. And, ultimately, the customer satisfaction level is the scorecard that measures the effectiveness of such proactive strategies.

Rapid Technological Change

The first change is the mushrooming rate of change in technology. Virtually every aspect of a business has been touched by the spread of technological innovation. Technology has changed the overall way businesses are managed by dispersing data quickly throughout an organization. This has flattened organizational hierarchies, reduced the number of managers, and empowered employees. Interactive training and development software can be loaded onto a local

1

area network (LAN) to enhance organizational learning, and e-mail puts the entire organization in contact.

Technology has changed production processes through better machine tools, automation, robotics, and computerized quality inspections and has reduced economical order quantities to one. Computer-assisted design (CAD), computer-assisted manufacturing (CAM), and flexible manufacturing systems (FMS) have changed the assumptions underlying manufacturing efficiency. Technology has played an important role in helping firms like Motorola reach a defect level of three or four defects per million.

Technology has helped shatter mass markets into splinter groups and microsegments. With computerized databases, market segments of one are possible for industrial firms, and consumer products aren't far behind. No longer is mass advertising adequate: promotional strategies must be personalized and customized, often using a diverse array of television networks, print media, direct marketing, and sales support. Customers order through fax machines or electronic data interchange, shortening cycle times.

These technological changes permeate virtually every aspect of a business. And the rate of technological change is increasing. A firm's technological base, product innovation, and traditional ways of doing things will rapidly go out of date. For instance, Micron Technology, a Boise, Idaho, DRAM (dynamic random access memory) computer chip manufacturer, feels that its existing production technology and the existing knowledge of its employees will be obsolete in three to four years. Micron must innovate rapidly in all areas or become extinct.

Increasing Global Competition

Rapid technological change, particularly in telecommunications, has enabled the second major economic change—increased global competition. The vast majority of industries in all industrialized countries are affected in some way by the increasingly interlinked global economy. In industrialized economies, the rate of growth in imports and exports between countries has been about twice the average rate of domestic economic growth. In other words, domestic producers in all countries are facing more intense foreign competition. The rate of international growth in services is not as clear, but it appears to be much more rapid.

International merchandise trade totals more than $3 trillion annually, and services add another $1 trillion. But these volumes of trade don't portray an accurate total picture of what is happening. World capital flows average more than $800 billion daily, and transactions through the Interbank Payments System have exceeded $1 trillion in a single day. While the annual rate of growth in merchandise trade has averaged 5–6% during the past ten years, foreign direct investment growth has averaged over 20% annually.

Foreign direct investment is evidenced in the Honda plant in Ohio, the Toyota plant in Tennessee, the Hewlett-Packard plant in Ireland, and the IBM plant in Japan. The output from these types of facilities substitutes for merchandise trade and masks international involvement. The Honda Accord produced in Ohio does not show up as an import, for example, but it is certainly a form of competition for GM or Ford.

Most firms can no longer define the competition as a group of only domestic rivals. If there are no foreign competitors today for a firm, there will be in a month, a year, or two years. Exports and imports will continue to increase faster than domestic growth. Foreign direct investment will grow even faster than exports and imports, blurring the term *international trade*. Capital flows will continue to link economies more closely together so that domestic economic policies have little impact. The only way for a firm to ensure its survival is to be a world-class player. Anything less will lead to extinction.

The Minnesota Mining and Manufacturing Company (3M), based in St. Paul, has dealt head-on with global competition in the VCR tape market. In 1984, two-hour VCR tapes sold for $24; in 1995, they sell for less than $1.50! Until a year ago, Korean tape manufacturers could compete effectively in terms of price and quality. Due to a continuous improvement process that included a focus on the customer, on gain sharing, and on management leadership, 3M was able to take the lead, even with labor rates three times the Korean rate. 3M is not resting on its laurels, however, because it now sees see the Chinese coming. Chinese tape manufacturing operations require ten workers for each one at 3M, but with a pay rate of 25 to 30 cents an hour, the total labor cost is still a third of 3M's. The quality of the product from China is substandard as well, but 3M expects it to improve dramatically over the next two years. 3M is therefore continuing to focus on improvement.

Demanding Customers
The third major change is among consumers and customers. Industrialized countries account for over 70% of the world's gross domestic

product (GDP), over 70% of world trade flows, and are the destination for over 70% of all foreign direct investment. Consumers in all industrialized countries share some common characteristics. Due to low birth rates and longer life expectancy, consumers are older, better educated, more knowledgeable, and far more demanding than ever before. They expect good product quality and good service quality at competitive prices. In short, consumers expect good customer value. Unfortunately, consumer expectations are not static; they continue to evolve in an upward spiral. The diversity of product offerings has conditioned consumers to higher and higher expectations.

The predominant factor that appears to influence consumer expectations is competitive intensity. The more intense the competition, the more rapidly new product alternatives are developed in an attempt to get ahead of the competition. Meeting last year's customer expectations will not ensure success—a firm must know what a customer wants today or will want in the future.

These changes are certainly not restricted only to consumers; they apply to organizational customers as well. As businesses face stiffer competition, they expect more and more of their own suppliers. They want high product and service quality, short cycle times, and shared research, problem solving, and training. The worldwide trend toward alliances requires that suppliers and customers blur the boundaries between them to develop synergistic, long-term, mutually beneficial relationships. Supplier firms are evaluated and selected on their ability to achieve or maintain a position as a world-class supplier.

As supply chains become more closely integrated, the old methods of competitive bidding and multiple sourcing fade into the archives of ancient business practices. The new view judges each member of the supply chain by its ability to create and deliver good value. If a firm cannot deliver good value, it will ultimately lose its place in the supply chain and be replaced by a more creative, innovative firm.

In total, these three changes—in technology, global competition, and customer expectations—along with a few lesser ones, have reshaped the environment of business. And as the business environment has changed, the prerequisites for success have also changed. No longer can a firm expect a low-cost position or a high-differentiation strategy to lead to industry leadership, as Michael Porter contended in the early 1980s. Now customers expect a firm to do both. Customers want high product and service quality and they want it at very competitive prices. In short, customers demand better customer value.

CUSTOMER VALUE

As the previous discussion implies, customer value consists of product quality, service quality, and a price based on those elements. Product quality and service quality are the pillars that support price level. But product and service quality are not evaluated on only a good-bad continuum. Corporate image also affects perception of value. Corporate image is highly correlated to product and service quality, but it also reaches beyond. Examples of corporate image are environmental responsibility, corporate citizenship, and overall integrity of the organization.

The concept of customer value is closely linked to customer satisfaction. If the customer's expectations of product quality, service quality, and price are exceeded, a firm will achieve high levels of customer satisfaction and will create "customer delight." If the customer's expectations are not met, customer dissatisfaction will result. And the lower the satisfaction level, the more likely the customer is to stop buying from the firm.

Numerous studies have shown that high levels of customer satisfaction and high rates of customer retention are strongly related to one another and to corporate profitability. These studies also find that it costs about five times as much time, money, and resources to obtain a new customer as it does to retain an existing customer. As customers become even more demanding and competition intensifies, achieving high customer satisfaction is essential for survival. Any firm with low customer satisfaction will experience a continual erosion of its customer base, resulting in declining market share. The realization that customer satisfaction is the best scorecard for measuring delivered customer value presents management in any business with a constant challenge.

MANAGEMENT CHALLENGES

The constantly increasing level of customer expectation means that no firm can ever be satisfied with current success. Customers simply demand that a firm improve upon current performance levels. But customers are

Table 1.1 Airline Attributes Contributing to Value

• No lost baggage	• On-time departure
• No damaged baggage	• Comfortable seats
• Clean toilets	• Prompt baggage delivery
• Courteous and efficient cabin crew	• Ample legroom
• Clean cabin	• Good-quality meals
• Comfortable temperature/humidity	• Prompt reservation service
• Being kept informed of delays	• Assistance with connections
• Well-organized boarding	• Curbside baggage check-in
• On-time arrival	• Quick/friendly ticketing
• Availability of blankets and pillows	• In-flight beverages and snacks
• Safety	

not concerned with just any type of improvement. They are concerned only with improvement that increases delivered customer value.

The major challenge for management in any organization, then, is finding ways to deliver better customer value. This leads to two distinct, but related, questions that must be answered over and over and over again. The first is, What can be done to improve customer value? and is focused predominantly externally, on the customer. The second question is, How can we align our processes to do the what better than anyone else? Thus, the second question is predominantly internal.

What to Do

The what question requires that a firm be able to identify clearly the attributes that convey value. For most products, a bundle of attributes add up to customer value. For example, the attributes of customer value for an airline passenger are presented in Table 1.1. If an airline were meeting or exceeding the customer's expectations on ten of the twenty attributes, the what question would be answered by the remaining ten attributes. Improving performance in the areas not meeting customer expectations will increase customer value and result in higher customer satisfaction. Improving performance in an area not important to customers, say, in-flight entertainment, may result in additional costs but have no impact on customer value or customer satisfaction. So the challenge for any business is to develop a clear understanding of exactly what makes up customer value—from the customer's point of view.

Table 1.2 Attributes Contributing to Value for a Tangible Product

• Durability	• Sample timeliness
• Appearance	• Technical quality
• Reliability	• Complaint resolution
• Shipment timeliness	• Telephone response
• No shipment damage	• Information accuracy
• Driver courtesy	• Invoice accuracy
• Sales rep's accessibility	• Invoice timeliness
• Sales rep's knowledge	• Inquiry responsiveness
• Sales rep's reliability/follow-up	• Market price
• Structural designs	• Supply cost
• Customer oriented	• Environmentally responsible
• Corporate citizenship	

There is a tendency for service businesses to overlook the tangible attributes of their "product." Of the list of airline attributes, clearly a service product, almost half are tangible in some way. Therefore, a firm must be very careful not to define a service product too narrowly.

There is an even stronger tendency for businesses manufacturing a tangible product to underestimate the role of service attributes in creating customer value. The list of attributes, again from a real firm, that contribute to customer value for a tangible product are presented in Table 1.2. The majority of the attributes that create value for this tangible product are service elements. If this firm has excellent, world class product quality and subpar service quality, it may fail miserably.

The answer to the what question requires a thorough understanding of that which contributes to perceived customer value. It requires breaking down a generic product concept into product, service, and image components. Then it requires measuring customer expectations, perceptions of performance, and perceptions of importance for each attribute. Finally, it requires analysis and dispersion of the data throughout the firm to employees. This is where the second question emerges: How can we align our processes to deliver the what?

How to Improve

The how question requires that a firm creatively and innovatively align its internal processes to deliver the attributes demanded by customers.

Answering the how question requires that a firm focus internally, continually rethinking the way things are done, challenging status quo assumptions. The firm must set up a mechanism for capturing innovative ideas wherever they exist.

But each innovative idea must be evaluated on its ability to deliver what the customer wants. What the customer wants must be the unifying theme that guides process improvement. Once the voice of the customer becomes integrated into the firm's culture, its decision processes, and its evaluation and reward systems, the firm is truly customer driven.

The highly successful organizations of the past ten years have mastered the art of linking what the customer wants with how to improve processes. Dell Computer, Home Depot, and NIKE have excelled at both. MBNA, State Farm, General Electric, Toyota, Motorola, and Xerox do both very well. The firms that have struggled either have lost touch with what the customer wanted or have lost the ability to creatively improve their internal processes.

In order to answer either the what or the how, a firm must continually be searching for, capturing, and implementing innovations. Firms must constantly revitalize themselves in a world that is less tolerant of complacency and less accepting of old products and old ways of doing things.

SOURCES OF INNOVATION

Innovations are often thought of as only technological breakthroughs: the new computer chip, carbon-fiber technology, or robotics. These types of innovations are important, but there are many types of innovations, each with a different source. Technological innovations can be divided into two types. One type deals with process technology, whose new and better machine tool, computer control, or optical scan technology speeds throughput, improves quality, or reduces labor inputs. A surprisingly large number of breakthrough ideas for process technology—more than half in some industries—come from the users of the products, both internal and external. The other type of technological breakthrough is product innovation. Most ideas for improvement come from customers asking questions. Some studies have indicated that up to 70% of ideas for innovations come from end users.

Whether the type of innovation is process or product oriented, customers are a valuable source of ideas for improvements that deliver better value. The clear implication is that a firm should set up some type of formal system to solicit and capture these ideas for improvement. If a firm does not do so, the ideas will be either lost completely or, worse yet, captured by a competitor.

The third major type of innovation is managerial. This involves new ways of organizing, structuring, leading, evaluating, and rewarding people. It is becoming increasingly clear that the old ways of managing are becoming less appropriate in today's turbulent environment. All current management trends suggest that business is in the midst of a managerial revolution.

The new concepts consist of: downsizing, team building, reengineering, emphasis on core competencies, time-based management, empowerment, and learning organizations. With all of these approaches, firms are encouraged to challenge every dimension of how they do business. Management strategy guru Peter Drucker talks of organizations that are structured like a symphony orchestra. Peter Senge, who promotes the concept of the learning organization, urges managers to shatter their mental models. Michael Hammer, mastermind of the reengineering craze of the 1990s, urges managers to obliterate their work processes.

At this point, a new, ideal business form is not clear. However, almost every organization can learn from the successes, experiments, and failures of others. Innovative, creative, and successful managerial practices can be copied, modified, and transferred to other organizations. There is certainly no need for everyone to reinvent the wheel.

These ideas do not naturally migrate to other firms, however. They too must be ferreted out. An organized system for locating, soliciting, and implementing managerial innovations is just as necessary and valuable as one for technological innovations.

Innovations can take many forms and arise from many places. To capture the innovations that can improve customer value, a firm must develop a mechanism for doing so. But a formal system alone will not lead to rapid innovation. The whole corporate culture must be oriented toward seeking and implementing innovation.

CORPORATE CULTURE

A primary responsibility of top management in any organization has to do with the shaping, molding, and guiding of a firm's corporate culture.

A loose definition of corporate culture might be "the informal rules, norms, and value systems of an organization that influence the way employees behave." McKinsey & Co. uses a framework (called 7-S) suggesting that a corporate culture consists of Strategy, Structure (both formal and emergent), Systems (information, budgeting, performance, evaluation, etc.), Style (the way management behaves), Staff (corporate demographics), Shared values (superordinate goals), and Skills (organizational and individual capabilities). Regardless of the way culture is defined, however, every organization has one.

If a corporate culture is allowed to evolve naturally, it is sometimes called an emergent culture. It represents the accepted way of doing things. But the most dangerous aspect of an emergent culture is that it reinforces the traditional way of doing things. It is self-sustaining.

Because rapid change is unnatural for most employees, those employees keep doing the things that made them successful, the things they learned through job experience or education. Employees continue to use their existing experience or knowledge.

In the business environment of the 1950s, 1960s, and 1970s, emergent or traditional cultures were not a problem, because the external environment was changing relatively slowly. But the rate of change accelerated rapidly in the 1980s and has increased even more in the 1990s. An organization that has not proactively shaped and nurtured an appropriate culture is definitely at risk. Emergent cultures that reinforce tradition can be compared to swimmers wearing lead belts. No matter how much the swimmers try, the additional weight will eventually pull them under. In the past fifteen years, many organizations have met that fate.

The New Culture

The appropriate culture for the present and future business environment is gradually becoming apparent. The new culture is based on the idea that organizations must be flexible, adaptable, responsive, and proactively anticipating necessary changes. The new culture is one that shuns complacency and constantly improves, learns, and seeks new ideas. New ideas are funneled into the organization from all directions: from customers, suppliers, competitors, or other industries.

To paint a picture of what the new organization and culture would look like, the key elements will be discussed using the 7-S framework. Then the issue of where a customer focus—and a customer satisfaction measurement program in particular—fit in the overall scheme of things can be critically evaluated.

The new role of Strategy is to develop a creative vision of what the organization can become. Central to that concept is the view that the true basis of competitive advantage is the stored knowledge of the organization and of each individual. Thus, the key thrust of the creative vision becomes the acquisition and application of new knowledge.

Organizational Structures, instead of being hierarchical boxes in an organization chart, become flatter, flexible, and fluid. Decision making is done by cross-functional, empowered work teams that share knowledge and seek to integrate and harmonize processes, not functional areas.

Systems of all types attempt to capture, assimilate, and disperse knowledge throughout the organization. Performance evaluation and reward systems reinforce knowledge acquisition, behavioral implementation, and cooperation.

Management Style goes far beyond simple participatory management. High-involvement, autonomous, or semiautonomous work groups predominate, blending the individual into a team environment. The manager becomes a coach, a facilitator, a teacher who helps employees gain and use knowledge and who exerts influence through expertise and persuasion, not power.

Shared values reflect the core competencies of what an organization is good at, what it can become, and what it stands for. Learning builds upon, reinforces, and modifies shared values as the environment changes.

The Skills of an organization deal not just with the maintenance of existing knowledge. The true skill that must be maintained instead is the ability to constantly learn and constantly push new frontiers by challenging existing thinking.

Finally, Staff are the people who implement all of the changes and collectively create the culture. A sound human resources plan is critical for developing and retaining good staff.

Collectively, the 7-S's contribute to form a dynamic and fluid corporate culture. The challenge becomes one of learning, improving, and innovating. Innovations can be either small, incremental changes or radical transformations of existing processes. Innovations will emerge only if they are consistent with the underlying culture, however. This has significant implications for customer satisfaction measurement and management programs.

A Customer Satisfaction Measurement Program

For a customer satisfaction measurement (CSM) program to be valuable, it must flow from and be embedded in the firm's corporate culture. If the CSM program is just a "program," another tacked-on activity, it will be of little real value. Even though it probably won't be a total waste of time, its full potential will never be realized. But when a CSM program is fully backed by the organization, the results can be impressive.

In essence, a CSM program is a formal mechanism for soliciting ideas for improvement and innovation from customers. It is a mechanism for acquiring, analyzing, and utilizing customer-driven input to the organizational learning process. It is an absolutely essential element of determining if good customer value is being created and delivered.

If you recall, the level of customer value is the extent to which customer expectations are met or exceeded. A CSM program is the best way to determine what those expectations are. Without a CSM program, the best that a firm can do is guess at customer expectations, and guessing is not a particularly good basis for decision making.

As the two examples in Tables 1.1 and 1.2 suggest, a "product" consists of a whole bundle of attributes. Decomposing a product into attributes and measuring each attribute's performance and importance allow a firm to identify clearly what can be done to improve value.

A good CSM program generates more than just empirical data about customers' expectations and perceptions of importance and performance. A good CSM program also captures those qualitative ideas and inputs that would never show up on traditional marketing research results. A good CSM program makes the customer a living, breathing part of an organization's learning and decision processes. A good CSM program captures ideas for process, product, and even managerial innovation.

A CSM program not only answers, What can be done to improve value? but also helps answer, How can processes be improved? This requires that both quantitative and qualitative information be widely dispersed and used in various ways. CSM data must be transferred to cross-functional work teams that can implement behavioral and process changes.

It is important to remember that a good CSM program looks beyond the customer's perceptions. A CSM program can gather data about competitors so that competitive profiles can be developed, identifying competitive strengths and weaknesses. A CSM program can also provide input for a firm's broader benchmarking effort by identifying world-class practices.

Regardless of the industry, studies have indicated there is a strong positive correlation between customer satisfaction, customer retention, employee satisfaction, and profitability. The most profitable firms are usually those that have the highest customer satisfaction levels. The most profitable firms typically are also those that have the lowest customer and employee turnover rates. The greater the customer satisfaction, the lower the customer turnover and, therefore, the fewer the direct and indirect costs of customer dissatisfaction.

As mentioned earlier, it costs five times as much to obtain a new customer than it does to retain current customers. Customer retention and loyalty directly affect the bottom line. Satisfied customers are more likely to increase their future reliance on your products and services and are likely to remain loyal customers. They will also recommend you to others, which represents a very effective and effortless way to obtain new customers.

Finally, business profitability is the final outcome of customer satisfaction measurement and management. Once your CSM process is up and running and data have been collected over a period of time, you can actually quantitatively determine the impact that customer satisfaction has on the bottom line in terms of profitability, share, or any other measure.

The CSM Process

Designing, implementing, and utilizing a CSM program are best thought of as constituting a sequential, iterative process. Each time, the CSM program gets better. But because the customer's characteristics, a firm's products, the competitive intensity, and the customer's attitudes continually change and evolve, the CSM program will also need to change. However, the process of designing, implementing, and utilizing a CSM program does not.

The general process is presented in Figure 1.1. It presumes that customer focus is a top management commitment and at least partially embedded in the corporate culture. This book has been organized around the process depicted in Figure 1.1. There are one or more chapters on each of these topics.

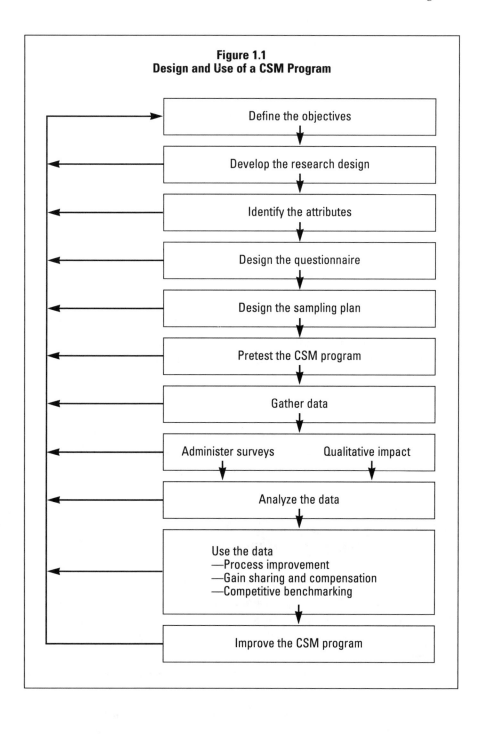

Figure 1.1
Design and Use of a CSM Program

Define the objectives

Develop the research design

Identify the attributes

Design the questionnaire

Design the sampling plan

Pretest the CSM program

Gather data

Administer surveys   Qualitative impact

Analyze the data

Use the data
—Process improvement
—Gain sharing and compensation
—Competitive benchmarking

Improve the CSM program

CHAPTER SUMMARY

In the rapidly changing business environment of the 1990s, becoming truly customer focused is essential for the survival and success of virtually any business. Meeting and exceeding customer expectations are no longer the domain of only innovative, world-class competitors. Satisfying customers should be the goal of every business in this highly competitive environment.

A CSM program should not be an add-on activity, another program, or the managerial fad of the month. A CSM program must flow from and be embedded into every aspect of the corporate culture. The voice of the customer must penetrate every corner of the firm. Only when the CSM program is a process and continually changing, evolving, and feeding new customer input into the firm will its real benefits be realized.

Finally, the CSM effort is not just about numbers and quantitative data. Certainly the latter are important, but other things are necessary to bring the voice of the customer to life. Complaint handling, proactive customer contact, and involving customers in decision-making processes are also necessary. Without these other elements, CSM data remain only numbers.

EASTMAN CHEMICAL COMPANY

Eastman Chemical Company's vision is to become the world's preferred chemical company. During the early 1990s, Eastman Chemical Company achieved several milestones toward that vision: In 1991 globalization was established as a major improvement opportunity for Eastman, in 1993 Eastman was awarded the Malcolm Baldrige National Award as well as the Tennessee and Texas Quality Awards, and in 1994 Eastman was spun off from Eastman Kodak as an independent company. To achieve such milestones requires a solid quality management process and program deployed throughout the company. Eastman's quality management process focuses on understanding the customer and managing the necessary systems, people, and products to continually improve the products and services Eastman provides customers.

As Earnie Deavenport said right after the spin-off from Eastman Kodak, "Our encore for 1994 and every year afterwards is summed up in two words: customer satisfaction." Eastman is looking to exceed expectations and create sustainable competitive value for the customer.

Collecting the data: Eastman has three major processes to capture the voice of the customer. The first process captures customer expectations or creating customer delight through first-line interface functions. The second process measures or captures customer dissatisfaction. The third process confirms customer needs. The model in Figure 1 shows the various inputs of the three major processes.

Sales calls; management visits to Eastman; contacts by manufacturing; quality assurance; health, safety, and environment; supply and distribution; technical service; customers visiting Eastman; business development contacts; quality partnerships; and trade shows are the "moments of truth" when Eastman is finding out what the customer wants and needs. To understand what the customer does not want, Eastman carefully analyzes customer complaints and lost business. Eastman considers customer complaints as opportunities for improvement.

To verify or confirm Eastman is working on the true needs of the customer, the company conducts a customer satisfaction survey. Eastman uses third-party surveys as well to confirm its own survey data and to gain information from potential new customers.

As described, Eastman has several methods for collecting information. The key, however, is what organizations do with such data.

Turning data into action: Immediate action is taken as soon as complaints are entered into Eastman's Complaint Handling System. A customer advocate is automatically assigned to every complaint. A customer advocate is an Eastman employee who champions the customer cause and who notifies the customer (1) to say Eastman is investigating the problem (i.e., searching for the root cause of the problem) and (2) to gather further information from the customer. The customer advocate then determines the solution and enters the recommended action into the complaint handling system. The sales representative follows up with the customer and makes sure the customer agrees to the resolution.

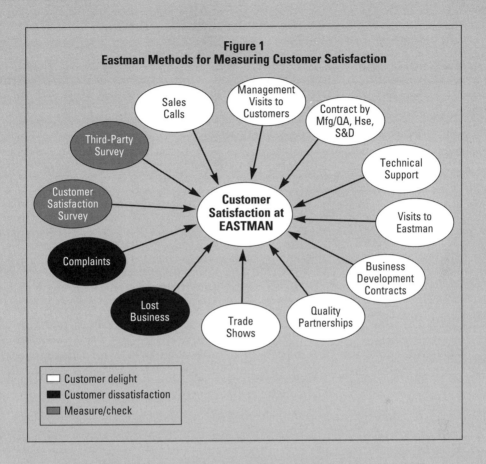

Figure 1
Eastman Methods for Measuring Customer Satisfaction

Another method Eastman has for taking action on the data is through Factor Stewardship. For every factor listed on the survey, a business or functional organization is assigned the responsibility for that factor. The business and functional organizations are responsible for monitoring their survey factors regularly, identifying improvement opportunities, and developing improvement plans and solutions to correct the process.

As teams work on projects to make improvements to Eastman's processes, teams can link into the MEPS process. MEPS stands for Making Eastman the Preferred Supplier. Improvement teams can be established based on feedback from customer survey data, complaint data, sales rep feedback, or any other input shown in Figure 1. The successes of these teams can be "merchandised" to the customer through a newsletter which is published in a regular basis. This type of communication is effective in helping to shape customer expectations.

Finally, Business Teams, consisting of members from business and functional organizations, review all needs identified. If there are projects that these teams want to work on to exceed customer expectations, these are documented and included in the company's annual business plans.

2

Objectives and Hypotheses

Clarifying objectives is the first and most important step in designing a CSM program. There is an old saying that "any road will do if you don't know where you want to go." However, as soon as you pick a specific destination, every choice can be evaluated on its ability to help you achieve your objective. If you throw in a few more details, like the amount of time you have to complete the trip, how far you are willing to travel in a day, and a desire to minimize the total mileage, you can then be specific in mapping your route.

If you want to drive from, say, Chicago to Los Angeles, with no other constraints, there is no best route. However, if you add three or four criteria, some choices become superior to others. Unfortunately, identifying the "best" route is still subjective and depends on the preferences of a particular traveler.

Designing a CSM program is much like that hypothetical trip from Chicago to Los Angeles. You know you should gather customer satisfaction data because it is the "right thing to do" in business nowadays. However, if you want to gather data simply to find out what customers think of your organization and products, you need to go back to the drawing board. You need to be much more detailed about what you want to accomplish. Only by clarifying your CSM program objectives will you be able to select from the many choices available and design a good program. Please note that *good* was substituted for *best*. It is unlikely that anyone ever designs the "best" program on the first try.

The purpose of this chapter is to discuss some of the issues that influence the selection of objectives. Those issues will be discussed first, followed by a discussion of the five most common objectives of a CSM program. Finally, the relationship between objectives and hypotheses will be addressed because that link is critical to a good research design.

GENERAL ISSUES

Three basic questions must be answered in order to develop clear, concise objectives. The first is, Why are we doing this? The second is, Who will use the data? The third is, In what form should the data be in order to be valuable? If you know the answers to these questions in detail, then you can develop good objectives.

Why Are We Doing This?

There are a surprisingly large number of answers to the question, Why are we doing this? Some firms may simply want to get "closer to the customer," trying to better understand a customer's needs and preferences. Other firms may want to measure the customer's perceptions of products and determine whether there have been any recurring problems. Still others may want to monitor customers in order to forecast changes in technology or product mix. Perhaps the goal is to get the customer's perception of product choices and to see how various competitors' products compare in terms of strengths and weaknesses. Maybe the company wants to see how customer satisfaction and employee satisfaction are related, possibly even to use customer satisfaction data as a basis for allocating incentive compensation. Perhaps firms will want to learn how customer satisfaction is linked to financial performance.

The answer to the why question could be even more detailed. Maybe the firm wants to measure the customer's perception of delivered quality, to learn whether continuous improvements are being noticed by the customer. Perhaps the answer is that the firm wants to solicit creative, innovative ideas for product improvement. Finally, firms will want to ultimately learn how customer satisfaction quantitatively impacts the bottom line.

The list of possible answers to Why are we doing this? can be quite lengthy. Unfortunately, every one of the possible answers suggested here has slightly different implications for the design of a CSM program. If you checked "all of the above," your CSM program will be complex.

Who Will Use the Data?

The answer to Who will use the data? flows directly from why you are doing CSM in the first place. Although a CSM program is typically housed in either a quality department or a marketing department, CSM data are normally dispersed widely throughout an organization. Production, engineering, R&D, administration, human resources, training, and sales development, in addition to quality, marketing, and executive management, are usually involved. In fact, virtually every value-added process in a firm (which should be all areas) can benefit from CSM data. This is especially true if internal customers are also included.

Although there are widespread potential benefits from the use of CSM data, there is rarely uniform ownership by everyone. Some managers use the data enthusiastically; others use it grudgingly. To identify objectives properly, you need to understand why some managers or departments are willing to use the data and why others stubbornly resist it. Much of the resistance can be avoided by a critical review of your corporate culture. In order for CSM to be successful, the culture must be willing to look at the organization with an eye toward removing barriers between departments. The culture must embrace the data, both positive and negative, and use them to understand the company's processes, not point fingers at the company's people.

Similarly, one department may have a specific reason or objective for using the data; another department may have a totally different reason. To design a good CSM program, you must know what support and departmental needs you have for each of the various objectives. You will probably set priorities for your CSM objectives by the level of support and needs for each.

In What Form Should the Data Be?

The answer to the question, In what form should the data be? flows from the previous two questions. If you know why the study is being done and who will use the information once it has been gathered and analyzed, then the data can be gathered in a form that is most usable to the client group (the internal customers of the CSM program). Because each manager may have somewhat different objectives and be in a different situation, getting each one to have ownership in the program means determining the desired form of the data before the gathering.

A production manager may want to measure attributes that can be directly linked to specific value-added processes. This manager may want precise data that can be displayed as tracking variables to let employees know how they are each doing in the eyes of the customer. A marketing manager may be most interested in how a customer perceives the product relative to competitive offerings. This manager needs data in a form that allows the identification of strengths and weaknesses of all products in the marketplace. An R&D manager concerned about new product development is probably most interested in creative ways that a product can be improved. This may be in the form of open-ended customer responses that spark new ideas. And, of course, executive management is interested in the overview of customer feedback that includes overall measures, corporate image, and competitive advantages.

As you can see, each of these situations requires data in a somewhat different form. In order for such information to be truly useful, it must be in a form desired by the internal customer. The only way this can be determined is to solicit the latter's input during the research design stage. A cross-functional task force is an excellent way to accomplish this. It is also helpful to understand how various groups best visually grasp data so that the results can be in a format that is easily understood and communicated.

With answers to the foregoing three questions, the objectives of a CSM program begin to emerge more clearly. The next section examines the most common objectives for a CSM program and discusses the implications of each.

THE MOST COMMON CSM OBJECTIVES

There are many possible objectives for CSM programs. However, the five presented in Table 2.1 are probably the most common. Because each has unique implications for CSM research design, each will be discussed individually to demonstrate the research implications.

To Get Close to the Customer

The virtues of getting close to the customer have been touted in the business literature for some time. It seems ironic then that many firms don't really understand what attributes are most important to customers. In fact, the process of initially identifying attributes is typically referred to as "discovery."

The discovery process normally concentrates on existing customers and begins with in-depth interviews and focus groups. Three types of information are sought from current customers:

Table 2.1   The Five Most Common CSM Objectives

1. To get closer to the customer
   The intent is to improve understanding of the customer's needs, preferences, and priorities.
2. To measure continuous improvement from the customer's perspective
   The intent is to determine if the continuous improvement efforts by total quality management are resulting in improved perceptions by the customer.
3. To solicit customer input as the driver for product and/or process improvement
   The intent is to use the customer as a source of innovation and as a partner in improvement efforts
4. To measure competitive strengths and weaknesses
   The intent is to guide strategy by providing external benchmark data that identify areas of distinctive competence or areas of strategic weakness.
5. To link CSM data to internal performance and reward system measures
   The intent is either to determine the relationship between customer satisfaction and employee satisfaction or financial performance, or to reward desired outcomes (an improved customer satisfaction level).

1. Which attributes affect the customer's decision-making processes and postpurchase evaluations in the product, service, and image areas.
2. The relative importance of attributes to the customer.
3. A performance evaluation by the customer of how well the firm is delivering each attribute.

This last type of information is probably the most common and widespread rationale for developing a CSM program. And it is probably one of the easiest to implement and achieve. The sample of current customers is easily identified and accessible. Once attributes have been identified by means of qualitative techniques (in-depth interviews and focus groups), importance and performance data can be gathered with a closed-end questionnaire, which allows easy compilation and analysis. The questionnaire can be administered only quarterly and still provide useful information about which attributes need improvement. The most significant benefit of this objective is improved understanding of the customer's needs, priorities, and perceptions.

Measure Continuous Improvement

In some respects, this objective is similar to the previous one. The major distinction here is that the attributes significant to the customer are linked directly to value-added processes in the firm. In essence, the customer conducts the ultimate performance evaluation.

The sample consists predominantly of current customers. However, this objective normally benefits from including lost customers as well. Lost customers are typically a good source of information on where a firm's value-added processes are competitively subpar. Such customers are not "lost" or "stolen." What has really happened is that they have stopped buying the firm's products, usually with good reason.

Whether the sample comprises current or lost customers, the data gathered need to be in a form consistent with the internal measurements used to evaluate the process. This means that the questions measuring the customer's perception of attribute-delivery performance are worded and scaled to measure the attribute as the customer understands it and also to yield data usable by the internal customer. This may also require adding questions directly linked to value-added processes. Ultimately the attributes will be used to identify the internal process that impact customer satisfaction.

To Achieve Customer-Driven Improvement

The previous two objectives have the intent of measuring customer perceptions of performance, and they can be achieved by using highly structured, closed-end questions. This objective is quite different and has implications for sample selection, methodology, and question structure.

Not all customers are equally valuable sources of innovation. Therefore, a firm must identify which customers are the best sources of ideas and then include them in a stratified sample along with a cross section of others. This requires a comprehensive database that tracks not only sales data but sources of innovation as well.

The questionnaire will have a larger proportion of open-ended probing questions designed to elicit customer creativity. Getting this type of information through a mail survey is unlikely. Computer-generated phone calls also limit the ability to obtain qualitative information. Telephone or face-to-face interviews are best. Computer network systems such as Internet are making inroads and have the potential to be as effective as the telephone. The interviewer must be flexible, as well as skilled in getting respondents to expand and clarify their ideas. The interviewer must also be able to quickly capture respondent ideas as they come out in the course of conversation.

Departed customers are particularly valuable in identifying areas for improvement. This is normally done through root-cause analysis. If root-cause analysis is conducted to determine reasons for departure, the methodology used is typically the telephone or personal interview that uses open-ended questions.

To Measure Competitive Strengths and Weaknesses

The intent of the objective of measuring competitive strengths and weaknesses is to determine customer perception of competitive choices. This is of great interest to top management, because it measures the success of the firm's overall strategies. Unfortunately, this objective is among the most challenging to achieve and requires a complex research design.

The previous objectives can be achieved by surveying only current or recent customers, who are easily identifiable through company records. For this objective, if only existing customers are included, the results will probably be biased: such customers continue to deal with a firm because either they are generally satisfied or they prefer the firm over competitors for specific reasons. Customers also don't want to feel they are using poor judgment by being your customer.

To survey customers' perception of the competition, a customer sample must include not only current and former customers, but potential customers and competitors' customers as well. By the inclusion of a more diverse sample, perceptions of different customer groups begin to emerge very clearly. This is precisely what the Cadillac division of General Motors found. When Cadillac surveyed only its own customers in the 1980s, customer satisfaction levels were quite high. Cadillac customers tend to be brand loyal and buy a number of Cadillacs throughout their lifetime. Hence, their views were favorably disposed, or biased, toward Cadillac cars.

When Cadillac started surveying potential customers several years later, however, it found a very different perception of Cadillac autos, one that was consistently less favorable. Then, when those who had bought competitive luxury cars were added to the survey sample, even more negative perceptions of Cadillacs were uncovered. Only by broadening the sample was Cadillac able to get an accurate measure of customer perceptions of competitive strengths and weaknesses.

There are two sampling difficulties with this objective. One is the challenge of identifying competitors' customers. The other is the issue of anonymity. The other objectives can be achieved by identifying who is conducting the research and why the research is being conducted. By identifying the sponsor, response rates are increased, and a more favorable image of the firm is created. However, in studies of competitive strengths and weaknesses, the sponsor is kept anonymous so as to remove a favorable-response bias. If respondents know who is conducting the research, they may be favorably impressed and allow that attitude to skew their responses. To avoid this, each respondent is asked to rate multiple firms—normally from three to five—but only one of the firms is the sponsor.

To Link CSM Data to Internal Systems

The second objective was related to linking CSM data to specific value-added processes. This objective is different in that the CSM data are linked to employee attitudes or reward systems. Some firms have found there is a positive correlation between employee satisfaction and customer satisfaction. Satisfied employees tend to go the extra mile for customers, thus boosting customers' perceptions of service quality. Research has also shown that employee satisfaction is strongly related to tangible product quality.

Unfortunately, measuring employee satisfaction is not as easy as it may appear. There are a number of ways to do it. It can be done by measuring overall satisfaction individually, or several measures can be aggregated to create a composite score. It can be done by determining employee satisfaction with various facets of the job, and each facet can be examined individually or combined for an aggregate score. It can also be done by measuring intrinsic and extrinsic satisfaction. Intrinsic satisfaction is the self-satisfaction that an employee derives from performing a particular job. Extrinsic satisfaction flows from the rewards bestowed upon an individual by the organization, such as recognition, promotions, or financial incentives.

As you can see, there are many ways of measuring employee satisfaction. The method chosen depends on what your internal customers want to do with the results. If you find that employee satisfaction and customer satisfaction are strongly and positively related (commonly the case), then you might want to improve employee satisfaction. This could be done by increasing employee involvement in decision making, improving supervisors' interpersonal skills, reducing job ambiguity, or changing the reward system. Your research will tell where improvement is needed most. Companies that strongly believe in improving customer satisfaction have, in some cases, linked customer satisfaction to employee incentives. They reward their employees monetarily for improving customer satisfaction and penalize them (by withholding such rewards) for not doing so. This logic sounds good, but in practice, some tough research issues emerge.

Linking individual rewards to something only partly under the control of the individual is risky. For example, many different attributes normally contribute to overall customer satisfaction. It is unlikely that any one individual or department has control over all the value-added processes that deliver those attributes. Therefore, identifying one individual's contribution is often arbitrary. If a firm insists on linking incentives to the results of the CSM program, the incentive system should be a very broad, group-based one that recognizes the whole organization as a value-creating entity and should only have up-side potential.

Some efforts to increase customer satisfaction have rewarded a 1 percent improvement in an overall CSM index. But CSM data are often not very precise. Most programs are subject to sample variation, construct validity, reliability, and bias problems to some degree. Any one of these could cause a 1 percent shift in the index. Further, customers' expectations are seldom constant—they go up. So a firm could be improving at the same rate as the customer's expectations are increasing, but the CSM index may stay constant.

For CSM programs that determine compensation, precision is important. It can be improved by increasing sample size—to a point. It can also be improved by being very careful in sample selection. And it can be improved by crafting the questionnaire, the questions, and the scaling techniques very carefully.

The preceding five objectives are those most commonly associated with CSM programs. Each has unique implications for the design of all aspects of the program. Failure to clarify the objectives is certain to present difficulty in developing useful data. However, the next step in the CSM design process serves as a preliminary check on the quality and clarity of objectives.

RESEARCH HYPOTHESES

Hypotheses are the link between your research objectives and the rest of the CSM program. If the initial objectives are clearly stated, then hypotheses flow nicely from them. If the initial objectives are ambiguous, then difficulty in formulating hypotheses is sure to follow. Thus, hypotheses serve as the litmus test for the quality of objectives. Hypotheses are questions that can be answered by the results of a CSM program. Hypotheses are normally presented as a statement of the relationship that you expect to find. Thus, CSM results will either support or refute your hypotheses. Let's return to our previous discussion of the relationship between employee and customer satisfaction. If the objective was stated rather generally, the hypotheses would be equally general. Assume that the objective was "to determine the relationship between employee satisfaction and customer satisfaction." The following hypothesis could flow from that objective.

H1: Employee satisfaction and customer satisfaction are positively related.

In order to test this hypothesis, all that is needed are a few questions measuring overall satisfaction for employees, and a few questions measuring overall satisfaction for customers. The data can then be analyzed to determine the correlation between the two levels. The results would indicate whether the hypothesis should be accepted or refuted. Unfortunately, these data are not very useful because they do not suggest how employee satisfaction could be improved.

Now, let's assume that the objective was stated more clearly and concisely as follows: "to determine the relationship between employee satisfaction and customer satisfaction and to determine what can be done to improve employee satisfaction." Several hypotheses could be derived from this objective. H1—stated earlier—would be the same, but it could be supplemented with several other hypotheses.

Many factors contribute to employee satisfaction, but let's keep it simple for now and use only four factors. Such factors as participation in decision making, role ambiguity, leadership consideration, and task variety are usually related to employee satisfaction. A separate hypothesis would be developed for each of these factors:

H2: The greater the participation in decision making, the more satisfied the employee.

H3: The greater the role ambiguity, the less satisfied the employee.

H4: The more considerate the leadership style of the immediate supervisor, the more satisfied the employee.

H5: The greater the variety of tasks, the more satisfied the employee.

Testing these hypotheses results in much more useful data. A test of the first hypothesis will indicate if an overall relationship does exist between employee satisfaction and customer satisfaction. Tests of the next four hypotheses will reveal what should be done to improve employee satisfaction: To reduce role ambiguity, the organization may need clearer job descriptions, better training programs, and clearer statements of management expectations. To improve task variety, the company may find it necessary to redesign jobs so that employees are allowed to perform a wider variety of tasks. Clear and detailed objectives should lead to clear and detailed hypotheses, which in turn lead to useful data.

Hypotheses such as the foregoing—usually referred to as research hypotheses—are the key ingredient to which all subsequent parts of a research design must be tailored. Attributes, data gathering, methodology, sample, questionnaire, scaling, and data analysis all have the goal of testing these hypotheses. A "good" CSM program is one that efficiently and accurately tests the research hypotheses. Some of the remaining chapters in this book are intended to help clarify or effectively test research hypotheses.

Implicit Hypotheses

Explicit research hypotheses flow from the objectives and can be tested by good research or "good science." Implicit hypotheses flow from the researcher's frame of reference and assumptions. Implicit hypotheses are seldom tested by the CSM program. If they are even recognized, they are tested only occasionally, in the pretest stage of research design.

One implicit hypothesis is that the respondent understands the question the same way the researcher understands it. However, the respondent may have a totally different understanding from that of the researcher and may be answering a different question from the one the researcher intended. This can be due to the wording of the question or to the scaling and response categories selected.

Take the example of a car polish manufacturer that wants to know how often a person polishes the car. The simple question is, How often do you polish? The first person who responds thinks, "I polish my furniture once a week," and responds, "once a week." The second person thinks, "I polish my car once a month," and responds, "once a month." The third person, a river-rafting guide, thinks, "I never polish my shoes," and responds, "Never." In this example, no conclusions can be drawn because of the difference in understanding of the question from interviewer to respondents.

Another implicit assumption is that the respondent knows the issue well enough to respond in a meaningful way. CSM researchers are often more concerned with the quantity of responses, or response rate, than the quality of response. However, the CSM questionnaire may not always get to the right person. A poorly informed respondent may complete a questionnaire only as a courtesy and thus not supply any useful information. In an organizational context, this assumption takes the form, "Because they buy our products, they can evaluate our products accurately."

A third implicit hypothesis is that the respondent is very concerned and interested in helping your firm improve. It may be that the respondent views completing the questionnaire as a pain in the neck. Or the respondent may have five minutes to complete the questionnaire before a meeting, so the questionnaire is skimmed quickly. The value of such responses is likely to be substantially lower than those from a respondent who reads each question and carefully selects a response category. Similar implicit hypotheses exist about the internal customers for the data: meaning, knowledge, and motivation can vary among managers using precisely the same set of data.

Implicit hypotheses constitute an insidious source of error because these assumptions are seldom tested. The best way to identify them is to put yourself into the respondent's shoes. If you were the respondent, would you be able to respond accurately? Would you be willing to complete the questionnaire? Ask your customers with whom you have an excellent relationship and rapport, to scan your questions.

CSM IS TWO-WAY COMMUNICATION

One final issue needs to be considered in the development of objectives and the derivation of research hypotheses. A CSM program is not a one-way process of communication administered to customers. It is a two-way, interactive process. First, a firm communicates a request for information to customers via some form of CSM. However, those customers must in turn communicate information back to the organization. The questions, words, and methodology of the CSM questionnaire are concerned primarily with the flow from the organization to the customer. However, the same issues are applicable to the customer's responses. The customer's words and meaning can be misinterpreted by the CSM researcher. This makes it important to allow respondents to answer in their own words. Accordingly, the appropriateness of response categories and formats should be carefully examined during development of the questionnaire pretest.

CHAPTER SUMMARY

Clarifying objectives allows a firm to adopt a clear direction for the CSM effort. The objectives must be custom designed to fit a firm's culture and environment. This usually requires an iterative, interactive effort, and it is often the responsibility of a high-level task force. Few firms begin the CSM effort with all five objectives for the whole organization. Often one or two divisions and one or two objectives are selected as a starting point. Then the CSM program is expanded to build on demonstrated success.

Clearly defined objectives lead to a cleaner, less ambiguous research design. A good initial test for the clarity of objectives is to identify the research hypotheses necessary to achieve the objectives. Ambiguous objectives invariably lead to difficulty in developing hypotheses.

The real litmus test of objectives and hypotheses is to take them to the people who will use the data. These internal customers of the CSM program typically provide uncensored feedback. If everyone is in agreement as to why the CSM effort is being done, who will use the data, and what form the data must be in, then the objectives and hypotheses are generally acceptable.

CERIDIAN CORPORATION

Ceridian Corporation (formerly Control Data) has an innovative approach to customer satisfaction in its Employer Services Division. The division provides services for payroll, human resources management, payroll tax filing, and employee assistance. It provides these services for many Fortune 500 companies. Ceridian has an overall corporate vision as follows:

Customer Satisfaction

Competitive Success

Increase Revenue

Profit

Ceridian's Customer Expectation Research Team (CERT) identified five objectives for its CSM process:

1. Determine the degree of customer satisfaction.
2. Measure factors associated with the quality of our services.
3. Identify opportunities for process improvements.
4. Establish a baseline to measure improvements over time.
5. Benchmark customer satisfaction relative to competitors and best of class.

In order to meet these objectives the team uses four surveys with different methodologies and timing: An application start-up phone survey is completed within 30 days of customer installment. A National Satisfaction mail survey is deployed quarterly. A Retention Survey is conducted by phone 90 days after the customer departed. And, finally, an annual comparative survey is conducted by phone.

Ceridian has taken the extra step to define five objectives for the surveying process:

1. Define information needed.
2. Enhance data collection tools.
3. Convert data into actionable information.
4. Develop and take ownership of action plan.
5. Achieve competitive advantage.

Every function in the company is involved in this process, for all are recipients of the data. Ceridian also uses a five-step process improvement model similar to other successful corporations: (1) determine customer requirements; (2) measure performance; (3) prioritize quality improvements; (4) implement changes; and (5) track improvements over time. Executive management reviews the process annually.

In the period from 1990 to 1993, Ceridian has made much progress by having CSM as a priority. Shipment error rates have been reduced almost 80%. On-time shipments increased from 94.4% to 99.7%. Overall satisfaction with the quality of one of their services has risen from 90% in 1988 to 94% in 1994. Lost customers in 1987 accounted for 21% of the customer base; in 1993 the rate was 8%.

Survey results are used for more than process improvements. Communications produces a CSM brochure, which sales representatives take to prospective customers as a point of discussion. Part of the executive management incentive plan and of the account representative bonus program is tied to CSM results.

The CSM process has helped Ceridian not only satisfy customers but also achieve a 13% growth rate and increase profitability.

3

Research Design

A research design is a description of the entire CSM program. The research design is really much like a puzzle of the United States. Each state makes a significant, unique contribution to completing the puzzle. Even though you could develop a pretty good idea of what the United States looks like without all the pieces, your puzzle would never be totally complete or totally accurate without each state in its proper place.

Similarly, to develop a very good CSM program, you must have all the pieces of a research design in place. You must do a good job on all activities such as sampling, question design, scaling and measurement, data analysis, and presentation of results to name but a few issues. Even if you neglect or perform poorly on a few of the activities, you will still have a rough idea of what customers think and how satisfied they are. Unfortunately, you won't have a totally accurate view of customer satisfaction unless all of the elements of research design mesh nicely together into a well-integrated program. Each element interacts with many other elements, so you must often consider many different issues simultaneously. No part of a customer satisfaction program stands alone.

This chapter focuses first on the general issues that influence design of a CSM program. Then a detailed discussion of the major research alternatives is presented.

FACTORS INFLUENCING RESEARCH DESIGN

Many different issues must be considered in designing a CSM program. Since each CSM program is unique to a particular company, competitive situation, and customer base, each CSM program should be custom designed. Simply borrowing a seemingly relevant customer satisfaction questionnaire and administering it to your customers is definitely not recommended. That is the same as taking a piece out of a U.S. puzzle and trying to force it into a puzzle of Europe. Sure, both are puzzles, but the specific pieces are quite different.

Therefore, the general issues are presented as if you are designing a CSM program from scratch, with no previous exposure to the various considerations. And the issues are presented roughly in the order in which they should be considered.

Objectives

As stated in the previous chapter, the most important step in research design is to develop clear, concise objectives. The whole research design should flow directly from the objectives. If you have only vague, ambiguous objectives, you are almost assured of having a vague, ambiguous CSM program. Clear, concise objectives don't guarantee that you'll have a good CSM program, but unclear, vague, ambiguous objectives almost certainly lead to a poor program that may not be actionable. Table 3.1 is a summary of objectives for the Milliken & Co. customer satisfaction measurement program.

Reliability

Reliability of a CSM program is the extent to which research results would be stable or consistent if the same techniques were used repeatedly. Reliability issues can be raised for most aspects of a CSM program. Sampling, questionnaire design, question wording, interviewer behavior, scaling, and measurement all present potential reliability problems.

In the sampling of respondents, personal factors such as health, fatigue, emotional state, and motivation can influence reliability. Characteristics of individuals such as education level, organization position, and experience can cause responses to vary. Situational factors such as a family crisis or an organizational restructuring can cause reliability problems. Questionnaire ambiguity, complexity, appearance, and question sequencing can also cause reliability problems. Throughout this

Table 3.1   Milliken & Company Customer Satisfaction Measurement

Key Objectives

- Fully supported by top management
- Addresses issues that are important to our customers
- Unbiased
- Statistically reliable
- Assesses strengths, weaknesses, and competitive advantage
- Determines relative importance of key performance measures
- Comparable across business units
- Consistent over time
- Backed up with corrective action

book, reliability will emerge as a significant issue in the design of a CSM program.

Validity

Validity is concerned with whether a CSM program, or a particular item, really measures what it is supposed to measure. A manager may want to measure customers' perceptions of a particular attribute, say, quality, and develop a specific question. However, the respondent might interpret the question to mean something quite different. The item might be worded like this:

	Very Poor					Very Good	
Please rate the quality of product A.	1	2	3	4	5	6	7

A respondent might interpret *quality* to mean how long a product will last. Therefore the answer would be an indication of durability, whereas the manager's definition of quality may not have included durability. Thus this item would lack validity because it doesn't measure the attribute it is supposed to measure. This is usually referred to as construct validity, with construct being roughly analogous to concept.

When multiple questions are used to measure a specific attribute—something that should be done whenever possible—another problem arises that is called convergent validity. Aggregating responses to questions is appropriate only when the questions all measure the same thing. If the questions are consistent with one another, then the survey has convergent validity.

Issues influencing construct and convergent validity are discussed in more detail in subsequent chapters, discriminating between validity, criterion validity, and sample validity. For now, however, it is important to recognize that a CSM program should actually measure the attributes under investigation if it is to be valid.

Bias

Bias occurs when some aspect of the research design causes the respondent to respond in a certain way, normally more favorably, regardless of what the respondent's true feelings are. Again, as with reliability and validity problems, bias can arise from many sources.

Bias can be introduced by the sample selection. A hotel chain decided to survey customers who stayed at the hotel at least four separate times during the previous year. The hotel felt that such customers, primarily business travelers, were valuable and it wanted to measure their satisfaction levels. However, by surveying high-frequency customers, the hotel had selected a brand-loyal segment that was not representative of its total customer base. Because brand-loyal customers typically have higher satisfaction levels, the hotel chain was almost certain to get favorable, but biased, results. The sampling procedure was certain to exclude those who had stayed only once, were dissatisfied, and never returned.

Bias can also be introduced by question sequence, wording, and scaling. For example, the following item appeared on a customer satisfaction questionnaire for a major airline:

	Strongly Agree						Strongly Disagree
The ticketing personnel were very helpful.	1	2	3	4	5	6	7

By wording the question in a highly positive way, "very helpful," respondents were led to formulate a positive response. This was reinforced by placing Strongly Agree on the left side of the scale, because respondents have a tendency to skew responses toward the left side of this type of scale.

The goal is to strive for an unbiased research design, because the results will be more actionable. However, as we shall see later, there have been instances when management didn't really want unbiased data. In some cases, management wanted some positive feedback from customers that documented what a great job they (management) were doing.

Meaningfulness

It is entirely possible to develop a research design that is both reliable and unbiased, as well as composed of very valid questions, but the issues being addressed lack importance to the customer. The issues may lack meaningfulness, and although respondents will answer most questions that you ask of them, the results from such an approach will be equally meaningless and of little value. Therefore, identifying meaningful issues is an important early step in the design process.

Responses may lack meaningfulness for several reasons. First, as just suggested, the wrong issues may be addressed. Second, the respondent may simply lie to protect the feelings of the interviewer or the company or to keep from appearing stupid. Third, respondents may not have any opinion about an issue, but we force them to respond. Fourth, respondents may lack knowledge the research assumes they have.

If the questions lack meaningfulness to the customer, the whole CSM research program will be of little value. This is the classic representation of garbage in, garbage out. It is precisely why it is important to spend so much effort on the up-front research design issues instead of rushing out to gather data.

Precision

Precision is the ability of a CSM program to accurately detect small shifts in customer attitudes. In order for research to be precise, the research design must first be reliable, valid, unbiased, and meaningful. However, a research program can be all of these and still lack precision.

One of the major obstacles to precision is sampling error. Although a sample usually yields a good approximation of the attitudes of total customer base, a sample usually does not exactly mirror the attitudes of all customers. Although there are ways of reducing sampling error, which are discussed in Chapter 10, the only way to eliminate this error is to have all customers respond to your survey. This is obviously an unlikely occurrence. Therefore, sampling reduces precision in virtually all research, but there are techniques that can be used to estimate this source of error.

The best examples of precision estimates are found in political polling. Most political polls give a preference rating and attach a margin of error, stated, "This is plus or minus three percentage points." As shall be shown later, this can also be done for customer satisfaction surveys.

Although the topic of survey precision is discussed later as it relates to question development, measurement, and scaling, precision is generally not a major problem in a CSM program. The only time precision does become very important is when incentive compensation is based on short-term changes in satisfaction levels. When individual or group compensation is tied to CSM data, then the organization has a responsibility to increase the precision of the research effort. Although the issue of linking CSM data to compensation is discussed later, if one of your objectives concerns compensation, precision *must* be designed into the research program.

COMPARING THE RESEARCH ALTERNATIVES

The issues discussed thus far in this chapter are relevant to any research design. Now, the specific considerations in choosing a specific type of data-gathering method are discussed. Please keep in mind that these are not mutually exclusive discussions. Your company's research objectives and the issues of reliability, validity, bias, meaningfulness, and precision also influence the choice of data-gathering method.

There are three basic types of data-gathering methods: mail, telephone, and personal interviews. Each approach has unique advantages and disadvantages, and there is certainly no best method. Further, it is possible, and sometimes advisable, to use all three approaches within one research design. For example, you may want to notify the sample for a telephone survey by first using a mailed introduction letter asking for respondents' cooperation. There are many different ways of combining the three approaches, but for now, the discussion will examine each as a discrete entity.

An additional emerging option for research design formats is the use of e-mail and global communications networks such as Internet. In the past year, "virtual" focus groups have convened on Internet to probe marketing issues, primarily with young, computer-literate individuals. The future of this option, as well as that of using focus groups conducted via teleconference, is wide open.

Costs

Accurate determination of research costs is difficult. Incremental costs associated with a given project are usually identifiable, especially when the CSM program is outsourced, or contracted out to an independent research firm. However, overhead costs are more difficult to identify, as are many indirect internal costs. Salaries at various organizational levels, time allocations for employees, computer time for data analysis, software programs, and telephone systems are all examples of cost elements that are often hard to determine and allocate incrementally to a CSM program. Despite the inherent ambiguity, certain general conclusions can be drawn about each approach, although the specific cost elements are highly company specific.

The predominant factors influencing the costs of a CSM program are sample size, number of attributes being evaluated, geographic dispersion of the sample, and frequency of administration. The larger the sample size, the greater the costs are. Because personal interviews represent the most costly technique per customer contact, followed by telephone and mail in that order, increasing sample size has the most dramatic impact on personal interviews. Telephone surveys experience a moderate increase in total costs, and the total cost associated with mail surveys increases the least as sample size increases.

For mail surveys, the increased costs are represented by postage, reproduction of the instrument and/or computer diskette survey materials, and incremental labor for mailings or data input. For telephone surveys, the increased costs consist predominantly of incremental interviewer compensation and long-distance phone charges. For personal interviews, the incremental costs are contained in interviewer time, travel, transportation, and, in some cases, lodging.

The number of attributes being evaluated influences costs in much the same way as sample size. The greater the number of attributes, the greater the costs. As the number of attributes increases, the length of the interview increases, so personal interviews and telephone surveys are affected most. The incremental costs of adding questions has a minimal cost impact on mail surveys, though it can affect response rates.

The number of attributes influences costs in another way. A large number of attributes being evaluated typically results in an even larger number of questions. The more questions that are asked, the greater the imposition on respondents. A long questionnaire can reduce response rates and therefore increase sampling costs.

When a respondent is asked to complete a mail survey, the normal evaluative process goes something like this: The envelope is opened, cover letter read, and questionnaire skimmed. If the questionnaire is considered too long, it is simply thrown away then. *Too long* can be determined by the number of pages, thickness, overall appearance, or number of questions. If the questionnaire is frequently discarded, the overall response rate will be low, and a larger number of respondents will need to be contacted to generate sufficient sample size.

The more widely dispersed the customers are, either domestically (in the United States) or globally, the higher the costs. Personal interviews are influenced most significantly due to travel, followed by telephone surveys, due to long-distance charges. Mail surveys, at least when administered in the United States, are affected relatively little by geographic dispersion.

If one of the initial objectives for the CSM program is competitive benchmarking, then geographic dispersion of customers becomes quite important. In the beverage industry, for instance, significant differences in competition occur in various locations. Coca-Cola may be the dominant soft drink in New York, but Pepsi-Cola may be dominant in West Coast markets. Budweiser may experience significant competition from Coors in Colorado, but in Texas, Coors may be a weak competitor, and Lone Star may be important. Further, customers in Texas may have a different perception of Coors from that of customers in Colorado.

In order to identify these variations in the nature of competition, the competitive benchmarking aspects of a CSM program must cover a widely dispersed customer base. The implication is that if your customers are dispersed widely and you have large variations in your competitors in different geographic areas and you want to conduct competitive benchmarking, then your CSM program will be much more costly.

Finally, frequency of administration of the CSM program influences cost. Basically, the more frequently you gather data, the more costly the program. If your industry is relatively stable, then gathering competitive benchmark data once a year may be completely adequate. However, if your industry has a very dynamic competitive nature, you may need to gather competitive data quarterly. If you survey your own customers monthly, the CSM program will be less costly than one that surveys customers on a transaction basis and has a continual stream of CSM data.

There are no golden rules that determine the appropriate frequency of gathering data. The primary determinants are managerial. What are the objectives the CSM program is trying to attain, how often must data be gathered to attain those objectives, and how much is the organization willing to spend? Answers to questions like these are what dictate the frequency of administration.

Staffing Characteristics

Human resource requirements play an important role in selection of a CSM program. The initial issue is whether to handle the CSM program in-house or to outsource the program to an independent firm. If an organization lacks the staff, in terms of either numbers or skills, the entire CSM program may be outsourced. If some human resources are available internally, then portions may be outsourced. For many firms this is not an easy decision due to cost variations and design complexity. Often an organization begins by hiring an experienced CSM firm to implement a program, and then the organization itself takes control once the necessary skills are developed internally. We will discuss this in depth in Chapter 4. Let's assume that the CSM program is being handled internally for now and compare the alternatives.

Personal interviews are the most labor-intensive and require a much larger number of interviewers and supervisory staff. Personal interviews require more initial training in conducting interviews and interpreting responses, because face-to-face contact results in much greater variability. The supervisory staff must be constantly available to the interviewers should unanticipated difficulties arise that require immediate resolution. For a national consumer survey, teams consisting of five interviewers and a supervisor each may simultaneously be gathering data in twenty different cities, for example. To ensure good-quality data, all interviewers should have the same training, questionnaire objectives, and a similar sampling situation such as mall intercepts.

Telephone surveys often require the same amount of interviewer training, but the number of interviewers is considerably smaller. Whereas 100 interviewers and 15 supervisors may be necessary for a national personal survey, a national telephone survey can be conducted by 10 interviewers and 1 supervisor. However, response rates for telephone surveys are influenced by the interviewer's interpersonal skills and ability to elicit respondent cooperation without the aid of the visual cues that exist in personal interviews. A CSM telephone survey is often longer than a normal telephone conversation (unless there are teenagers in your household), but more usable responses are generated per hour of interviewer time than in personal interviews. Although completion rates vary significantly from study to study, five or six completed interviews can usually be completed per hour in a telephone survey, which is about twice the normal rate for personal interviews.

Once a questionnaire for a mail survey is designed, the human resources requirements are minimal. A staff of one or two people could administer a survey, analyze the data, and present the results. The mail survey, therefore, is far less labor-intensive and requires less technical skill and training. The same is true for surveys on diskette. Computer e-mail or Internet surveys may elicit questions or action items from customers. Internal staff must have a procedure for responding to these.

Implementation Time

How fast the organization wants the data is another important consideration. If management wants the data "yesterday," then telephone surveys have a significant advantage. With the computer-assisted-telephone-interview technology, the questionnaire appears on a computer screen, and responses are entered instantly into the database. The most time-consuming activity often is development of the sample frame of telephone numbers.

Mail surveys may take three or four months due to questionnaire development and printing, mailing time, and completion delays. A respondent may have a questionnaire for a week or two before completing and returning it, for example. Personal interviews may take three or four months, but for different reasons. Interviewers must be recruited, selected, and trained, and even then, completion rates are low.

This discussion is concerned with implementation time, or the time it takes to actually gather the data. In terms of the whole CSM program, the most time-consuming portion consists of the initial identification of objectives, hypotheses development, determination of the attributes, development of a database of customers, and design of the questionnaire. This process normally takes months to complete.

Data Quality

The goal of every CSM program is good-quality data, and a number of factors influence the quality of various types of data. The factors are influenced by the choice of mail, telephone, or personal surveys as data-gathering techniques. These issues relate to sample selection, identification of correct respondents, and question complexity.

The term *customers* is rather generic and can include channel inter-mediaries of various types such as brokers, agents, business organiza-tions, and ultimate consumers. The term could also apply to internal customers within the same organization. The discussions in this chapter are applicable to all types of customers. Among external customers, con-sumers present the greatest research challenges due primarily to the difficulty of accessibility and lack of motivation to assist in a firm's continuous-improvement effort. For business customers, an organization should have a much better description of the sample frame and a more highly motivated respondent group. These characteristics have a signifi-cant impact on data quality.

Data quality is highest when all customers are known (names, ad-dresses, phone numbers, etc.). This allows all customers an opportunity to be included in a survey, thus reducing the potential bias that results from an incomplete sample frame. Whereas obtaining a complete cus-tomer list is possible for businesses, it is very difficult to get one for con-sumers.

More than 90% of U.S. households have telephones. However, sam-pling can still be difficult because of unlisted numbers, new numbers, temporary disconnects, and households in transition and without phone service. Telephone consumer surveys can also be complicated by house-hold composition. Single individuals are harder to reach than those in a larger family unit. Vacations, part-time residences, and a respondent's working hours all influence accessibility. Households without a tele-phone tend to be lower income, elderly, and rural. The normal noncon-tact rate for consumer telephone surveys is about 40% of all those num-bers dialed. Depending on the objectives of the CSM program and the characteristics of the total customer base, such issues may not present a problem. However, in some cases, these factors could reduce data quality in a telephone survey.

The same concept also applies to mail surveys. Mailing lists are seldom accurate, particularly in a highly mobile population such as that of the United States. Although most individuals provide a forwarding ad-dress, you can never be certain if the questionnaire was forwarded, re-ceived, discarded, or lost. Mail surveys are, however, a good method to contact hard-to-reach respondents such as those who are rarely home. Unfortunately, you can never be certain if the characteristics of those who do respond are the same as those who do not respond. Because re-sponse rates of 25% are not unusual in mail surveys, nonresponse can be a data-quality problem. If the nonrespondents are quite different, data quality can suffer.

Personal interviews have the highest response rate—75–85%—so obtaining respondent cooperation is highest with this method. However, if the individuals who are asked to respond are not representative of the total customer base, data quality may suffer. For example, research indicates that interviewers tend to select (sample) respondents who are similar to themselves in some way. Older interviewers tend to interview view older respondents, women prefer to interview women, Hispanics prefer to interview Hispanics, and so forth. Even when that issue can be overcome by the stratified sampling technique of interviewing a certain number of individuals in various categories, data quality can still suffer.

Even if the sample frame is completely accurate, reaching the correct respondent is not guaranteed. With a mail survey, a questionnaire may reach a household, but may be completed by someone other than the desired respondent. Perhaps the wife or a son or daughter completes a questionnaire intended for a male, head of household. Perhaps a daughter completes a survey intended for an elderly parent. In research vernacular, this issue is referred to as substitution, wherein someone other than the desired respondent is substituted. In telephone and personal interviews, the problem of substitution can be documented. However, in mail surveys, documenting substitution is difficult.

Reaching the correct respondent is not a problem only with consumers. The same situation also exists for business customers. In most business situations, a variety of individuals, often from different functional areas or departments, are involved in purchase decisions and postpurchase evaluation. This group of individuals, typically referred to as the buying center, presents a thorny research dilemma. Which individual or individuals should be surveyed?

The situation assumes, of course, that you can identify which individuals were involved in the purchase decision for a particular product. To have an accurate sample frame, you would need to know who represented production, engineering, purchasing, quality assurance, and research and development, for example. Then you would need to decide which respondents you would want in your survey, for each would possibly have somewhat different perceptions. Once you've identified who the buying center members are and whom you want to survey, the substitution problem arises.

You may try to reach the top purchasing manager, but that person may not be available for numerous reasons. You must then decide whether *any* purchasing agent will suffice as a respondent or whether there is a preferred second-choice respondent. If you allow substitution in a situation like this, you must monitor the responses to see if the substitute's responses differ from your preferred respondent's. If there is a difference in responses, you then try to determine whether the variation is due to differences in the respondent or is a normal variation due to different experiences by that organization.

Whether the respondents are consumers or business customers, reaching the correct respondent is not an easy task. If substitution occurs, either intentionally or unintentionally, then data quality can be compromised.

A third major factor influencing data quality is the complexity of the topic being examined. Mail surveys, in most cases, are not well suited for very complex issues. A high degree of complexity normally requires a commensurately high degree of respondent effort. If the respondent perceives too much effort is required, the conclusion may be reached that completing the questionnaire is "too much trouble." Also, a question on a mail survey may have a scaled response category followed by an open-ended probe like the following.

Please rate the quality of your dining experience.   ☐ Above expectations
                                                          ☐ Met expectations
                                                          ☐ Below expectations

If you answered the previous question with "Below expectations," please describe in as much detail as possible why your dining experience was below your expectations.

The first question seems simple enough. It is an overall quality measure with three reasonably clear categories. However, many possible factors could contribute to the quality of a dining experience. Everything from valet parking, to furnishings, service, food, or price could contribute to perceived quality level. Therefore, the open-ended probe could raise a complex set of issues, and few respondents would answer in detail. It would simply be too much trouble to write a paragraph explaining the cause of unmet expectations.

However, if the same questions were asked in a telephone survey or personal interview, answers to the probe would be much more detailed.

Respondents would probably be willing to explain in great detail the specific reasons for the "Below expectations" response.

Conversely, if respondents in a telephone survey were queried with an item like the following one containing many response categories, they may have difficulty recalling all of the categories.

Please identify the percentage of times that the following alternatives are used in the event that your customers' pet food orders cannot be filled by their normal or requested delivery date.

a. Backorder—hold until all product is available and ship complete.   ___%
b. Cancel unavailable items and ship balance by committed date.   ___%
c. Split-ship—ship quantities available now and out-of-stock
    items as they become available.   ___%
d. Cancel order and go to another distributor.   ___%
e. Substitute.   ___%
f. Other   ___%
                                                                             100%

Such an item would present no difficulty at all to respondents in a mail survey.

If your objective is to solicit a good deal of free-form customer response to open-ended questions, then telephone or personal interviews will generate better data quality. On the other hand, if your objective is to solicit responses to closed questions, especially those that are scaled or have many response categories, then a mail survey that allows respondents to visually analyze the categories will probably produce better data quality.

Anonymity/Confidentiality

Most customer satisfaction surveys are neither anonymous nor confidential. A CSM survey lacks anonymity because in most cases, the customer knows immediately, in the introduction, who is sponsoring the research, and the firm obviously knows who the customer is. This is normal in CSM research, for the very act of conducting a CSM survey often creates goodwill among customers. The implicit message in any CSM program is that the customer is important. Responses are not confidential in that if a complaint is voiced by a customer, a closed-loop program implies that complaining customers will be contacted directly at the customer's request.

There are two situations in which anonymity and confidentiality are important. When CSM surveys are reaching consumers, very often respondents would like their responses to remain anonymous. Assume that your dentist conducts a CSM survey and you receive a questionnaire that is numbered. If you have a complaint, would you be hesitant to respond honestly when you think that the number can identify you? Would you be hesitant to respond if you had an appointment in two weeks? For situations like these, it is generally advisable to keep respondents anonymous, allowing respondents to identify themselves if they so choose.

The other situation in which anonymity and confidentiality become important is the one when competitive benchmarking is done. As is discussed in a later chapter, competitive benchmarking is most effective when the sample includes both your own customers and competitors' customers. In these cases, more unbiased data can be obtained by keeping the sponsor of the research anonymous. Some respondents might skew their responses positively if they know who is conducting the research.

CHAPTER SUMMARY

Research design is a fundamental part of the CSM process. A number of factors influence the design process. The research design flows directly from the stated objectives. The design must be developed so as to ensure reliability, or the extent that the results are consistent, as well as to ensure validity, or whether the CSM program is really measuring the original intent. Care must be taken to eliminate bias from the research. Questions must be meaningful to the customer. Finally, precision, or the ability of the CSM program to detect shifts in customer attitudes, is important to include in the design process.

The main design formats are personal interview, telephone, and mail. Each one of these formats has strengths and weaknesses. In order to choose the best methodology, the factors of costs, staffing, timeline, and data quality must be analyzed. Anonymity and confidentiality must be addressed as well.

The overall research design provides a shell within which other parts of the CSM program are constructed. As a CSM program is developed, the initial research design is invariably modified. However, to the extent possible, the initial research design will provide guidance and consistency to the remaining steps.

NCR CORPORATION

Since its acquisition by AT&T in 1994, NCR is now known as AT&T Global Information Solutions. However, because its CSM program was developed while it was known as NCR, that name is used here. AT&T has an equally strong commitment to CSM.

Research Design at NCR

NCR is committed to a company-wide, worldwide CSM program. The initial impetus for its focus on customer satisfaction came from the chairman of the Board of Directors. The strong support of top management led to rapid acceptance throughout NCR, but the process was not painless.

NCR partitioned its customer base into two groups. The first, and smaller, group comprised the critically important customers that were vital to NCR's future success. The second group consisted of the rest of the customer base. The research design required that the first group be subject to a census, and the second group be subject to a stratified random sample.

Four questionnaires were administered to respondents in customer firms. Each questionnaire shared common elements with the other three questionnaires, but all were customized to fit the respondent group. The shortest questionnaire contained 67 questions, the longest over 100 questions.

In each customer firm, four types of respondents were surveyed. The first group contained the most-senior-level executives with any impact on the purchase of NCR products. These respondents typically held the title of vice president, executive vice president, chief operating officer, or chief executive officer. In a customer firm, there were usually two or three such individuals who were surveyed. Incidentally, the questionnaire for these respondents was the shortest.

The second type of respondent surveyed was the top technical executive. Typically, this would be a vice president of data processing or vice president of store operations. This individual was concerned with the technical view of products and services.

The third group contained individuals in the administrative position responsible for paying bills and tracking invoices. This group was more diverse and could include a director of purchasing or materials, director of accounts payable, or some other functional area. Such individuals tended to be concerned with the procedural interaction between their firm and NCR.

The fourth group consisted of the managers in charge of users of NCR products. They could be a department head or a store manager at the outlet of a retail chain. This group was sampled for each customer firm, whereas individuals in the other three groups were all surveyed.

Whenever possible, NCR used telephone survey methodology. But in some countries that lacked an adequate telephone research infrastructure, mail surveys were used. In other countries such as Japan, personal interview methodology was necessary.

The telephone questionnaire took about twenty minutes to administer. Initially, NCR managers thought that respondents weren't likely to agree to such long interviews. But because the topic was of high interest and importance to the respondents, cooperation was no problem.

Because NCR believed the attitudes of customers were fairly stable, the survey was administered only annually. But the program has not remained static; it has continued to evolve.

NCR has added an additional customer partition—the small business customer. And the four groups in each customer firm were expanded to include the actual users of NCR products, such as the checkout clerks in a grocery store.

NCR also has included lost customers—those who had recently switched to a competitors' products. Then NCR also began surveying competitors' customers to develop a competitive profile. Then NCR encouraged functional areas, such as field engineering, to gather more-detailed CSM data that would be more actionable for its needs.

NCR's customer satisfaction research design is very thorough and includes a variety of qualitative and quantitative techniques. But the most important characteristic is the company's willingness to improve research design and allow it to continually evolve, getting better and better.

4

Selecting Consultants

Imagine for a moment that you and your CSM task force/management team are on a white-water rafting adventure. You have just reached a point where there is a deep gorge. Once you enter the gorge, you are committed for the next portion of the journey. There are no escape routes. You can hear the roar of the first rapid, which fills you with both excitement and apprehension. This stretch of the river has been rafted before, but there are only sketchy maps. The reason the maps are only sketchy is that the river changes constantly due to water level, weather, and geologic activity; the element that is always consistent, however, is your rafting team. Your team has been planning this river journey for some time now, and the prior portion of the journey has required some maneuvering and teamwork, but no one has been in danger. Now you are approaching the most challenging part. You know that you have talent in your group and maybe even appropriate technical expertise to conquer the rapids, but you are not sure that you want to do so without an "expert." The question is, Do you look to each other to determine if you have a rafting-guide-turned-corporate-exec in your group or do you hire a professional guide? Coincidentally, at the entrance to the gorge are a number of rafting outfitters who will guide you down the gorge. All of the outfitters have the ultimate goal of getting you through the gorge, but they all also have different philosophies, practices, and of course charges. If you want a guide, do you look for the least expensive guide, the guide with the most experience, or the guide with the most innovative ideas? Or do you just decide to go for it on your own?

The process of determining how to begin your CSM journey is not unlike the scenario described. Obtaining commitment to CSM and identifying common CSM objectives can be very intense and time-consuming; once your organization decides to embark upon the CSM path, however, the technical and organizational details that involve initiation of the process require some thought and appropriate decisions. Organizations that have been through the CSM process have used one of two approaches at this point. You must decide whether to conduct the CSM work through in-house expertise or to outsource some or all of the process with the use of consultants. For most organizations, use of an outside consultant has definite advantages in the initial stages of development, design, and implementation; long term, however, the CSM function has the most effectiveness as a integral part of the organization.

WHY START WITH A CONSULTANT?

Every organizational culture has its own preferences and idiosyncrasies with respect to consultants. Some organizations love them, and instant credibility is gained whenever someone with the title consultant on a business card shows up. Other organizations have only a preference for the brand-name consulting firms from either historical dealings with the firm or the feeling that if it costs a lot of money, it must be good. Still other organizations prefer to use local academic talent or perhaps even displaced employees with expertise who are out on their own. And finally, a few organizations such as cash-strapped entrepreneurial ventures don't like consultants—period. Taking into account your corporate culture and preference, or building a case to go outside the norm for the CSM process, represents the first consideration.

In our experience, we believe that it is best to hire a CSM consultant to assist you with the initial process. A professional who is well acquainted with qualitative and quantitative research methods specific to customer satisfaction can be the catalyst to move the CSM process rapidly in a company. The person can bring expertise and objectivity to the issue and ultimately teach you how to deploy the process in-house should you so desire. Selected carefully, your CSM consultant is a team member who works with your task force, quality and marketing department, and senior management to drive the voice of the customer into your organization.

HOW TO FIND A CONSULTANT

Finding the right consultant for your organization requires a great amount of attention and energy. CSM consulting is now a $200 million business, so there are many firms from which to choose. Many marketing research firms have a specialty division or department that focuses on CSM. There are also specialty "boutiques" that specialize in customer satisfaction research; such boutiques can offer instant credibility and recognition in your organization but often at quite a high price tag. It is important to look for consultants who can both educate and adapt to your corporate culture. As discussed earlier, some corporations demand brand-name consultants, and others look for academic talent. The best results we have seen come from consulting firms that have both a stellar reputation and academic talent. You want to make sure that the consulting firm is not just resting on its laurels due to the work it has done in the past, but that it is also on the cutting edge of research. Examples of cutting-edge research would be in the areas of linking customer satisfaction and employee satisfaction and financial performance; discussions in this exciting area of linkage occur later in the book. Aligned with the research is the objective that your consulting firm intends to implement the research and move from theory to practice.

The best source for identifying appropriate CSM consultants consists of your peers at other companies that have implemented CSM. Another resource for identifying CSM firms is the annual review of CSM consultants in *Marketing News*. Local universities can also be a source for some of the pieces of CSM, particularly assistance in the areas of qualitative interviews and statistical analyses. And displaced employees who understand the unique characteristics of CSM research and also understand the culture of your company can be valuable as a resource.

EVALUATING THE CONSULTANT

Evaluating consultants or consulting firms is exactly like interviewing potential employees. You will be spending a lot of time with your consultants, and your personal performance within the company will be greatly influenced and ultimately judged by the consultant's performance. The consultant becomes a component of your next merit increase or team bonus. Excellent rapport, communication, and "fit" with you, your team, and your company are critical. Just as with potential employees, an evaluation process, reference check, interview, and legal agreement are all appropriate and necessary to good decision making. Table 4.1 lists the seven key evaluation topics that are critical to setting the foundation for a successful CSM process.

CSM Expertise

It is important that the consulting firm or individual you are considering have CSM experience. Such experience verifies the fact that your consultant is not just trying to get on the CSM bandwagon without an understanding of the entire process. There are also some subtle but important differences between CSM research and marketing research that are essential to driving a customer focus into your organization. Traditional marketing research is generated from the company or supplier perspective, which may have no relevance to the customer. For example, you may believe that it is critical that your customer service representatives answer the telephone within the first two rings to take customer orders. You may find out, however, that when you listen to your customers' concerns and needs, your customers tell you that they prefer to send their orders via electronic data interchange and don't want to place orders by phone at all! Questionnaires developed from customer interviews have attributes identified by the customer, not your management. Marketing research objectives are internally driven; CSM is externally driven. CSM consultants must articulate their abilities to differentiate the two types of research. Failure to do this results in a CSM process that does not address true customer needs. Your customer service representatives may be answering the telephone within two rings, but there won't be many calls as customers move their business elsewhere to meet their needs.

Industry Experience

If you can find a consultant who has worked in your industry, you may gain some insight about your competitors. You may also get a sense of some of the customer-identified attributes. You also need to remember that the extent of your consultant's willingness to bestow or withhold competitor information will be reciprocated with your competitors.

Table 4.1   Key Evaluation Areas for CSM Consultants

CSM EXPERTISE
INDUSTRY EXPERIENCE
PROJECT MANAGEMENT SKILLS
CONTRACT AND PAYMENT SCHEDULE
INTERPERSONAL SKILLS
COMMITMENT TO TOTAL QUALITY AND CSM
WILLINGNESS TO ASSIST IN TRANSITION TO IN-HOUSE PROCESS

Consultants with experience in a number of industries can provide you with some insight into overall best practices. Some of the areas you will be measuring such as delivery and customer service may have common attributes regardless of the industry. An industrial manufacturer can learn from a service industry about delivery just as the service provider can learn about corporate image from the manufacturer. Your consultant should be able to help your organization learn from industries completely different from your own. A consultant with a variety of clients often is more willing to share overall insights and tends to have a more global view and understanding of the CSM process.

Project Management Skills

Many a project has started with innovative concepts, grandiose goals, and brilliant objectives only to die on the vine. We've all seen it happen, and if it hasn't happened as the result of a corporate change in direction, it has happened as the result of poor project management skills. Project management skills can truly make or break a CSM program. As a consumer, you know that the best product or service means nothing if it is not delivered. The ability of your consultant to develop a time line and anticipated completion dates and deliverables is a key evaluation area. Your consultant should provide you with a time line that outlines the key activities and deliverables, the responsible party, and the due date.

Figure 4.1 is an abbreviated example of a project time line. There are four major areas in every CSM project. The first is the qualitative com-

Figure 4.1
CSM Time Line

Activity	Due Date	Complete
Qualitative work—customers and company	1/15	
Qualitative work—summary report/transcripts	2/1	
Questionnaire draft	2/21	
Questionnaire final	3/7	
Updated database organization	3/14	
Prenotification letter mailed	3/18	
List of business terms to interviewers	3/18	
Daily report format	3/20	
Interviewer briefing	3/21	
Pretest	3/22	
Rollout	3/23	
End of interviewing	4/15	
Thank-you card mailed	4/20	
Data tabulations	4/20	
Analysis complete	5/6	
Report and presentation prepared	5/20	
Presentation to senior management	6/20	
Final billing	7/1	

ponent, when your consultant will be learning about your organization, your management, and your customers. Much of this time is spent listening to these audiences, and transcripts or summary notes of the information form the basis for development of the quantitative survey.

The second area is the development of the questionnaire. Your consultant needs to provide you with a timetable for developing the instrument and determining an appropriate time to obtain feedback. Contrary to what you may believe initially, fine-tuning the instrument can take time. Part of that fine-tuning is also the pretesting of the instrument with customers to ensure that it is covering the attributes and issues important to customers. It is also important to schedule the prenotification letter (if used) to arrive just before the survey deployment.

The third area is the actual deployment of the survey. You will want not only an idea of the amount of time that your surveying will be in the field but also some agreement on a progress report during this period. A process should be identified for any problems or customer concerns that arise during interviewing, if, say, a phone number is incorrect. The consultant should also indicate when the thank-you postcard to customers should be ready to mail based on that successful deployment and the end of the field-calling period.

The final area of the project time line comprises the data analysis, reporting, and presentations. Once you have finished in the field, your business units will be very eager for the data, your managers will be looking for the reports, and your senior executives will be interested in the data. In most organizations, the scheduling of meetings between middle- and senior-level managers must be done months in advance, so your consultant must be willing at the beginning of the process to agree to a schedule and make a commitment for reporting and presentations. Timeliness and ability to meet the deadlines are very important, for both your own career and the future work of the consultant, so it is critical that you be involved in this scheduling.

Contract and Payment Schedule

In a perfect world, a handshake and complete understanding between two people would be all that is needed to begin the CSM process. As we all know, however, what we say and mean is not always heard and understood in the same way by the other person or party. Therefore, apropos of the development of a project management time line are contract negotiation and a payment schedule. Contract negotiation and payment terms must be discussed and agreed upon prior to any work.

Many of the large CSM firms have boilerplate contracts that cover all of the essential areas; most of the smaller firms and academic consulting firms, however, do not. In addition, you may have some special concerns or particular process areas that are not standard. In any event, it is important to cover five main areas in your contract, as shown in Figure 4.2. Contracts addressing these issues and signed by both parties are recommended to avoid unpleasant and potential legal action.

Figure 4.2
Recommended Contents of Legal Agreement for CSM Process

Area	Content
CSM project issues	• Intellectual property ownership • Ownership of the data • Time line • Confidentiality and nondisclosure statements • Protection from conflict of interest
Deliverables	• Reports • Presentation materials • Data in specific format
Billing	• Travel parameters and reporting requirements • Entire project fee or daily rate schedule • Reimbursable expenses and daily/hourly charges • Billable travel time • Charges for additional analyses outside the project • Payment schedule
Insurance policies	• Workers' compensation • Proof of indemnification and insurance • Copy of certificate of insurance
Other issues	• Adherence to your company's drug and alcohol policies • Requirements for any notices or demands

The first area covers CSM project issues. It is important that you determine who owns the intellectual property. Unless your consultant develops a proprietary model, your company should be the owner of the intellectual property. If you use a model similar to the one illustrated in this book, your company and not the consultant is the owner of the intellectual property. You may also wish to discuss ownership of the model and intellectual findings if a proprietary model is being tested with data from your organization. It seems that in that case, both parties benefit and therefore the property belongs to both.

As part of the project, ensure that your consulting firm will keep your data confidential and not disclose it at any time. Since you are embarking on a process that will ultimately assist you in becoming more successful and you are paying for it, you should keep your data confidential. Many consulting firms mask the client company name, input all of the data onto a normative database by industry, and sell the information to other companies. Specify in the contract that this is acceptable to you. If you are well into the CSM process (i.e., several rounds) and wish to change the focus from internal improvement to external comparison, you may want to participate in normative studies. Your consultant may also use your data in presentations and sales calls to potential clients, so if you don't want that to happen, you must specify it. The bottom line is that your consultant should agree to keep your data confidential and to destroy your data in accordance with any records retention schedule your company may require.

The remaining project issues include the agreement that you own the data and require it in a particular format (ASCII files, spreadsheet, etc.). You may also require that your specific consulting project managers not become involved in other CSM research with your competitors for a period of time. The usual protection-from-conflict-of-interest time period is two to three years. Finally, an outline of the project time line should be a part of the contract.

The second area covers all of the physical deliverables from the process. You need to specify the types and number of reports, the style and number of presentation materials to be provided, and the format of the data. The more specific you can be at this point, the less hassle and last-minute runaround you will encounter as the process reporting and presentation deadlines loom.

The third area concerns billing. Every consulting firm has a different way of approaching this, and it is usually negotiable (if the consultant wants your business!). It is important to note whether the process billing is on an entire project or a daily rate. Specify ceilings and appropriate charges for travel, administrative work, presentation materials, and additional analyses, as well as any other charges outside the project or daily rate. Delineate the reporting requirements necessary to your auditing department for consultant travel and billing. Specify whether travel time is billable; this can add up to a substantial amount and depending on the travel itinerary can be a source of perceived gouging. Specify the entire payment schedule, from up-front payments (usually either 30–50% of the project fee or monthly billing if on a daily rate) and the interest charge for late payment (usually 1% per month.)

The fourth area covers primarily insurance issues. Your consultant must provide you with proof of indemnification, insurance, and workers' compensation coverage. Copies of the certificates that so attest must be filed with your legal department or in your own secured files. Make certain that the policies are up-to-date, and require that consulting firm provide updated policies if the current ones expire during the project period.

The fifth area represents a miscellaneous category to cover any other issues. Most large companies have a drug and alcohol policy that applies to their employees and ask that consultants working with them adhere to those policies. If you have nonsmoking premises, your consultants should be expected to adhere to that practice. Finally, identify the format and time period requirements for any notices or demands that may arise during the course of the project. In the event of a misunderstanding or a special circumstance, you want to be certain that you will have adequate notification (usually thirty days) to respond.

Interpersonal Skills

Interpersonal skills probably represent the most critical characteristic of the consultant. Your consultant will be meeting with executives, customers, middle managers, and frontline employees. A person who can empathize and communicate with anyone is necessary. Professional yet appropriate demeanor can make the difference regarding client receptivity.

Probably the key element in the interpersonal skill set is the ability to listen. Remember: The goal of CSM is to drive the voice of the customer into your organization. Your consultant must be able to listen to your customers and provide you with their views. The consultant must also be able to listen to you and your company employees. The consultant is often in the middle of controversy between your company perceptions and your customers' perceptions and must be able to effectively represent your customers while effectively working within your company. It's not an easy task, but there are such people in the world.

How do you measure listening skills? When you interview the consultant, take note of the amount of time consultants talk versus the amount of time you talk. Does the consultant ask probing questions about your company and your customers? Seek clarification by restating what you said? Capture the nuances of your process? If your consultant spends most of the time emphasizing personal abilities and greatness and you rarely get the opportunity to speak, you may want to broaden your search. As mentioned earlier, the individual selected is integral to your personal success.

Commitment to Total Quality and CSM

All of the total quality literature and all of the total quality gurus have extolled the necessity of walking the talk, be it talk about quality principles, cost containment, or the focus on customer satisfaction. Any CSM consultant worth considering has an individualized CSM process in place and will be willing to share survey results from clients. Of course you will also expect to be interviewed as your CSM process progresses at appropriate intervals. If a firm is not measuring its performance as a CSM provider and improving on areas that are important to its clients, you should not even consider it. Ask your prospective consultants to provide you with information, communications, or reports about their CSM procedures. This process will narrow the field considerably.

Willingness to Assist in Transition to an In-House Process

Depending on your organization you may want to have the option of conducting most of the CSM process in-house at a later date. There are a number of good reasons for this. First and foremost is that bringing CSM in-house signifies the importance of the voice of the customer in the company and culture. Company employees are recognized, developed, and rewarded for being customer advocates. The second reason is that CSM requires organizational learning to bring the necessary expertise into the organization. That expertise can be utilized in other areas such as business planning, employee satisfaction, and marketing research, not to mention the benefits of the cultural change to a learning organization. Finally, the costs attributed to CSM can be substantially less to your organization if implemented appropriately. Organizations are always looking for ways to operate more effectively, and in-house CSM has the potential to contribute to that.

Finding a consultant who is willing to assist you in making the transition if you so desire in the future is not effortless. Some consulting firms feel that their expertise is best used for the entire CSM process and are not at all interested in helping companies bring CSM in-house. Some firms will do so only if you agree to do all of the data collection and reporting through them. Some firms will educate you while you are going through the entire process so that you have the option of bringing the process in-house. We recommend that you choose the latter, as they probably also embrace the organizational learning philosophy. If you decide not to bring your CSM process in-house, you have not lost anything.

REFERENCE CHECKS

Once you narrow down the number of CSM consulting firms or individuals capable of meeting your specific needs, a reference check is critical. Due to the time and effort involved, you probably want to reduce your list to three to five. Most consultants have lists of CSM clients who are willing to discuss their experiences candidly with you. Of course, most consultants or consulting firms will refer you to individuals who will give them a positive recommendation! While it is helpful to call those clients, you may also want to use the reference list of clients provided in the consultant's literature. Several calls or transfers usually result in reaching the person responsible for CSM at other companies.

For each consulting firm you are considering, call three references. A telephone survey is the best way to obtain the information, for much can be probed, and conversation will encourage your referral to be honest. A short, concise series of scaled questions is appropriate for the reference, particularly if the CSM firm decision will be made by a team or task force within your organization. Figure 4.3 contains a script that can be used on the telephone. In order to obtain the best results, ensure that your call is made at a convenient time, or reschedule it for a time convenient to the reference. Specify the amount of time that the survey will take; five minutes should be adequate unless specific ancillary issues arise that need to be probed. Once you have finished, extend your thanks for the time. You may be surprised when the person on the other end requests that you call back with your decision; companies are always curious to see whether other companies are selecting the same consultants or to learn the reasons different consultants were preferred! Once you have implemented your CSM process with a consultant, you will in turn probably receive this type of call from others, and hopefully you will feel that you chose the right firm.

Figure 4.3
Referral Script

Hello. This is _____(your name)_____ from _____(your corporation)_____.

We are about to embark on a customer satisfaction measurement process with

_____(consulting firm)_____. You were given as a referral for their prior work.

Could I ask for five minutes of your time to answer a few questions about them?

When was the last time that you used _____(consulting firm)_____'s services?

Using the scale of excellent, very good, good, fair, or poor, how would you rate

_____(consulting firm)_____'s:

Activity	Excellent	Very Good	Good	Fair	Poor	DK
Preresearch assistance						
Qualitative research						
Quantitative research						
Data collection process						
Analyses						
Reports						
Presentations						
Overall project mgmt						
Overall quality of products and services						
Value						

Would you recommend this consultant?

Are you planning to use them in the future?

Are there any specific comments that you have about _____(consulting firm)_____?

Thank you for your time and input.

CHAPTER SUMMARY

A good CSM process requires specific expertise in order to be successful. The person or persons responsible for CSM have the ability to make or break the process. While a few companies have developed and implemented CSM entirely through an in-house process, virtually all firms initially obtain the services of a CSM consultant and consulting firm. Properly obtained and managed, the CSM consultant can add tremendous value, credibility, and organizational learning to your company.

Selecting an appropriate consultant is not a difficult process, but it requires some discipline. CSM consulting is a large business, and both very experienced and very inexperienced firms do business in the market. There are seven critical areas of evaluation of a CSM consultant. The first area is to determine the consultant's CSM expertise. The second area is to determine the consultant's experience in your industry as well as any other industries. The third area is to ascertain the project management skills of the consultant. The fourth area is to establish your needs by cooperatively developing a contract and associated payment terms with your consultant for the CSM project or process. The fifth area is to determine if your consultant has the appropriate interpersonal skills. The sixth area is to investigate the commitment your consultant has to total quality management, particularly the consultant's own CSM process. And the last area is to ensure that your consultant is willing to teach your team or organization how to deploy CSM through an in-house process should you so desire.

Reference checks are critical and can easily be made to select the best consultant for you. Remember that the capabilities and services of your consultant will ultimately be reflected in your performance evaluation, so a rigorous process of selection is important not only for your company but also for your own future success.

RELENTLESS CORPORATION

Selecting a CSM Consultant

A Fortune 200 company we'll call Relentless Corporation initiated a task force to research customer satisfaction measurement practices. The task force found that most companies that were measuring and acting upon customer satisfaction information tended to be leaders in their industries and were financially successful. Most of these firms also used outside consultants specializing in CSM to initiate the process. Since Relentless had neither a dedicated corporate marketing or quality department nor CSM or marketing research expertise in the company, the task force decided to embark on its CSM process by using a consultant; at the same time, the company created and filled the position of CSM director. The rationale for hiring a consultant was based on the belief that the consultant brought to the process an objectivity that was unclouded by corporate history. Relentless also knew that a consultant selected and managed well is a tremendous trainer for ultimately bringing the CSM process in-house if desired.

Relentless Corporation initially chose an academic consulting firm to begin the CSM process. This academic consultant had an unusual but enticing conceptual model for tying in CSM with financial performance. The principals of the firm were bright and impressive marketing academicians. It seemed like the opportunity to get in with a firm at the entrepreneurial stage and learn from the experience. The CSM director of Relentless, who had selected the academic consultants on the basis of their intellectual horsepower and entrepreneurial spirit, was soon concerned when it turned out the firm couldn't deliver as promised.

Despite Relentless's numerous requests, the academic firm worked for nearly seven months before providing a bill. When the bill did arrive, the amount was astronomical, and excessive charges had been made for travel days and administrative duties. Included in the bill were a $500 charge for four hours of word processing and a $3000 charge for a travel evening (a four-hour flight). Relentless Corporation was also billed a daily rate for an individual who became ill and did not deliver the necessary product. Although Relentless did truly have sympathy for the individual and the illness, it was not responsible to the individual and did not receive the deliverable anyway. After several negotiations involving attorneys and a tremendous amount of time, a settlement was reached and further work with the consultant was terminated.

Relentless next sought a reliable consultant and chose a boutique consulting firm, which indeed provided an excellent product and service. Management presentations were well received. After some time, however, Relentless wanted to take more ownership in the process by bringing it in-house. The boutique firm, however, was not interested in the process of educating the company by assisting with the transition process; it specialized only in outsourced processes. Relentless proceeded anyway and successfully made the transition to an in-house process. Ownership and interest in the data and process have increased. The purpose of this book is to help you avoid these types of difficulties.

5

Identifying the Attributes

The accurate identification of attributes important to the customer is the foundation upon which all subsequent portions of the CSM program must be built. Errors, flaws, and biases in this step will limit the usefulness of the whole CSM effort. Therefore, this chapter discusses the many different sources and techniques that can be used in the identification of attributes. The discussion focuses first on internal sources and then discusses a variety of customer-driven external sources.

INTERNAL SOURCES

Most firms have a wealth of information available internally although it is usually not systematically organized. However, the first places to look are probably with the areas that have compiled the best records of some type.

Warranties and Guarantees

Most firms closely track warranty and guarantee problems. The data normally indicate what was so unacceptable to customers that the product was returned. From the data, management can normally glean a rough idea of what the customer's expectations were and how successfully the firm has been meeting the most basic expectations. Complaints are also a source of information that is covered in a separate chapter.

Customer Service Records

The use of 800-number hot lines that provide access to customer service departments has mushroomed in recent years. Many customer service personnel are on-line on a computer network, and they log calls into a record-keeping system of some type. The frequency of inquiries about various attributes can shed light on what is important to customers.

At Hewlett-Packard all customer service personnel log questions into a database that is accessed by new product development engineers. The engineers scan the data to determine which areas are of concern to customers and what product modifications might be valuable.

Customer Contact Personnel

All employees who have contact with customers should be the subject of surveys, interviews, or focus groups to determine what is important to customers. Since normally less than 10 percent of a customer base initiates contact with a firm at a time other than a sale, customer contact personnel should include more than only personnel in the customer service department. Sales representatives, service personnel, or managers that have direct customer contact should be included. In many cases, this also requires contacting sales personnel in a retail outlet if products are sold through retailers.

Managers

In most organizations a variety of managers read a diverse array of trade journals, attend professional conferences where presentations are made by leading firms, or participate in benchmarking visits. Each of those exposures could indicate the relative importance of various attributes to customers. Many materials from benchmarking visits include questionnaires that indicate which attributes are important to that firm's customers. The managers at various levels and in different disciplines should be contacted to obtain their perceptions of which attributes are relevant to customers.

Typically, a good deal of knowledge about customers is dispersed throughout a firm. The goal of the attribute identification process is to systematically explore each of those sources to dredge up a list of all possible attributes. Although the internally generated attribute list is often long, it is also usually incomplete and should be supplemented with external sources. Be aware that internally generated lists can also be myopic and focus only on what has been traditionally done in a firm.

EXTERNAL SOURCES

To this point, the process of identifying attributes has focused on sources of information internal to the firm. Although such efforts identify a good portion of the attributes important to customers, some of the important attributes are almost always neglected or overlooked. There are a number of reasons for this.

Some managers may simply lack the knowledge and exposure to generate an accurate list. Some firms may have a poor, or nonexistent, system for tracking customer perceptions. The firm may have been operating in a make-it-and-sell-it culture; perhaps time constraints did not allow enough time to do a thorough investigation.

But the most common reason for an inaccurate list of attributes is probably a self-attribution bias. Typically, it is hard for us as individuals to comprehensively describe our strengths and weaknesses to someone else, especially to a friend. We are simply too close to objectively observe ourselves. One of the most difficult tasks for any artist is to paint a self-portrait. And the same concept applies to attribute identification for most firms.

Most managers know what customers want, or at least what customers should want. After all, that is why they are managers: because of their knowledge, expertise, and skill. Collectively, the organization is much the same. The organization really should know what the customer wants. Unfortunately, those rose-colored glasses of self-analysis often paint a rosy picture, but not necessarily an accurate one.

Eliminating self-attribution bias is the primary goal of depth interviews and focus groups—the two best external techniques. Customers' views may be somewhat ambiguous and ill defined at times, but they tend to be reasonably objective. Therefore, obtaining input directly from customers helps to eliminate inherent blind spots.

There are two techniques that are used most often to identify the customers' perceptions of attributes, depth interviews, and focus groups. Each of these techniques will be discussed in detail in the following sections.

DEPTH INTERVIEWS

A depth interview is a one-on-one interview with one party being a customer of some type and the other party being the interviewer. The interviewer could be a member of the firm, such as a quality or marketing manager, or the interviewer could be an unbiased third party, such as a consultant or researcher. The normal length of an interview is one to two hours, although some may last for three or four hours in rare instances. In most cases, the customer tends to wear down after a few hours, and response quality subsequently declines.

As part of a larger research effort, depth interviews are rarely done singly. Normally, from six to ten interviews are done with customers, depending on the diversity of a firm's target markets. If a firm targets one primary segment that is fairly homogeneous, six depth interviews may be adequate. If a firm has three relatively distinct target markets, then six or so depth interviews from each segment may be necessary.

There is no magic number for depth interviewing. When the marginal contribution of each successive interview tails off, then you have probably done enough. On the other hand, if each interview raises new ideas and opens new avenues to travel, you probably need to do a few more. Because the purpose of the depth interview is to generate an unbiased customer view that will be explored further in focus groups, this step is not an exact science. It is really a quality check to make sure no major issues have been neglected by a manager's self-analysis.

The Interviewer

Even though a good interviewer either could be selected internally—from the firm—or could be selected externally, there are some benefits to having an unbiased, external source conduct the interview. The most significant benefit is that an external individual is probably more objective. Objectivity is not only essential in the interview but also an advantage in debriefing the results and preparing a report. Objectivity thus leads to more credibility about the whole interviewing process when the results are analyzed and discussed by various managers within the firm.

In some cases, a third-party interviewer may get more-open responses from customers, particularly when consumers are involved. For a variety of reasons, customers may be hesitant to share their true feelings, especially when the opinions are negative. Making negative comments to a neutral third party has less social stigma than making negative comments to a representative of the firm.

When dealing with complex products, as with many industrial goods, or with organizational customers, there are some advantages to having an employee conduct the depth interview. An interviewer's deep technical knowledge of products may be necessary to obtain the desired information in the interview. Such knowledge may be difficult for an external interviewer to acquire quickly. In some cases, the customer may be more willing to deal directly with a representative of the firm, believing that such a representative's comments may make a difference.

Regardless of who actually conducts the interview, there are a number of other issues that must be kept in mind. A depth interview is a form of social interaction. Accordingly, the interviewer's interests, attitudes, actions, and reactions influence the interview process. The interviewer's attire, speech, organizational position, and organizational affiliation all provide cues to the customer that can influence the process. For example, if the interviewer wears a designer-label suit, silk shirt, and imported loafers, a middle- or lower-income respondent may develop a resentment that would constrain the interview results.

The most important characteristics of interviewers are being open-minded, socially sensitive, and adaptable. The interviewer must enter each interview with no preconception about the outcomes; otherwise, the interviewer's bias will subtly shape the discussion.

The interviewer must be socially sensitive to verbal and nonverbal cues. Because the goal of depth interviews is to get a deeper understanding of customer perceptions and decision-making processes, an interviewer must be sensitive to areas customers experience difficulty in discussing or areas that customers may avoid.

Because each interview is a unique interaction, the interviewer must be adaptable. The approach used very successfully in one interview may yield poor results in another interview. Therefore, the interviewer must be willing to change the interview style to fit the customer's preferences.

There is some research that suggests that if an interviewer is formal and professional, a trusting interviewing environment will be created more quickly. A depth interview is not just a casual discussion with customers about products. If it is perceived as such, responses may be very superficial and of little value.

The Respondent

No pretenses can be made that a sample of one is representative of the whole customer base. However, the customer, or respondent, should be the average customer. The respondent should not be a friend or acquaintance who is willing to participate. Normally, the respondent should have no unique knowledge or characteristics that would not be found among average customers.

For both consumers and organizational customers, an array of demographic data should be obtained. The typical variables would be items such as age, education, occupation, and organizational position. The purpose of such data is to determine if any variances in responses can be linked to individual or organizational characteristics.

The two most important issues in respondent selection are relevance and commitment. The topic of the depth interview must be relevant to the respondent. Therefore, getting occasional users to participate in interviews may not yield good results, for a particular product may not be particularly relevant.

Respondent commitment can normally be created in the recruiting process by stressing that the interview is "action research." The results of action research, as the name implies, lead directly to specific improvement actions by a firm. Thus, respondents would feel commitment because their responses would have a positive outcome.

Overall, the greater the relevance and commitment, the more likely the respondent will get deeply involved in the interview. And the greater the involvement, the better the responses are likely to be.

The Depth-Interviewing Process

Depth interviewing is a process with four major phases, or sequential steps. This concept is presented in Figure 5.1. The first step is background research, followed by interview design, conducting the interview, and analysis and summary. Because each interview is unique and builds upon the existing knowledge base, each interview is somewhat different. In fact, it is quite common for the issues raised in one depth interview to lead to modifications in the agenda for the subsequent interview. Because of that fluidity, depth interviewing is a process that allows new issues to be explored as they emerge. Nevertheless, there are certain guidelines that are relevant to each stage of the process.

Background Research

The purpose of the background research is to identify the key themes that must be explored in the depth interviews. The first portion of this chapter identified typical sources of this information. However, this background research clearly establishes the domain of the interview and the general flow.

From a CSM standpoint, the primary purpose of depth interviews is to see whether the customers can generate a different list of attributes that are used to evaluate products. As mentioned previously, customers

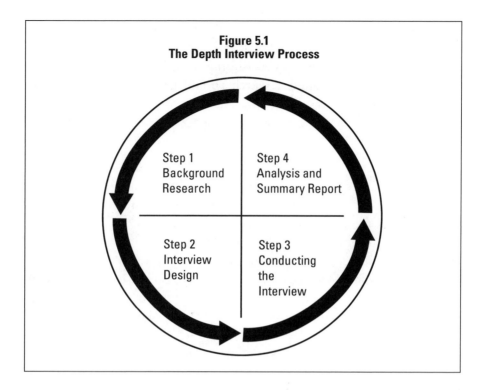

Figure 5.1
The Depth Interview Process

Step 1
Background
Research

Step 4
Analysis and
Summary Report

Step 2
Interview
Design

Step 3
Conducting
the
Interview

normally are able to supplement the attribute list generated by management. At this stage, the relative importance of each attribute is not an issue; that will come later.

One issue related to attributes is important to note in depth interviews, however. That issue is, how do customers evaluate each attribute, or what does a particular attribute mean in the customer's language? An example may better illustrate the point.

Suppose that a customer is in the market for a hammer for use around the house. Let's further assume quality is an attribute identified as important by both the customer and the firm selling the hammer. To the manufacturer of the hammer, quality may be determined by the tensile strength of the steel in the head of the hammer, the grade of oak used in the handle, and the finish on both the steel and wood. From a customer's viewpoint, quality may be determined by the feel of the hammer, the appearance, and the price. Both the customer and the firm viewed quality as important, but the attribute was conceptualized in different ways.

Therefore, when conducting background research, any existing data that indicate customer's perceptions, conceptualizations, or language should be of particular importance. Unfortunately, in most situations, the customer's views are quickly translated into the language of the firm—and something is usually lost in that translation.

In total, the background research should generate a list of topics and issues in need of investigation. The next step—interview design—translates those topics into a specific agenda.

Interview Design

A depth interview is not a nondirected, ambiguous discussion with customers. Nor is it a highly structured interview around a tightly developed set of specific questions. Somewhere between those two extremes lies the appropriate interview design.

Generally, the previous step, background research, identifies the issues and attributes under study. In some fashion, the various attributes need to be grouped into broad categories and the categories sequenced in some logical manner. Normally the sequence flows from broader, easily identifiable attributes into more specific, detailed issues.

For each category, the desired additional information should be identified. At this point, questions should be developed that will elicit the desired information. The list of questions should cover all the relevant issues and provide direction for the interview without leading the respondent. The questions should be low-profile queries that give impetus and momentum to the interview but allow respondents to tell their story in their own words.

The questions, like the sequencing of topical categories, should descend from broad to specific. Therefore, the first questions should be broad and easy to respond to so that the right atmosphere is established quickly—in the first few minutes. If any sensitive information is desired, such questions should be positioned toward the end of the interview, after a climate of openness has been established.

For each question, follow-up probes should be identified before the interview. The probes can be key-word, contrast, category-process, or stimulus probes. A key-word probe may include all or some attributes such as quality, value, and appearance. When a customer indicates that quality is important, the use of the key word *quality* should cause the interviewer to ask the follow-up question, "What do you mean by quality?"

A contrast probe would be a follow-up to a broader lead-in question. Let's assume again that quality emerged as an important attribute for photographic film. The interviewer would then follow up with a question such as, "How would you compare the quality of brand A film with brand B film?" The respondent would then normally proceed with a discussion of what constitutes quality for film and provide a subjective evaluation of each brand. Thus, the interviewer would lead the discussion from a broader issue, "What are the key attributes?" to a more specific one, "How would you compare these two products on that attribute?"

A category probe would be a follow-up to a broad question such as, "What are the important attributes that you would use in evaluating product X?" Once the attribute list was generated, the interviewer would then request of the respondent, "Group the attributes into as many categories as you like." This would identify how the customer perceives relationships among attributes. Another follow-up probe might then be, "What criteria did you use to group the attributes into the various categories?"

A process probe would again be a follow-up to a broader question. It might take the form of, "How does your firm reach a decision on that issue?" or "In your family what is the process for buying a so-called high-quality television?" The intent of the process probe is to identify how attributes are evaluated in some fashion. This often allows the key players in an organizational context to be identified.

A stimulus probe would involve the use of props of some type. The prop could be a picture, a video, an advertisement, or several actual products. Normally, props would be introduced at will into an interview to rejuvenate a discussion. Such stimuli could be used to bring a category of issues to closure or to open another series of questions on a different topic.

Regardless the nature of the interview, the desired questions and probes should be carefully planned beforehand. A depth interview is time-consuming for respondents and can be intellectually challenging, so careful planning of the questions and flow will enhance the productivity of the process.

Carefully crafted questions enhance the professionalism of a depth interview and also help to create social distance between the interviewer and respondent. Social distance leads to more objective interviewing, for an interviewer is less likely to lead respondents subtly toward preconceived conclusions. Although questions are essential, respondents must always be allowed the freedom, flexibility, and variability to respond in their own words.

Conducting the Interview

Since all depth interviews should be audio- or videotape recorded, the interviewer should never take notes; that will come later in the analysis stage. There is even debate over whether a respondent should see or know that an interviewer has a detailed list of questions. Opponents argue that the list, especially if it is on a sheet of paper and visible to the respondent, will inhibit the free flow of the discussion, as the respondent will wait for the next question and monitor progress down the list. Proponents of written-question lists say there is greater continuity between interviews and that the chance of omitting some questions is reduced.

Probably the best advice we can offer is that the questions should appear on index cards that are less conspicuous and can be held or kept out of sight. The cards can be referred to periodically throughout the interview to ensure that all relevant topics have been addressed.

The purpose of predeveloped questions is that the interviewer can focus more completely on the respondent. This is the primary reason why the respondent should not take notes either. The interviewer must be perceived by the respondent as an eager listener, and anything detracting from that should be eliminated.

An atmosphere of trust and openness is critical to successful depth interviewing and must be established quickly. This is usually done during the introduction and first few questions. Some argue that five to ten minutes of casual conversation between the respondent and interviewer before the introduction serves as an ice-breaker and enhances friendliness.

When the questions are being asked, the interviewer should allow ample time for the respondent to answer fully. Such "space" indicates the respondent is not being rushed. If the interviewer cycles through the questions too quickly, a hurried pace to the interview emerges and answer quality normally deteriorates as the respondent adjusts accordingly.

The interviewer must be sensitive to key terms, patterns of responses, and interrelationships. An abrupt change of topics often indicates topic avoidance, something the respondent would rather not discuss. The interviewer must also watch for misunderstanding or inconsistencies that might indicate a lack of comprehension by the respondent.

The interviewer must also be aware of nonverbal cues that a respondent may be communicating. Body posture, eye contact, facial expression, and voice intonation provide indications of interest, boredom, or annoyance that may require a new direction in the interview.

At points when the interview begins to bog down, the introduction of props or exercises often helps. For example, a respondent could be asked to map products spatially. Spatial mapping may require having a variety of products or advertisements ready and then asking the respondent to develop a perceptual map. Regardless of the prop or exercise, the items or activities should be injected into the discussion when the interviewer deems it most appropriate.

If the questions have been carefully crafted and sequenced, then most interviews flow well. Inherently, the success of a depth interview is a result of interview design, interviewer ability, and respondent willingness. Fortunately, all three of these issues are at least partially controllable. Once the interview is complete, the next step is analysis.

Analysis and Summary Report

After each interview, the interviewer should immediately write a summary that captures the overall impressions. If the interview went well, why? If it didn't go well, why not, and what can be done to improve it? Was the respondent distracted, comfortable, relaxed? Any important perceptions should be captured quickly, while the ideas are fresh. Once the interviewer has written a comprehensive report, then review of the tapes can begin.

Soon after the interview, the audio- or videotapes should be reviewed by the interviewer and analyzed. In the case of attribute identification, responses can be allocated to predefined categories. The use of predefined categories makes the analysis process faster and easier, but it also introduces some potential bias because attributes may be forced into the wrong categories.

The analysis should identify key words and comments that indicate the customer's perceptions of patterns and relationships among the attributes. The interviewer should note where the conclusions were consistent or inconsistent with the expectations.

Finally, a verbatim transcript should be made of the tape. With most of the current word processing programs, a key-word scan can be run that indicates the variety and frequency of various terms used by respondents. This can help to clarify the patterns underlying the responses in the interview. Software is also available that scans key words, analyzes context of comments, and determines importance of attributes based on an iterative process. Until sophisticated artificial intelligence can be programmed into software packages, however, this application has less appeal.

The analysis should comprise three components: the interviewer's summary, the interviewer's detailed analysis of the tape, and a verbatim transcript. Both the summary and the detailed analysis should be completed soon after the interview is completed, so an appropriate time between interviews should be allowed.

Depth Interview Summary

Properly designed and implemented, depth interviews can yield detailed information about product attributes. Due to small sample sizes—usually no more than six or so for each segment—there is an inherent danger of both interviewer and respondent bias. Despite their limitations, depth interviews are a valuable precursor to larger and more costly focus groups. The use of depth interviews often clarifies issues much more sharply so that focus groups, the subject of the next discussion, will be more effective.

FOCUS GROUPS

The use of focus groups is so widespread and commonplace that most readers are generally familiar with what they are and how they operate. However, to provide a common base for subsequent discussion, we'll define what focus groups are and describe their advantages and disadvantages, and then move on to more detailed analysis of how to conduct a focus group.

A focus group is a small group of individuals, normally from six to twelve, who are brought together, along with a moderator, to openly discuss a particular topic or series of issues. A focus group discussion usually lasts for two or three hours and is held preferably in a room specifically designed for that purpose.

Focus groups can be used for many purposes. They can be used to evaluate new products, concept ideas, or advertising programs, for example. For a CSM program, focus groups can be used to identify attributes—the primary subject of this discussion—or used to reduce an attributes list, identify the relative importance of attributes, discuss customer decision processes, or evaluate questionnaires. Another good use of focus groups is to identify emerging trends in customer expectations—normally difficult to do with only a standard CSM questionnaire.

Because of their inherent subjectivity, focus groups are rarely held singly. Usually, from four to six focus groups are conducted on a specific topic. The more important the issue, the greater the number of focus groups conducted.

But, as with depth interviews, there is no magic number that is correct. The total number of focus groups conducted is a subjective managerial decision influenced predominantly by time and budget decisions.

Advantages

Focus groups are able to identify very well issues that are key to the customer. Therefore, when deeper understanding and insight about customer preferences and processes are needed, focus groups are a valuable tool. Accordingly, focus groups are an excellent technique for identification of attributes or perceived benefits of products. Focus groups allow participants the opportunity to build on the comments of others and even brainstorm possible innovations.

Focus groups are well suited to the generation of new ideas. If a firm is trying to solicit ideas for new product development or modification of product and service attributes, then the group discussions are a good vehicle to screen the viability of ideas. Likewise, focus groups are good for identifying emerging trends in the use of products, ideas, and so forth that may not become generally apparent in the marketplace for a year or so. Therefore, some firms use focus groups regularly as an early warning system to identify shifts in customer preferences.

When a focus group is used as action research, results have been favorable. Participants are often very committed and involved when they know that their ideas can change the behavior of organizations.

Focus groups are useful when a firm needs a social context in which to evaluate ideas. The dynamics of a group are often more representative of the way decisions are made in both organizations and family units than are individual depth interviews.

Although each focus group can easily cost $1000 or more, this is a relatively low figure for obtaining quick feedback from customers. Hence, the low cost and speed of response are advantages of using focus groups.

Disadvantages

Although focus groups have a number of advantages, they also have some disadvantages as well. The group situation may be a limiting factor for some participants. Social pressures may cause individuals to condition their responses, such as when one individual opposes what has already been said by others. In other cases an individual may be hesitant to discuss sensitive or controversial issues with relative strangers.

More pragmatically, a focus group doesn't allow individuals much time to fully express themselves. A two-hour focus group of twelve people allows an average of only ten minutes for participation by each person. Such a short amount of time is not conducive to deep discussion. Therefore, the size and duration of a focus group should be adjusted to fit the level of desired detail. For true detail, a three-hour focus group of six people may be appropriate.

Focus groups are not good for identifying an individual's awareness and knowledge. Each participant is influenced by what others say and do, so each learns from the comments made by other participants.

The subjectivity of focus groups is a disadvantage. The effectiveness of each group is a function of the participants, the moderator, the structure and objectives, and the facilities. Changes in any one of those variables can alter the outcome of a focus group. Of those variables, getting the right participants is probably most important. If participants aren't representative of the target market, then focus group results will be skewed accordingly.

Because focus groups are a form of soft research, the same problems that plague all soft research also accompany focus groups. Subjectivity, lack of representativeness, and variability should be considered in interpretations of the results. Despite those disadvantages, however, focus groups are a valuable research tool when used properly. The next sections describe such proper usage.

Planning

As with depth interviews, effective planning is critical to the success of focus groups. Clarifying the objectives and strategy, selecting the moderator, recruiting participants, and selecting facilities all contribute to the success of groups. Each of these issues requires exploration.

Objectives

The most important part of the planning process is to clearly define what you hope to accomplish—the objectives—because all other aspects of the focus group flow from that element. For the purpose of a CSM program, the most common objectives are to develop a customer-driven profile of attributes and to pretest and evaluate the first draft of the CSM questionnaire.

Specific objectives dictate the nature of the introduction and directions to be used at the beginning of the focus group discussion. Subsequently, the design of the questions and the direction of the discussion flow from the objectives. The approximate time allocation for each topic should be planned so the moderator can subtly steer the discussion through the agenda.

Any stimulus materials and activities should be planned and debugged before the focus group begins. The focus group might critically evaluate the set of competitive product offerings. The focus group may try to identify ways a product could be improved. All of these are indirect ways of evaluating attribute importance that would require preplanning and the use of props. A more direct approach may be to simply try to identify salient product attributes through a guided discussion.

If an objective is "to see what customers think of our products", the focus group is likely to be equally vague and yield poor results. If the goal is "to see how customers determine quality" or "how customers evaluate value," then the design of the focus group can be built around that more specific objective. And the results will probably be much more useful.

Moderator

Having a good moderator is a key to the success of a focus group. A moderator must be a good listener and possess good conflict resolution skills should a difference of opinion arise. Although a moderator should know the topic reasonably well, he or she must also understand and appreciate group dynamics and allow the group perspective to emerge without being tainted by moderator bias.

In order for the latter to occur, the moderator and client must have a close dialogue in formulating the goals, objectives, and design of the focus group. This should be an interactive process so that the client gains the full benefit of the moderator's experience. For example, the moderator usually prepares a written moderator's guide that includes objectives, detailed plans for conduct of the focus group, actual questions, and time allocations. This is discussed in detail with the client to make the client aware of how the moderator plans to steer the conversation so as to cover all of the issues.

A good moderator should have enthusiasm for the subject matter, for enthusiasm is contagious in a group context. A moderator must also be technically competent with regard to any exercises or activities that will be conducted such as perceptual mapping or development of a commercial. Normally an experienced moderator can assist in recruiting the right type of participants in order to enhance the group dynamics. A moderator should also share the client's urgency to get the results and produce the written summary report within a week.

Because the moderator plays such a key role in the success of a series of focus groups, careful selection of an experienced moderator is critical. By jointly clarifying the objectives and design of the focus group, the client and the moderator can likely reduce problems.

Participants

The participants must be roughly representative of the target market under study. Therefore, a client may provide a list of customers that could be used to recruit some or all of the participants depending on the objectives. Recruiting participants is not a random process, as stratified quotas are typically used. For instance, an electric utility company may have one focus group consisting of builders, another owners of small businesses, and another of homeowners. Mixing these three disparate segments at one time would render the focus group useless.

Each participant should be interested in the topic of the focus groups. Even though participants are paid, money should not be the only motivating factor in participants' involvement. This has obvious implications for recruiting technique.

Organizational respondents in particular are seldom motivated by the payment. Such participants are usually motivated by their desire to share their knowledge and help another organization to improve.

When a series of focus groups are planned, the initial group should be fairly general and broad based. Subsequent groups can then be more specific, targeting a more detailed respondent group. This allows the issues to be more generally discussed before isolating subsequent differences between various segments.

Facilities

When possible, a focus group should be held in a room designed specifically for that purpose. Normally, such a room is relatively soundproof so as to minimize external distractions such as traffic or other background noise. The room should be equipped with microphones built in so the discussion can be tape recorded. One wall is typically a mirrored one-way glass with a video camera so the group discussion can be video-taped. Another wall typically is mirrored with one-way glass to create a client viewing area.

Some focus group facilities have video teleconference capability so that the focus group can be broadcast live, or on a taped basis, to managers across the country. Having cross-functional teams jointly view actual focus groups is an excellent way to encourage interaction and break down functional differences.

The client viewing area almost becomes a miniretreat, especially during the debriefing period between focus groups. These client discussions often generate additional or more refined questions for the next focus group.

Regardless of where the facilities might be, all equipment should be pretested beforehand and backup equipment obtained when appropriate. Some focus groups have been largely wasted because a cassette tape broke, unknown to the moderator. The saying "An ounce of prevention is worth a pound of cure" certainly applies to the use of focus group equipment.

Conducting the Focus Group

The first ten minutes of the focus group discussion should attempt to put all participants at ease. Some refer to this as creating a "talking environment" in which participants talk to one another instead of a series of two-way conversations with the moderator.

The introduction and directions should explicitly identify the agenda and attempt to create a nonthreatening environment that is reasonably unstructured. The first questions should be very general in an attempt to get everyone's opinion and to draw all participants into the discussion quickly.

From this general beginning, the subsequent open-ended questions, with probes like those discussed with depth interviews, can gradually lead the discussion into more specific topics. The moderator should be flexible and adaptable, allowing the discussion to naturally evolve in the desired direction.

In some cases, clients in the viewing room may pass written questions to the moderator for further discussion. However, that practice tends to break up the flow and continuity of the discussion. When possible, such questions should be written down and then built into the next focus group.

Immediately after each focus group, a debriefing period of several hours should occur. This allows the viewers and moderator to discuss results, insights, and questions that may have been raised. Often, slight modifications to the moderator's guide are made before the next focus group.

Analysis

Both the moderator and a viewer should independently complete a summary report of their perceptions and conclusions. Then the moderator and viewer should jointly go over their separate reports and compile a single report. This process helps to remove bias on the part of any one person.

The primary objective of the analysis process is to identify customers' needs, customers' expectations, and relevant product and service attributes. Normally, a lengthy and diverse list of attributes are identified.

While the moderator and viewer are compiling the joint report, they normally review a verbatim transcript of the focus group that has been subjected to a key-word count. The verbatim transcript is useful in identifying the underlying trends in the discussion.

Summary

Focus groups are an excellent vehicle to make managers aware of the voice of the customer. Any effort to identify a comprehensive list of product and service attributes should include the use of focus groups as part of the overall effort. When used properly focus groups constitute a valuable supplement to other, more quantitative approaches. Focus groups are especially good for identifying evolving customer expectations much earlier than would be noticed through the use of questionnaires.

REDUCING THE ATTRIBUTE LIST

In most cases a very lengthy list of product and service attributes can be created, a list that often includes approximately fifty attributes. Such a lengthy list would present some real problems for questionnaire design, which is addressed in subsequent chapters. However, for now, suffice it to say that a workable list normally has fifteen to twenty-five attributes.

A good example is the process that Boise Cascade's newsprint division went through in its attribute selection. Originally, more than seventy-five attributes were identified through customer focus groups, previous survey instruments, input from sales representatives, and all other sources. The newsprint group took the customer-defined attributes first and eliminated overlap from internal sources. Next some attributes were refined. In the case of newsprint, the appearance attribute was one of these. Internally, Boise Cascade has many subattributes for appearance: color, brightness, opacity, and so on. The customer, however, is interested only in the *overall* quality of appearance. The first study, therefore, went out asking the overall question. If it turned out that appearance was affecting overall satisfaction, Boise Cascade went out again to determine specific attributes. In the case of this study, newsprint appearance did not have an impact on overall perception of quality, so the refinement of the process was correct.

You might ask, Why go through all the trouble of generating all possible attributes when half of them will be thrown out? The answer lies with the self-attribution problem discussed earlier. Even if a manager is very in touch with customers, 80 percent accuracy in the attribute identification process is quite good. Pragmatically, that means that sixteen of twenty attributes would be identified by management.

The problem is that those other four attributes may hold the key to success or survival in a highly competitive marketplace. There is a saying that if something is really important, it should be measured and tracked. If your important attributes are left unmeasured by the CSM program, then your company's performance on those attributes seldom improves and normally deteriorates. A manager may be only 60 or 70 percent accurate, and there is no way of knowing it without soliciting input directly from customers.

There are three ways to reduce the attribute list; two are subjective and one is quantitative. The subjective approaches are to use managers or to use focus groups. The quantitative approach is to use factor analysis or regression analysis to identify the key themes among the attributes.

Managers
The long list of attributes would normally be reviewed by a cross-functional team of managers. The first step in the process is to group the attributes into categories that correspond to value-added processes in the firm. The logic behind this is that the attributes represent process outcomes that are evaluated by the ultimate judge of quality—the customer.

Once the attributes are in the appropriate categories—normally from five to eight—they are gleaned for redundancy. A number of the attributes might be quite similar, with very minor wording differences. The cross-functional team should read each category, carefully synthesizing redundant attributes into one attribute description. The intent should be to maintain the customer's meaning as closely as possible, for it is very easy to throw out the wheat with the chaff.

Once the redundancies have been removed, the shorter list is then used as the basis for a rank ordering. Each manager independently rank orders the attributes within each category. (The reason the long attribute list is not rank ordered is that ranking works well for up to about ten items, but after that, rankings become very inconsistent.) Then the team members meet and jointly negotiate the rankings in each category so that a composite ranking results.

Although it is not recommended due to potential bias, the team could gradually reduce the attribute list by evaluating the salience of the lowest-ranked items in each category successively. Ultimately, a list of keepers would emerge from this process.

Focus Groups

A more unbiased approach to reducing the list is to use focus groups and let customers make the decisions. The focus group should receive the attribute list, grouped by category but unranked. The task of the focus group would be to rank the attributes in each category. Then the focus group reduces the attribute list to the most critical twenty or so attributes regardless of the category.

When focus groups are used in order to reduce the attribute list, it is normally preferable to apply the process with at least two groups to observe the consistency of results. Lack of consistency means more work needs to be done in reducing the list, normally through more focus groups.

Comparing the rank ordering of the manager's or cross-functional team's rank ordering with that of the focus group is often enlightening. The rank orderings are seldom the same. This is a real eye-opener for many organizations, because long-held assumptions about what is important to the customer are quickly shattered.

Reducing the List Statistically

In many cases, what people say they do and what they actually do are not the same. This concept also applies to CSM research. What customers say is important while they are in a focus group may not be completely consistent with the way they actually respond to a questionnaire.

When customers say something is important, it is often referred to as self-report or self-explicated data. Yet when a database is subject to sophisticated statistical analysis, other relationships may emerge. And those other relationships may be more reliable and better at predicting which attributes contribute to overall customer satisfaction.

There are two statistical techniques that are useful in identifying which attributes are most important. The two techniques are factor analysis and multiple regression. Both of them require that customer perceptions be gathered for all possible attributes. As a rough rule of thumb, a minimum sample size of about 200 is necessary. This preliminary database is then subjected to one or both techniques.

Factor analysis is so named because the individual attributes are grouped into a number of categories or factors. The attributes that share common patterns of relationship with one another are loaded into a factor. The relative strength of the relationship between the individual attributes and the dependent variable—normally a customer satisfaction index—can then be identified. Also, the relationship between the dependent variable and the factor groupings can be identified. Attributes displaying a weak relationship with the overall customer satisfaction can then be trimmed from the attribute list.

The primary problem with factor analysis is that the factor loadings or underlying themes may not necessarily correspond very well with a firm's value-added processes. Therefore, the outcome of the factor analysis—a reduced attribute list—is usually massaged and adjusted until it fits more closely with specific value-added processes.

The other statistical technique that is used to reduce an attribute list is multiple regression. As with factor analysis, the whole attribute list is examined at one time. All of the attributes are regressed against the dependent variable—a customer satisfaction index. The strength of the relationship between each attribute and overall customer satisfaction is indicated by a regression coefficient.

There are several types of multiple regression techniques. The most useful type for reducing an attribute list is probably stepwise regression, in which each attribute is sequentially introduced and evaluated for its ability to explain variation in the dependent variable. If an individual attribute adds little or nothing, it is dropped. So stepwise regression culls the wheat—the important attributes—from the chaff—the unimportant attributes.

In order to use either factor analysis or multiple regression, a preliminary database must have been gathered. Since the data gathering is the hardest, most expensive, and most time-consuming activity, both statistical techniques should be used. It really takes very little additional time.

By comparing a reduced attribute list generated by managers, focus groups, and statistical analysis, common themes typically emerge. If big differences exist, then the research design issues need to be carefully re-examined.

CHAPTER SUMMARY

There are many possible ways to identify attributes that are important to customers. Relying only on internally generated attributes carries a real danger of biasing the whole CSM effort. You can ask great questions and do a good job of sampling and analysis, but if you include the wrong attributes, the whole CSM program will be of marginal value.

Identifying customer-driven attributes is not technically difficult, but the process can be time-consuming. A good deal of patience should be exercised to make sure that the process is done correctly because all the successive steps in the CSM program assume that it has been done.

Therefore, all internal sources of attribute information should be exhausted. This information should be used to clarify the issues to be addressed in depth interviews and focus groups. Even though many firms skip the depth interviews and go directly to focus groups, that approach is not quite as efficient. Depth interviews are very good at clarifying the blind spots that need to be addressed in focus groups.

Focus groups usage is almost mandatory in CSM research. For most firms, having customers identify forty to seventy-five attributes when management has identified twenty to thirty is a real eye-opener.

And the same concept applies to reducing the attribute list. An attribute list reduced by focus groups is seldom the same as one reduced by management. But reducing the attributes should also involve validity. It is upon this reduced list that the questionnaire will be built.

GTE CORPORATION

Identifying the Attributes Application

GTE Telephone Operations (GTE-TO) is a unit of GTE Corp. GTE-TO sells local phone service and equipment to residential and business customers in thirty-one states, as well as Canada and the Dominican Republic. GTE-TO generates revenue of more than $12 billion in an increasingly deregulated and competitive industry.

As the industry has deregulated, customer satisfaction has become increasingly important. Initially GTE-TO focused its research efforts on residential customer satisfaction. However, the unit expanded its business research and now conducts a CSM survey involving 20,000 interviews annually.

Prior to designing a telephone survey instrument, GTE-TO conducted both qualitative and quantitative research to determine which attributes were most important to its business customers. The primary qualitative technique was focus groups.

Five focus groups involving thirty-one customers were held at different U.S. locations. In total, these focus groups identified seventy-five different attributes for telephone services. Customers identified such issues as voice transmission quality, repair responsiveness, network quality, and system reliability. Terms such as quality were further decomposed. Voice transmission quality could include voice clarity, no echo, no background static, and no background conversations, for example.

To reduce this list, depth interviews were conducted with 280 telecommunications managers from different regions. For objectivity, the interviews included both GTE customers and competitors' customers. The interviews resulted in the identification of thirty-one key attributes, which then became the subject of quantitative analysis. The quantitative analysis helped shape the attributes into related groups and identified their relative importance to the customer. This reduced and refined attribute list then became the heart of GTE-TO's business-customer CSM survey.

For GTE-TO, the identification of seventy-five attributes was a surprise to management. However, by using customers to generate an attribute list, GTE-TO was assured there were no blind spots overlooked that would lead to competitive weakness.

INVESTORS DIVERSIFIED SERVICES

Identifying the Attributes

As an American Express subsidiary, Investors Diversified Services (IDS) has stressed high-quality customer service. As part of that tradition, top managers would routinely staff the customer service telephones to hear the unfiltered voice of the customer. IDS also regularly conducted in-touch customer focus groups so management could stay in touch with customers. Often the managers were surprised at what customers were saying. And this type of customer feedback was not very actionable.

As a result, IDS conducted a study of customer expectations so that managers in each division could assess their own performance. The first portion of the study utilized focus groups from which four broad categories of expectations were identified. All four categories were concerned primarily with the characteristics of the individual financial planner. IDS managers were again surprised that corporate image was not a dominant factor.

From the focus groups, twenty-two attributes of an individual financial planner and fifteen attributes relating to the corporate headquarters were identified. IDS used a sample of 600 clients to develop a database to study the attributes statistically.

Of the twenty-two financial planner attributes, fourteen emerged as important and included an individual's product knowledge, taking responsibility for problem solving, ability to communicate clearly, and prompt responsiveness to requests.

Of the fifteen overall corporate attributes, only three emerged as important. They dealt with accurate paperwork, prompt responsiveness to requests, and offering a variety of investment products. Once again IDS managers were surprised at the heavy emphasis placed by customers on individual planner attributes compared with corporate attributes.

The reduction of the initial thirty-seven attributes to a reduced list of the seventeen most important yielded very actionable data. Both corporate and division managers were able to develop strategies to improve each attribute.

6

Basic Issues in Questionnaire Design

Designing a questionnaire of any sort is an art, not an exact science. Thus, as with any art, beauty is in the eye of the beholder, to an extent. But the beholder of most concern is the customer, not the designer of the questionnaire. Therefore, in the design of a questionnaire, everything must be done from the perspective of the customer. This is precisely why pretesting, discussed briefly in the introductory chapters, is so important, because a pretest is a formalized way to solicit customer reactions to the questionnaire.

Communication Model

It is often helpful to think of a questionnaire as a communications tool. But it is not a one-way communication device, only obtaining information from customers. A questionnaire is a two-way communication tool whereby the company communicates a request for information and the customer communicates a response in some fashion. In the case of mailed questionnaires, the process is completed by means of a written questionnaire and a written response.

This two-way communication process is presented very simply in Figure 6.1. Each of the eight steps shown holds the potential for error in some way. Because this is a sequential process, errors in any step will affect subsequent steps in some way. An error early on can be very costly. The following discussion, while illustrating the process through a mail survey, is relevant to all types of questionnaire formats.

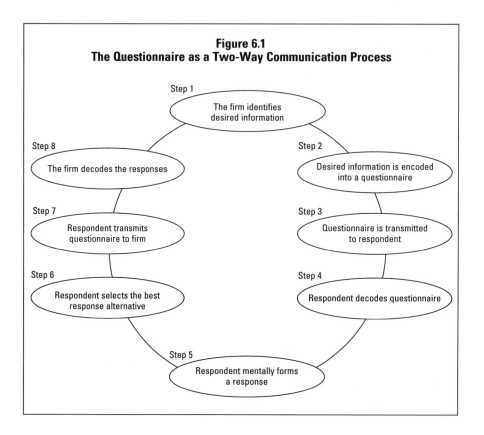

Figure 6.1
The Questionnaire as a Two-Way Communication Process

Step 1
The firm identifies desired information

Step 8
The firm decodes the responses

Step 2
Desired information is encoded into a questionnaire

Step 7
Respondent transmits questionnaire to firm

Step 3
Questionnaire is transmitted to respondent

Step 6
Respondent selects the best response alternative

Step 4
Respondent decodes questionnaire

Step 5
Respondent mentally forms a response

The first step has been the subject of the previous several chapters. Identification of the objectives leads to the need for certain types of information. The need for information normally requires that the relevant attributes be identified. Once this is done, the task of developing a questionnaire comes next.

Step two implies that the request for certain information, which is usually stated in the language of the firm, can be translated into language that can be clearly understood by the customer. This translation and encoding of desired information represent a complex process that is discussed in detail in this chapter.

Step three is discussed subsequently in the sampling chapter. Essentially, it requires a means of getting the questionnaire to correct respondents. Generally, an accurate mailing/phone list must be available, and the desired respondent must complete the questionnaire. As discussed later, this does not always happen.

The next step, step four, occurs when the respondent reads the cover letter and questionnaire and tries to determine what is being asked. The respondent normally has several things in mind at this point such as, How long will this take? and How difficult will it be? Answers to these questions are usually formed very quickly by scanning the cover letter and questionnaire. The word *scanning* is used because most respondents do not bother to read every word of a cover letter, an introduction, the directions, the questions, and so forth.

After the respondent decodes the purpose of the questionnaire, in step five a mental response is made. The first and most obvious decision is whether to complete the questionnaire or to throw it away. The cover letter, introduction, appearance of the questionnaire, and first few questions play a dominant role in this process. However, let's assume for a moment that the respondent decides to complete the questionnaire. In this case, the respondent must read each question and formulate some type of response. The assumption here is that when the respondent decodes the question, the respondent develops the same understanding of the question that was intended by the designer of the question.

Once the respondent has decoded a question, in step six the respondent reviews the response categories, which can be in the form of open or closed responses. Technically, this is referred to as measurement and scaling. From the set of alternatives, the respondent selects or provides the best alternative. The response categories should allow a respondent to present true feelings and attitudes, but this is not always the case.

In step seven, the respondent transmits the questionnaire back to the firm. This is a simple and straightforward step that is usually accomplished through the use of a stamped or postage-paid, self-addressed return envelope.

The final step, step eight, occurs when the firm decodes the responses communicated by respondents. Again, for accuracy, the receiver of the information, now the firm, must interpret the responses as the respondent intended. This interpretation process is directly related to the initial design of the questionnaire.

Too often, a questionnaire is thought of as a one-way communication device designed to allow a customer to furnish information to a firm. In reality, the questionnaire is only a highly visible instrument in a two-way communication process involving many sequential steps. By thinking of the questionnaire as a two-way tool, the firm must place added importance on step two, encoding the desired information into a questionnaire. However, before we move into technical discussions of questionnaire development, several other issues that influence questionnaire design must be addressed.

BASIC ISSUES IN QUESTIONNAIRE DESIGN

CSM research is concerned predominantly with attitudes, so a common understanding of attitudes must be developed. Related to attitudes are issues of volatility, bias, validity, meaningfulness, awareness, and reliability. Each of these constitutes a rather general issue that is important to all aspects of questionnaire design, including the cover letter. Therefore, a brief discussion of each is presented.

Attitudes

The purpose of a CSM questionnaire is usually to accurately capture the customer's attitudes toward various attributes of products and services. The most common attitudes studied are performance (How are we doing?), importance (How important is this attribute to you?), and comparison (How are we doing compared with the competition). On the surface, such attitudes appear reasonable and easy to understand.

However, attitude formation is a complex process that involves unique interaction between an individual and a specific environment surrounding a particular situation. Attitudes can be formulated toward a person, an object, a specific situation, or a more general referent. A specific attitude toward one of these referents can overpower attitudes toward the others. This is what Jan Carlzon, CEO of SAS Airlines, was implicitly referring to when he said, "One negative offsets six positive experiences."

A customer can have a negative, or positive, experience with an employee and conclude that the firm is either uniformly bad, or uniformly good, based on that one interaction. This is especially true in the service industries that have a higher degree of direct employee-customer interaction. As an example, a customer goes to a bank to open a new account by depositing a portion of a check and taking some cash. The teller acts sullen to the point of rudeness, so the customer picks up the check and walks out of the bank. One person—in this case the teller—created a negative overall customer attitude toward the bank.

Likewise, a customer might buy four tires for a car, have one go bad, and conclude that the brand is no good. Or a customer might go to a restaurant eight times, and on the ninth time have a problem with the food and conclude that the restaurant is lousy. A student may have difficulty completing the registration process at a university and conclude that the whole university is inept.

For attitudinal information to be useful, a researcher must be able to understand why a customer has developed a particular attitude. Unfortunately, decomposing attitudes by causal factors is difficult to do with a mail questionnaire. A mail questionnaire is good for identifying overall attitudes, but the "why" probes used in a telephone survey are probably better for digging more deeply into the customer's mind so as to improve understanding.

Volatility

Volatility is concerned with the stability of attitudes over time. For example, a student satisfaction survey would indicate registration is more of a problem if the survey is completed two weeks after registration in September than if the survey were conducted in December. Attitudes toward registration would be fairly volatile and vary considerably over time. Attitudes toward student parking, something experienced daily, would be much less volatile and would demonstrate very little change over time.

A large western electric utility surveyed all its customer groups once a year in late October. The residential users were pretty satisfied, but the agricultural users were very dissatisfied. Because September and October were mild weather months, very little electricity was required by residential users for either air-conditioning or heating. Because monthly bills were low, the recency of customer evaluation on this attribute dominated other attributes and led to high satisfaction levels.

On the other hand, agricultural users used electricity predominantly for irrigation pumps, and their October bill usually represented the last of five months of high electrical usage. The result was that the agricultural users had a consistently more negative satisfaction level than if their survey were conducted in March or April.

There is some evidence that the more important a particular issue is to a customer, the less volatile the attitudes will be. Because electric bills are more important to agricultural users, their attitudes would be less volatile over time than the attitudes of residential users. They might have generally negative attitudes all year long, for example.

Also, attitudes tend to be more volatile when a customer experiences conflict among different attributes. If a firm is performing well on some attributes and poorly on others, customer attitudes tend to be more volatile. The more uniform a customer's attitudes toward various attributes, the less volatile each attitude is individually and generally.

Bias

Bias occurs when a customer's response is influenced by factors other than true attitudes. Bias can be introduced through any number of factors. One of the most obvious ways is through sampling errors such as using an unrepresentative sample, but that issue is discussed in a subsequent chapter. In this chapter, bias is discussed as it is relevant to cover letters, introductions, question wording, scaling, and sequencing.

For now, an example from a recent customer satisfaction survey will be used to illustrate the problem. The U.S. Postal Service (USPS) recently started surveying customers by using a variety of instruments. One of the pieces that was used was a trifold using heavy paper. The front of the trifold carried the typical address label directed to the "Residential Customer" at a particular address.

On the back of the trifold, which was sealed lightly with glue, the following statement appeared. Please keep in mind that most individuals would read this statement before ever opening the trifold and getting to the cover letter and questionnaire.

> The United States Postal Service wants you to know—
> Currently 87% of American households rate United States Postal Service performance and prices as "Good," "Very Good," or "Excellent." It is the USPS goal during the next year to significantly *raise the percentage of Americans rating it in these categories.*
>
> *No tax dollars are used to subsidize the U.S. Postal Service,* which, based on international postage cost and performance statistics, is rated as the most efficient and least expensive postal system in the world. *But the Postal Service recognizes that it must improve service performance and continue to reduce operating costs in order to meet your needs and expectations.* You can help us provide service that better meets your expectations by *reading the message from your Postmaster inside this mailer and by completing and mailing the response card enclosed.*

In the first sentence the reader is told that virtually everybody rates the U.S. Postal Service a "Good" or better. The second sentence, in italic print, states the goal is to get even higher ratings. The third sentence educates the reader that the USPS is the best in the world. The fourth refers to "continue to reduce costs." As you shall see later, the cover letter inside the trifold provides more of the same. Finally, an equally biased question is presented.

After the customer is thus educated and basically told that anything less than "Good" is a stupid response, there isn't much doubt about the impact on respondent attitudes. It would be interesting to see the extent to which such a statement skews responses.

As we shall see, bias does not have to be nearly so blatant. It can be done by simply changing one word in a question or slightly modifying the end point in bipolar scale. To the extent that a firm wants unbiased responses—an assumption made in this chapter—the goal is to remove bias as much as possible.

Validity

In Chapter 3, the issue of validity was raised and briefly discussed. There are a number of validity conceptualizations—such as construct, or criterion, validity, convergent validity, discriminant validity, and sample validity—on which we will elaborate.

Construct validity indicates whether a question actually measures what it is supposed to measure. This is influenced by the wording of a particular question and in the case of a closed-end question, by the scaling and measurement used.

For CSM purposes, the best way to determine construct validity is to have a customer-based focus group go over each question in the questionnaire and discuss the interpreted meaning. In the communication model in Figure 6.1, this would be a testing of steps four, five, and six. The results would indicate whether customers decoded the same meaning from the question as intended by the researcher. The results would also indicate whether the response categories were broad enough to accurately capture customers' true attitudes.

For example, the following questions, drawn from actual CSM surveys, lack construct validity because of the ambiguity associated with each. The questions are taken from a convenience survey form placed in each room of a national hotel chain.

Please rate and comment on the following areas:

Service   □ Excellent   □ Good   □ Fair   □ Poor
    Comments:

Facility   □ Excellent   □ Good   □ Fair   □ Poor
    Comments:

The reason that the foregoing lack construct validity is that each attribute is so ambiguous that ten different customers could interpret each attribute ten different ways. *Service* could be front desk service, bell service, laundry service, maid service, restaurant service, or any number of other services.

Facilities could mean recreational facilities, such as exercise rooms, tennis courts, putting greens, or jogging track. Or it could mean business facilities, such as meeting rooms, tables, chairs, microphones, and projectors. Or it could mean a spacious lobby, nice restaurants, or charming shops. Or it could mean a comfortable bed, spacious room, relaxing chairs, a desk for working, or a computer table and modem line.

Further, the measurement scale doesn't allow a very wide range of response categories. What if the customer thought facilities were downright terrible? Is "Poor" a close enough alternative to capture the customer's true attitudes? Probably not. When the range of actual response categories doesn't accurately mirror the respondent's true attitudes, problems of construct validity begin to emerge. The extent of the problem depends on just how close, or how far off, the categories might be.

The following items come from the customer satisfaction survey of a bank. Both of the items appeared toward the end of a brief questionnaire and were apparently trying to obtain a demographic profile.

Please tell us about yourself:

Lifestyle
_____ Single / No children
_____ Married / No children
_____ Single / Children
_____ Married / Children
_____ Age(s) of children at home

Your Employment
_____ Professional Managerial
_____ Technical
_____ Retired
_____ Clerical / Labor
_____ Student
_____ Other

The first question is supposedly about lifestyle. Yet in the most commonly used form, the response categories have absolutely nothing to do with lifestyle. The response categories appear to be a cross between marital status and family situation. Further, the response categories have even more problems. Single / No children and Married / No children are pretty straightforward. But does Single / Children mean single and never been married? Or does it mean divorced? Or does it mean both? In our society, *single* and *divorced* have different meanings to many people.

Then, in the trailer at the bottom of the response category, reference is made to children at home. Does the respondent of, say, 45 years of age, who has two grown children who no longer live at home now go back and change the response category Married / Children to Married / No children? The implication is that children don't count if they don't live at home.

This question lacks construct validity not only because of the ambiguous term *Lifestyles*, but also because of the inappropriate references to children. All three of these issues, which render the question worthless, are correctable and would have become apparent had this instrument been subject to focus group pretesting of any sort.

The second question is just as bad. Apparently, the question was trying to evaluate type of employment. In the previous question, the diagonal slash, /, seemed to imply *and* as in "single and no children." Does the slash now mean *and* again? Or does it mean *or*? My guess is that it means *or*, but that is only my opinion. Yours might be different and we'd both be correct.

The response categories appear pretty narrow. Where would an entrepreneur, a teacher, a fireman, or an IRS (heaven forbid!) employee be placed in this set of response alternatives? The Other category is probably the best bet, and when the Other category gets heavy usage, it indicates a construct validity problem. The response categories simply don't provide enough in the way of alternatives to capture reality.

Further, there appears to be a sequential bias from better to worse employment status reading from top to bottom. The Clerical / Labor category has the potential to insult people because it is a lower category. Some clerical personnel have college degrees and are highly skilled at computer applications, and they may resent being grouped with laborers. Conversely, a laborer may operate a piece of equipment worth $200,000 and make $40,000 a year and resent being grouped with secretaries.

One final question should illustrate another problem of construct validity. This comes from a different U.S. Postal Service survey that was a little more refined than the one discussed previously. But it presents the respondent with a fairly difficult task.

The directions for this questionnaire anchored the respondent's opinion "of the U.S. Postal Service's performance *during the past three months* on some general topics." One of the subsequent questions appears below.

Please rate the U.S. Postal Service on . . .
Consistency of delivering *mail from outside your local area* in the same number of days each time.

(Poor		Fair)	Good	(Very Good	Excellent)	Don't Know
1	2	3	4	5	6	7
☐	☐	☐	☐	☐	☐	☐

The question attempts to measure the respondent's attitudes toward the consistency of mail service. However, for respondents to accurately respond, they must partition incoming mail by whether it is local versus nonlocal mail. Then, for the nonlocal mail, the respondent would apparently look at the postmark date, many of which are illegible, compare it to the date of receipt, and calculate the days in transit. Then the respondent would have to track the in-transit days for some period of time within the stipulated three months to determine the degree of consistency, that is, whether it is the same.

Realistically, the respondent will not make the necessary computations. Therefore, the responses are not likely to answer what the question is asking for. Hence the question lacks construct validity because it asks for one thing and gets something else as a response.

Further, the response scale has problems. When an uneven scale is used, seven points in this example, the midpoint is normally viewed as neutral, or average, by respondents. By placing Good at the midpoint, with only two of the seven responses that could be viewed as Poor—1 and 2—the response categories don't mirror reality. Also, there are five descriptors—four grouped into parentheses for some reason—and seven boxes. This leads to respondent ambiguity. Hence, the problems with the requested information are compounded by a biased scale that limits responses. The result is a question that lacks construct validity.

Convergent Validity
Convergent validity is the ability of each question to measure some different dimension of an underlying concept. Let's presume for a moment, that the stated goal is to measure overall customer satisfaction. To improve reliability—a subject to be discussed shortly—aggregating several questions is normally a preferable approach.

The following three questions appear on the Toyota CSM questionnaire that is sent to the customer after one of the periodic new car service checkups. There are quite a few other questions, and these three are interspersed at different points throughout the questionnaire. Spreading these types of questions out is a useful technique to reduce the likelihood of a sequential pattern developing on these global questions.

Would you recommend this dealership to a friend as a place to have a Toyota serviced?

Definitely Recommended	Probably Recommended	Might or Might Not Recommended	Probably Not Recommended	Definitely Not Recommended
5	4	3	2	1

Please explain why: _____

If for any reason you had to replace your Toyota, do you think you would buy from this dealer?

Definitely	Probably	Might or Might Not	Probably Not	Definitely Not
5	4	3	2	1

If for any reason you had to replace your Toyota, do you think you would buy another Toyota?

Definitely	Probably	Might or Might Not	Probably Not	Definitely Not
5	4	3	2	1

Although these three questions are very general, each has a different referent—service, the dealer, and the brand. The underlying concept is overall customer satisfaction, but each question draws on a somewhat different dimension. These three questions would probably have a pretty high degree of convergent validity.

Whereas construct validity is somewhat ambiguous and relies on the subjective perceptions of both managers and customers, convergent validity can be determined. Without going into the mechanics of the statistics, suffice it to say the analysis measures the ability of each construct to contribute to the overall satisfaction score. Thus it is possible to determine which of the three is the best predictor of overall satisfaction. It is also possible to tell whether a particular question contributes little or nothing to the overall score and should therefore be dropped from the questionnaire.

Discriminant Validity

Discriminant validity is the ability of each question to measure something that is somehow distinct from the other questions. Normally, if a very long attribute list is developed and each attribute is converted into a question, there is conceptual overlap between some of the questions. For example, three or four questions may measure essentially the same underlying characteristic. Thus, there may be a high degree of redundancy among the questions and no real need to include all of them in the final draft of the questionnaire. Questionnaire length is often a problem, so deleting repetitious questions is usually helpful.

If the attribute list has been reduced properly, as discussed in the previous chapter, the reduced list should contain only attributes that are unique and relatively distinct from one another. Again, discriminant validity can be measured by examining the incremental ability of each question to contribute to an understanding of overall satisfaction. Several statistical techniques exist that allow this to be done once a database has been compiled.

Meaningfulness

A common assumption is that because a specific topic, issue, or series of questions is important to the researcher, it is equally important to respondents. However, that assumption is not always valid. Therefore, a great deal of importance can be placed on data, when in fact the respondents really didn't care much about the issue.

A respondent's answers may lack meaningfulness for a variety of reasons. A respondent may be very sincere when making a response but simply lack the knowledge necessary to form accurate answers. This is especially true when asking respondents to make comparative assessments of competing products. A customer may have little actual knowledge and thus responds based on vague perceptions. This has been demonstrated in the auto industry when both U.S. and Japanese cars are produced on the same assembly line, but consumers perceive the Japanese cars to be of significantly higher quality, more reliable, and so forth.

A respondent may give sincere answers based on partial or incomplete information that is extended to the whole issue. This is analogous to the four blind men who tried to describe an elephant by each feeling a portion for themselves. Each was completely accurate in describing what was felt, but each was completely inaccurate in total when describing the whole elephant. Therefore, it is important to try to determine what the basis of the respondent's attitudes might be.

Respondents may not know why something was done or may not have thought of an issue. For example, most consumers have difficulty explaining why they bought a particular piece of clothing, such as a shirt or blouse, from among all the alternatives available. The typical response is they "like it." The respondent may respond with an answer that sounds good logically, but may not depict what really went on at the time of purchase.

The way that meaningfulness is determined is by measuring the respondent's level of awareness and the salience of a topic. These issues are closely related to meaningfulness and are discussed next.

Awareness and Salience

Awareness and salience are two related and important issues. Awareness is self-explanatory: greater knowledge of and experience with an issue lead to greater awareness. Generally, the higher the level of respondent awareness, the more meaningful the responses will be, and therefore the better the data set.

Salience concerns the importance of a particular issue to the respondent. The more important the issue, the higher the level of awareness, and therefore the greater the meaningfulness of responses.

Awareness

The issue of gay rights, for instance, has stirred a good deal of debate. However, the average American probably has a relatively low awareness of the key issues either for or against gay rights. The average respondent probably has an attitude about whether being gay is socially acceptable or unacceptable and simply extends that "for or against" attitude to the gay rights debate. Overall awareness is low.

However, if a series of questions are developed to measure awareness and salience, then a better respondent profile will emerge. For example, answers to the following questions would result in a more accurate profile. Have you discussed gay rights initiatives, such as those in Colorado or Oregon, with an individual or group in the past sixty days? Do you have a friend or relative who is gay?

The same concept could be applied to any number of other issues such as abortion, nuclear energy, environmental damage, and endangered species. However, the topic of this book is CSM, so let's return to that issue.

A good CSM program determines what the respondent's attitudes are. This is the answer to the general, How are we doing? question. A good CSM program also determines how strongly the respondent feels about the issue and measures both awareness and salience. The following questions, taken from the United Airlines in-flight CSM questionnaire, provide a good example of measurement of awareness.

Including today's trip, how many total air round-trips have you made in the past 12 months on United Airlines and all other airlines, *including* United?

	None	1 or 2	3–5	6–10	11–20	21–40	41–59	60+
a. Number of business trips								
— On United	○	○	○	○	○	○	○	○
— On all airlines, including United	○	○	○	○	○	○	○	○
b. Number of pleasure/personal trips:								
— On United	○	○	○	○	○	○	○	○
— On all airlines, including United	○	○	○	○	○	○	○	○

These questions provide a quick profile of the awareness of respondents. A business traveler who flies exclusively on United, say, once a month, will have a good awareness level for evaluating United's performance across a variety of attributes. However, that same traveler would have a low awareness of how United compares with other airlines. Instead, a traveler who frequently flies on various airlines has a higher awareness level of competitive performance.

By asking this type of question, United can segment its database in a variety of ways. It can determine whether the attitudes of infrequent fliers are the same as those of frequent fliers and then use the information to develop more effective marketing strategies. Also, by focusing on the responses of frequent fliers, United can use these data as an accurate customer-driven measure of service quality.

The following question appeared on the CSM questionnaire of a national hotel chain. The questionnaire was mailed to the customer's address after the customer's visit. The awareness questions appeared as follows:

a. How many overnight business trips have you made during the past 12 months?
   None   1 or 2   3–5   6–14   15–24   25–49   50 or more

b. On how many of these trips did you stay at a _____ hotel?
   None   1 or 2   3–5   6–14   15–24   25–49   50 or more

These questions accomplish somewhat the same end as the United questions but with an important difference. Earlier in the hotel questionnaire, the respondent was asked to indicate whether the trip was for pleasure, business, or convention. But the awareness question, only a few questions later, asked about business trips only. Perhaps the hotel didn't really care about pleasure travelers or convention attendees. As a result of not asking about other user groups, or customer segments, the richness of the data is reduced and of less value. The point is that awareness levels should be monitored for all customer segments, not just one. The marginal impact on the questionnaire is usually slight, just another line or two, but the contribution to improved data quality is usually worth it.

One final question on awareness will illustrate the problem of not measuring awareness level. The series of questions presented in Figure 6.2 comes from the CSM questionnaire of a hotel and casino in Nevada. The hotel has six different restaurants, and the names have been changed to protect the identity of the hotel. The respondent is asked to grade the hotel restaurants using a report card grading scale of A through F, with A being excellent and F being failure.

Nowhere in the directions does it say what to do if you haven't eaten at a particular restaurant. And the question of frequency of use is not asked. Therefore, the hotel doesn't really know if respondents have even eaten in a particular restaurant or how many times the respondent has dined there. Because awareness was not measured in any way, the hotel doesn't know how meaningful the responses are. The value of such data is relatively low.

This problem is really very simple to correct. A Did-not-dine-there column could be added to the right of the grading scale. The customers would then be partitioned into users and nonusers of each restaurant. Or conversely, frequency of use could be measured by six questions, one for

Figure 6.2

4. Dining		A	B	C	D	E
a. Red Room	Service	☐	☐	☐	☐	☐
	Food quality	☐	☐	☐	☐	☐
	Price/Value	☐	☐	☐	☐	☐
b. Blue Buffet	Service	☐	☐	☐	☐	☐
	Food quality	☐	☐	☐	☐	☐
	Price/Value	☐	☐	☐	☐	☐
c. Showroom	Service	☐	☐	☐	☐	☐
	Food quality	☐	☐	☐	☐	☐
	Price/Value	☐	☐	☐	☐	☐
d. Green Room	Service	☐	☐	☐	☐	☐
	Food quality	☐	☐	☐	☐	☐
	Price/Value	☐	☐	☐	☐	☐
e. Orange Café	Service	☐	☐	☐	☐	☐
	Food quality	☐	☐	☐	☐	☐
	Price/Value	☐	☐	☐	☐	☐
f. Room Service	Service	☐	☐	☐	☐	☐
	Food quality	☐	☐	☐	☐	☐
	Price/Value	☐	☐	☐	☐	☐

Comments _____

_____

_____

5. Casino	A	B	C	D	E
a. Friendliness of cocktail servers	☐	☐	☐	☐	☐
b. Atmosphere/decor	☐	☐	☐	☐	☐
c. Personnel friendliness	☐	☐	☐	☐	☐
d. Personnel service	☐	☐	☐	☐	☐
e. Cleanliness & upkeep	☐	☐	☐	☐	☐
f. Space to gamble	☐	☐	☐	☐	☐

Comments _____

_____

_____

6. Cocktail service	A	B	C	D	E
a. Speed of service	☐	☐	☐	☐	☐
b. Service friendliness	☐	☐	☐	☐	☐

Comments _____

_____

_____

each restaurant. Either way, awareness level will be measured and more meaningful data will result.

Salience

Salience, as mentioned previously, concerns the relative importance of an attribute, product, topic, or issue to the respondent. Whereas awareness is usually measured indirectly in some way through product usage, salience is usually measured more directly.

When we get to the scaling and measurement discussion contained in the next chapter, technical issues of measurement will be discussed. For now, several examples will be provided to illustrate how and why salience should be measured.

In most situations, a CSM questionnaire includes ten to twenty attributes. It is pretty unlikely, however, that all the attributes are equally important to the customer. Very often three or four attributes dominate the others.

The need to know the salience of each attribute grows out of resource allocation and competitive positioning. Virtually all organizations have scarce resources, so resources must be allocated where they'll do the most good. Within a CSM context, that means the resources for process improvement should be allocated first to the areas of predominant importance to customers. Once performance is high on those attributes, resources can be allocated to process improvement in areas of moderate, and then low, importance to customers. The following are some examples of how salience can be measured. The first example is for a restaurant in a hotel.

How important was each of the following food and beverage items in determining your overall satisfaction with your hotel stay?

	Extremely Important								Not at All Important
Overall dining experience	10	9	8	7	6	5	4	3	2	1
Overall breakfast experience	10	9	8	7	6	5	4	3	2	1
Overall lunch experience	10	9	8	7	6	5	4	3	2	1
Overall room service	10	9	8	7	6	5	4	3	2	1

Although this question is general, the responses will provide a rough idea of the relative importance of each type of dining experience. The problem with this type of scale is that respondents tend to view everything as relatively important. Therefore, the mean responses are usually above the midpoint. On this scale the mean response would probably be around 6 or 7 for each item, so the issue becomes which is relatively more important.

To correct the problems with an interval-scale salience measure, some firms use a forced allocation approach. The following is an example of this type of question:

Please allocate 100 points among the six items listed below to indicate how important each of these was to you in selecting today's flight. The more important an item, the more points should be given to it. You may allocate all or none of the 100 points to any item, but your total must equal 100 points.

Friendliness of personnel
Departure convenience
Recommendation of travel agent
Mileage program
Price of ticket
Airline reputation

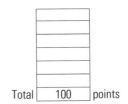

Total [100] points

This type of question forces the respondent to make a more difficult choice. The allocation process is based on the salience of each attribute, relative to the others. Although this technique works well for six or seven items or fewer, it breaks down for larger numbers. However, these kinds of salience measures do indicate, reasonably accurately, the relative importance of each attribute and the distance between attributes.

The issue of salience can be addressed for individual attributes, as in the preceding examples, or it can also be examined on a broader level. If a product is relatively unimportant to the customer, then the customer may not be very excited about completing a questionnaire. On the other hand, if a customer—a business in this case—buys several million dollars of products annually, the customer is much more concerned about supplier improvement.

Therefore, measuring the relatively importance of your products or services overall to the customer should also be done. The greater the importance of your products, the more meaningful the responses are likely to be. The techniques for doing this are much the same as the awareness questions presented earlier and could take the form of number of items used, dollar amount of purchases, or some other relative importance measure. Regardless of how it is done, salience is an issue that should be considered in the design of each CSM program.

Reliability

Reliability is the ability to get consistent results, time after time, with repeated samples. Reliability has been deferred until the end of this chapter because reliability is largely a function or a result of the other issues. Attitudinal volatility, bias, construct validity, meaningfulness, awareness, and salience all influence reliability.

The reliability of a questionnaire, or even the whole CSM program, will be damaged if any of the other issues are handled poorly. If you ask the right things of the right people, using well-crafted, unbiased questions, you will achieve reliability. Conversely, if there is a weakness in any one of the topics discussed previously in this chapter, reliability will deteriorate. A well-designed program that checks for each of these components during the preparation stage will help you avoid this problem.

SOME BASIC GUIDELINES

The issues discussed thus far in the chapter have been broader, more conceptual issues that must be considered in the design of questionnaires. Now, we'd like to provide some more specific guidelines that are relevant to all types of questionnaires.

Keep It Simple

Strive for simplicity in all aspects of the questionnaire, introduction, directions, question wording, and scaling. The more complex and difficult the task is for the respondent, the greater the likelihood of misinterpretation and confusion. When the respondent is uncertain, reliability usually declines rapidly.

The directions and questions should be short. Respondents often do not read long introductions, directions, or questions completely. Many respondents read enough so that they *think* they know what is being asked and then skip the rest. For personal or phone surveys, respondents may listen attentively and then allow their mind to wander when they become bored. Therefore, all aspects of the questionnaire should be as short and concise as possible and still achieve the research objectives.

For written questions, a rough guideline is that questions should not exceed twenty words. For verbal questioning, longer questions are generally viewed as more acceptable, and, in some cases, long questions seem to elicit longer, more detailed responses by the respondent. Some researchers have suggested that longer, verbal questions, delivered slowly, provide the respondent more time to think about the question and formulate a response. However, the best counsel is to keep questions as short and concise as possible and still convey the desired meaning.

The counsel for simplicity also applies to the words used. Long words, technical jargon, and ambiguous words (those with multiple meanings) should be avoided. The best advice is to write questions in common conversational format. Therefore, some questions may not be technically correct grammatically, but may still be very good questions. An interesting guideline for wording is that questions should be worded for an individual with an eighth-grade education. That is the average level of everyday spoken English.

The need for simple wording also applies to response categories and scaling. The more difficult it is for a respondent to interpret response categories, the less reliable the questionnaire.

Be Specific

Except for a few general lead-in questions to start a questionnaire, each question should be as specific as possible. Normally, the common rule of one concept per question is good advice. This item appeared on a CSM survey: "Please rate our product and service quality." Such double-barreled questions lead to respondent confusion. How should the respondent answer if product quality is good and service quality is terrible? It would be far better to break this into two items and aggregate the responses or weight them differentially for an overall score.

Such terms as you, regularly, and recently are vague in many cases. For business customers, does *you* refer to the respondent personally, or to the respondent's department or functional area such as engineering or purchasing, or to the company in general? It would be far better to say, *you personally* or *your department* or *your company*. In a family situation does *you* refer to the family unit, the husband, the wife, or anyone who happens to complete the questionnaire?

Instead of *regularly* or *recently*, a question should be worded *in the past week*, *in the past 30 days*, or *the last time you used* . . . This type of conceptual anchoring provides the respondent with a specific referent and makes it easier to respond.

Make the Tasks Manageable

The respondent should be able to easily perform the requested tasks. If computations are necessary, the questions should be broken down into simpler, separate issues, and the researchers should perform the computations themselves. The following question is a difficult one for respondents to answer: Has our company's proportion of your total purchases for this product decreased from last year's purchases, stayed about the same, or increased from last year's purchases?

This question requires that total expenditures be determined, that a particular company's purchases be segmented out, and that a proportion be calculated. And it must be done for two time periods and the results must be compared. For the time period, which years are to be compared? Will it be a comparison of 1993 and 1994 calendar years? But what should be done if the survey is conducted in September 1994 and only partial-year data are available? As you can see, this is not a very manageable task for respondents, as few would actually perform the calculations.

Most respondents would respond based on opinion or attitude rather than fact. That being the case, the question could be reworded to obtain a total figure and a company-specific figure. And the researcher could make the computations in a computer program.

A Questionnaire Is a Funnel

A questionnaire should be thought of as a funnel. There should be a logical transition from the opening introduction all the way through to the last question. The broader, easier-to-respond-to questions should come first, and the more detailed, specific, and sensitive questions later.

There may be a series of filters in the questionnaire. Such filters screen and route respondents to the next appropriate question. For a written questionnaire, the routing may be done with arrows to graphically lead the reader. For verbal questionnaires, respondents may not even be aware that they are being screened. Screening questions avoid the problem of asking irrelevant questions of respondents and losing their interest.

Whenever possible, related questions should be clustered together in distinct segments with a specific transition statement about the topic. An example of a transition would be, Now I'd like to ask some questions about the service that you experienced in your last visit. This would be followed by three to five service-related questions. Then another transition to another topic would appear followed by another cluster of questions.

This allows respondents to feel they are progressing through the questionnaire. Also, a long list of, say, twenty to twenty-five similarly scaled questions is visually unattractive in a mail survey. Respondents may scan the questionnaire and file it in the garbage because it doesn't "look good."

The process of completing a questionnaire educates the respondent about many issues. The questionnaire may raise some issues to a top-of-mind awareness. Therefore, the sequential relationship between specific questions or separate segments should be considered in this educational context. If the questions do a lot of educating, they should appear late in the questionnaire. Because general questions often do little educating, this is another reason they are usually located at the beginning of the questionnaire.

No Opinion/Don't Know

Awareness and salience measures indicate something about a respondent's overall knowledge of a subject, but they do not suggest that a respondent knows something about every attribute of interest to the researcher. Yet most respondents offer a response to most reasonable questions even though they may know very little about the topic. If the researcher doesn't mind, or indeed desires, uninformed responses, then omission of the No-opinion/don't-know category doesn't present any conceptual problem.

However, if accurate, precise data are desired, then inclusion of the No-opinion/don't-know category is also desirable. It has been shown that up to one-third of respondents who would give a response would select No opinion were it offered. Inherently, these uninformed responses are less reliable and could skew the overall results if a consistent response pattern were shared by respondents.

The only way to estimate the impact of the No-opinion/don't-know category is to conduct a split-sample comparison in a pretest. Half the respondents would have a questionnaire with the category, and the other half would not. The comparison of the results of the two samples would indicate the magnitude of the impact. You may also wish to distinguish between No opinion and Don't know, particularly for an image attribute. For example, if a paper company wants to know how it is perceived and what it can leverage in the area of environmental responsibility, and the results show 60% Don't know/no opinion, it may be difficult to understand the issue. Breaking out the 60% and finding that 5% have no opinion and 55% don't know provides the paper company with information that can be used for marketing communications to inform customers (provided, of course, that they have a good story!).

This discussion applies to both open and closed questions and to both written and verbal questionnaires. Although estimating the magnitude of

---

Figure 6.3

Global Measures
- Value
- Satisfaction
- Overall product and service quality
- Future reliance
- Willingness to recommend
- Price
- Meeting or exceeding expectations

Corporate Image
- Customer-oriented
- Socially responsible
- Reputation

Specific Attributes
- Product area
- Service area

---

impact of the category on open-ended questions is somewhat more difficult and subjective, the same split test can be used.

With using open-ended questions it is not necessary to repeat the option with every question. The use of No-opinion/don't-know is usually built into the initial discussion and occasionally into the transition statements between sections for reinforcement. By building the No-opinion category into the initial directions, the company implicitly sends the respondent the message that thoughtful, knowledgeable answers are important.

The CSM Questionnaire

When designing your questionnaire for CSM, you want to incorporate your CSM model into its design. This will assist in the analysis phase so that you can uncover the attributes driving customer satisfaction.

There are three major components measured in a CSM questionnaire. The components are shown in Figure 6.3. The first component comprises the global measures, which are really the overall perceptions your customers form based on performance on attributes. The most common global measures used by firms are value, overall quality, satisfaction, and future reliance. The second component is the corporate image area. Corporate image includes customer-defined attributes concerned with customer orientation, social responsibility, and reputation. The third component covers the customer-defined attributes specific to the product or service being measured. Together these components constitute the questionnaire skeleton.

CHAPTER SUMMARY

Designing a questionnaire is definitely an art. But it is certainly a complex art subject to many problems. This chapter has attempted to discuss the problems that influence the design of questionnaires of all types. Most of the problems flow from the fact that a CSM questionnaire is only one part of a far more complex two-way communication process.

Issues of attitude formation, volatility, bias, validity, meaningfulness, awareness, and salience must be considered during questionnaire design. And all of these issues interact to influence the reliability of a questionnaire. Fortunately, all of them can be addressed through good science.

Even when all of these issues are addressed, numerous concerns must be faced. A questionnaire should be as short, simple, and manageable as possible. It should have some logical flow, continuity, and transition from section to section.

In the final analysis, a questionnaire is not just a collection of individual questions. It should be viewed as a whole, one piece of a complex communication process.

DEERE & COMPANY

Exciting Quality

Deere is a manufacturer of agricultural, industrial, lawn and garden care equipment and financial services. Deere's total quality objective is to provide "Genuine Value through Continuous Improvement." The three guiding principles are Customer Focus, Process Orientation, and Involvement and Empowerment.

Deere is integrating customer feedback into its approach to providing products or services. In the past, a product was designed, tested, produced, and delivered, and aftermarket support was provided. Recognizing changes in consumer needs and wants, new technologies, global market demands, and the regulatory environment, Deere implemented a customer-focused approach that begins with the voice of the customer translated into a design:

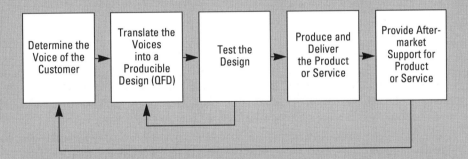

Deere collects information directly from customers through four main methods: personal and telephone interviews, focus groups, questionnaires, and direct observation via videotape. Deere also gathers customer input from other areas: routine customer contacts, warranty claims, requests for assistance, customer help lines, and secondary sources. The company then uses three methods for understanding what the customer is saying. The first is an affinity process whereby employees brainstorm what they have heard from customers. The second method involves an editing and coding process of the feedback. The third method uses cluster analysis and an analytical hierarchy process to distill key attributes and areas. Deere then transforms the voice of the customer into customer requirements:

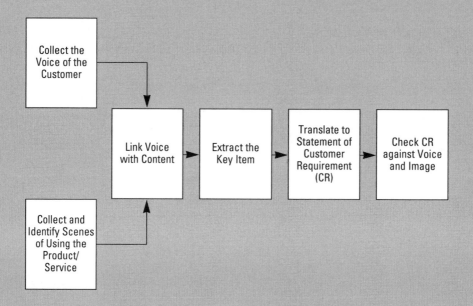

Deere then aligns and prioritizes the customer requirements with the technical descriptors that it calls the Voice of the Company to identify product and service components that can be continually improved to surpass customer expectations and provide Exciting Quality. An example of this process was in the design process of logging equipment. During the past century, North American logging operations were focused primarily in the Northwest. In the past few years, however, concern about endangered species such as the spotted owl has greatly affected logging access and practices. There has been a major shifting of logging operations from the Northwest to the Southern states, and logging in the South is conducted very differently. Deere, anticipating the changing needs, began to design specific features into its logging equipment based on information from customers as well as field testing. In this way, Deere was able to meet and surpass expectations.

More than 150 years ago, founder John Deere said, "I will never put my name on a product that does not have in it the best that is in me." It is clear that his spirit lives on in the values and focus of his employees.

7

Designing Mail Questionnaires

As should be apparent from the preceding chapter, designing a questionnaire is not an exact science, it is definitely an art. And as a form of art there is no exactly correct way to design the different components. We can, however, provide guidance about the key issues and describe the most commonly used or successful techniques.

A word of caution is appropriate before we begin. There are many books written on the subject of questionnaire design. This chapter does not delve into all of the many diverse issues relevant to all types of questionnaires. Instead, the discussion is restricted to issues that relate directly to CSM questionnaires.

The discussion begins with the cover letter and then moves through the introduction, question design, and scaling. Examples, both good and bad, are provided along the way. The three or four most common techniques are described so that readers can select from an array of choices in designing their own questionnaire.

COVER LETTER

The primary purpose of the cover letter is to induce the respondent to complete the questionnaire. This is normally done by piquing the respondent's interest in some way, normally in the first sentence or two, for that is all that may be read. Often this task is accomplished by a plea for help in some fashion.

Then the cover letter moves into a benefit section, which usually answers the respondent's question, Why should I do this? or What's in this for me? In some way, the reader is told how completing the questionnaire will be beneficial. Perhaps the firm will be better able to serve the customer's needs, create a better product, provide better service, and so forth. You may also want to offer an incentive, though such is not as necessary in CSM as in a marketing research study.

The next portion of the cover letter moves into a request for specific action: Do this now. If you can get the reader to act immediately, your questionnaire is much more likely to be completed and returned. If the questionnaire is set aside to complete later, very often it is never completed. For most mail surveys, for example, about 90% of total responses are received within two weeks of being mailed to respondents. This section also has an estimate of completion time, particularly if the physical appearance of the questionnaire is long or complex.

Finally, the last portion of the cover letter expresses gratitude to the respondent for cooperation. This is the same as the assumed sale in personal selling, in which the assumption of a sale is made. In this case the assumption is that the respondent will complete the questionnaire. At this point there is also a statement saying, If there is anything we can do . . . or If you have any questions, please call 800 . . ."

The signature on the letter is usually that of someone of high organizational stature so that the importance of the research is reinforced. To illustrate these concepts let's evaluate several actual cover letters currently in use.

The first cover letter is presented in Figure 7.1. The cover letter personally identifies the customer on a generic letter. Given the current state of computer technology, it is possible to personalize all letters, although it is more costly to do so. Nevertheless, personalized letters usually result in a higher response rate.

The letter is reasonably good. The customer is thanked for patronage and provided with an explanation of why the survey is being conducted and how the data will be used. The customer is asked to make additional comments to either the local dealer or the 800 number.

The closing with a signature is common, but the signatory is not identified organizationally as a vice president. If the title were prominently displayed below the name, the respondent might be more favorably impressed. However, signatures on form letters don't have nearly the impact that signatures on a fully personalized letter have on response rates. For smaller samples, personalized letters are probably worthwhile, but for large-scale sampling, personalization is unrealistic.

Figure 7.1

(Customer's name and address)

Dear _____ Customer:

Thank you for servicing your _____ at the _____ dealer shown on the front of the enclosed survey form.

Your opinions regarding your recent service experience (the repair date is shown in the upper right corner of the survey form) are very important to us as they will help us provide _____ products and services that satisfy your needs. We would like you to share with us your impressions and experience with your vehicle and the dealership where it was recently serviced. Please take a few moments to complete the enclosed survey.

We use the information gathered on the front page of the survey to evaluate the dealership's performance in handling your recent service needs. The data collected are used to determine your satisfaction with your _____ vehicle.

Please return the completed survey directly to _____ in the enclosed, self-addressed, postage-paid envelope. If you have additional comments, please contact your dealership's customer relations manager or our Customer Assistance Center at 800–_____–_____.

We appreciate your business and thank you for taking the time to share your opinions with us.

Sincerely,

(vice president's signature)

The second letter is presented in Figure 7.2. This letter is also a cover letter for an automobile CSM survey, but the research is not handled by the company directly. A marketing research firm administered the survey and compiled the data.

The advantage of third-party administration is that customers might be willing to say things to an independent third party that they would be unwilling to say directly to the company. Hence, the data may be more unbiased.

The disadvantage of this approach is that the customer is not dealing directly with the firm. Therefore, the customer might feel that the re-

---

Figure 7.2

(Customer's name and address)

Dear _____ Customer:

We need your help! You recently contacted _____. Your answers to the enclosed survey will be vital to _____ in evaluating current customer relations programs and procedures and in providing direction for the future.

You will find that this questionnaire is easy to read. It only should take a few minutes to fill out.

Please complete your survey carefully including written comments if desired, and return it to us promptly in the self-addressed, postage-paid envelope provided.

Your opinions are important to _____. _____ continually strives to refine products and procedures. For your answers to be used in guiding future decisions by _____, it is essential that you mail the completed survey **as soon as possible**.

Why not complete yours right now? Thank you for your time.

Sincerely,

(name of marketing research firm)

---

sponses won't make as much of an impact, that they won't be taken as seriously.

As with the previous cover letter, the customer is identified personally by name and address at the top of a generic cover letter. The remainder of the letter is shorter and more direct.

The "help!" plea is intended to grab the reader's attention and probably does so reasonably well. The benefits—improved service—are made apparent to the reader.

This cover letter, however, makes a more forceful plea for quick response in the third, fourth, and fifth paragraphs. "Promptly return it," "as soon as possible," and "complete yours right now" are intended to generate quick compliance. The danger in being too forceful is that the respondent may resent being told so directly what to do and may simply throw the questionnaire away.

The signature is weak. There is no personalized signature at all, just the name of a marketing research firm. The implication of this approach is that having an individual name makes no difference in the respondent's willingness to cooperate. This issue of signature would be a relevant one for focus group analysis during a pretest, the subject of a subsequent chapter.

The final cover letter, presented in Figure 7.3, is an example of what not to do. This one educates the reader far too much about the various attributes. The wording and detail create enough bias so that the results will have very little real value. This cover letter is on the flip side of the trifold from the statement discussed in the previous chapter for the U.S. Postal Service. Taken together, the previous statement and cover letter strongly lead the respondent.

That leading is reinforced by the design of the questionnaire card. The seven response categories are unequally spaced, which creates greater perceptual distances between the response alternatives. The line "If response is less than VERY GOOD, please give us your comments" is almost surely read before a response is given. What is surprising is that only 87% of respondents rated the Postal Service as GOOD or higher.

In summary, a cover letter does not have to be a candidate for a creative writing award. It must get the reader's attention and lead smoothly into the questionnaire. Because most terminations in a mail survey come *after* the cover letter is read but *before* the first question is completed, a good cover letter is an absolutely critical, but often overlooked, component of the questionnaire.

INTRODUCTION

Questionnaires that are mailed to respondents are usually accompanied by a cover letter that explains the rationale for the study. Such questionnaires typically have little, or nothing, in the way of an introduction. The questionnaire simply begins with a set of directions.

The questionnaires that are given to a customer at the time of the transaction, provided in businesses such as hotels and restaurants or other convenient locations, are quite similar to mail questionnaires. Even though these questionnaires lack a cover letter, the introduction fulfills the same role.

The introduction is normally a condensed version of a cover letter, typically three or four sentences long, that tries to elicit customer coop-

Figure 7.3

Dear Customer:

All of us at the U.S. Postal Service want to provide you with the best postal service possible. Therefore, we would appreciate it if you took a moment to complete the questionnaire below, tear it off, and drop it in any mailbox.

In today's U.S. Postal Service, our primary focus is satisfying our customers. Like many other businesses, we have restructured and reduced our overhead. That and other steps have enabled us to reduce our costs by $2 billion this year. As a result, we are now in a good position to keep your rates the same until 1995.

And we've listened to your suggestions. Here are some of the things we are doing across the nation to serve you better.

- Redelivering parcels either only when you are at home or, if you wish, leaving them at your doorstep
- Reducing waiting time in our post office lobbies
- Extending window hours to make our retail operations more convenient
- Bringing innovative approaches to your purchasing of stamps. (For example, you can order stamps by calling 800–STAMP–24 and pay for them with credit cards; you can mail in stamp requests by using Stamps by Mail forms; you can purchase stamps at face value in many locations such as grocery stores and stationery stores; and in some areas you can even purchase stamps through automated teller machines.)
- Establishing an active Customer Advisory Council: many post offices have volunteer members who represent a cross section of postal customers who meet to discuss the concerns of the community with postal managers.

We are genuinely committed to improving our service and are interested in what you have to say. Your feedback to us now will provide us with a starting point to measure improvements in the future. Thank you again—on behalf of all the employees at the U.S. Postal Service—for filling out our questionnaire card.

Sincerely,

Your Postmaster

- -

Zip Code of Local Office _____
Please rate the U.S. Postal Service on its overall performance.

(Poor–Fair)			Good	Very Good–Excellent			Don't Know
1	2	3	4	5	6	7	8
☐	☐	☐	☐	☐	☐	☐	☐

If response is less than Very Good, please give us your comments.

_____
_____
_____

(Please print carefully.)
Name _____
Address _____
_____

eration in completing a questionnaire. The following is an introduction from an airline CSM survey.

Dear Passenger,

_____ Airlines is pleased you have chosen to fly with us today. In order to provide you with the best possible travel experience, we would like to know a little more about you and why you are traveling today. You can help us by taking a few moments to complete this questionnaire. Your flight attendant will collect the completed form.

Thank you for your assistance.

(Signature)
Senior Vice President of Marketing

This short, succinct introduction informs customers why the survey is being done, asks for cooperation, tells what is to be done with the questionnaire, and offers thanks for customers' patronage and assistance. And, of course, it helps to have a captive audience strapped securely in their seat! Maybe the airline even keeps the "Fasten seat belts" sign on while the questionnaire is being administered.

The following introduction for a hotel is a bit longer and more detailed but is a good introduction.

Dear Guest,

At _____ Hotels we are determined to provide our guests with the highest standards of hospitality and to make your stay with us so comfortable and memorable that you will want to return.

Your evaluation of our performance is our most valuable source of information. Please take a few minutes to complete this form. Let us know of anything that did not measure up to your expectations and also tell us what pleases you.

In order to be able to quickly address any concerns you may have, this form is directed to the general manager of the hotel. You may, however, prefer to write to me directly at (address).

Thank you for choosing to stay with us.

(Signature)
President

The customer is asked to contact the president of the company directly and is given the address. This tends to increase the credibility of the questionnaire.

The next introduction is much shorter, almost to the point of being useless. It is taken from the form attached to the rearview mirror of a rental car: "Because we value your patronage, may we hear from you if there is anything _____ can do to serve you better?"

This is then followed by about half a dozen questions. The problem with this introduction is that it is conditional. The respondent is to complete the questions only if there is something either wrong or at least substandard. If a customer is pleased, then implicitly, the questionnaire should not be completed.

The introductions presented here are diverse, ranging from one sentence to three paragraphs. Regardless of the length, the purpose of the introduction is the same as for cover letters: to solicit the respondent's cooperation and involvement. The introduction should lead the customer smoothly into the directions.

DIRECTIONS

The directions can range from nothing to complex. If complex directions must be provided for a section, that section should not appear at the beginning of the questionnaire. Move the complex section toward the end of the questionnaire. The first set of directions should be as short and simple as possible.

The reason for short introductory directions is that they should be easy for the respondent to read. The following statement is from the latter portion of a consumer survey that was evaluating four different types of companies. What do you suppose the respondent's reaction would have been if this had been the initial set of directions encountered?

> We realize that there are several attributes or characteristics about companies that influence how you feel about them. Obviously, some things are more important to you than other things, and some features, while important to you about one company may not be as important to you relative to another company. Therefore, we are interested to learn how important the following attributes are to you for each company. So please rate each feature below on a scale of 1 to 10 on each line for each company and feature listed below.

Following this long direction were fourteen rows of attributes and four columns of companies. Answering this one question required making fifty-six separate evaluations, after the directions were read, reread, and understood. This type of question early in a questionnaire would be a real turnoff to respondents.

Therefore, the early directions should be as short and succinct as possible to quickly get the respondent into the flow of answering questions. The logical extension of this discussion is that the first question should also be easy.

THE FIRST QUESTIONS

The first few questions should be general, easy to answer, and directly related to the research purpose that was stated in the cover letter and/or introduction. If an unrelated question is quickly introduced, the continuity of the transition into the questionnaire may be destroyed.

These first questions should not be throwaway questions. They should be general questions related somehow to CSM. Some questionnaires begin with general demographic or background questions. However, the most common first question is, How do we rate overall, followed by some easy awareness and demographics.

After five or six questions, the questionnaire then transitions into importance, performance, satisfaction, or expectations type questions, which we'll explore shortly. If the respondent is still with you after these easy warm-up questions, the probability of completing the entire questionnaire is quite high.

The initial questions should not create too much of a leading environment, or the questionnaire may lack credibility to the respondent. For example, the initial directions for a CSM questionnaire for a national hotel chain read as follows:

Example
• This example shows that the respondent thought that overall the hotel was excellent

How would you rate our hotel on an overall basis?

Excellent   **Poor**
(●) (9) (8) (7) (6) (5) (4) (3) (2) (1)

And what do you suppose the first question was? "How would you rate our hotel on an overall basis?" The questionnaire directions suggested the rating was excellent, and the response also was given with the 10 shaded in. So, subtly, two cues were given that suggested an excellent response was appropriate. For many respondents, leading like this leads to terminations due to reduced credibility.

MEASURING IMPORTANCE

There are three primary issues that form the heart of a CSM questionnaire. These topics are the relative importance of attributes, performance or satisfaction measurement, and expectation fulfillment. One other topic, competitive assessment, is closely related to these and is discussed in the chapter on benchmarking. For now, the discussion will be restricted to importance measurement.

There are three different ways to measure importance: interval scaling, rank ordering, and forced allocation. Interval scaling is probably the most commonly used, and abused, technique. Rank ordering is probably the most difficult to use, and the least used of these three techniques. A forced allocation is probably the most accurate, but it works well only for small clusters of attributes.

Interval Scaling

Interval scaling is a technique whereby the respondent is asked to read a statement and indicate the importance of the attribute or issue. Importance is usually measured on a 7- or 10-point scale with the end points labeled Extremely important and Not at all important, or something similar. Respondents are supposed to pick a point on the scale that represents their attitude, in this case, importance.

The choice of the bipolar adjectives is critical because many sets of adjectives are not perceptual opposites of one another. If one adjective conveys a much stronger intensity than the other, the respondent's perceptual midpoint on the scale is skewed. The following example may illustrate this point.

Important									Unimportant
10	9	8	7	6	5	4	3	2	1

Extremely Important									Unimportant
10	9	8	7	6	5	4	3	2	1

On the first scale, respondents would probably perceive 5 or 6 as a neutral midpoint and anchor their responses above or below that point based on their perception of relative importance. On the second scale, the presence of *extremely* creates an uneven perceptual balance between the end points. Now, the neutral midpoint may be skewed to 6 or 7 because the use of *extremely* may overpower the *unimportant* adjective. In this case, the average rating may be skewed higher by the addition of one word: extremely. Using even more divergent bipolar adjectives could have an even greater impact on responses.

This scale has another typical response characteristic that a researcher should be aware of. Respondents in many countries read from left to right, and this obviously includes English. What is implied is that respondents begin on the left side and move to the right until they have gone "far enough." They then select a response point.

This process tends to skew responses to the left side of the scale. Again, consider the following two scales:

Important									Unimportant
10	9	8	7	6	5	4	3	2	1

Unimportant									Important
10	9	8	7	6	5	4	3	2	1

If the same statement were used for both scales, the first scale would usually produce a higher mean-response level than the second. And this brings us to an important characteristic of interval scaling: The absolute-importance rating is less important than the relative-importance rating. That is, this type of scale allows the comparison of scores between attributes, but it doesn't do a good job of determining the magnitude of difference in importance. Some actual data may better illustrate the point.

The following set of data is from the CSM survey of an electric utility. The questionnaire measured the relative importance of fourteen attributes by using a 10-point interval scale with 10 representing Extremely important and 1 representing Not at all important. The figures presented below are the mean response figures for the top six attributes.

Attribute	Mean Importance Rating
Trustworthiness	9.44
Billing accuracy	9.44
Value	9.36
Problem solving	9.31
Easily reachable	9.24
No service interruptions	9.18

As you can see, the difference between these attribute ratings is slight. A statistical comparison of means would probably show the figures are not statistically different from one another, for the most part. Therefore, the magnitude of difference between these six attributes is difficult to determine by using this scale. The lowest-rated attribute of the fourteen had a mean rating of more than 5.50, which is the numerical midpoint. However, the results do indicate which attributes were relatively more important or relatively less important, though all fourteen means were on the Important side of the scale.

The next example is for a firm in the electronics industry that regularly surveys its customers, measuring the importance of about twenty attributes. Respondents are asked to indicate the importance of each attribute on a 10-point scale, also. However, *unimportant* is represented by 10. Thus, on this scale, the numerical midpoint is 5.

The results of the firm's survey for the top ten most important attributes are presented in Figure 7.4. The mean values for the ten attributes are clustered between 9.4 and 9.0, again indicating the mean differences are slight.

However, the three years of historical data indicate important characteristics of importance ratings: (1) The relative importance of attributes tends to remain relatively stable over time. (2) Variation in the ratings from year to year is most likely due to sample variation rather than real shifts in attitudes. The implication is that gathering importance ratings annually is normally adequate, whereas performance ratings should be gathered more frequently.

The small differences between mean values among the attributes suggest that this firm should be cautious in making refined judgments based on the results. Unfortunately, that is just what this firm does. However, the data are not precise enough for what the firm is trying to do.

While the firm is gathering the importance data, it also gathers satisfaction data. The scale that is used for each attribute is given below:

Unimportant   Very Important
  O — O — O — O — O — O — O — O — O — O
  0   1   2   3   4   5   6   7   8   9   10

Dissatisfied   Very Satisfied
  O — O — O — O — O — O — O — O — O — O
  0   1   2   3   4   5   6   7   8   9   10

Although the argument could be made that both sets of bipolar adjectives are unequal and would tend to skew results, let's ignore that flaw for a moment and focus on some larger ones. By positioning these scales adjacent to one another, which is how they appear on the questionnaire,

Figure 7.4
Ten Most Important Factors
AVERAGE IMPORTANCE RATING

Element	1988	1989	1990
Software support	9.5	9.6	9.4
Hardware quality	9.5	9.4	9.4
Service technical ability	9.3	9.4	9.1
Hardware performance	9.3	9.3	9.2
Commitment to market	9.2	9.3	9.4
Service responsiveness	9.3	9.3	9.0
Spare parts availability	9.5	9.3	9.2
Software quality	9.3	9.2	9.3
Product maintainability	9.2	9.1	9.0
Attitude of supplier	—	9.0	9.0
Sales responsiveness	9.0	9.0	9.0

the questionnaire is made shorter. However, a significant sequential bias is introduced. Once the respondent indicates importance, that response will influence the satisfaction rating due simply to the close positioning. Satisfaction and importance are two distinct issues and should be physically separated.

Unfortunately, this firm, when using the data, *subtracts* the satisfaction score from the importance score to create a gap. The firm is confusing importance with ideal performance. It is mixing apples and oranges without knowing the difference. What is worse, this firm has a sophisticated system for evaluating the gaps and prioritizing the results.

For example, if satisfaction exceeds importance, the firm's conclusion is that it has overinvested in that attribute. Resources should thus be reallocated to a different area, accordingly.

The point of this discussion is that a manager needs to understand what is being measured and what the results really indicate. Importance is conceptually different from performance or satisfaction ratings. Although both are really necessary, each is a distinct concept and should be treated individually.

Let's go back to our interval-scaling discussion. Interval scales are easy to design, use, and interpret, from a researcher's standpoint, and easy to use, from a respondent's standpoint. However, it is very easy to skew the responses through the use of leading statements, direction of the scale, and use of bipolar adjectives. Probably the biggest weakness is the fact that respondents are usually hesitant to say anything is unimportant, so responses are skewed to the important side of the scale, resulting in small, and often statistically insignificant, mean differences.

Rank Ordering

Rank ordering occurs when respondents are asked to rank a series of attributes according to their perceived importance. This can be done with up to twenty attributes.

Even though rank ordering accurately indicates the order of importance, the technique does not provide any information about the magnitude of difference between attributes. One particular attribute may be twice as important as the next attribute, but such intensity would not show up in rank-order data. Rank-order data indicate the consistency with which a specific attribute is ranked second, third, or fourth, however.

A common error committed in using rank-order data is to calculate mean values for each attribute. The lowest mean value would be considered the highest ranking and so forth. This is simply conceptually and methodologically incorrect.

Once a rank ordering has been obtained, some type of weighting can be subjectively assigned to each rank for further computations with satisfaction or performance data. However, subjectively assigning weights is arbitrary and is usually not recommended.

While rank ordering is possible with up to twenty or so attributes, accuracy diminishes with the number of attributes to be ranked. Ranking six attributes is easy for most respondents. Ranking ten attributes becomes more difficult. Ranking fifteen or twenty attributes becomes very problematic for respondents.

Most respondents can identify the four or five top rankings and the four or five lowest rankings. However, the remaining attributes tend to become an inconsistent mass of rankings somewhere in between.

All in all, rank ordering of attributes is a viable technique for short or moderate-length attribute lists that solves the problem of everything being rated important. Unfortunately, ranking doesn't tell the researcher whether the real difference between ranks is quite small or quite large. Because of the empirical difficulties encountered, rank ordering is probably the least popular of the three approaches to measuring the importance of attributes.

Forced Allocation

The forced allocation technique requires that the respondent allocate a specific number of points, normally 10 or 100, across categories of attributes, usually six or fewer, based on each attribute's importance. This technique forces respondents to make choices about the relative importance of attributes *comparatively*. All attributes cannot be rated Very important, as with interval scaling.

The technique requires that respondents make more difficult, discrete distinctions between attributes. Therefore, this approach is a bit more refined and discriminating than the previous techniques. Because the data for each attribute are truly interval, from 0 to 100 points could be allocated to each attribute and the data can be analyzed using a wide variety of statistical techniques. This approach, too, is easy for respondents to understand and use.

There are a few limitations, however. When allocating points, most respondents do so in units of ten, some in units of five. Relatively few respondents segment the allocation in units of fewer than five. What this means from a technical standpoint is that the data are not truly interval, but they are certainly closer to being interval than a 10-point scale is. For practical purposes this is not much of a problem.

A bigger problem is that respondents have difficulty in using this technique with more than six or seven categories. The greater the number of categories, the more variable and inconsistent the responses tend to be. Because most firms are usually trying to evaluate the relative importance of fifteen to twenty attributes, this can be a real problem. Simply allocating 100 or 200 points, across twenty categories, would be viewed as what researchers describe as an unmanageable task.

The solution to the problem is to decompose the attribute list into a number of groupings. The process for doing this is to use managerial judgment, focus groups, or statistical analysis (factor analysis), which were discussed in a previous chapter.

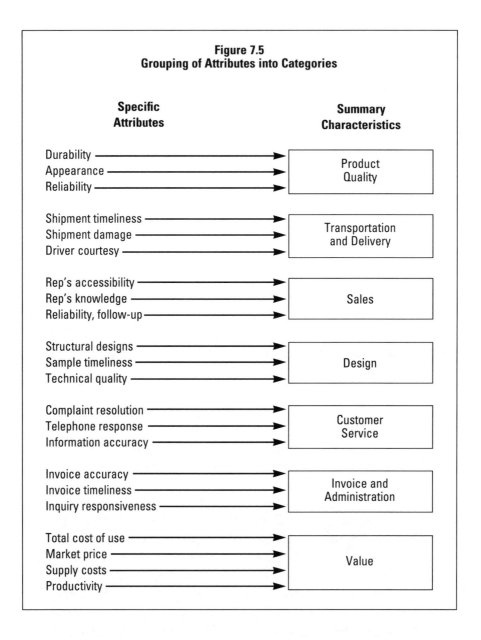

Figure 7.5
Grouping of Attributes into Categories

Specific Attributes	Summary Characteristics
Durability, Appearance, Reliability	Product Quality
Shipment timeliness, Shipment damage, Driver courtesy	Transportation and Delivery
Rep's accessibility, Rep's knowledge, Reliability, follow-up	Sales
Structural designs, Sample timeliness, Technical quality	Design
Complaint resolution, Telephone response, Information accuracy	Customer Service
Invoice accuracy, Invoice timeliness, Inquiry responsiveness	Invoice and Administration
Total cost of use, Market price, Supply costs, Productivity	Value

An example of how this might be done is presented in Figure 7.5. The twenty-two attributes are grouped into seven categories. Respondents could be given a figure like this and asked to allocate 100 points across the categories, based on the relative importance of each category. Then, in a separate question for each category, respondents could be asked to rate the relative importance of each attribute within a category. The process generates a series of weightings that allows the relative importance of each attribute to be determined relative to other attributes within the category and in other categories.

The forced allocation technique is probably the most discriminating approach to measure the relative importance of attributes. However, it is cumbersome to use for large attribute lists, and the calculation of weighting factors may make the interpretation of results a little more difficult.

Since importance data do not need to be gathered as frequently as performance data, once a year is usually sufficient. Creating a questionnaire that measures only importance is not an unreasonable alternative. When this is done, ample room is available for constructing forced allocation questions, even for long attribute lists.

STATISTICAL ANALYSIS

When using any of the three techniques just described, the analysis should consist of more than simple rank ordering by mean values or self-reported rank. The data should also be analyzed through the use of regression analysis. Regression analysis indicates whether respondents are giving "socially acceptable" responses that mask true attitudes.

In the use of regression analysis, variation in each attribute is analyzed as a predictor of the overall satisfaction index. Usually, two or three overall satisfaction questions are aggregated. This normally improves the reliability of the satisfaction index. Then, regression analysis is done, simultaneously evaluating the ability of each attribute to predict the satisfaction index. The best predictors, statistically, are the most important attributes, and this is expressed as a regression coefficient.

Earlier, the mean-value results were presented for a CSM survey by a utility company. Table 7.1 presents those results and an expanded analysis of the rankings.

If only the mean values are used, the Mean rank column indicates what the rankings are. However, when the mean rank is compared with regression rank, major discrepancies emerge. Even though the top four regression ranks are in the top six mean ranks, there is little consistency in the order.

There are two reasons for this disparity in rankings. First, the mean values for the top six ranks are so similar that they are not statistically different from one another. Therefore, distinguishing ranks for each attribute based on mean values is methodologically inappropriate and rather arbitrary. The same comment could be made for the rankings presented in Figure 7.4.

Table 7.1   Regression Analysis of Importance Data

Key Objectives	Mean Value	Mean Rank	Regression Rank
Trustworthiness	9.44	1	6
Billing accuracy	9.44	2	4
Value	9.36	3	1
Problem solving	9.31	4	3
Easily reachable	9.24	5	13
No service interruptions	9.18	6	2
Friendly employees	—	9	5

The second reason for the disparity is the socially acceptable issue mentioned earlier. Some respondents may be hesitant to admit that money, a key component of value, is the dominant decision criterion. They may feel it is nobler and more humanitarian to reward trustworthiness. Also, respondents may have a more difficult time determining an importance rating for an intangible; in this case, regression analysis can determine underlying importance.

When there is conflict between self-reported importance measures and statistical analysis, the use of statistical data is more objective and unbiased. This is particularly true when the mean differences are slight, as in Table 7.1.

If there are major differences between the self-reported measures and the statistical analysis, there may be a problem with either the descriptions of the attributes, inappropriate scaling, or some other problem. In these cases, it is generally advisable to bring the results to a focus group for discussion, for customers are usually able to identify the underlying problems or inconsistencies.

PERFORMANCE RATINGS

There are two approaches to measuring a customer's perception of performance. One way is to have respondents indicate whether the firm's performance is good, bad, or something in between. The other way is to simply ask respondents if they are satisfied or dissatisfied with the firm's performance. Both of these approaches have strengths and weaknesses that should be considered in the design of a questionnaire.

Also, there are two levels of performance questions. One level is at the broader, overall level, and the other level is for individual attributes. We'll begin the discussion with overall measures and then move to the good–bad, satisfied–dissatisfied discussion of individual attributes.

OVERALL RATINGS

Overall performance rating should be done by aggregating the responses to two or three different, but related, questions. The use of multiple questions improves both reliability and consistency over the use of a single overall question.

The three most common global measures are some derivative of:

1. Overall, how do we rate?
2. Would you buy from us again?
3. Would you recommend us to a friend?

There are many possible ways of wording and scaling these questions, as the subsequent examples indicate.

Normally, these questions do not appear sequentially. Instead, the first question usually appears at the beginning of the questionnaire, and the other two are interspersed at intervals throughout. This reduces the problem of sequential response bias common to very general questions.

Examples of overall performance measures are included in Table 7.2. There is really no best format among these, for it really depends on the objectives and the researcher's preferences. However, these are some of the more commonly encountered overall measures. The following discussions provide a more detailed analysis of the response categories.

Before moving on, you should notice that none of the overall measures include a No-opinion/don't-know category. The assumption is that all customers have at least a very general opinion that the researcher is trying to obtain. Absence of the No-opinion category forces respondents to make some type of rating. For more specific evaluations, a No-opinion option should be included for each question.

Good–Bad Ratings

Good–Bad ratings can take a wide variety of formats. They could be scaled using 4, 5, 7, or 10 points. Or they could be three, four, five, or seven categories. The fewer the response categories, the cruder the measurement.

Table 7.2   Overall Performance Measures

1. How would you rate (product) on an overall basis?
   Excellent   Poor
   10   9   8   7   6   5   4   3   2   1

2. Overall, how do we rate?
   Excellent   Adequate   Poor
      ☐   ☐   ☐

3. Overall, how satisfied were you with your (brand)?
   Very   Somewhat   Neither   Somewhat   Very
   Satisfied   Satisfied   Satisfied nor   Dissatisfied   Dissatisfied
                                 Dissatisfied
      ☐   ☐   ☐   ☐   ☐

4. Compared with other (products), overall how would you rate us?
   Among   Better   About the   Not as Good   Among
   the Best   than Most   Same as   as Most   the Worse
                                 Most
      ☐   ☐   ☐   ☐   ☐

5. If you were in the area, would you stay at our hotel again?
   Definitely   Probably   Might or   Probably   Definitely
   Would   Would   Might Not   Would Not   Would Not
      ☐   ☐   ☐   ☐   ☐

6. If you were now in the market for another (product), would you
   buy a (brand) again?
   Definitely   Definitely
   Would   Would Not
      10   9   8   7   6   5   4   3   2   1

7. Would you recommend (product or brand) to a friend?
   Definitely   Probably   Might or   Probably   Definitely
   Recommend   Recommend   Might Not   Would Not   Would Not
                                 Recommend   Recommend   Recommend
      ☐   ☐   ☐   ☐   ☐

For example, a commonly used, scale is the excellent–good–fair–poor format of some type. Fair is a very ambiguous term that has a vaguely positive connotation to most respondents. Thus, three of the response categories are positive and only one is negative, and poor may not be a strong enough description for some respondents.

Also, four alternatives are purely a categorical approach. Mean values should not be calculated for categorical data, although this rule is often violated.

For methodological reasons, primarily for easier statistical analysis, interval scales should include from 7 to 10 points plus a no-opinion option. Some researchers recommend an even number of points, such as 8 or 10, because such scales have no neutral midpoint. Respondents must make either a positive or negative response. However, the odd or even decision is really a matter of personal preference.

For scaling, the bipolar adjectives could be excellent–poor, very good–very bad, or among the best–among the worst. A common problem plagues most interval scales, especially the agree–disagree version, which we do not recommend for CSM questionnaires. The problem is response-set acquiescence.

With agree–disagree, respondents tend to agree to everything, just as they tend to rate everything important. Individual responses have a tendency to be skewed toward the positive side of the scale. Just as with importance, the differences in performance ratings among attributes are sometimes very slight.

This is especially true with the excellent–poor bipolar adjectives that are commonly used. Excellent and poor are not truly conceptual opposites of one another the way very good and very bad are. This use of unbalanced adjectives tends to create a positive bias to the results, and respondents acquiesce that performance must be reasonably good.

When categories, instead of interval scales, are used, either five or seven categories, plus the No-opinion/don't-know option should be present. Although this does not yield truly interval data, at least it is better than three or four categories. Further, the categories should be balanced with an equal number of positive and negative alternatives.

The following two sets of seven-category responses are both reasonably good and allow the respondent a wide range of choices. Remember, the response set should provide a broad enough array of alternatives to mirror reality for respondents. The use of only three or four categories generally does not do that.

Among the Best	Better Than Most	Slightly Better Than Average	About the Same as Most	Slightly Worse Than Average	Worse Than Most	Among the Worst

Excellent	Very Good	Good	Neither Good nor Bad	Bad	Very Bad	Terrible

Seven categories such as the foregoing can be converted into point rankings, and the results would be meaningful to managers. Such categories are user-friendly to respondents and user-friendly to users of the data as well.

Satisfied–Dissatisfied Ratings

Rather than having respondents evaluate whether performance is good or bad, some researchers prefer to measure satisfaction. The argument is that evaluating performance as good or bad requires the respondent to think of a standard or benchmark and then compare a firm's actual performance to that standard.

Proponents of satisfaction measures contend that the satisfaction measure is easier for respondents to conceptualize. Respondents would simply formalize their opinions, which result from expectations, perception of performance, and perception of quality. Inherently, satisfaction is supposed to be more internal to the respondent.

As with other performance ratings, satisfaction can be scaled intervally. The most commonly used end points are very satisfied and very dissatisfied, which are clearly preferable to the excellent–poor adjectives. However, interval scaling for satisfaction also tends to suffer from response-set acquiescence, for respondents tend to be satisfied with most attributes, and the mean differences turn out to be minor.

The use of five or seven response set categories solves some of the response-set acquiescence problems of interval scaling. Some respondents complain that five alternatives are inadequate to mirror reality, so they prefer seven categories. Both formats are given below.

Very Satisfied	Satisfied	Neither Satisfied nor Dissatisfied	Dissatisfied	Very Dissatisfied		

Very Satisfied	Moderately Satisfied	Slightly Satisfied	Neither Satisfied nor Dissatisfied	Slightly Dissatisfied	Moderately Dissatisfied	Very Dissatisfied

Some researchers contend that performance ratings, of either the good–bad or satisfied–dissatisfied variety, are not actionable. They contend that the results are difficult to use managerially. That may be true if only performance measures are evaluated. But when importance measures and performance measures are used together, the data are very actionable. If an attribute is very important to customers, the firm should closely monitor performance on that attribute. Low performance on an important attribute is a guaranteed recipe for failure if significant competition exists.

EXPECTATIONS MEASURES

During the past few years there has been an increasing use of expectations measures in CSM questionnaires. There are several reasons for this. The first is that most managers now realize that customers' expectations are constantly moving upward as competition intensifies. A firm's actual performance can remain constant and satisfaction ratings will go down. Or a firm can actually improve but at a slower rate than customer expectations increase and satisfaction ratings will go down.

The second reason is somewhat related to the first. More firms are embracing the idea that the customer is the ultimate judge of quality. Thus, meeting the customer's expectations is critical for a firm that is trying to deliver high quality. Meeting customer expectations is central to being a customer-driven firm. And some of the more innovative firms are realizing that to create so-called customer delight, the customer's expectations must be even exceeded.

Given that brief introduction, let's now examine the different types of expectations measures. In simplest form, expectations measures have only three response categories. A sample of expectations measurement by a hotel is presented in Figure 7.6. This type of question is generally user-friendly to respondents; respondents can easily identify an appropriate response category. This particular questionnaire is flawed, however. Suppose that a respondent did not use valet parking, the concierge service, or the toll-free reservation number. It is not clear what the appropriate response should be. Therefore, this type of question should also have a no-opinion/don't-know option available.

The use of only three categories obviously requires that calculating mean-response data is inappropriate. Instead, proportions, or percentage response, for each category normally are calculated and tracked over time. This type of data is user-friendly to managers that use the data also.

The implication from this type of data is that respondents who check Below expectations are dissatisfied, those who respond Met expectations are satisfied, and those who respond Exceeded expectations are de-

---

Figure 7.6
The Use of Expectations Questions

In the following areas, how did the service you
receive compare with your expectations?

	Exceeded expectations	Met expectations	Below expectations
Hotel reservations	☐	☐	☐
Toll-free central reservations	☐	☐	☐
Check-in	☐	☐	☐
Checkout	☐	☐	☐
Housekeeping	☐	☐	☐
Bellhop	☐	☐	☐
Doorman	☐	☐	☐
Concierge	☐	☐	☐
Telephone	☐	☐	☐
Valet parking	☐	☐	☐
Maintenance	☐	☐	☐
Quality of your room	☐	☐	☐

---

lighted. Sometimes *met* and *exceeded* are simply aggregated together as satisfied customers.

The use of only three categories is viewed as too narrow and simplistic by some so five- and seven-category versions of expectations questions might be preferable. The use of five or seven response categories also is assumed (incorrectly) to be an interval scale and allows the use of a wider range of statistical techniques. The expanded versions of these expectations are presented below.

Much Better Than Expected	Somewhat Better Than Expected	Same as Expected	Somewhat Worse Than Expected	Much Worse Than Expected		

Far Exceeded Expectations	Moderately Exceeded Expectations	Slightly Exceeded Expectations	Met Expectations	Slightly Below Expectations	Moderately Below Expectations	Far Below Expectations

Use of these scales gives some indication of the size of the gap between expectations and perceptions of performance, both positively and nega-

---

Figure 7.7

When a customer phones an excellent firm, the phone should be answered within four rings.

Strongly Disagree	Moderately Disagree	Neither Agree nor Disagree	Moderately Agree	Strongly Agree

When you phone our company, the phone is answered within four rings.

Strongly Disagree	Moderately Disagree	Neither Agree nor Disagree	Moderately Agree	Strongly Agree

Or the question might be worded like this:

Thinking about your company's requirements and expectations, how much do you agree that a supplier should have sales representatives who are technically knowledgeable in solving problems facing your type of business?

Completely Disagree   Completely Agree

10	9	8	7	6	5	4	3	2	1

Now, to what extent do you agree that our sales representatives are technically competent?

Completely Disagree   Completely Agree

10	9	8	7	6	5	4	3	2	1

---

tively. A firm could link its internal performance metrics to a response category and get some idea of how much improvement is necessary. Unfortunately, none of these types of questions indicate precisely what the customer really expects. Only a rough estimate is possible. Also, it is not possible with these scales to determine how much customer expectations are changing over time. To remedy these deficiencies, a slightly more complex approach has emerged.

The respondent is asked two questions. The first question determines how much of an attribute *should* be present in an ideal firm. The second question basically asks, How do we compare to that standard? In a fairly simple format, it might appear as shown in Figure 7.7.

The score on the first question indicates roughly what the customers think the ideal level of performance should be. The second question indicates how a firm stacks up against that standard. If a firm's performance is below ideal level, expectations have not been met. If a firm's performance is equal to ideal level, expectations have been met. If the firm's performance is above ideal level, expectations have been exceeded. However, the use of agree–disagree is ambiguous, and the questions could be improved by being more specific. For example, the first two questions could be reworded.

When a customer phones an excellent firm, the phone should be answered within how many rings?
    1   2   3   4   5   6   7 or more

When you phone our company, within how many rings is the phone answered?
    1   2   3   4   5   6   7 or more

This question is more actionable for several reasons. First, the respondent gets to pick the ideal from a concrete set of alternatives. Then the ideal can be used as a standard. Probably also as important, however, is the ability to determine the accuracy of the customer's perceptions of your performance.

Let's say the ideal answer time is within three rings. Then the customer responds it takes four to reach your firm. The performance standard could easily be monitored to determine whether it takes two, three, or four rings. If customers' perceptions of performance are incorrect, then the implication is that the firm needs to educate customers about actual performance levels.

If the possible response alternatives are not as easily identified as rings on a phone—and most are not—then the question can be reworded so that it is in a completion format. In this way, the respondent freely decides the response criteria, as in the following modification.

When a customer phones an excellent company, within how many rings should the phone be answered? _____

When you phone our company, within how many rings is the phone answered? _____

All of these more sophisticated types of expectations questions allow three things to be done. First, the customer's expectations can be tracked over time to determine the rate of change. Second, the customer's perceptions of the firm's performance can be tracked over time and in some cases be compared to actual data to measure accuracy of perceptions. And third, the size of the gap between ideal and actual performance can be precisely calculated with a view toward suggesting the magnitude of change necessary to improve the firm's competitive position. Once the magnitude of change necessary is known, more-accurate assessments of the financial costs can be made as well.

OPEN-ENDED QUESTIONS

Most mail and convenience questionnaires are highly structured, consisting predominantly of closed-ended questions. The reason for this is apparent: most respondents won't bother responding to open-ended questions. When a request is made in some fashion for additional comments, usually only 5 percent to 10 percent of respondents bother to respond. And many of those responses are short, terse comments of just a few words.

A few things can be done to improve the quality of open-ended responses. The more specific questions will result in better responses. Items such as the following have a better response rate:

- Please list the three things we need to improve the most.
- What was your most positive experience?
- What was your most negative experience?

These questions make very clear what is requested of the respondent. Thus, respondent difficulty is reduced and responses will be more frequent. Also, a Why? probe following an important question may elicit a response, especially for very important issues. Usually though, if good, open-ended responses are desired, then the telephone or personal interviews should be used. And those questionnaires are the subject of the next chapter.

SURVEYS BY DISKETTE

During the past ten years, some firms have deployed their mail survey in the form of a diskette. The diskette is inserted into the respondent's computer and the questionnaire is completed on the computer. Afterward, the diskette is returned to the research firm for tabulation. Mail surveys by diskette have several advantages. From the respondent point of view, they can be appealing if the respondent has computer skills. Since the content of the survey is completely unknown until called up on the computer, it can create some curiosity and therefore encourage responses. If areas of your questionnaire jump sections, a computer survey can do that automatically. From the company point of view, the data are easily tabulated by being formatted as respondents completed the questionnaires.

There are also some disadvantages to this technique. If your respondents are not familiar with computers, they will probably throw the diskette out. If the survey was not adequately pretested and debugged, the data may not be in a recognizable form. Finally, the cost involved is somewhat higher for both mailing materials.

Nonetheless, for a CSM process targeting computer-literate and curious individuals, a CSM survey by diskette can be a useful technique. All of the issues of concern for mail surveys are also pertinent for surveys by diskette.

CHAPTER SUMMARY

Designing a good mail questionnaire really consists of much more than just designing good questions. A good cover letter is essential, an introduction that pulls the respondent in is necessary, and directions and transitions must be clear and understandable. Once these general issues are addressed, then attention can shift to the questions.

There are four types of questions, each with advantages, disadvantages, and design and data implications. Most questionnaires have advanced beyond the very simple, biased questions of a few years ago that were easy to write but yielded poor data. Now, questions can be much more sophisticated so that very actionable data will result.

But in spite of all the alternatives and a higher level of understanding of how to measure attitudes and expectations, designing a questionnaire is still very much an art. The questionnaire must be customized to fit the needs of internal customers, the firm's objectives, and external customers. And all this is typically done by a relatively few people in the organization. Nevertheless, this chapter has presented many alternatives that can, collectively, create an excellent mail questionnaire.

GRANITEROCK

Using a Mail Questionnaire

Graniterock is a 1992 Malcolm Baldrige award winner in the small business category. Based in Watsonville, California, Graniterock produces rock, sand, and gravel aggregates, ready-mix concrete, asphalt, and road treatment, and it also has a highway paving operation. In addition, the company sells a wide range of building materials, such as brick, concrete block, wallboard, and decorative stone, some of which are manufactured by outside suppliers.

The industry in which Graniterock competes is fiercely competitive, and most competitors are now large, publicly traded firms. Traditionally, the industry has consisted of a commodity business, with most customers buying from the lowest-bid supplier. Further, the industry has been adversely affected by recession, and the overall demand has decreased. Despite that highly competitive and shrinking industry, Graniterock has achieved notable success.

The first of Graniterock's nine corporate objectives is concerned with customers:

> *Customer Satisfaction and Service.* **To earn the respect of our customers by providing them in a timely manner with the products and services that meet their needs and solve their problems.**

Graniterock measures the customer satisfaction levels of both customers (contractors) and the end user of its products. A five-step process is used:

Discover customer needs

Ask for a grade from customers

Analyze information

Inform employees of feedback

Form action teams

Graniterock uses an annual mail survey of customers and noncustomers to rank the importance and performance of satisfaction attributes. It uses a report card format. Buyers write in the three suppliers they use most often and then grade the suppliers in all the attributes. The mail format allows Graniterock to obtain comprehensive information that would be awkward to obtain over the telephone. Response rates run at about 20%. More than half of the respondents identify themselves on the survey, which allows Graniterock the opportunity to customize its approach so as to meet the specific needs of those customers. The mail survey is also relatively cost-effective, running about $1.50 each for printing and mailing. Development and analysis are done internally. A copy of Graniterock's questionnaire is included in the Appendix.

8

Designing Telephone Questionnaires

To the novice, the primary goal of a telephone survey appears to be to quickly gather data from customers. Although that may be an accurate goal, it is far too general and simplistic. It is roughly analogous to stating the goal of a business as "making money." Even though making money is what business is ultimately all about, many other goals must first be achieved. Similarly, in order to gather good data, a number of other goals must first be achieved.

The respondent must be motivated to participate in the study. The respondent must be motivated to provide serious, thoughtful responses, not superficial answers. Communication between the interviewer and the respondent must be clear, concise, and complete. The data must be in a form that is usable to the firm. And all this must be done verbally within a few minutes, over the phone, without the aid of visual cues.

TELEPHONE INTERVIEW AS SOCIAL INTERACTION

The primary reason that telephone surveys are more difficult to design than mail surveys is that telephone surveys are a form of interpersonal, social interaction. Although most of the issues of questionnaire design discussed in the previous two chapters are relevant and applicable to telephone surveys, a whole new layer of issues is now laid over the research design. These issues are the factors that influence the social interaction, and therefore the communication process, between the interviewer and the respondent.

Four major types of variables influence the social interaction (Figure 8.1). Each respondent is unique, bringing his or her own experiences, knowledge, values, biases, and frame of reference to the interview. The same can also be said of the interviewer; no two interviewers are precisely the same. And the specific situation that the respondent is in at the time of the phone call certainly influences the respondent in some way. Finally, not all research topics are uniformly interesting to the respondent—or, for that matter, to the interviewer. Since these four groups of variables interact to both shape the social interaction and determine the quality of the data, each needs to be discussed more fully.

The Respondent

The three major types of respondent characteristics that influence the communication process are the respondent's social characteristics, knowledge of the subject, and willingness to respond. The respondent's social characteristics such as age, geographical location, ethnic background, cultural values, organizational position, and educational level collectively contribute to a frame of reference that may be encouraging or hostile to an interview.

If we examine an admittedly extreme situation, the impact of these characteristics may become more apparent. Let's assume that the interviewer is a woman in her twenties, a lifelong New Englander and college graduate, and has been interviewing for a few months. Let's assume that the respondent is living in the Deep South, a lifelong Southerner 55 years old, who worked his way up through the ranks straight out of high school and who happens to have very traditional views of the role of women in the workforce (i.e., they don't belong!). There is the distinct possibility that the dramatic and obvious differences in linguistic accents, age, gender, and geographical background could inhibit the respondent's commitment to the interview. This same type of disparity can be an inhibiting factor in many telephone interviews, although probably to a lesser degree than the example presented here.

In order to minimize the impact of social distance, the researcher needs to consider the respondent's profile and match the interviewers to that profile whenever possible. Unfortunately, there is no research that suggests the magnitude of this issue's impact on data quality.

Just as each respondent brings a different social profile to the interview, each also brings a unique knowledge level. Not all respondents are able to express their ideas equally well even if their knowledge levels are

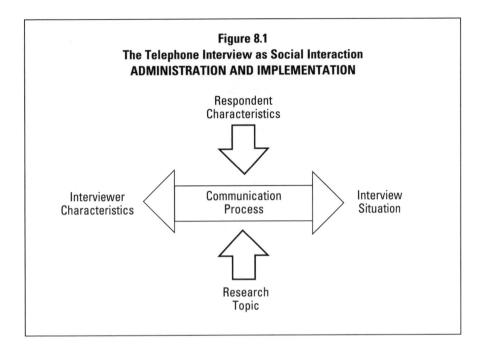

Figure 8.1
The Telephone Interview as Social Interaction
ADMINISTRATION AND IMPLEMENTATION

Respondent
Characteristics

Interviewer
Characteristics

Communication
Process

Interview
Situation

Research
Topic

equal. Since knowledge, awareness, and salience were discussed previously, we won't go into further detail here. However, an implicit assumption in most research projects is that respondents have either some knowledge of the issues or, at least, opinions. Knowledge level certainly influences the communication process in that a respondent with a low level may conclude the interview is a waste of time.

As any interviewer knows, there is a tremendous variability in respondents' willingness to participate and respond. Some respondents are inherently altruistic, and will do anything they can to help the interviewer. Some respondents see the interview as a challenge intellectually and want to demonstrate how smart they are and how much they know. Some respondents feel a responsibility to participate, especially business customers, for they would expect other companies to help them improve similarly. And some respondents are flattered to be asked their opinions, as the interview may make them feel important and they see the interview as a form of self-expression. There are many reasons why respondents are willing to participate in telephone interviews and most of these are enhanced by the direct, interpersonal contact of the interviewer.

Unfortunately, there are also several reasons why respondents are unwilling to respond. Some respondents feel that a telephone survey is an imposition, an invasion of their privacy. As telemarketing efforts increase due to improved technology, databases, and cost considerations, consumers will be increasingly bombarded by unsolicited telephone requests. Therefore, consumer resentment of telephone requests of any type will probably grow. The increasing portion of unlisted telephone numbers nationwide is an indication of this.

Some respondents may simply not want to take the time or devote the energy necessary to complete an interview. Others may be uncertain about the real purpose of the interview, fearful that they will get themselves into something. And some respondents, due to a bad experience, may be openly hostile to an interviewer representing a particular firm.

One of the goals of the pretest, discussed in the following chapter, is to identify why respondents will or will not participate in a survey. If a researcher is armed with information about the factors influencing respondents' willingness to participate, then the introduction can be modified accordingly. The introduction could be worded to specifically elicit feelings of altruism in respondents or to allay their fears and uncertainty.

The Interviewer

As discussed previously, the interviewer's social characteristics interact with the respondent's to influence the communication process. In CSM surveying, professional and personable interviewers are critical. In addition, there are a variety of other interviewer characteristics that can influence the interview.

The skill level of all interviewers is not uniform. Some interviewers are better listeners than others and are better able to sense what a respondent is saying or avoiding. These interviewers are described as socially sensitive, and it's probably easier for them to establish a rapport with the respondent.

The experience and knowledge of interviewers is variable. A well-experienced interviewer is normally more effective in eliciting respondent cooperation. An interviewer who knows a lot about a subject can make more effective use of probes and can more easily understand responses. More-experienced interviewers are also more likely to stick precisely with the questionnaire, with fewer modifications or deletions of questions.

The motivation of interviewers influences the communication process. An eager, enthusiastic interviewer will obtain better results than a bored, dissatisfied, uninterested interviewer. It has been said that enthusiasm is contagious, and that is especially true for telephone interviewers. However, if the interviewer appears to be going too fast or in a hurry to complete the interview, respondents usually provide shorter responses in order to comply with the interviewer's implicit message.

A knowledgeable, motivated, self-assured interviewer who paces the interview smoothly nearly always obtains better results. The researcher, therefore, should exercise caution in selecting interviewers. The researcher also needs to consider the needs of the interviewer when designing the questionnaire. Soliciting input from interviewers after the pretest is usually a valuable activity.

The Interview Situation

A respondent's situation normally does not remain uniform throughout the day. For a business customer, there may be reports to complete, meetings to attend, phone calls to make. A request for an interview when a respondent is swamped is probably going to result in a refusal. However, a request to reschedule on a different day or at a later time of convenience for the respondent may result in cooperation.

The same guidelines apply to households. Certain times of the day are much more hectic for family members than others. Calling at the wrong time reduces response rates. Therefore, researchers should try to anticipate the respondent's situation throughout a day, week, or month and cluster interviews at optimum times to enhance the communication process. It is always important to ensure that the time is convenient for the respondent.

The Topic

The more interesting the topic, the more likely the respondent will be to communicate openly and freely. However, the more difficult an issue is, the less respondents are normally willing to discuss it.

The issues relating to respondent interest in a topic have been discussed elsewhere so they won't be rehashed here. But these items interact with one another. A bored respondent may be willing to discuss an uninteresting topic. However, at a different time, that same respondent may be much busier and simply "not have time" to complete the interview. For CSM interviewing, the topic is generally of interest unless the respondent has had chronically negative experiences.

A telephone survey should not be thought of simply as an introduction and a series of questions. Many behavioral considerations involving the respondent, the interviewer, the interview situation, and the topic interact to influence the communication process. A broader view of this social interaction usually results in correction of the most common weaknesses in telephone questionnaires.

MOST COMMON ERRORS IN TELEPHONE QUESTIONNAIRES

The most common errors made in telephone questionnaires are that such questionnaires are often too complicated and overwritten, not conceptually clear, too demanding, and too long. Because researchers often want hard data, or numbers, to evaluate, telephone questionnaires are also too structured. The remedy to all of these problems is normally simplicity.

The reason that telephone surveys are prone to these problems is that the designer of the questionnaire knows the subject well and doesn't consider the questionnaire as complex or difficult. Most designers of questionnaires have a biased frame of reference because of their own knowledge. Length is often a problem, too, because researchers want to gather all of the information possible once a respondent agrees to participate.

For these reasons, pretesting a telephone questionnaire is even more important than pretesting mail questionnaires. The behavioral issues create an expanded margin of error.

Remember: a telephone interview should allow respondents to have their say—in their own words as much as possible. Forcing responses into inappropriate categories should be avoided. For these reasons, telephone questionnaires should usually be shorter, less complex, and more unstructured and should make greater use of open-ended questions than mail questionnaires. Having addressed these concepts, let's move on to more specific issues.

THE QUESTIONNAIRE

These are many issues to consider when designing telephone questionnaires. The following discussion begins with the broader issues of questionnaire design, then progressively shifts to more detailed analysis of introductions, directions, question structure, routing and transitions, and data analysis.

General Guidelines

A telephone questionnaire should be viewed as a whole, not just a collection of well-designed questions. The purpose of the whole questionnaire, which includes the introduction, is first to obtain the respondent's participation; second, to elicit high-quality responses; and third, to maintain the respondent's interest throughout. Failure on any of these three points reduces the value of any results that might be obtained.

The primary goal of the introduction is, therefore, to obtain the respondent's participation and motivate high-quality responses. The goal of the directions and first few questions is to motivate respondents and smoothly pull them into the flow of the questionnaire. The goal of the remaining sections is to maintain the respondent's interest by smoothly transitioning through the different subjects.

In order to accomplish this, the whole questionnaire must be clear, logical, and understandable to the respondent. Normally, this requires a conversational presentation instead of a "canned" or "read" style. Thus, the questionnaire must also be easy for the interviewer to administer.

A questionnaire is not a test, but it definitely does educate the respondent. The sequence from section to section or from question to question should reflect the consideration of this education effect. Specific, detailed questions may cause a respondent to elevate the importance of items not otherwise considered. This education effect is also sometimes referred to as sequential bias.

To reduce the impact of sequential bias, a telephone questionnaire is often thought of as a funnel with a series of filters. With regard to the overall questionnaire, the broader, more general issues are normally addressed first. Then subsequent sections address more specific issues. Between the sections are the routings and transitions that screen and filter respondents.

Within a particular section, or series of questions, the more general questions appear first followed by more specific questions. This is because general questions allow the respondent a wider frame of reference, resulting in more variability in responses and more susceptibility to sequential bias. Each question should also be evaluated within the context of the questionnaire. In particular, each question should be considered with regard to the immediately preceding several questions and subsequent several questions for flow, consistency, and potential bias.

Each section should focus on a specific topic or issue, and all questions should relate to that topic in some way. Normally, there are from three to seven questions in a section, usually with the same response format. For example, the section may cover the attributes associated with customer service. With long series of routine questions, respondents tend to lose interest. Therefore, after a small cluster of similar questions, the respondent should be transitioned to a fresh, new topic with a different response format.

If certain items are especially important to researchers, multiple questions should be developed for each item. The use of multiple questions significantly improves reliability, but in most cases, this is impractical to do with all questions due to questionnaire length. Thus, identifying the critical few issues and developing multiple questions for each is advisable. The multiple questions should not appear sequentially due to potential sequential bias and the appearance of redundancy. The multiple measures should be dispersed throughout the questionnaire, but normally should not appear either at the very beginning or at the very end.

At the beginning, respondents may not be into the flow of the questionnaire and may still be uncertain about their participation and commitment. The first multiple questions should appear after the respondent has warmed up to the questionnaire a bit. At the end of a questionnaire, respondents may become bored, uninterested, or fatigued. Their primary concern is getting the interview completed, so their responses may be superficial. Accordingly, important questions should not be placed at the end of the interview.

The interviewer controls the pace and flow of the interview. The most common interviewer weakness is that of going too fast and rushing the respondent. This is especially true after the interviewer has administered the questionnaire twenty, thirty, or forty times. To combat this tendency, each interview should be timed so that interviewers can monitor their pace. As a general rule, when the respondent is quite familiar with a topic, the questions can be longer and the pace faster. However, when the topic of the research is complex, difficult, or unfamiliar to the respondent, the questions should be shorter and the pace of delivery slower, allowing the respondent more time to think and to formulate a response.

As concluding advice on these general guidelines, the researcher should keep in mind that the respondent's normal routine has been interrupted by a telephone request for an interview. In all likelihood, the topic of the interview is not a terribly important, top-of-mind issue to the respondent. And if the respondent does agree to participate, the respondent does not have a questionnaire to visually examine, so all communication is verbal. In this situation verbal communication is seldom 100% accurate, so the questionnaire should be clear, concise, and relatively simple.

Introduction

The introduction is a critically important but frequently neglected aspect of questionnaire design. The vast majority, usually around 80%, of refusals to participate come after the introduction but before the first question. For many in the sample, the introduction is the only part of the questionnaire that will ever be heard. However, many researchers devote virtually all of their effort to designing questions at the expense of the introduction.

The dominant, overwhelming purpose of the introduction, then, is to get the respondent to participate. If the respondent's reasons for refusing to participate can be determined in the pretest or from previous experience, the introduction can be designed to overcome the most common objections. Certain aspects of introductions should always be included: personal identification of the interviewer, nature of the study, benefit to respondent, and approximate length of time for completion. But an introduction should contain more than just this type of information.

The introduction should be thought of as a sales presentation, but instead of selling a product, the introduction is seeking the respondent's participation. Instead of money, the respondent is spending time and mental effort. As a reward, instead of a product, the respondent gets some intrinsic satisfaction such as those discussed previously in this chapter. Just as all customers don't desire the same product, all respondents don't have the same reasons for deciding whether or not to participate. Understanding the respondents and designing the introduction based on that knowledge are important.

The characteristics of the customer are, then, a determinant of what goes into the introduction. If a firm has a close relationship with its customers and is quite well known, then a very brief introduction stressing sponsor identification may get a high participation rate. If the sample is randomly generated from a large list of consumers, conversely, the same introduction may get a low participation rate.

Because of considerations such as these, there is some debate as to how long the introduction should be and how much information should be provided. Some argue that a long introduction may lead to more bias in the results; while others argue that a short introduction makes for a poor sales pitch and leads to lower a participation rate.

Some researchers argue that a long introduction gives respondents time to think about how to get out of participating. They suggest a one- or two-sentence introduction that catapults the respondent into the first one or two questions. This assumes an implied consent unless the respondent interrupts with a refusal. Unfortunately, there is no research that helps us to resolve these issues. Therefore, the length and detail of the introduction represent a judgment decision for the researcher that should be closely examined in the pretest.

Testing several different introductions is quite easy to do in a pretest. This can be accomplished by using a split-sample approach and calculating participation rates for each introduction.

The researcher should keep in mind that a respondent may decide within the first few seconds not to participate. Rather than interrupt, however, the respondent may politely allow the interviewer to complete the introduction and then give a, "No thank you." In that situation, the complete introductory message may have very little impact on the respondent.

This raises an interesting point that should be remembered. Many researchers assume that the introduction, and other parts of the questionnaire, are heard completely by the respondent. Studies in listening effectiveness indicate that this is probably not the case at all. Most respondents filter communication for the "important" parts, selectively perceiving what is said by the interviewer. This seems to provide good support for keeping introductions simple and avoiding complexity.

One technique that helps to improve participation rates is the use of a prenotification letter. While this is not always practical, in many cases the sample can be identified by address beforehand and mailed a prenotification letter introducing and "selling" the subsequent CSM study. The letter can cover the objectives, time frame, and benefits the respondent can expect. It can also confirm the call is important and that the interviewer will schedule the call to fit the customer's schedule.

In other cases, the prenotification can be included in customers' monthly statements if consumers are to be surveyed. A sample of such a prenotification is presented in Figure 8.2. This notice was included in the monthly statement for a bank. It was printed on bright-blue paper to catch the reader's attention. The primary weakness of this prenotification is that it was mailed in the March statement and the survey was to occur during April, May, and June. A prenotification is normally most effective when it reaches a respondent within two weeks prior to the survey.

As you can see by now, writing a good introduction for telephone surveys is not an exact science. The nature of the respondent and the goals

---

Figure 8.2
Prenotification of a CSM Survey

ATTENTION

_____ Bank is committed to providing high-quality customer service. Therefore we have employed _____ Marketing Research to conduct telephone interviews during April, May, and June with randomly selected customers.

If you should receive a call, we encourage and appreciate your participation. Your responses will help us determine your satisfaction with our service.

Any questions can be referred to (name), Vice President of Quality, ___-____-_____.

Thank you.
_____ Bank

---

of the survey are probably the most important factors leading to variability. However, most introductions share some common characteristics.

Normally, interviewers quickly introduce themselves to personalize the interview. They usually identify their employer, the sponsor of the study, and the purpose of the interview. The selection process for selecting the respondent and an assurance of confidentiality then follow, along with the approximate length of the interview. Often the respondent is offered the opportunity to ask questions.

There is a difference of opinion among researchers whether a formal request for participation should be asked, such as, "Will you help us by participating?" Those in favor of this type of question feel that respondents who explicitly agree to participate are committed to the interview and will provide higher-quality responses. Those opposed feel it gives respondents an easy opportunity to bail out of the interview, an option many will take.

The alternative to the direct request for participation is the implied-consent approach, in which the last sentence of the introduction transitions into the directions for answering the first question. Those favoring the implied-consent approach feel that a respondent who has not decided

---

Figure 8.3
Sample Introduction with Implied Consent

Hello, may I speak to (customer name)?

This is (interviewer's full name) calling from (research firm's name). We are conducting a customer satisfaction study for XYZ Company, and we would like to obtain your view of the company's performance.

You were randomly chosen from XYZ's customers, and all your responses will remain confidential. The interview should take approximately ten minutes. Please feel free to ask questions at any time, and if you have no opinion on a question, please let me know.

Is this convenient time for you?
(If no, reschedule. If yes, continue.)

---

about participation can be drawn into the interview. Given the option to terminate with a direct question, some of the undecided respondents would take the graceful exit.

A fairly simple introduction is presented in Figure 8.3. It does very little selling of the survey and is very neutral. The last sentence illustrates an implied-consent approach. This basic shell could be modified if the specific reasons for terminations by respondents were known.

One final consideration is relevant regarding introductions. The introduction in Figure 8.3 assumes that the customer is known by name. If that particular individual is not known or available, a contingency plan should be developed. In an organization, there may be several "customers" who would be viable respondents. In a household, there may be several viable respondents as in the case of a car that is jointly registered. Or there may be no viable substitutes. Thus, the introduction often contains the first screen that filters respondents. An example for that situation is shown in Figure 8.4.

Directions

Fortunately, writing directions for a telephone questionnaire is much easier than writing introductions for a mail questionnaire. The best advice is to keep directions as simple and clear as possible. In most cases this requires short directions.

Figure 8.4

Hello. This is (interviewer's full name) calling from (research firm's name). We are conducting a customer satisfaction study for XYZ Company. Are you the person responsible for the purchasing decisions for (product/service)?

(If yes, continue. If no, ask for the name and phone number of the person who is responsible.)

The various segments of a questionnaire should each have separate directions. Within each segment the question format and response categories should be the same. The only exception would be when open-ended probes follow and expand certain responses.

Informing the respondent of the response categories in the directions before the questions has several benefits. The respondent can think about the question as the interviewer is talking, thus identifying and formulating an appropriate response. This reduces the respondent's burden in answering questions. Also, by stating the response categories in the directions and after each question, the respondent is exposed to a redundancy that reduces misunderstanding or ambiguity. As with all aspects of telephone interviews, the respondent probably does not accurately hear everything correctly the first time.

As we shall see in the subsequent sections of this chapter, the need for simplicity normally requires that telephone surveys utilize simpler response formats. Where seven categories might present no problem for a respondent in a mail survey, the respondent in a telephone survey would probably not remember all seven categories.

When respondents can't distinguish between categories, a response-category bias is introduced. Respondents tend to remember the first alternative—a primary bias—or the last alternative that they heard—a recency bias. Therefore, instead of the wide range of response categories found in mail surveys, telephone questionnaires usually have only four or five response categories.

If a question, or set of questions, requires very complex directions, consideration should be given to redesigning the questions. Complex issues can often be decomposed into a series of much simpler questions. Three simple questions are usually superior to one complex question with a long, involved set of directions.

First Questions

The first questions should draw the respondent easily into the interview and establish a rapport between the interviewer and respondent. This requires creating an atmosphere of trust and the willingness to respond by the respondent.

This is usually enhanced by linking the first questions closely to the introduction. The first questions are usually rather general and should be easy to respond to. Some researchers like to use a closed-response first question with very broad categories that require little or no directions. Then the respondent's answer is followed with an open-ended probe. In CSM the question generally pertains to overall quality or value.

Since the first few questions often set the tone for the whole interview, the broad-category closed question lets the respondent know the closed questions are easy to answer. The open-ended probe encourages the respondent to verbalize in more detail and helps to create a talky atmosphere. If the interview began with, say, six or so closed questions, the respondent's willingness to respond verbally would not be encouraged.

A telephone questionnaire should not start with a demographic profile. Some of these questions may be viewed as sensitive and annoy the respondent. But even if they don't, the questions are not directly related to the research topic and therefore contribute very little to creating the tone of the interview. Besides, demographic questions are very easy for the respondent to answer and should be placed at the end of the questionnaire when respondent fatigue may be a problem.

Question Structure

The questions used in a telephone questionnaire tend to be simpler and less structured than those in mail surveys. Less structured does not mean that the questions are vague or general, however. In fact, it may be possible to ask much more specific questions during a telephone interview. Less structured simply means that open-ended questions are much more frequently used, and, when closed questions are used, fewer alternative-response categories are provided. And when closed questions are used, they are often followed by open-ended probes to find out why a particular response category was chosen.

The same two categories of questions, open and closed, are available to researchers. Open questions take two forms. With completely open questions, the response is captured verbatim. With precoded response categories, the respondent's answer is evaluated by the interviewer and placed into the appropriate, preestablished category.

All types of closed questions can be used: interval scale, categorical, and ranking. Interval scaling (i.e., like the measures on a thermometer) can be much the same as with mail surveys, but categorical questions have fewer categories, and the rankings utilize much shorter lists of variables. Before examining the various types of questions, reviewing issues relevant to all questions may be useful.

Question-writing Guidelines

The words used in questions should be simple, direct, and familiar to all respondents. Also, the words should be unambiguous and free of double meanings. The problem with words like *you, regularly,* and *recently* was discussed in previous chapters. However, with telephone interviewing, the problem of phonetically similar words also becomes relevant. *Allow* could be mistaken for *outlaw,* for example.

The questions should be clear and specific. The more specific questions tend to provide cues that may aid respondent recall. Instead of asking a respondent, "How satisfied are you with the service that you have received in the past six months?" the question could be improved by asking, "How satisfied are you with the service that you have received in the past thirty days?" or "How satisfied are you with the service that you received during your last visit?" Although the six-months question was attempting to put limits on the respondent's frame of reference, for long periods of bounded recall such as this, the six-months boundary is blurred for most respondents. Events that occurred a year ago would probably influence the response. Even the past-thirty-days period would not be clearly delineated, although the margin for error in the reference period is much smaller. Most respondents can form a relatively concrete image about what happened on the last visit though.

With regard to specificity and simplicity, questions should never have multiple referents. The question, "How would you rate our product and service quality?" is double-barreled. Product and service are usually conceptually different to the respondent, so conflicting or at least different attitudes could exist for each.

Leading questions should be avoided. This is the problem with many interval scaled questions that have Very Important–Very Unimportant or Agree–Disagree types of end points. A statement is provided and respondents are asked to indicate the extent of their agreement. Unfortunately, writing completely neutral statements is very difficult. As soon as a statement is phrased positively, responses are skewed somehow. In the following questions, most responses would be skewed by the phrasing of the statement.

	Strongly Agree					Strongly Disagree	
Being served within five minutes of entering a bank is very important.	1	2	3	4	5	6	7

	Strongly Agree					Strongly Disagree	
Our sales personnel are very friendly.	1	2	3	4	5	6	7

	Very Important					Very Unimportant	
Being served within three minutes is:	1	2	3	4	5	6	7

All three of these questions are leading because of the positive slant on the statements, particularly the first two with the use of the word *very*. Even the third statement is leading in that respondents are very likely to acquiesce and think, "Sure, that's important."

Care should be taken to make sure that each question asked of a respondent is relevant for that individual. This is the purpose of screening and routings. Asking obviously irrelevant questions is viewed as a waste of time by the respondent and can quickly destroy the tone of the interview.

The respondent should also have the option of choosing a don't-know response. It does not need to be given after every question as in a mail questionnaire, but should be provided in the initial directions and reinforced throughout the interview during some transitions. The don't-know option has little impact on respondents who have strong feelings about an issue, but overall, about 20% of respondents select this alternative when it is available in telephone surveys.

During the interview, the interviewer should watch for signs of respondent fatigue, loss of interest, short answers, or more don't-know responses. This is particularly true for pretests so that the questionnaire can be subsequently modified. However, even during a regular interview, the interviewer can assure the respondent that the interview is almost over, only a few more questions, and so forth.

With these general guidelines in mind, let's move on to a discussion of specific question format. Since the more extensive use of the open question is a distinctive characteristic of telephone questionnaire, we begin our discussion there. Then structured questions will be discussed subsequently.

Open Questions

Open-ended questions provide the opportunity to gain insight and understanding about customers that could never be obtained by using only structured questions. Yet open-ended questions are often avoided or used with disdain by some researchers. Because of the diverse opinions about this type of question, reviewing the advantages and disadvantages may be helpful.

Open questions are essential with any exploratory research when the researcher doesn't already know the key concepts and issues. By allowing the respondent to answer freely, the range and variety of responses will emerge from the spontaneity of conversation. The respondent's frame of reference, intensity of feelings, and logic will become apparent. Particularly valuable is the vocabulary that the respondent uses to describe attitudes and opinions. Intentions for future actions and behavior can be solicited. Thus, open questions provide the researcher with a rich understanding of the respondent's attitudes and thought processes. Unfortunately, these very advantages lead to disadvantages as well.

The disadvantages primarily involve analysis and control. Data analysis for open-ended questions is inherently subjective and some researchers feel that soft, nonempirical data do not constitute "real research." The responses can be either short and concise or long and rambling, and weighting the equivalence of ideas may be difficult. For example, a short answer may concentrate on one point important to the respondent, whereas another answer may include three or four concepts none of which are really important to the respondent.

Capturing a long, rambling response verbatim may be difficult for the interviewer, particularly if a respondent speaks quickly or doesn't enunciate clearly. And multiple ideas in a response may present difficulty for allocating the answer to precoded categories. In such cases, interviewers may have a tendency to selectively filter responses for key ideas, thus injecting interviewer bias.

Open questions are more susceptible to variability caused by the respondent's specific situation at the time of the interview. Length of responses may have little to do with the respondent's attitudes or intensity of opinion. Length of responses may be influenced more by a forthcoming meeting, an unfinished report, or a crying infant.

Depending on the specific objectives of the research, these disadvantages may or may not be a problem. The use of open questions should be determined by the research objectives. If the goal is to get closer to the customer through better understanding, then open questions are valuable. If the primary goal is to provide tracking data for process improvement or for compensation, then open questions are inappropriate.

Types of Open Questions

Completely open questions are typically used as stand-alone questions or as follow-up probes. Precoded response categories could be used in either situation, although precoded categories are probably used more frequently as stand-alone questions. The ability to develop precoded categories is really a function of the researcher's knowledge.

Precoded response categories should be based on specific knowledge, not a researcher's assumptions, speculation, or gut feel. This implies that categories should be based on focus group and pretest results that clearly indicate the range and frequency of various response tendencies. If this is not done, precoded categories should not be used.

Probably the best evaluator of the appropriateness of the categories is the interviewer. If a full range of accurate categories is available, interviewers have little difficulty allocating responses. However, if the categories are deficient, then the interviewer will experience real difficulty in allocating responses. This usually results in the forcing of responses into marginally suitable categories that cloud and blur the respondent's true feelings. Inappropriate response categories can be a source of significant bias.

On the positive side, precoded categories can be a tremendous asset to the interviewer. A good interview maintains an easy-flowing, conversational tone. If the interviewer is trying to capture all responses verbatim, then making the interview conversational is a real challenge. The interviewer may be rapidly interpreting a poorly phrased response, trying to type it verbatim, and simultaneously thinking about which of several probes might be most appropriate as the next question. Or if the question is a screen, the interviewer may be trying to decide which routing is appropriate. And the interviewer must always seem interested, an eager listener to the respondent.

The use of precoded categories removes the burden of trying to capture the verbatim response. It allows the interviewer to concentrate more fully on the respondent and where the interview is headed. Although the interview should never appear rushed, the use of precoded categories typically allows a little faster pace, as the respondent does not have to wait for the interviewer to catch up.

The reason that precoded response categories are not as useful with follow-up probes is that the variety of responses is greater. This is particularly true when respondents with extreme positions are asked to expand their response further. The following question illustrates this.

How would you rate the service during your experience?

> Very satisfied
> Somewhat satisfied
> Somewhat dissatisfied
> Very dissatisfied

IF VERY SATISFIED OR VERY DISSATISFIED PROBE: What factors caused you to say that?

Respondents with a strong position would usually select one of the extreme points for specific factors that occurred. Because there could easily be fifteen to twenty positive or negative factors, capturing the full range of possible responses in precoded categories would be difficult. And when the precoded categories don't match the respondent's views of reality, bias in some form will be introduced.

The best advice on precoded response categories is to use them when possible because the interviewer's task will be much easier. However, they should be used only when there is a good, factual basis for the development of the alternative categories.

Most stand-alone, open-ended questions should adhere to the guidelines provided earlier in this chapter, so those won't be discussed further. Placement of open questions during an interview is a consideration that does merit further discussion.

Open questions are normally best positioned toward the beginning and middle portions of an interview. The respondent needs to be drawn into a talking mode early in the interview, usually in the first few questions. But as an interview progresses, respondent fatigue and boredom lead to shorter, more cursory responses. An open question that would generate a long response early in the interview may generate a short response if placed at the end of the interview.

The use of open-ended probes and their placement also presents a dilemma. It is normally impractical to use follow-up probes with every question; the interview would simply take too long. The question then becomes, "How many probes should be used and where would they be used?"

The number of probes used is determined by the overall length of the questionnaire, the respondent profile, and the respondent's interest in a particular issue. Probes should be used whenever the researcher has a need to gain more insight. Therefore, some general sort of importance ranking of the issues should be done by the researcher, and probes should be allocated to the more important issues. This, of course, suggests that all respondents are asked exactly the same questions.

An alternative is to rotate the use of probes across questions for successive interviews. Let's assume that 34% of the questions include the use of a follow-up probe. Over the course of three interviews, probes would be asked once following every question. For a sample of 600 customers, 200 responses would be available for each question. But, realistically, probes do not need to be used for every question, so a number of responses greater than 200 is more likely.

As with all questions, there should be a specific purpose for using a probe. Probing because it would be interesting to hear what a respondent would have to say is a poor justification. So, probes should be used judiciously to achieve a specific research objective. The most common objective is to gain a better insight into and understanding of customer behavior. Probes are used primarily for low ratings and occasionally exceptionally high ratings to uncover the serious issues and areas of customer delight, respectively.

Closed Questions

There are four types of closed questions: interval scaled, rankings, forced allocation, and categorical. All are affected in some way by the need for more simplicity in telephone interviews.

There are two primary concerns with interval-scaled questions. The first deals with the anchoring statement. As discussed earlier in this chapter, writing completely neutral statements is difficult. It is even more difficult for telephone surveys because each statement is usually shorter and less complex, conveying less information to the respondent.

But the bigger concern rests with the response format. When a Likert-type scale is used, the end points must be conceptually clear and appropriate and easily remembered. Then the respondent must remember the scaling alternatives—whether it's a 10-, 7-, or 5-point scale and which end point is which. The following are three examples of scales frequently used.

Very Important	1	2	3	4	5	6	7	Unimportant
Very Satisfied	10	9 8 7 6 5 4 3 2 1						Very Dissatisfied
Excellent		1	2	3	4	5		Poor

Some respondents may feel that the better something is, the more important, or more satisfied, then the more points it should be rated. But Very Important and Excellent are at the low end of these scales. The result could be a confused respondent who thinks service was excellent, and give it a rating of 5.

In addition to the potential lack of conceptual clarity, there is the old problem of sequential bias. With interval scales, some respondents may not really think of the end points for each question. The respondent may consider the end-point alternatives for the first question and give it a rating of 6 on a 10-point scale.

After that, subsequent answers may be anchored not to the end points of the scale but to the previous response. For the next question the respondent may think, "Well, on the previous question I rated ____ a 6, and this is a little better, so I'll give it a 7." It becomes obvious then that the response to the first question or two exerts a strong influence on subsequent responses.

Response-set acquiescence was discussed earlier for mail surveys, but the same concern arises for telephone questionnaires. Respondents have a tendency to indicate that they "agree" that performance is "good," that they are "satisfied". This invariably skews the responses to the positive side of the scale.

Ranking, as a closed format, is even more conceptually difficult than interval scaling. To rate an attribute, the respondent must hear all the items correctly, compare them with one another, pick the first attribute, and then repeat the process until all are ranked. If respondents change their mind about an attribute, all subsequent attributes must also be reevaluated. The need for a respondent to memorize a list places a significant burden on the respondent. Even though the burden can be lessened by having the interviewer read the list of remaining variables, the process is still awkward and difficult for the respondent.

Due to this heavy respondent burden, ranking works well for only three or four attributes. Five or six attributes becomes pretty marginal, and seven or more is unworkable. The need for simplicity limits the use of ranking in a telephone interview.

The use of a forced-allocation approach results in a similar problem. With forced allocation, the respondent is instructed to allocate a certain number of points, normally 100 or 10, across a set of attributes. With ranking, the "best" of the alternatives is selected sequentially. With forced allocation, the respondent must simultaneously consider all the alternatives because the allocation to any one attribute influences the remaining allocations. Thus, the allocations are all relative to one another.

Therefore, a forced allocation is even more complex because the list of attributes must be memorized. The respondent must then make a series of mathematical computations correctly. Forced allocation, as a closed format, is workable for three or four variables in a telephone survey. Beyond that number, the task presented to the respondent becomes too challenging and complex.

So far we have greatly reduced our closed-format choices. Interval-scaled questions are not terribly difficult for the respondent to understand, but they are subject to significant response-set bias. Ranking and forced-allocation formats are conceptually difficult without the use of visual cues. What is left?

Because of the problems with other closed formats, categorical questions are the winner, in frequency of use, by default. Categorical questions still have limitations, but the limitations are still workable in a telephone interview.

With categorical questions, the response choices, or categories, are read to the respondent during the directions for a particular section. Then each question is read by the interviewer, and the response categories are repeated once again. This removes the task of memorizing anything and makes the respondent's task more manageable.

The primary concerns with categorical questions are the number of categories offered to the respondent, whether the categories should be balanced or unbalanced, and whether the number should be odd or even. The assumption for this discussion is that an additional no-opinion/don't-know category is always available to the respondent.

The number of categories is determined by the research objectives and flow of the interview. If the research design requires sensitivity to small shifts in customer attitudes, then a larger number of categories, say six or seven, may be necessary. When a respondent has a limited set of alternatives available, the "best" among the categories will be selected even though it may not really represent how the respondent truly feels. Therefore, a larger number of response categories give the respondent more opportunity to accurately portray reality.

However, as the number of categories increases, the length of time devoted to each question also increases. So, for the same number of questions, the total interview length increases slightly, which may or may not be a problem. More troubling, though, is the impact on the flow and continuity of the interview.

A larger number of response categories, repeated over and over, becomes monotonous to the respondent, who may lose interest more quickly and display respondent fatigue. When the respondent is fatigued, the larger number of response categories may not be conducive to the sensitivity desired by the researcher. The number of categories is an issue that is often decided by using focus group and pretest feedback.

The next concern with categories is whether categories should be balanced or unbalanced. A balanced set of categories means there are an equal number of good or bad, satisfied or dissatisfied, important or unimportant categories. An unbalanced set of categories means there are more positive than negative alternatives.

The argument for a balanced set of categories contends that respondents should be offered a neutral set of response choices. If three out of four or five alternatives are positive, the respondent may be led by the response set to provide a positive answer. Negative categories may be viewed conceptually by the respondent as way out in left field. This is a form of the response-set acquiescence discussed earlier.

The argument for unbalanced categories is that a positively skewed set of choices more accurately depicts reality. At any one point, most respondents will hold generally positive attitudes. The vast majority of respondents wouldn't select a negative option of any type, so providing three or so negative options is really just a waste of time. By reducing the number of negative categories, often to just one, the researcher can offer a more discriminating set of positive choices. For example, three or four positive categories could be provided with only one negative alternative.

The danger with unbalanced categories comes in the managerial use of the data. Some managers may say, "Look, the vast majority of people think we're doing pretty good, so what's the problem?" This type of misinterpretation of unbalanced scales is fairly common. A better approach would be to say, "Why isn't everyone in our top or top two categories?"

The final issue in developing categories is whether there should be an odd or even number of categories. This issue is relevant when a balanced approach is used. An odd number of categories—three, five, or seven—provides a neutral midpoint that is neither positive nor negative. When a neutral choice is provided, a significant number of respondents may sit on the fence and thus not commit themselves. This is especially true when the no-opinion/don't-know category is not offered.

With an even number of categories, normally four or six, there is no neutral midpoint. The respondent is forced to get off the fence and make a decision. The argument goes that no one is truly neutral, that everyone has some basis for making a response. Interestingly, the use of an even number of categories does not result in a big increase in the use of the no-opinion/don't-know response. Apparently, respondents do select one of the adjoining categories.

After all of the foregoing discussion about response categories, it turns out that for telephone interviews the most common number of categories is four or five. There is probably a slight preference for positively skewed, unbalanced categories, but the preference certainly is not overwhelming. And when unbalanced categories are used, an even number of choices is often provided, again with four categories. The most common balanced approach is five categories, providing a neutral midpoint.

CHAPTER SUMMARY

In the United States, Canada, and some European countries, telephone surveys are the most commonly used approach to gather CSM data. That popularity is often due to telephone ownership levels, technological advances, cultural acceptance, and speed.

Despite their popularity, however, telephone questionnaires are more difficult to design than mail questionnaires. This is largely due to behavioral considerations flowing from the social interactions between the interviewer and respondent. Many factors can, and do, subtly influence that social interaction. Verbal communication without the aid of visual cues is simply a difficult way to gather technical data.

Because of the difficulty, virtually all aspects of a telephone questionnaire must be shorter, simpler, and clearer than aspects of mail questionnaires. These imperatives influence both wording and scaling.

Because of the lack of visual cues for customers, the use of focus groups to critically evaluate telephone surveys is often undertaken. This allows errors to be isolated and corrected early in the design process. And this is why it is also critically important to pretest the telephone questionnaire, the subject of the next chapter.

COMPUTER-ASSISTED TELEPHONE SURVEYS

Computer applications have benefited virtually every aspect of business, so the distinction is no longer between high tech and low tech. The issue now is *how* computer applications will affect a particular business or activity.

The marriage of telecommunications and computers has resulted in a major change in the nature of telephone surveying. The term that describes the new approach is computer-assisted telephone interviewing, or CATI.

There are generally two components in a CATI system. One focuses on managing the questionnaire and its administration. The other focuses on managing the sample and the telecommunications interface. Both components yield major benefits.

With CATI there is usually no hard-copy questionnaire; everything is computerized. This allows a variety of checks to be built into the system so that errors and invalid responses are reduced or eliminated. The biggest benefits come from the ability to implement more-complex research designs.

With CATI, everything is on-line, so interviewers can more easily enter responses for precoded-response categories or verbatim comments. When appropriate, interviewers can skip patterns and routings automatically triggered by the response to a specific question. This creates a smoother, more consistent interview flow during administration.

A variety of split-sample tests or rotations can be done. For example, two or three or four different forms of a questionnaire could be used by interviewers to test different issues. Or rotations could be done on response categories, question sequencing, or even whole sections of the questionnaire.

CATI systems also can identify a variety of productivity issues such as quotas, interview length, and completion success to be tracked. This can identify which interviewers need which type of training to improve performance.

The second component of a CATI system, managing the sample, yields similar benefits. Virtually all aspects of the sample can be randomized more easily so that each subsequent respondent is allocated across interviews.

Automated dialing, interviewer directions, and callback management are common. Scheduled callbacks emerge at the correct time. The sampling procedure can consider time zones, lunch hours, quitting time, or commute times automatically.

If the survey involves a census of customers, then a historical database for each customer can be developed. If a nonrepeated sample is desired for each survey, then the telephone numbers used in previous survey can be deleted.

And all of these types of issues can be handled on a real-time basis. Supervisors or researchers can evaluate an ongoing survey at any time to examine costs, interviewer productivity, response rates, or interim results. All of these benefits have led to a rapid increase in CATI during the past several years.

9

Pretesting the CSM Program

Pretesting is an absolutely essential step in the design of a CSM program. Although no respectable researcher would ever argue against pretesting, few guidelines exist that indicate exactly what should be pretested and how the pretest should be conducted. Therefore, the goal of this chapter is to provide some guidance on how to conduct a pretest effectively.

WHAT IS A PRETEST?

Designing a CSM program is an iterative process. We would be very skeptical of any program that was implemented with no revisions. But revisions are not necessarily a pretest. In fact, most revisions are done well before the first pretest.

One of the authors was recently involved in the design of a fairly complex CSM project. A rough draft of a questionnaire was developed. The questionnaire was then revised by the researchers two more times to clean it up and improve the wording, the scaling, and the overall appearance. Then the questionnaire was circulated among colleagues for their input and suggestions. This resulted in a third revision. The questionnaire was then circulated among managers in the client organization to get their input. This resulted in the fourth revision. The revised questionnaire went back to the managers again to make sure their concerns had been addressed properly. This resulted in one more revision.

If you are keeping track, that created the sixth version of the questionnaire. That sixth version was used in the first pretest, and the feedback warranted another revision. So, the seventh version was used in the second pretest. At this point, the changes were very minor so the questionnaire was not pretested again. But it was the eighth version that was ultimately used in an actual CSM survey. This is a pretty normal sequence of events in the design of a moderately complex questionnaire.

The first six versions of the questionnaire were not pretests; they were simply revisions based on internal feedback. The sixth version was used in the first pretest, but the pretest was concerned with much more than just the questionnaire. It was concerned with every aspect of the research.

This brings us to what a pretest is. A pretest is simply a test of a miniature CSM program. Everything is evaluated, from sample composition to introductions, to questionnaire issues, to data analysis, to use of the data. A pretest is *not* merely a test of the questionnaire. If you examine only the questionnaire, you may be asking excellent questions, but using the wrong respondents. Or you may be analyzing the data in a way that the internal customers—the users of the data—cannot use. Essentially, then, what you are trying to do is to critically evaluate every aspect of the miniature CSM program.

MANAGERIAL ISSUES

Before a discussion about how to actually conduct and evaluate the pretest, certain subjective managerial decisions must be described. Pretests cost money and take time. Most organizations never have either the budget they would like for research purposes or enough time, so the number and size of pretests often are constrained by how much money is available for the activity and how much time is available for pretests.

Budget Constraints

A pretest is not the place to save money! If you must save money, do it someplace else in the research effort. Reducing the sample size is often more palatable than scrimping on the pretests. The reason that pretests are so important is contained in the old garbage-in, garbage-out adage. If weaknesses, errors, or faulty assumptions exist, correcting them before full-scale data gathering begins is mandatory. Otherwise, a good deal of effort may be expended gathering that proverbial garbage, or, worse yet, important decisions may be based on flawed data.

A pretest will not lead to the elimination of all research limitations. But if a pretest is done properly, at least the major problems will be corrected.

Time Constraints

The other major constraint is time. Management usually wants the CSM results yesterday, if not sooner. Therefore, a tendency to rush or skip pretests may exist. For precisely the same reasons, this can be just as dangerous as trying to save money.

When you are designing the CSM program, developing a timeline for project completion chart is often helpful (this topic was discussed in Chapter 4). If you do this, you need to have a rough idea of how many pretests will be necessary and how long each will take. Normally, the number of pretests is between one and five, with two being fairly common.

The primary determinants of the number of pretests are the complexity of the questionnaire, how accurately the targeted respondents can be identified, and how well the respondents' perceptions are known. The more complex the issues, the greater the uncertainty about who the best respondents are, and the less that is known about the respondents, the greater the number of pretests required. For simple, clear issues with an easily identified respondent group, one pretest may be completely adequate.

The other time-related issue is how long each pretest will take. This will vary according to the data-gathering methodology to be used. For telephone surveys, a pretest, complete with revisions, can be done in one or two weeks.

Mail surveys usually take about a month for a pretest. Mailing time, respondent completion time, and return-mail lags take longer than a week in most cases. Typically, 80%–90% of all responses come back within two weeks. Then, depending on exactly how the pretest is conducted, another week or so is lost in analysis, revisions, and the printing of a new questionnaire. If things go well, the whole pretest and revision can be completed in a month.

Conducting multiple-mail pretests can be frustrating indeed. To reduce the time delays, some firms hand deliver or fax questionnaires to nearby customers for the initial pretests and complete only one full-scale pretest by mail. The advantages and disadvantages of this are discussed shortly.

Declared versus Undeclared Pretests

In addition to budget and time constraints, a decision must be made about whether the pretest will be declared or undeclared. A declared pretest is one in which respondents are told that they are participating in a pretest. An undeclared pretest is one in which respondents are not so informed. Each approach has advantages and disadvantages.

There are two ways of declaring a pretest. One is to inform the respondent in the introduction. The other is to inform the respondent at the completion of the questionnaire.

By informing the respondent initially in a telephone or personal interview, the interviewer can ask the respondent very detailed probes about the questions and answers. The respondent's perceptions of questions, phrases, or key words can be examined very specifically. For example, the following probes could be used by the interviewer:

- What did the question mean to you? How would you word it differently?
- What did (word or phrase) make you think of?
- Did the response categories fit your real attitudes accurately?
- When you responded to this question, what were you thinking?
- What led you to respond in that way?
- If the question were worded this way: _____, how would you respond? Why?

When probes such as these are used, unless the questionnaire is very brief, only a few questions can be examined. Doing this for twenty or thirty questions would be too much of an imposition on respondents, particularly in an organizational context.

The advantage of declaring the pretest initially is that the probes can immediately follow a question. Thus, the respondent's interpretation of the question and the thought process used in answering are top of mind and more easily and accurately resurrected. In fact, in some cases, a protocol approach can be used in which the respondent is asked to think aloud about what questions mean, what the thought processes are, and why a particular answer was selected.

The disadvantage of this approach is that it does not reflect the normal and natural flow of the questionnaire. Respondents may be much more careful and cautious in their initial answer to the question. Therefore, a respondent may exhibit a treatment effect whereby responses to a particular question are influenced by the nature of the probes asked about previous questions.

When a pretest is declared after the respondent has completed the questionnaire, there are again both advantages and disadvantages. The advantage is that the respondent was left to complete the questionnaire in a natural manner. Thus, individual responses more closely approximate the actual CSM survey, and the treatment effect of conducting the pretest will be minimized.

However, declaring the pretest after the questionnaire is completed has two disadvantages. The first deals with the respondent's reaction. The respondent may agree, in good faith, to participate in the survey, thinking that the responses will be helpful to the sponsoring firm. When told the questions were a pretest, the respondent may feel like an unknowing guinea pig in an experiment. Therefore, you need to be very careful about how you inform the respondent. Normally, the declaring would be in the form of a request to help improve the instrument.

Even when a respondent is willing to go back and debrief the answers, a time effect may exist. After completing thirty or so questions, the respondent may give a somewhat different interpretation of the question than would have been obtained immediately after a specific question. This is particularly true when a general question is followed sequentially by more detailed questions on related topics. The mere act of asking questions may raise new issues for respondents and change their interpretation of previous questions. In most cases, respondents learn something about the issues by completing a questionnaire.

In conducting a declared pretest for a mail questionnaire, respondents are normally contacted through the use of a telephone or personal follow-up. To an extent, the same disadvantages of declaring the pretest after completion exist. The only difference is that the follow-up probes occur within ten to fifteen minutes in a telephone survey, but the follow-up in a mail survey may come as much as a week later. Thus, the respondents may have even more difficulty debriefing their interpretation of questions, thought processes, and answers.

An undeclared pretest most closely simulates the actual CSM program. The respondent is never informed that the questionnaire was a pretest and so cannot help to identify any difficulty encountered in completing the questionnaire. Although a few probes can be built into the pretest questionnaire, the burden of identifying problems rests with the researcher, who must evaluate the responses to see whether they make sense and are what was expected or whether new issues are raised that need an explanation.

There is a compromise version that falls somewhere between a declared and undeclared pretest. In this situation, the respondent is not informed that a pretest is taking place. However, the respondent does not complete the normal questionnaire. The respondent is asked the regular questions that would be on the CSM questionnaire, but additional probes are built into the questionnaire to explore the most important concepts in more detail. Due to the increased time constraints resulting from the use of open-ended probes, a split-sample pretest is often used.

One half of the pretest sample would be pretested using the first half of the questionnaire. The other half of the questionnaire would be used with the remaining portion of the pretest sample. The results of the pretest would then be pooled for evaluation and determination of whether subsequent revisions are necessary.

CONDUCTING THE PRETEST

Once again, the point should be made that a pretest is not just a pretest of specific questions or of an entire questionnaire. A pretest is a critical evaluation of a complete CSM program. It is a test of the sampling assumptions and procedures, the questionnaire, the data analysis, and the expectations of internal customers. However, each of these aspects has unique characteristics that must be evaluated in a somewhat different manner.

Sample

One of the first issues that typically arises is the appropriate sample size for a pretest. There are no set rules or formulas that can tell you how large the pretest should be. As stated previously, the more complex the issues being studied, the more diverse the respondents; and the less that is known about respondents, the larger the pretest sample should be. However, the pretest sample size is ultimately a subjective, managerial decision. But there are some rough guidelines that may help in making this decision.

A normal-size range for a pretest is between twenty-five and seventy-five, with fifty being fairly common. If several pretests are anticipated, the initial pretest may be smaller, relatively, with subsequent pretests getting progressively larger. There is also a general relationship between your targeted sample size for the full CSM program and your pretest sample size.

If you plan to use a monthly sample of 200 customers to provide tracking feedback, a pretest of 50 is very adequate. However, if your CSM program calls for a monthly sample of 2,000 or more, then a pretest of 100 to 200 is more appropriate. The larger the CSM sample, the larger the pretest sample should be.

Another reason for a pretest sample of around fifty is due to statistical analysis. If you've taken a course in statistics, you may recall that there were normally two sets of formulas for many types of statistical procedures. Small-sample procedures were for samples of fewer than thirty, and large-sample formulas and procedures were for samples of thirty or more. Although a pretest sample of forty or fifty will not yield very precise results, the sample is at least large enough to make a test run for most forms of statistical analysis.

One final consideration comes into play if telephone or personal interviews are to be used. If the interviewers are experienced, then they are normally more sensitive to respondent difficulty and more perceptive of potential problems. If inexperienced interviewers are used, interviewer sensitivity is normally lower. Therefore, the more experienced the interviewers, the easier it is to identify potential problems in the research design. Accordingly, the use of experienced interviewers typically reduces the size of the pretest sample to 1% to 2% of the sample. Assuming that a desired pretest sample size has been determined, the next issue that emerges is who should be in that sample.

A pretest sample should *not* consist of friends, colleagues, managers, or employees. Using such individuals for revisions is fine, but a pretest sample should approximate the desired customer group as closely as possible. This sounds very straightforward, but in practice, it can be difficult for both consumers and other types of customers.

As discussed in a previous chapter, identifying the various customer groups is a necessary early step in the research design process. In the pretest, all the assumptions made about the appropriateness of the sample should be examined.

Assume for a moment that you need to survey consumers for your product or service. Precisely who should the respondent be? The male head of household? The female head of household? Any adult in the household? Does *adult* mean anyone older than 18? The pretest should indicate the appropriateness of the desired consumer respondent. Perhaps those in the desired respondent group don't possess the knowledge that you thought they had.

In an organizational context, sampling problems often become even messier. The respondent group could be a horizontal slice of the customer organization, including individuals from production, quality assurance, purchasing, and research and development. Ultimately, a decision must be made about which individual from each area is the appropriate respondent. Also, the respondent group may include a vertical slice of the organization.

The objective, then, is to determine which organizational level from each functional area constitutes the best respondent. In conducting a pretest with organizational customers, the willingness and appropriateness of the targeted sample must be evaluated. Are the desired respondents individually identifiable, accessible, and knowledgeable enough to provide meaningful responses? These issues become readily apparent in a pretest.

Questionnaire

There are several issues related to the questionnaire that need to be examined in the pretest. The first is the reaction of the respondent to the overall questionnaire. The second is the respondent's perceptions of the questions. The third consists of scaling, measurement, and response categories.

Overall Questionnaire Issues

In the design of a questionnaire, there should be a smooth, natural flow from one section to another, with some sort of logical consistency. Unfortunately, all of this is very subjective, and a person who has read the questionnaire many times is not a particularly good judge. Thus, the overall questionnaire must be evaluated from the perspective of the respondent, to the extent possible.

The topic and direction of the questionnaire are set by the cover letter or introduction. The pretest should begin with these items and flow from there. The sequential groupings of questions are linked by transition statements and directions for completing the next group of questions. These items should also be evaluated. The transitions and directions should be clear and concise and should pique the respondent's interest in the next section.

Respondent interest and attention should be uniform throughout the questionnaire. If respondents become impatient and hurry through the questions, then later questions may yield only very cursory, superficial responses. Therefore, the various sections should be timed, and the interviewer, when appropriate, should note where interest begins to wane. If the pretest indicates that respondents lose interest after, say, fifteen minutes, there are two options.

The first option is the obvious one: shorten the questionnaire. Current research has shown that twelve to fifteen minutes is the optimum amount of time unless the respondent is very engaged and interested. If shortening compromises the objectives of the research, then restructuring the questionnaire to provide more variety for the respondent often helps. This could be done by using a wider variety of response formats so the respondent doesn't get bored with using the same response categories, such as Agree–Disagree. In either case, a second pretest is normally warranted to determine if the respondent's attention is measurably improved.

The second option is to split the questionnaire into two or more versions. United Airlines regularly administers questionnaires to its customers. But even on one flight, United may have three or four different questionnaires being randomly handed out. United's CSM objectives are simply too complex and diverse to use only one reasonable-length questionnaire.

Another important issue is the sequencing of the topics or questions. If you feel that there may be a sequential bias in the topics or questions, a split pretest may be necessary.

Let's assume for a moment that a firm's product quality is pretty good, but customers complain continually about service performance such as invoicing and billing. If you position questions about product quality first, you may be conditioning respondents to think positively about your firm in general. This positive anchoring may cause respondents to rate invoice and billing performance higher. On a 1-to-10-point scale, with 10 being the best, a respondent might rate product quality as an 8. Then, a lower rating of 6 may be given for a service-quality attribute.

If the sequence were reversed, so that service evaluations came first followed by product evaluations, the opposite may occur. The service attribute may be rated a 3, and then the product-quality rating would be compared to the service anchor rating. Perhaps product quality would be rated a 6 in this situation.

The split-sample pretest would indicate very quickly if a sequential-bias effect is present. This means ratings for, say, for service attributes in our example would be compared from the two questionnaires. If the means are different for each position, then a sequential-bias effect normally is present.

A word of caution is necessary regarding pretest sample size. If a split pretest is being conducted, you should have at least thirty, and preferably more, responses in each half. Thus, a split-sample technique normally increases the pretest sample size.

Question Issues

There are a number of things to look for in pretest results that pertain to specific questions. Variation in responses, the meaning of words or questions, respondent difficulty, and respondent interest may all indicate bad questions.

If the responses are skewed toward one end of a scale or toward a specific response category, the cause may be a leading or biased question. Ideally, responses would display some sort of normal distribution around a mean. Anytime there is significant deviation from a normal distribution, further investigation is justified. In some cases, a skewed response profile is indeed an accurate description of respondents' attitudes. However, be sure to closely examine any question that generates a very skewed response.

When we, as individuals, ask questions, we usually know exactly what we mean. Unfortunately, the respondent doesn't always interpret the meaning the same as we do. On a pretest, differences in meaning usually show up very quickly through the use of probes. In a telephone survey, respondents often ask interviewers, "What do you mean?" or "Please repeat the question." Such responses are a good indication that the meaning of key words or the entire question is not very clear.

In a mail survey, unclear meaning normally results in many neutral or no-opinion responses. Respondents usually answer a question somehow, but if the question is unclear, they seldom have extreme tendencies. As a result, a safe, neutral response is given, or the easy out of a no-opinion option is checked.

Developing a good understanding of respondent meaning is one of the most important reasons for doing a pretest. You can be virtually certain that some respondents will interpret the questions differently from what you meant. To illustrate, in one study that used difficult questions, respondents accurately interpreted the meaning of only 30% of the questions. This was determined through a follow-up interview with all respondents, incidentally.

One reason for inconsistent meaning is selective perception by the respondent. Respondents often do not read the entire introduction, directions, or questions. Some respondents read enough so that they think they know what the question means. Respondents may selectively perceive words, phrases, and sentences.

The same situation also occurs in telephone surveys. The respondent may not hear all the words or may misinterpret words. Most of us can recall, as kids, sitting in a circle and verbally passing a message along from one to another. Each person slightly alters the message by interpreting it and sending it in different form. The message that results at the end of the circle usually bears only a vague resemblance to the one that started. In every telephone interview, the same thing happens to a degree, and the result is inconsistent meaning.

Respondent difficulty is typically an indicator of a poor question. This occurs when we ask a question that requires respondents to do computations, for example. The following question was intended to determine market share, but it illustrates a difficult task.

"What proportion of your company's purchases of commodity X does our product Y constitute?"

This question, on the surface, appears simple enough. However, to answer accurately, the respondent must determine the total amount of the commodity purchased. This could be a vague estimate—determined by taking last month's consumption times twelve—or more exact—by going to the purchase records. Then the respondent must determine how much of product Y was purchased. Since the question did not state a specific time period, the respondent will be unsure of what the appropriate time horizon might be.

Even assuming that the respondent can determine the total consumption of the commodity, the total purchases of product Y, and the appropriate time horizon, the respondent must now remember how to calculate a proportion. Which goes on top of the equation—the numerator or denominator? (The numerator does.) Which figure is which?

This apparently simple question presents the respondent with a reasonably high level of difficulty. The question could be broken down into several subquestions, which individually would be easier for the respondent to answer. And the more specific questions would probably yield better data.

Again, the use of probes would give some indication of respondent difficulty. When the respondent is unsure or needs additional information, the cause is often a difficult question.

One other issue relevant to evaluating questions in a pretest is the salience of a question to the respondent. If a question is very important to the respondent, interest is likely to be quite high. Conversely, if a question is unimportant, respondent interest is often very low. Low interest by the respondent is typically manifested in one of two ways.

Respondents tend to select the same category, such as Agree, time after time. Or respondents may respond "no opinion." If a particular question has a large proportion of these types of responses compared with the other questions, the question may be irrelevant and of little interest to respondents.

Scaling and Measurement Issues

Additional important issues to evaluate in a pretest are scaling, measurement, and response categories. Although these issues are of most concern with closed questions, the concepts are applicable to open-ended questions as well.

When conducting telephone or personal interviews, interviewers can ask questions that are completely open or use precoded categories. In the pretest, the interviewer's ability to capture verbatim, open responses should be evaluated. If the interviewer condenses the open responses to capture only the essence of the ideas, valuable ideas may be filtered out inadvertently.

The use of precoded categories allows the interviewer to concentrate more fully on the interview. The appropriateness of the variety of categories should be closely evaluated in the pretest. If a large number of responses end up in the Other catch-all, then the precoded categories probably don't capture the range of responses. Some researchers have used pretest results to identify the categories that should be available to interviewers.

Closed-end questions require the respondent to answer in a manner specified on the questionnaire. If the response formats exactly mirror the respondent's perceptions, then no problems arise. Unfortunately, that is not always the case. The following scale is one of the most popular but brings a few problems with it:

Strongly Agree	Agree	Neutral	Disagree	Strongly Disagree
—	—	—	—	—

In a telephone survey pretest, a respondent complained about this scale. In his words, he only "partially agreed" with the statement. He admitted he wasn't neutral, but he felt that Agree was too strong a statement. Therefore, the scale was modified to provide a wider range of responses as follows:

Strongly Agree	Agree	Somewhat Agree	Neutral	Somewhat Agree	Disagree	Strongly Disagree
—	—	—	—	—	—	—

Another respondent wanted a no-opinion category. Her comments indicated that she wasn't really neutral with regard to the statement. She simply had never thought about the issue and had not formulated any opinion. As a result, a "no opinion" category was added. In the full CSM survey, nearly 30% of the respondents checked one of these three new alternatives.

In a mail pretest, respondents sometimes circle two categories or check a space between two alternatives. When this happens, respondents are trying to tell you that your response categories are inadequate to capture the full range of perceptions.

When responses are equally distributed over all response categories, there are probably too few categories to pick up the true variation in respondent perceptions. However, the flat distribution could also be caused by ambiguous category descriptors. Descriptors are the terms or phrases used with each category on the end points of a scale. As discussed previously, the end points of Excellent and Poor are not true opposites of one another. The responses on this scale would tend to be skewed toward Excellent because it overpowers Poor.

The response formats should mirror the range of possible respondent perceptions, and the words used should correspond to the respondent's true attitudes. The pretest results should be examined for any unusual distribution indicating that respondents are artificially constrained in some way.

Data Analysis

Once the pretest is complete, the results should be analyzed statistically using the same techniques and procedures that are to be used in the full CSM program. There are two reasons for this.

One reason is simply to make sure all the input procedures, whether manual or by optical scan, are designed properly. With even a small data set like those generated with a pretest, any problems can be quickly identified. Trying to isolate a problem with a data set of a thousand or more can be quite challenging, to say the least.

In one case, a researcher had misspecified the data field for a large data set. The variables were one column off, so when the statistical analysis was done, many strange results emerged. It was immediately obvious that a problem existed, but finding the error during a pretest period would have saved a good deal of anguish and time. Debugging the data analysis procedures is essential in any CSM program, and even small errors can completely alter the results.

Another reason to pretest the data analysis procedures is to make sure that data are in the correct form for the desired statistical technique. Responses should be dichotomous (yes or no), scaled intervally (0–100), categorical (four response categories), or rank ordered (1–10). Some types of analysis techniques can be used for interval data, others for categorical, and still others for rank ordering. The surest way to check for problems is to try to analyze the data. If problems arise, the easiest alternative is almost always a change in the wording of a question or in the response format.

Although the authors have done a lot of fairly sophisticated statistical analysis and have a pretty good understanding of the procedures, it seems that we always have to cycle through data analysis a couple of times to fully debug everything. We suspect that we are not alone.

Internal Customers

As a final step in pretesting, the results should be presented to the internal customers. The intent is to make sure the data are in a form that can be confidently used by such customers. It is a sort of speak-now-or-forever-hold-your-peace opportunity.

If the customers prefer to see the data in a different form, it may be necessary to use different analysis techniques. And if different statistical techniques are required, the wording and measurement of questions might need alteration. It is much easier to change questions and analysis techniques in the pretest stage than at a later point.

There are probably some behavioral benefits to running the pretest results past the internal customers. Involvement of individuals in the decision-making process will reduce resistance to the CSM program and help increase widespread buy-in. If a customer wants data in a slightly different format, then customizing the program to fit that need may well be worth the extra effort in the long run.

CHAPTER SUMMARY

A pretest is an absolutely essential part of the CSM process, but there is often a tendency to minimize or rush this activity. In many cases, it is due to the mistaken view that a pretest is concerned only with the questionnaire. After many revisions and refinements, some may feel that a questionnaire has become good enough. In other cases, management may want the CSM yesterday, pressuring the researchers to rush the process.

The major reason that pretesting is so important is that it is a pretest of the whole CSM program, from the questionnaire, sampling, and data analysis, to using the data. In most cases, improvements and refinements can be made that improve data quality. And in most cases, those benefits greatly outweigh the costs.

There are many issues that need to be addressed in the design of a pretest. Probably most significant is the decision to make it declared or undeclared. Ultimately, this decision boils down to one of managerial preference based on what is to be accomplished.

Invariably, difficult decisions must be made about issues involving the sample, questionnaire, measurement and scaling, and data analysis. As discussed, these issues are much more complex than having customers look at a questionnaire and give vague overall feedback. The more carefully designed the pretest is, the better the ultimate data quality.

INTERCEPT RESEARCH

Questionnaire Pretesting

Intercept Research is a multifaceted marketing and CSM research firm in Portland, Oregon. Intercept conducts CSM surveys for companies and public opinion surveys for preelection polling statistics. Part of every process consists of pretesting a questionnaire before actually deploying the entire process in the field.

"Pretesting is critical for identifying potential problem areas in the interviewing process," says Dean Bolon, president of Intercept. "No matter how many times you deploy a survey, even the same CSM survey six months or a year later, you must pretest the instrument again. Perceptions and language nuances can be entirely different in the next research cycle. Often in a prior CSM study, we might be notified of potential areas of change from the verbatim comments, but it is a mistake to assume changes or status quo and forge ahead."

Intercept generally pretests telephone questionnaires until they achieve consistency of responses and customers stop asking for clarification. Intercept then checks with its client company to discuss changes, and if everyone is in agreement, it rolls out the CSM process. Sometimes it is helpful for the client company to listen to an actual customer interview via a listen-only phone to hear the questionnaire and understand the problem areas. Of course, you will want to make sure that confidentiality is ensured either by connecting the company and the customer after the initial identification is made or by asking the customer to waive confidentiality and anonymity.

Not only does the pretest process save the interviewer's time with the customer and shorten the time that the customer is on the phone, but it also increases the reliability of the data. In the long run, pretesting is a very wise and considerate investment.

10

Designing a Sampling Program

This chapter implies that the customers be clearly identified, a surprisingly difficult task for some firms. Each major target market must be defined in some logical fashion. In addition to end-user customers, the channel intermediaries should be identified as customers. The CSM objectives discussed in Chapter 2 should indicate which customer groups are to be examined.

Once the customer groups have been identified and prioritized, the determination of how many customers from each group to survey must be made. This sample-size discussion includes considerations of cost, precision, and reliability and is linked to the objectives. The discussion includes some simple sample-size computations, but more-complex sample-size computations are available in most marketing research books.

The pragmatic sampling issues of frequency, seasonality, time of day, and identifying the right respondent are examined. This section also includes a discussion of the use of internal and external personnel to gather the data.

Finally, a decision must be made whether the CSM and, therefore, the sampling procedure will be open loop or closed loop. An open-loop CSM program gives no feedback to respondents when negative comments or complaints are voiced. A closed-loop system means that every negative comment gets a direct response from the company. This has obvious implications for sampling procedures.

Because implementation of a comprehensive CSM program that samples all customer groups can be a formidable challenge, a phased-in approach is discussed. Specifically, a CSM program can begin with one or two small business units, divisions, or market segments and gradually spread to other areas. The strategic implications of which groups to select first are discussed.

A CENSUS OR A SAMPLE?

The decision to survey all or part of the customer base should flow directly from the objectives of the CSM program. If the CSM program is viewed as a tool to build stronger relationships with all customers, then perhaps a census is most appropriate. If the goal of the CSM program is to track customer attitudes in some way, a sample is probably most appropriate. Because both censuses and samples have advantages and disadvantages, each is examined. However, because using a sample is the most common approach, the majority of the discussion in this chapter is devoted to that topic.

CONDUCTING A CENSUS

On the surface, conducting a census may seem simple enough. And for a firm with a small, clearly identifiable customer base, this may be true. However, for most firms, the task is difficult.

Defining the Term *Customer*
Defining the term *customer* is the first challenge. The customer could be an individual or a firm that used a product once in the past year. Or *customer* could be a regular user of a product, perhaps on a daily basis. Typically, some specification of usage rate is part of the definition of *customer*.

If a product is used in a group context, then defining a customer may be even more complex. In a household unit, is the appropriate person to contact a male head of household, female head of household, any adult male, or the person who uses a product the most? Or is the customer a composite that should include several individuals?

In an organization, the customer could be the purchasing agent. But since the purchasing agent usually does not act alone, other individuals from other departments are typically involved in the purchasing decision process and the postpurchase evaluation. If four departments, such as purchasing, production, engineering, and quality assurance, are involved in the decision process, the next challenge is determining which individual to contact from each department.

To make matters even more complex, many firms use a channel of distribution of some type. The customer could be the end user of the product. But the customer could also be a channel intermediary such as a wholesaler, distributor, agent, or retailer. And each of these customers normally has a different view of product attributes and decision criteria.

Researchers could simply throw up their hands in despair and just send one questionnaire to each firm. But in one firm the questionnaire may be completed by a secretary because the boss is too busy. In other firms, the questionnaire could be completed by a general manager or a newly hired purchasing agent or an experienced production manager or someone from quality assurance. These responses on the questionnaire would probably vary significantly because each individual's view of the situation would be quite different, even though all respondents are completing the same questionnaire and evaluating the same firm.

The point of all of this is that the customer must be carefully specified. If the objectives are unable to guide identification of the appropriate customer, the objectives of the CSM program should probably be revised and tightened up. Since it is beyond the scope of most research efforts to contact all possible customers, normally the best customers are identified. The best customers are those capable and willing to share the information necessary to achieve the objectives. Those best customers are the ones who should be included in the census.

Costs

Conducting a census is more costly than sampling. For a firm with 100 or 200 or even 1,000 customers, a census is not prohibitively expensive. But for a firm with 10,000 or 50,000 or a million customers, conducting a census could be quite costly.

As discussed in a previous chapter, sample size has a much greater impact on the costs of telephone and personal interviewing due to the labor intensity. Because both methods are labor-intensive, marginal costs for each additional interview remain high. Therefore, telephone and personal interviews are generally not used when a firm is conducting a census, unless the customer base is relatively small.

The marginal cost for each additional customer is often low in a mail survey. For example, some firms send out a questionnaire with all customers' monthly statements. Although this approach may introduce significant bias, the cost is low and the questionnaire is certain to be seen. Even when a separate mailing is used, the additional cost of each questionnaire is often only a few dollars. Mail questionnaires are also predominantly closed-end questions, which are well suited to optical-scan data input. The use of optical-scan questionnaires greatly reduces data input costs, which are often labor-intensive.

Time Considerations

Because all customers are surveyed, conducting a census is often more time-consuming than a sample. This is partly due to the facts that mail surveys are more commonly used for a census and that mail surveys have a longer turnaround time than telephone or personal interviews. This is particularly true when one or two follow-ups are sent to nonrespondents.

When a survey is used to conduct a census, the frequency of administration is no different from the frequency for a sample. Data could be collected monthly, quarterly, semiannually, or annually. Some firms utilize a sequential approach to gathering data rather than a survey, however.

With a sequential approach, every customer is contacted after specific activities. Most often this is after direct contact with a firm in some way such as a complaint, a service call, a reservation, or the purchase of a product. With a sequential approach, the primary decision concerns when to administer the questionnaire.

The customer could be given a questionnaire at the time of the contact and asked to complete it and mail it back to maintain anonymity. Or a questionnaire could be mailed to the customer a day, a week, or two weeks later. The lag between the contact and the administration of the questionnaire should be determined by the objectives.

Regardless of how the sequential contact is made with customers, however, the sequential approach is usually more time-consuming than a survey. A survey of all customers can be treated as a project that is implemented and then put aside until the next survey. With a sequential approach, the program must be continuously utilized, and data are continuously flowing into the firm from customers.

The continuous nature of sequential programs usually requires more time, effort, and costs to administer. Although a sequential program consumes more managerial resources, the firm does get more frequent feedback that can indicate early shifts in customer attitudes. Normally, the sequential data are aggregated, compiled, and analyzed on a weekly or monthly basis. This type of data has obvious advantages over CSM data that are gathered annually—if the firm is prepared to respond quickly.

Census Summary

The primary disadvantages of a census are the difficulty of identifying a comprehensive list of all customers, the increased cost, and the greater time commitment. Each of these disadvantages can be ameliorated by modifications in the research design.

The primary advantage is that all customers are periodically contacted. The mere act of soliciting input from customers helps to create goodwill, especially when customers see tangible improvements as a result of their inputs.

A census does not necessarily yield a more accurate profile of customer attitudes than a well-designed sample does. In a census, even though all customers may be contacted, not all customers will respond. And because sampling is usually less costly and takes less time, the most common approach to gathering CSM data is to design a sampling plan.

USING A SAMPLE

Sampling should be thought of as a sequential process that consists of several interrelated steps. The quality of each step is dependent upon and limited by the quality of the previous step. Therefore, errors made in one step will directly influence and reduce quality in each of the subsequent steps. The sequential process for sampling is presented in Figure 10.1.

Define the Customer

The first step in the process is to define the customer as accurately and specifically as possible. The issues here are the same as those previously discussed for census taking. Surprisingly, many firms have a lot of difficulty with this step. This is particularly true for those businesses selling a product or service that is used by several rather distinct customer segments.

For example, a regional electric utility had customers that included farmers who were heavy users due to irrigation pumps, businesses ranging from sole proprietorships to multibillion-dollar manufacturing operations, single-family residential customers, multiple-family residential (apartment) customers, residential-construction companies using temporary power, real estate development companies building new subdivisions, and rural resort cabin owners. For each of these different seg-

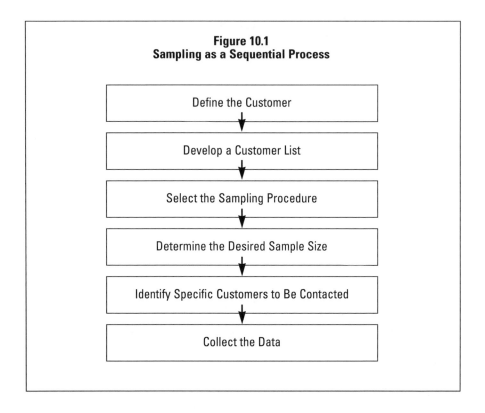

Figure 10.1
Sampling as a Sequential Process

Define the Customer

Develop a Customer List

Select the Sampling Procedure

Determine the Desired Sample Size

Identify Specific Customers to Be Contacted

Collect the Data

ments, deciding exactly who the customer is presents a real challenge. Unfortunately, ignoring the differences between these diverse segments and simply developing an aggregate profile has severe limitations.

Since each segment often has a different decision process, each should be treated separately when defining the customer. The decision criteria, and the relative importance among criteria, are often different for each customer group. Simply lumping all customers together often results in very significant aggregation bias, which would render the data managerially useless.

The implication is that each major customer group should be defined as distinctly and specifically as possible. The distinction should be made both between segments and within each segment.

Develop a Customer List

From company records, a comprehensive list of specific customers, by name, should be developed. For some firms, this is relatively easy. Telephone companies, utilities, banks, doctors, dentists, and a wide variety of other businesses maintain detailed, and usually current, customer profiles. When such information is fully computerized, as it is for most businesses nowadays, developing the customer list is a simple task.

However, for organizational customers, developing the customer list is more challenging. Many firms maintain customer information only in general for organizations. In these cases, each customer firm will need to be contacted individually to identify the appropriate respondent by name. Depending upon the research objectives and research design, specific customers could be identified through a series of screening questions at the time the data are gathered. However, if mail or personal interviews are used, having the names of specific individuals is immensely more valuable and effective.

The researcher should, therefore, gradually develop a comprehensive list of key customers and update the list continually rather than wait to do so at the time the questionnaire is administered. Such a comprehensive list makes sales calls far more efficient and profitable as well.

The comprehensive customer list constitutes what is often referred to as the sample frame. The sample frame is a pool of customers from which a sample will be drawn. If all customers in the sample frame are contacted, the research is a census. If only a portion of the customers are contacted, regardless of how large a portion, then the research is a sample. There are many specific ways that a sample can be drawn, and this step is commonly referred to as selecting the sampling procedure.

Select the Sampling Procedure
There are a wide variety of sample procedures, or ways to draw a sample from the pool of customers in the sample frame. The major distinctions are the sequential sample versus the fixed sample. Both of those categories can be further classified into probability method and nonprobability method. And each of those categories could be further divided into several more types of sampling procedures. Every type of sampling procedure carries with it a unique set of advantages and disadvantages. The final choice of sampling procedure should flow, as do most other research decisions, directly from the objectives of the CSM program.

Sequential Sample
Sequential samples are far more commonly used in CSM programs than in other types of research for one predominant reason. Many firms are trying to stay close to their customers and to use timely customer data to drive continuous process improvement. Since most of these firms are fa-

miliar with and widely use statistical process control for internal operations, a continuous flow of external, customer-driven data is a logical extension of internal improvement practices. These firms are culturally and managerially able to use such continuous-flow data.

Other firms may be less able to change and adapt their production processes as quickly. These firms don't need the continuous flow of customer data for their decision-making purposes and may be better off gathering CSM data only periodically, say, once or twice a year, through the use of a survey, or fixed sample.

The primary advantage of the sequential sampling procedure is the continual flow of data. Process variations can be quickly detected and corrections or improvements made. The primary disadvantage is that data are generated only from existing customers. Feedback from potential customers or competitors' customers is normally not included in a sequential procedure. Therefore, sequential sampling of existing customers is often combined with a periodic survey of other potential respondents. Once or twice a year is normally an adequate frequency for this competitive benchmarking approach.

As noted previously, in the census discussion, the most common form of sequential sampling is used after some type of customer contact. It could be after a purchase transaction, after a service call, or after an inquiry or complaint, for example. The problem is that each type of contact may influence the customer's responses. Therefore, a manager must decide which type of contact is most appropriate given the research objectives. Then the manager must decide how soon after a contact to administer the questionnaire. Surveying a customer at the time of complaint is likely to elicit a different response from surveying that customer one week later, after a cooling-off period. Generally, a customer should be surveyed within one week of contact so that the issues being addressed are fresh, recent, and, hopefully, more accurate.

The issue of how many customers to contact is addressed in the section on sample size determination later in this chapter, but first a variety of other issues must be addressed and the first of those is the fixed sample.

Fixed Sample

A fixed sample is just what the term implies: a fixed number of customers are surveyed. Normally, fixed number refers to usable responses rather than the number of customers contacted or the number of questionnaires mailed. A fixed sample suggests that a manager has used statistical formulas or made a managerial judgment about the necessary sample size.

On the surface, determining a fixed sample seems pretty straightforward, for example, surveying 1,000 customers quarterly. But the same problem of deciding how the sample of 1,000 should be allocated among subgroups or market segments again emerges. That issue is discussed in the following sections a bit more and the ultimate decision is a subjective one, although there are some heuristic rules that can help.

With a fixed sample, data are normally gathered on a periodic basis, and each round of data gathering can be treated as a project. Therefore, estimating and controlling costs are easier tasks with a fixed sample than with sequential samples.

Probability Method

Probability samples are those in which customers are selected through the use of some objective process, rather than an arbitrary selection by a manager. The most common type of probability sampling is simple random sampling. With simple random sampling, all customers would have a known and equal chance of being included in the sample. For example, if a firm were selecting a sample of 30 randomly from a customer base of 100, the probability that any individual customer would be included is .3.

The most common way of using simple random sampling for a CSM survey is to assign each customer a number. Then a random-number generator, available on most statistical and many spreadsheet software programs, is used to generate a sample list. If the customer is an individual or a consumer, this process works pretty well. But for an organization, even after the customer firm has been selected, an objective process for selecting the appropriate respondent must be developed.

Another type of probability sampling is stratified random sampling. The total customer base would be divided into subgroups, or strata, and then a random sample of customers in each group would be drawn. This type of sampling is appropriate when a firm has a number of distinct market segments or groups that have different decision criteria or attitudes. When separate groups can be identified and segmented out, the responses within each group are usually more homogeneous and precise. Stratifying a customer base allows the commonalities, and the differences, between different customer groups to be quickly identified. Such knowledge is helpful in improving the processes that deliver value to customers.

Proportionate stratified sampling occurs when the sample size in each strata is in the same relative proportion as in the entire population. For instance, if a firm has three customer groups in which 60% are in group A, 30% are in group B, and 10% are in group C, then 60% of the total sample would come from group A, 30% from B, and 10% from C. The data could then be either examined for each group or aggregated together for overall satisfaction statistics.

Disproportionate stratified sampling occurs when the sample distribution is not the same as in the total population. Say, for instance, that a firm generates 80% of total sales from 20% of the total customer base, a fairly common situation. To ensure an accurate profile of the heavy users, 50% of the total sample could be drawn from the 20% of customers who are heavy users, and the other 50% could be drawn from the 80% of customers who are light users. The data could be aggregated together or examined individually.

Cluster sampling is similar to stratified sampling in that the total customer base is segmented into subgroups. Stratified sampling is usually used when there are fewer than ten or so subgroups. Cluster sampling is used when there are a large number of customer groups, such as those served by different sales offices, stores, or regional territories. A sample of different groups is randomly determined, and then customers are randomly selected within each group. If a firm has fifty retail stores, ten stores might be randomly selected, and then customers from each of those groups would be surveyed. The data could either be examined individually or aggregated for an overall customer satisfaction score.

For all types of probability sampling, customers are chosen randomly, either from the entire population or from various subgroups. Most of the statistical formulas and measures assume that a probability sampling technique is being used, as in the calculation of confidence intervals or sampling error. However, many CSM efforts use nonprobability approaches.

Nonprobability Method

Nonprobability sampling occurs when customers are not randomly selected from the total customer base. Instead, managerial judgment contaminates the sampling process somehow. If a good research design is used, the contamination may be quite small. However, contamination may result in very biased, skewed data if the research design is careless and sloppy. The problem of potential error exists with all three types of nonprobability sampling: convenience, judgment, and quota.

Convenience samples are those that occur when the customer is accidentally exposed to the questionnaire. A common example is the CSM questionnaire found in hotel rooms. A particular customer may be exposed to the questionnaire and may or may not complete it. The concern in this situation is whether respondents who respond are representative of the total customer base. Potentially, respondents could be extremely satisfied and eager to heap praise on the hotel, or respondents could be very upset and seize the opportunity to complain. In reality, most customers may be somewhere in between. But the hotel would have no way of knowing how representative the respondents were.

A large hotel chain conducted a split test to compare the responses from convenience samples with those from a randomly selected sample who were administered telephone interviews. The results indicated that some very significant differences existed. However, some of the differences may have been due to the different sampling techniques.

Convenience samples are quite common in CSM research. Those little tell-us-what-you-think questionnaires seem to be everywhere—in restaurants, hotels, rental cars, banks, and retail outlets. But most of them are so brief and superficial that nothing more than a very crude, overall measure is usually generated. Still, in some cases, if well done, convenience samples can generate actionable data.

Judgment samples are those that are selected by the researcher in some way. Perhaps a particular individual at a customer firm is selected because that person would be the best respondent. Judgment samples are generally not representative of the entire population, because the customer is selected based on unique characteristics such as education, experience, knowledge, or accessibility.

A hotel chain based in the state of Washington, decided to survey its customers. After some discussion, heavy-use businesspeople were selected as the sample frame. The hotel management thought that business travelers, because of their high frequency of use, were more knowledgeable and could provide what management considered a better response. That assumption of better responses may or may not have been valid, but the sample certainly was not representative of the total customer base.

Some firms have designed CSM programs that contact the same key individuals weekly, monthly, or whatever the frequency might be. The logic behind this is that key customers can provide accurate feedback and longitudinal consistency. Often there is indeed a good deal of longitudinal consistency with this type of judgment sample, but it is not necessarily more accurate, which is due to potential built-in biases. One key individual may not have the same perceptions as others in the organization or as other customers in general.

One final type of judgment sample is the referral. If the interviewing firm contacts a customer firm but doesn't know who the appropriate respondent is, the interviewer often asks to be referred to the best respondent. In this case, the judgment about who might be the best respondent is made by someone in the customer organization who has little knowledge of the research objectives. Therefore, this referral type of sample selection does not necessarily result in representative data.

Another type of nonprobability sample is the quota. In a CSM program, a quota approach ensures that a certain number of customers possessing certain characteristics are included in the total sample. A sample of 100 customers could be split so that 50 are male and 50 are female. Or a firm desiring a total sample of 300 could split the sample so that 100 respondents are engineers, 100 are production managers, 50 are from quality assurance, and 50 are from purchasing. Normally, quotas attempt to reflect frequency of occurrence in the total population. Thus, the use of quotas is often an attempt to ensure representativeness of the sample.

The characteristics used to describe the quota groupings may not be the most appropriate descriptive criteria. Let's examine the case in which the interviewing firm wanted 50 men and 50 women in the sample because that proportion roughly represents the total population. Men might actually buy and use 60% of product sales, and women might actually buy and use the remaining 40%. The use of a 50-50 quota therefore would skew the data toward the lighter users, women. Utilizing gender as the discriminating criterion ignored other important characteristics—in this instance, the usage rate.

There are a wide variety of sampling procedures. Probability samples are generally preferred in CSM programs because the randomness leads to higher statistical reliability by eliminating some sources of bias. However, nonprobability sampling procedures can be used effectively if care is taken to reduce the potential bias introduced by managerial judgment. As with most other research decisions, initial research objectives play the dominant role in the selection of a sampling procedure. In other words, given the CSM objectives, who must be sampled to get the right kind of data?

Determine the Desired Sample Size

Determining the appropriate sample size is a complex decision involving many trade-offs. Whereas the formulas found in most statistics books lead us to believe that sample sizes are calculated based on a few criteria, in practice a wide variety of factors influence the decision. And in reality the formulas aren't extremely helpful either. The following sections discuss some of the key factors that influence the sample size.

A significant consideration is the amount of time available. The larger and more complicated the sample, the more time it takes to gather the data. Because managers may want the data yesterday, intense time pressure tends to depress sample sizes. Also, large data sets take more time to enter and analyze, and thus smaller sample sizes lead to a faster turnaround of the whole project, not just the data gathering. With intense time pressure, there is also a tendency to compress or streamline some of the up-front steps of identifying customer groups and developing a sampling frame for customers.

The design of optical-scan mail questionnaires and computer-assisted telephone questionnaires takes additional time for initial preparation but can save a considerable amount of time on subsequent sampling efforts. Depending on the amount of resources that a firm puts into the research effort, the larger the sample size, the more time it takes to gather the data. However, if a firm is willing to throw a lot of money and resources into a research project, even large samples can be gathered very quickly.

Resources

The two most obvious resources that influence sample size are money and people. Since no firm has an unlimited amount of money to pour into a research project, there are invariably budget constraints. Some research managers may have a budgeted amount that was squeezed out of the financial allocation process. They may simply survey "as many as possible at a cost of $30,000," for example. First, the overhead charges are factored out, and then the balance is allocated on a per-observation basis. The per-unit costs of a mail survey, from printing to data analysis, might be $2 each. The researcher would simply divide $2 into the total budget. If, in our $30,000 example, it costs $10,000 in overhead charges for the design and pretest, $20,000 would be left for sampling. Dividing the $20,000 by $2 yields a mailing of 10,000. Assuming a response rate of 25%, the total usable sample would be approximately 2,500. So essentially, the budget provides an upper constraint on sample size: the smaller the budget, the smaller the sample size.

The other resource that influences sample size is staffing, and this is a constraint only if all activities are performed in-house rather than outsourced. Some firms may have a customer satisfaction measurement department that consists of only a few people. In such firms many of the necessary CSM activities are outsourced to marketing research or survey research organizations. The primary constraint in these instances once again becomes budgetary. Because the independent organizations are specialists at a given activity, such as telephone interviewing, outsourcing can be considerably cheaper than using in-house staff.

When the whole CSM program is handled internally, staffing can be a constraint. If a mail survey is used, labor intensity can be quite low. Mailing lists, personalized cover letters, and personalized envelopes can be printed easily from computer files. Follow-up contact can also be automated. Optical-scan questionnaires can facilitate a large volume of data input. But for labor-intensive data-gathering methods, such as telephone or personal interviewing, staffing becomes a real problem.

Ideally, data should be gathered over a fairly short period of time to reduce any longitudinal variation in customer perceptions. Usually a week or two is the normal length of data gathering for periodic surveys of customers. Therefore, the size of the staff and the length of interviews directly influence sample size. Perhaps an individual interviewer could complete 20 telephone interviews in one day. If there are six interviewers, 600 interviews could be completed in one week (6 interviewers × 20 per day × 5 days) or 1,200 over a two-week period.

In the outsourcing of CSM activities, budget is usually the primary constraint. When CSM activities are brought in-house, staffing becomes a significant constraint, particularly when using labor-intensive data-gathering techniques.

Type of Sample
The nature of the sample influences sample sizes. If all customers are more or less homogeneous, then one sample can be drawn from the overall customer base. If a firm has a diverse array of subgroups or market segments, larger sample sizes are usually necessary to ensure adequate customer representation within each grouping.

For example, a firm may get by with a sample of 300 if a customer base is relatively homogeneous. But if six market segments are present, it may be necessary to have a sample of 600 or more. Therefore, well before the sample procedures are designed, a researcher should have a good idea of exactly how a sample will be decomposed for data analysis.

Type of Questionnaire

The longer and more complex a questionnaire, the more expensive it becomes to gather a large sample, particularly when a labor-intensive data-gathering procedure is used. For mail surveys, long questionnaires generally depress response rates. Therefore, to achieve a given desired usable data set, more surveys must be mailed out. For personal or telephone interviews, long questionnaires obviously lengthen interview time, which increases costs. Long questionnaires usually increase sample size for another reason, however.

Questionnaires are usually longer when a researcher is trying to satisfy multiple objectives in one study. Having several objectives normally result in additional questions. A large number of groupings and questions result in a larger sample size so the data can be sliced in more ways and with adequate observations in each slice. As we shall see shortly, long questionnaires typically increase the likelihood of respondent variability, and greater variability increases sample sizes.

Variation in Customer Base

The more consistent customers are in their views, the smaller the necessary sample size. The greater their variability, the larger the necessary sample size. In statistical terms, this variation within a population is referred to as the variance. The exact variance of a population is seldom, if ever, known, but an estimate for the population can be calculated from a sample. That calculated estimate is known as the standard error of a sample. It is one of the key components of sample size formulas and will be addressed shortly.

Although size of the customer base is not used directly in formulas for sample sizes, it does exert an indirect influence. As the customer base increases, there is more potential variability, and hence the variance increases. As the variance increases, sample sizes always go up as well. So, potentially, an increase in the customer base can lead to an increase in sample size, but does not always do so.

Precision

Precision is the width of an estimate. Political polls are often described as being within plus or minus percentage points, a statement of precision. The mean percentage of voters in favor of a candidate may be 60%, with the width of the interval from 56% to 64%. The narrower the interval, the more precise the statement about a characteristic.

In a customer satisfaction context, the proportion of customers who are satisfied may be calculated in a variety of ways. If a researcher states that 90% of customers are satisfied, without providing an accompanying statement of precision, a very crude indicator of satisfaction is being determined. A satisfaction level of 90% with a ±10-percentage-point interval is far less useful than a satisfaction level of 90% with a ±2.5 percentage-point-interval. In the first instance, the researcher is fairly certain that the true satisfaction level of the customer base is between 80% and 100%. In the second situation, the researcher is fairly certain that the true satisfaction level is between 87.5% and 92.5%.

The desired precision can be specified in sample size formulas. As precision goes up, narrowing the precision interval, sample size also goes up. However, the relationship between precision and sample size is nonlinear. If the width of the precision interval is reduced by a factor of 2 (halving the interval), the sample size increases by a factor of 4. In our example, reducing the precision interval from ±10 percentage points to ±5 percentage points would require a sample four times as large. Reducing the interval from ±10 percentage points to ±2.5 percentage points requires a sample sixteen times as large as the original, if everything else remains unchanged.

If a customer base is very homogeneous—having a small variance—then the exponential relationship between precision and sample size may not be a big problem. If a ±10-percentage-point precision interval is desired, a sample size formula may indicate a minimum sample size of 50. Reducing the precision interval to ±2.5 percentage points would require a sample of 800.

But if a customer base is very heterogeneous—having a large variance—then the initial required sample size may be 200. To reduce the precision interval for this study to ±2.5 percentage points would require a sample of 3,200, an increase of 3,000 respondents.

The point of all this is that a high degree of precision can be costly in some situations, most notably in the case of a very diverse customer base. The desired precision level is, again, one of those managerial decisions that should flow from the objectives of the research. If a primary goal is the improvement of value-added processes, then the level of precision shouldn't be a big issue, within reason. But if customer satisfaction levels are used in the performance evaluation and reward systems, as when allocating incentive compensation, then precision becomes extremely important. Indeed, the researcher has a responsibility to be very precise when an individual's career and compensation are on the line.

Confidence Level

The third major component in sample size formulas, in addition to variance and precision, is the confidence level. The confidence level indicates how certain we are about our conclusions. The most commonly used confidence levels are 90, 95, 97.5, and 99%.

A researcher might use a 90% confidence level in a CSM project. Using our earlier figures, that researcher would be 90% confident that the mean customer satisfaction level is 90%, ±2.5 percentage points. However, to be more confident, and maybe to impress the users of the data a bit more, a researcher may decide to use a 95% or 97.5% confidence level. As the confidence level increases, sample size also increases.

The same relationship exists between sample size and confidence level as with precision. A 90% confidence level implies that a 10% chance of being wrong exists. If the chance of error is reduced by a factor of 2 (again halving the error), sample size goes up by a factor of 4. Increasing the confidence level from 90% to 95% increases the sample size four times. Increasing the confidence level from 90% to 97.5% increases sample size sixteen times.

Some rough guidelines that describe appropriate sample size are presented below. Please keep in mind that the table addresses a confidence level of only 95% and precision of plus or minus 5%. It does not take variance into consideration. Populations with a small variance may require a smaller sample size; a population with a large variance would require a larger sample size than those indicated.

Sample Size Requirements
95% Confidence
Error = ±5%

Population Size	Required No. of Respondents
100	80
200	132
300	169
400	197
500	218
1,000	278
1,500	306
2,000	323
2,500	334
3,000	341
5,000	357
10,000	370
20,000	377

"Required No. of Respondents" identifies
the number of surveys that you must **get back**.

If a researcher desires to be very confident, say 99%, and very precise, say ±2 percentage points, very large sample sizes will result. The more conclusive and detailed the results, the larger the sample size and the greater the costs. This is especially true when a customer base displays a good deal of heterogeneity, resulting in a large variance. But there are a few other issues that must be considered as well.

Multiple Segments and Measures
The discussion so far has assumed that the variance, precision, and confidence level are easily determined. And these factors are easily calculated or determined for a *single* question. Unfortunately, a one-question customer satisfaction questionnaire is pretty rare. *Each question* has its own accompanying variance. And the same question, used on six different customer groups, may have a different variance in each group.

The impact of multiple questions and multiple segments is that, when sample size is held constant, both the precision and confidence level vary somewhat from question to question. For questions with a large variance, precision and confidence are lower (wider precision intervals and lower confidence level). For questions with a small variance, precision and confidence are relatively higher.

The conservative approach would be to determine the variance for all questions and use the largest variance in sample size calculations. This would result in the largest possible sample size. A more realistic approach would be to examine the variance for the key, most important questions and use that variance in calculations.

Another problem in deciding which variance to choose is the use of multiple measurement scales. A variance of 1.7 is greater on a 5-point scale than on a 7-point scale. Because most CSM questionnaires utilize a variety of response categories, the same absolute variance may be relatively more, or less, important from question to question.

Sample Size Guidelines
Sample size formulas suggest that an exact figure can be calculated for each study. In reality this is not the case. Constraints of time and resources, the nature of the sample and subgroups, length and type of questionnaire, and consistency in the variance can all influence the sample size. In addition, the desired precision and confidence levels are important considerations. Collectively, these factors all work together to muddy the waters, making the final decision rather subjective.

To assist managers in dealing with these issues, Sudman developed the guidelines presented in Table 10.1. These guidelines provide a basis of

Table 10.1   Sample Size Guidelines

Number of Subgroup Analyses	People or Households		Institution	
	National	Regional	National	Regional
None or few	1,000–1,499	200–499	200–499	50–199
Average	1,500–2,499	500–999	500–999	200–499
Many	2,500+	1,000+	1,000+	500+

Source: Seymour Sudman, *Applied Sampling* (New York: Academic Press, 1976), p. 87.

comparison during a determination of sample size. For each situation, a researcher should still attempt to calculate the precision and confidence level based on the variance associated with key questions.

Identify Specific Customers to Be Contacted

Once the sample size has been determined, the next step is to draw the actual customer names from the total sample frame of customers. Because sample size refers to the number of *usable* responses, the sample size is not the number drawn. Instead, sample size is the starting point for determining the number of customers to contact. The researcher must know the approximate response rate, particularly for mail surveys.

If the estimated response rate is 25% for a mail survey and a sample size of 200 is needed, then at least 800 surveys must be mailed out. If the response rate is 25% and a sample of 2,500 is needed, 10,000 surveys must be mailed.

For telephone and personal interviews, the interviewers can simply keep going until the desired sample size is reached. The response rate does influence the total amount of interviewer time and therefore may affect the budget. But a low telephone response rate may mean only that the interviewers must add on one or two more days of interviewing.

If a randomized sample procedure is used, each customer is assigned a number. Then a random-number-generator program is used to select the actual individuals to be contacted. When a nonprobability sampling procedure is used, the sample list is managerially selected based on whatever criteria are being used. When a sequential approach is being used in which every nth (i.e., 4th, 10th, 30th, 50th) customer is contacted, some method of tracking each customer transaction is necessary. Regardless of the specific sample procedure, sample size, or sample frame, however, there remain a variety of other issues that must be considered when the data are actually collected.

Collecting the Data

The results of a sample rarely *exactly* mirror a population. Therefore, a CSM researcher can usually be assured that the results are in error. Good research normally minimizes the error associated with a study; sloppy research allows the error to extend all the way to the results in significant proportions. There are two types of error that result when samples are conducted: sampling error and nonsampling error.

Sampling error results when a sample is not representative of an entire customer base. The previous discussions of precision and confidence level dealt directly with sampling error. A 90% confidence level implied that there was a 10% chance that the results were in error. A 97.5% confidence level implied that there was a 2.5% chance that the results were in error. The same situation existed for precision. Increasing the confidence level and increasing precision both required an increase in sample size. So the way to reduce sampling error is to have a larger sample size. The larger a sample absolutely or as a proportion of the total customer base, the less significant the sampling error.

Because sampling error is easily remedied by an increase in sample size, it is not normally a significant issue in a well-designed sampling procedure, even when nonprobability procedures are used. Instead, the nonsampling errors are clearly more troubling and difficult to correct. Because of their perniciousness, nonsampling errors are the predominant focus of the remaining discussion.

Nonsampling error is a result of inherent bias, flaws in logic, or improper implementation. These types of error are unaffected by sample size. Since sampling error decreases as sample size increases, nonsampling errors actually become relatively more important in large samples and are the *primary source of error*. The effect of non-sampling error is normally five to ten times greater than sampling error. The only way to reduce non-sampling error is through better research design and implementation. And to do that, an understanding of the types of nonsampling error is necessary.

Types of Nonsampling Error

Nonsampling errors can flow from virtually every aspect of research design, from the initial focus groups to the data analysis. No attempt is made here to address *all* possible sources of error. Rather only the major types of nonsampling error are discussed.

Faulty Questionnaires

The potential sources of error in questionnaires are extensive. Misleading introductions, ambiguous directions, biased questions, inappropriate response categories, and improper sequencing are just a few sources of error. These and other problems were discussed in detail in previous chapters. But flaws on any type in questionnaires are serious because they systematically influence every respondent. The solution to this error lies in careful questionnaire design and pretesting.

Inconsistent Interviewers

The chapter on telephone questionnaires presented the interview as a two-way, interactive process. A variety of factors independently or jointly influence the quality of the interview. Age, experience, education, and interpersonal sensitivity are a few of the interviewer characteristics that influence data quality. Each interviewer may have different attitudes and expectations that influence communication with the customer. Different interviewers may have a different voice inflection that may alter interpretation by the customer. Some interviewers may paraphrase a question slightly rather than read it verbatim, particularly at the end of a long day of interviewing. Other interviewers may inadvertently drop a word or a response category or skip a question. Others may misinterpret a customer's response or may mark the wrong response category. The solution to this error consists of good training, evaluation, and reward of interviewers.

Noncoverage Errors

Noncoverage occurs when the sample frame does not include the total customer base. Some firms may use warranty cards as a sample frame, but significant portions of the customer base may not complete warranty cards. For business customers, the sample frame may include only purchasing agents, when engineering and quality assurance are important customers. A telephone interviewer may attempt to reach a busy executive, but settle for a more accessible respondent, possibly biasing a study toward lower-level managers. The primary solution to noncoverage errors consists of careful definition of the customer and compilation of an appropriate customer list. To a lesser degree, the interviewer must be instructed as to who is the most appropriate respondent and what degree of substitutability is allowed.

Nonresponse Errors

Nonresponse error occurs when those who don't respond are somehow different from those who do. In the hotel industry, for example, non-respondents tend to be more dissatisfied than respondents. In this case, many nonrespondents simply refused to participate because they were annoyed in some way. An understanding of the reasons for refusal is necessary in order to develop corrective managerial action.

Nonresponse can also occur because the respondent is not available. For telephone interviewing, some of the possibilities are no answer, busy signal, answering machine, disconnected line, or out of order, or desired respondent is home sick, on vacation, on a business trip, or in a meeting, or has terminated employment. Each of these situations requires a different managerial response.

One study indicated that one telephone attempt reached 24% of respondents, five attempts reached 75% of respondents, and eight attempts reached 89% of respondents. However, it took seventeen attempts to reach all respondents. Nonresponses are strongly influenced by the timing of the interviews. Dual-income households seldom yield anyone home during the day. Monday mornings may be very busy times for businesspeople. Businesspeople may frequently be at lunch between 11:30 a.m. and 1:30 p.m. If nonrespondents are no different from respondents, nonresponse will not produce any nonsampling error. But if nonrespondents are somehow different, then nonsampling error will be introduced. The solution, therefore, is to determine through the use of a separate, follow-up study whether nonrespondents are different.

Data Errors

Data errors are those that occur during the input, compilation, or analysis of data. If data are entered manually, keypunch errors can occur. If optical scanning is used to input data, sloppy marks and smudges can cause problems. Errors have been known to occur in the format specifications, thus causing all subsequent responses to be shifted over by one column. The data could be analyzed using an incorrect technique, such as calculating a mean response for categorical data or rank-ordered data. Data errors are relatively minor compared with other non-sampling errors and are corrected by careful handling and analysis of the data. Problems with format specifications can be found by printing out an entire data set and randomly validating twenty or thirty questionnaires.

CHAPTER SUMMARY

Sampling is a highly visible element of the research design. Whereas some firms with a small customer base may use a census of all customers, most CSM programs may use a sample. Although both a census and a sample require the clear definition of who the customer is, samples typically cost less, take less time, and are easier to conduct.

Sampling is a sequential process that has six interdependent steps, as indicated in Figure 10.1. The successful completion of each step has a direct influence on the quality of the CSM data. Each step has its own unique challenges and managerial implications.

The final sample design should flow from the research objectives. Samples could be drawn from customers sequentially, after a particular transaction. Or fixed samples could be drawn periodically by utilizing simple random, stratified, cluster, convenience, judgment, or quota procedures. Each of these approaches carries with it a unique set of advantages and disadvantages that must be weighed carefully.

Calculating sample sizes is also a complex decision. Factors such as time, resources, sample procedure, type of questionnaire, variation in the customer's attitudes, and desired precision and confidence all work together to determine the appropriate sample size. Calculating sample size is more complex and subjective than simply using a few sample size formulas.

Once the process of data gathering actually begins, a variety of other variables tend to rear their ugly heads, causing nonsampling errors. The more common nonsampling errors are caused by faulty questionnaires, inconsistent interviewers, noncoverage of the total customer base, non-responses by customers, and mistakes in data handling.

In order to design a good CSM sampling plan, all of these issues must be carefully considered. Ultimately, many of the decisions are subjective, flowing from the overall research objectives.

THE PRAXIS INSTITUTE

CorporatePulse™

The Praxis Institute is an organizational development and change consulting firm whose mission is "to improve individual and organizational vitality." Praxis's primary change strategy is to work jointly with leaders to develop positive, lasting change in organizations.

Over the years, Praxis has been involved with helping corporations develop their employee opinion surveys. After struggling for weeks, even months, gathering data, Praxis observed that leaders either paid little heed to the findings or didn't know what to do with the results. Praxis also learned that infrequent employee survey results were meaningless compared with other output measures that leaders pored over daily. Because of this, Praxis pulled together a team of trainers, researchers, software designers, and consultants to create an integrated system called CorporatePulse™.

CorporatePulse™ is a computer program that designs custom employee surveys or provides generic surveys, calculates sample sizes, tabulates data through survey scanning, and generates reports. The result is a program that is icon driven and collects real-time data for pertinent organizational questions in a cost-effective manner. CorporatePulse™ also takes much of the agony out of the survey administration and data collection process by computerizing the tedious components. And finally, the survey questions can be drawn from a question bank in order to receive actionable data.

Even though CorporatePulse™ was developed with employee opinion and satisfaction surveys in mind, it can be used for CSM surveys. CSM questions must be developed, but the CorporatePulse™ program helps to determine sample size based on your own parameters and precision level. The built-in database can link up to your database and generate mailing labels. Data can be entered through scanners. And you can track and graph results over time.

CorporatePulse™ takes the drudgery out of the survey process by using the power of a computer to do the tedious work.

11

Analyzing the Data

Determining what is driving customer satisfaction requires good data analysis in order to effectively allocate an organization's physical, financial, and human resources. Data analysis is a common-sense, logical process that should not be intimidating. Unfortunately, many managers neither understand nor trust some of the more advanced statistical techniques. This chapter explores the conceptual, technical, and motivational aspects of data analysis necessary to address these issues.

There are two types of data analysis required. The first consists of the techniques used to create the CSM model. In Chapter 5, "Identifying the Attributes," those issues were briefly introduced. The two most commonly used techniques for model construction are factor analysis and multiple regression. Chapter 5 examined how these techniques can be used to reduce the attribute list. But reducing the attribute list is really only the first step in creating a CSM model.

The second category of data analysis comprises those techniques that are used to examine the ongoing data generated by a CSM program. Therefore, those techniques are concerned with sequentially tracking variations in customer satisfaction levels. They tend to be simpler than those used in model construction, and they include descriptive statistics, computing aggregate indices, and so forth.

Because a CSM model must be constructed first, that process is discussed first. The three levels of measurement of the model—global measures, corporate image, and specific attributes—were introduced previously. We now discuss the components of the model

215

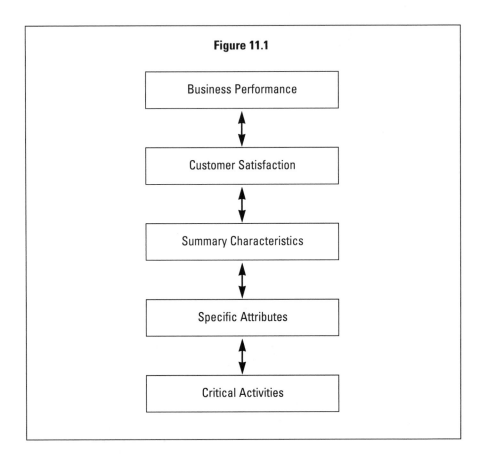

Figure 11.1

Business Performance

Customer Satisfaction

Summary Characteristics

Specific Attributes

Critical Activities

and the linkages between components. Discussions in the remaining portion of the chapter then focus on analyzing the ongoing CSM data.

COMPONENTS OF A CSM MODEL

Probably the best way to understand and communicate the data collected is through the use of a model. A number of CSM models have been developed, but the one covered in this book is the most comprehensive. The model encompasses five key levels, from the external customer environment to the internal processes: business performance, overall customer satisfaction, summary characteristics, specific attributes, and critical activities. The model, shown in Figure 11.1 is a reflection of the external and internal process that create customer satisfaction. As the arrows indicate, the model moves in both directions. A

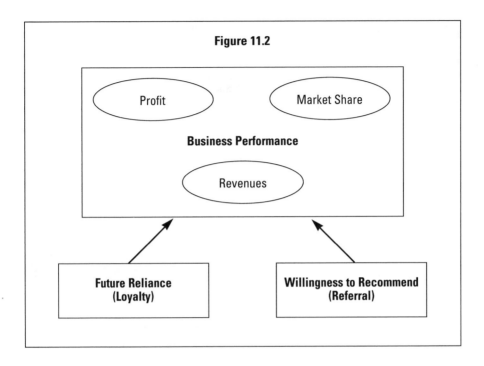

journey through the model will help set the conceptual framework for the analytical process.

Business Performance

The ultimate outcome of the customer satisfaction process is business performance. Business performance means different things to different businesses. For small businesses and corporations, it usually refers to market share, increased revenues, and/or profit. For nonprofits, it usually means increased donations and volunteer commitment. For government agencies, it should mean lower taxes and more social services for us! In essence, business performance is whatever it takes to stay in business and achieve the strategic business objectives. Over time, you will be able to quantitatively link customer satisfaction measures with the bottom line. Companies such as AT&T, Harris Corporation, and Marion Merrill Dow are successfully doing this. Until that time, business performance is determined by customers' willingness to recommend you to others and by customers' future customer loyalty (Figure 11.2). Thus, one aspect of data analysis links business performance with the overall aggregate CSM measures.

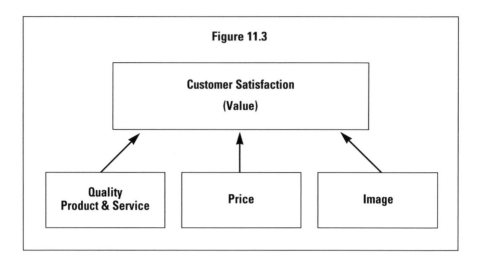

Figure 11.3

Overall Customer Satisfaction

The next level in the model is overall customer satisfaction (Figure 11.3). Overall customer satisfaction influences the future reliance and willingness to recommend in Figure 11.2. But overall satisfaction is determined by the degree to which customer value expectations are met. Customer value is composed of three major elements: overall product and service quality, price, and corporate image. These three elements all influence the customer's perception of value. The impact of each of these three elements is unique to every business unit, product, service, or industry.

The first element of customer value is overall quality, which is a combination of product and service quality. Product and service quality often have the greatest influence on perception of customer value. The measures of quality capture top-of-mind perception of the overall quality provided, which includes issues such as the customer's time and the ease, or hassle, of doing business with you as well as the specific product and service attributes. Overall quality will be discussed in detail as we decompose the model into summary characteristics of products and services in the next section.

Price is the second element of customer value. Measuring a customer's perception of the price charged is important and also difficult to measure. For example, you may ask if your product or service is in a range anchored by low priced and high priced. Some biases naturally come into play in this pricing question. Customers who say your products are high priced could be indirectly admitting that they are making a poor decision when purchasing your product or service. On the other hand, customers may be reluctant to indicate your products are low priced, because they may believe you will then raise prices based on their feedback. Asking if your product or service is comparably, competitively, or fairly priced may yield more accurate data. If customers' perceptions of benefits exactly match price, customers will be satisfied, but not extremely so. If the benefits are viewed to be less than the price, then customers will feel they are not getting their money's worth and will indicate very low levels of satisfaction. Please keep in mind that the term *price* is used very broadly here. Price could include price paid, life-cycle costs such as depreciation and maintenance, and risk. The competitive benchmarking questions discussed in Chapter 14 further address this issue.

Corporate image is the third element of customer value. Corporate image could include the attributes of general business practices, ethics, and social responsibility. Examples of image attributes are shown in Figure 11.4. Many of these attributes are generic, though some could be identified by customers in your focus groups. Perceptions about corporate image are derived from many areas. A customer can develop perceptions about your corporation from your products and services, from business interaction with your employees, articles in popular magazines, print and television advertising, public relations and marketing materials, an acquaintance who may work for your corporation, articles or publicity from communities, environmental influence, social activities, or a myriad of other areas. The bottom line is that you do have a corporate or business image that customers perceive. The impact of corporate image on customer value varies with differing business units and tends to generate issues that need to be addressed by senior management.

Corporate image is important because customers may use image as a surrogate cue in their decision-making processes. For example, customers may be unable to accurately evaluate the product and service attributes. But the customer can evaluate the image of the firm and transfer that image to a specific product. For instance, a consumer buying a personal computer may not have much technical knowledge about them, but the IBM image might convey respect and trust. The consumer may conclude that product quality *must* be good; it's an IBM. And IBM, as a respected company, must stand behind its products, so service quality must also be good. So the real value of corporate image is that it serves as an indicator of what a customer might expect. A positive corporate

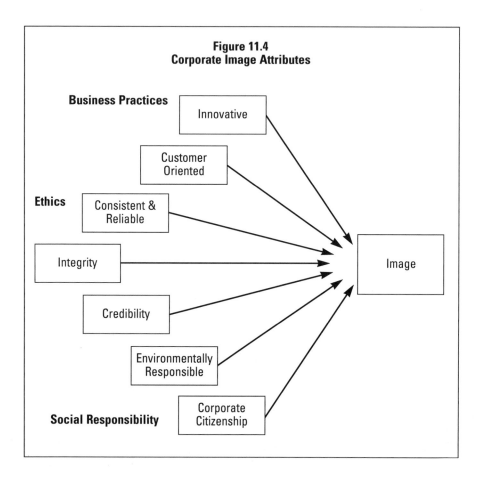

Figure 11.4
Corporate Image Attributes

Business Practices

Innovative

Customer Oriented

Ethics

Consistent & Reliable

Integrity

Credibility

Environmentally Responsible

Social Responsibility

Corporate Citizenship

Image

image creates positive expectations. A negative corporate image creates uncertainty and risk for the customer.

Summary Characteristics

Summary characteristics are the aggregations of specific quality and service attributes. An example of summary characteristics is shown in Figure 11.5. Summary characteristics are determined by your customer, not your organization. You may believe that there is no difference, but this is not always the case. For example, a paper company had a third-party consultant conduct a focus group with some of the company's key customers to determine product and service attributes. The consultant found that customers identified paper smoothness with the summary characteristic of printability. In the paper company, marketing and oper-

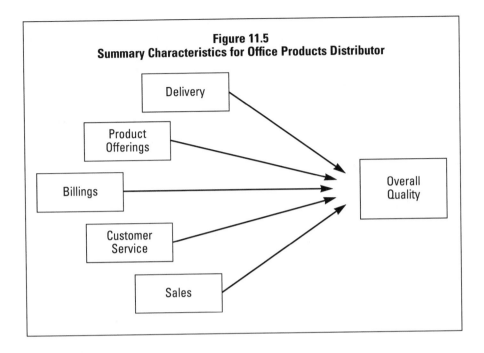

Figure 11.5
Summary Characteristics for Office Products Distributor

Delivery

Product
Offerings

Billings

Customer
Service

Sales

Overall
Quality

ations managers considered the smoothness attribute part of the appearance summary characteristic because that was where smoothness was measured. By placing the attribute in the correct place from the customer's perspective, the paper company came to understand different perceptions and the need for new measures to make the product perform to customer expectations.

Summary characteristics should, to the extent possible, reflect a firm's major value-creating processes. As we shall see later, this linkage facilitates using the data. For most firms there are relatively few—normally from three to seven—major value-creating processes. All other activities in a firm should support one of those processes. Each of these processes produces a variety of outcomes. Those outcomes are usually expressed as product and service attributes.

Specific Attributes

Specific attributes are the individual components of the summary characteristics. These attributes are the ones that the customer defined in the qualitative research discussed in Chapter 5. Figure 11.6 shows the specific attributes for delivery for an office products distributor. In the qualitative work, customers identified four attributes that constitute the

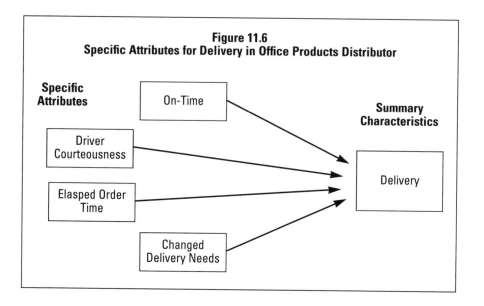

Figure 11.6
Specific Attributes for Delivery in Office Products Distributor

overall summary attribute of delivery: on-time shipments, driver courte-
ousness, elapsed order time, and changed delivery needs. Performance on
each of these should be individually measured and recorded.

Critical Activities

The final component of the model is where the voice of the customer enters the organization in identifying those activities that are critical for
meeting customer expectations and satisfaction. In the example used for
the office products distributor's delivery performance, we must look at
each attribute (Figure 11.7). Analysis of data identified on-time delivery
as having the greatest impact on customer perception of overall delivery
quality. In examining on-time delivery, one looks within the organization
to identify which activities affect whether or not an order is delivered on
time. In this example, four critical activities were identified. Orders are
not delivered on time if they are not delivered complete. Orders are not
delivered on time if the order was not entered accurately into the computer system by the customer service staff. Orders are not delivered on
time if no trucks are available on the schedule to deliver product to the
customer's facility. Finally, orders are not delivered on time if the product
is not in stock in the office products distributor's warehouse. These four
activities and the underlying critical processes that drive them must be
the focus of process improvement efforts. The next chapter is completely
devoted to this topic.

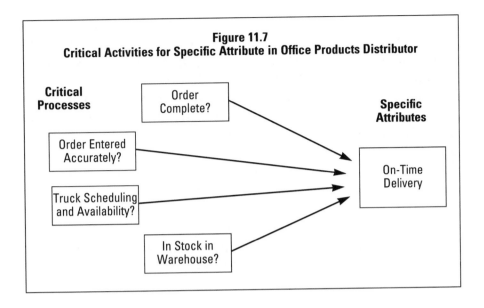

Figure 11.7
Critical Activities for Specific Attribute in Office Products Distributor

In summary, improving overall business performance is the ultimate goal of customer satisfaction measurement. Business performance is strongly influenced by future customer reliance upon and recommendation of your organization's products and services. Customers' future reliance on you and willingness to recommend you are based on their satisfaction or their perception of customer value. Customer value is determined by overall product and service quality, price, and corporate image elements. Overall product and service quality are driven by perceptions of the categories called summary characteristics that are aggregates of specific attributes. Specific attributes have differing impacts on customer satisfaction. Through data analysis, the attributes of greatest impact are determined. Knowing this, organizations can then identify the critical activities and therefore the critical processes in their organizations toward which quality improvement efforts should be directed.

BUILDING A CSM MODEL

As mentioned previously, there are two groups of techniques used in the analysis of CSM data. The first group deals with how to statistically derive a model from a database, and these techniques are rather complex. The second set of techniques deals with how to track CSM levels from one time period to the next, and these techniques tend to be much simpler.

To begin data analysis, a firm must obviously have gathered data in some way. The design of a model is usually derived from a large-scale pretest sample. As described in Chapter 5, the first step in model construction is to reduce a long attribute list down to a shorter, more manageable one. These key attributes are then grouped by value-added processes as discussed in the previous section. Then the relative importance of each attribute or process can be determined by analyzing the relationship to overall customer satisfaction measures. The overall customer satisfaction measure can then be linked to key business performance criteria.

Identifying the Key Attributes and Processes

There are several ways to reduce an attribute list and then group the attributes into categories linked to a firm's value-added processes. The two most common techniques are factor analysis and multiple regression. However, in some instances, canonical correlation is also useful. Each of these techniques carries with it certain differing assumptions and constraints.

Factor Analysis

Factor analysis is a statistical technique that examines the relationships between a single dependent variable and multiple independent variables. We discussed this technique briefly in Chapter 5. Because it considers many variables, it falls into the family of multivariate statistics.

Factor analysis condenses a long list of attributes by simultaneously evaluating all variables and then identifying common trends, or factors, that exist in the data. If, for example, a firm has identified forty to fifty attributes during the qualitative process, factor analysis may reduce the list down to, say, six factors with clusters of four to seven attributes each. Individual attributes that have a weak statistical relationship could then be dropped out, leaving only the more important factors.

In order to use factor analysis, several assumptions are made. From a CSM standpoint, factor analysis generally assumes that the data are interval scaled. Although factor analysis can be used for categorical data, the results are less robust and meaningful. So if a questionnaire uses a three- or four-category measurement scale, factor analysis really won't be valuable.

A second assumption is that there exists an adequate sample size. At the bare minimum, sample size should be twice the number of variables being examined. However, the preferred sample size is four to five times the number of variables. Therefore, if a firm has an attribute list of forty variables, the minimum sample size is 80–100, but the preferred sample size is 160–200.

Factor analysis is not a single technique; instead there are several types of factor analysis. Since most researchers have a reasonable understanding of the attributes, principal components factor analysis is most commonly used for reducing an attribute list and determining the underlying constructs and relationships in the factors.

With principal components factor analysis, factors are extracted from the data until successive factors add little in the way of explanatory power. The most important factor is extracted first, so for each iteration the marginal contribution of each factor can be evaluated. As a rough rule of thumb, factors adding less than 4 to 5% are deleted from the model. When a factor is deleted, the attributes composing that factor are also deleted.

Factor analysis is seldom used alone in constructing a CSM model. Instead, factor analysis is most often used as a preliminary screen to reduce an attribute list and form groupings. The reduced list is then subjected to regression analysis. In other instances, the full attribute list is evaluated using *both* factor analysis and multiple regression. The results of both approaches are then compared for similarities.

Multiple Regression

Multiple regression is a technique that analyzes the relationship between a single dependent variable and multiple independent variables. As with factor analysis, the dependent variable, a CSM index, is assumed to be interval. However, the independent variables need not be interval. Thus, if attributes are categorically scaled, multiple regression is more appropriate than factor analysis.

Multiple regression does not identify common underlying trends in the data and then use that as the basis for loading individual variables into factors the way factor analysis does. However, multiple regression does allow the relationship between each independent variable, or attribute, and the dependent variable to be examined in more detail. The strength, or importance, of the relationship between each attribute and the dependent CSM index is easily identified.

There are a variety of types of multiple regression. Using a full-model approach, all attributes would be forced into a model simultaneously. A researcher could then drop the variables that demonstrate a statistically insignificant relationship. In this instance, the researcher could determine the ability of all variables to predict the CSM index as well as the relationship between each attribute and the index.

Unfortunately, two or more independent variables may interact with one another in some way, and the full-model approach provides little insight into that phenomenon. However, stepwise regression provides more insight into how variables relate to one another.

With stepwise regression, the attribute most strongly related to the CSM index is entered first. Then each additional variable is sequentially entered into the model. If a variable makes a significant additional contribution to explain variation in the CSM index, the variable is kept in the model. If an attribute makes no significant contribution, it is automatically dropped. The researcher can specify the cutoff level of significance. Most researchers use a .05 level.

For each variable entered in stepwise regression, the impact on all other independent variables is also examined. Thus, if a new variable is redundant with an existing variable but adds additional explanatory power to the model, the existing variable will be dropped.

Therefore a stepwise regression approach automatically builds a model that contains only those variables that have good explanatory power. Once the variables are identified, it is then up to the researcher to group them according to value-added processes.

A regression model is usually evaluated based on its ability to explain variation in the dependent variable. This explanatory power is referred to as an R^2. An R^2 of .75 means that a model explains 75% of the variation in the dependent variable. An R^2 of more than .70 means the model is pretty good and that the researcher has identified most of the influential attributes.

An R^2 in the range of .60 to .69 means that the model is getting marginal in terms of its acceptability. An R^2 of less than .50 usually means there are some other variables that should be included in the model. A low R^2 is an indication of conceptual problems somewhere in the earlier steps.

Each attribute can also be evaluated individually or in a group. Depending on how the regression analysis is done, a t or F statistic can be calculated for each variable or each group of variables. Hierarchical regression is similar to stepwise regression and the results of a hierarchical regression analysis of CSM data are presented in Table 11.1.

Table 11.1 Hierarchical Regression of Customer Satisfaction and Predictor Variables

Variable	t	F	Significance Level
Product quality		12.164	.0001
Durability	0.556		.5788
Reliability	4.456		.0001
Appearance	2.034		.0438
Structural design	3.733		.0003
Technical quality	0.535		.5937
Service quality		11.588	.0001
Complaint resolution	5.074		.0001
Telephone response	1.001		.3187
Information accuracy	2.072		.0400
Inquiry responsiveness	2.695		.0079
Shipment timeliness	0.865		.3883
Other attributes		9.211	.0001
Market price	3.829		.0002
Productivity benefits	2.655		.0088
Corporate image	2.916		.0041
Full model		13.118	.0001

For this study thirteen attributes were grouped into three categories. The groupings were categorized by management into product quality, service quality, and other attributes. For hierarchical regression, each group is entered as a separate, full-multiple-regression model. This allows the evaluation of each group. Then all three groups are combined into a full CSM model.

The F statistic column indicates the strength of the relationship between each group and the customer satisfaction index. Product quality is the category with the strongest relationship, followed by service quality and other attributes, because the larger the F statistic, the stronger the relationship. However, all three categories are important, for all have a significance level of .0001, which is quite high. Of the five product quality attributes, reliability, appearance, and structural design exceed a .05 cutoff level and should be kept. Durability and technical quality should be dropped. Of the five service quality attributes, three should be kept—complaint resolution, information accuracy, and inquiry responsiveness. Telephone response and shipment timeliness should be dropped. All three of the other attributes should be kept because all exceed the .05 significance level.

Even though this example is a bit simplistic because the original attribute list of thirteen was trimmed to nine, it shows how regression analysis can be used to develop a model. Obviously, an attribute list of forty or so attributes grouped into six or seven categories would be much more complex. But the process would be conceptually the same. Because of its versatility, regression analysis in some form is probably the most important statistical technique used to build a CSM model.

Canonical Correlation

For both factor analysis and multiple regression, the assumption was made that there was a single dependent variable, normally a customer satisfaction index of some type. However, there may be instances when a manager would like to know if the attributes are related to satisfaction and repurchase intent in different ways. Perhaps a manager may want to pay particular attention to repurchase intent as part of a customer retention effort.

Canonical correlation allows a researcher to examine the relationship between a set of independent variables, such as attributes, and a set of dependent measures. For CSM purposes, the most common dependent measures would be an overall satisfaction question, a repurchase question, and a referral or recommendation question.

Canonical correlation is a flexible technique that accommodates categorical and interval data as both dependent and independent variables. Accordingly, canonical correlation is viewed as less rigorous than multiple regression or factor analysis.

The key statistic in canonical correlation is the correlation coefficient. It is the same as an R statistic in multiple regression, so an R^2 statistic is the percentage of variation in the set of dependent variables explained by the set of independent variables.

A canonical correlation was performed on the same set of data as used in the previous regression example. The results of the correlation are presented in Table 11.2. In this example, overall customer satisfaction and intent to repurchase are the two dependent variables.

The standardized canonical coefficients, or canonical weights, indicate the strength of the relationship. As a set, the attributes are a better pre-

Table 11.2 Canonical Analysis

Variable	Standardized Canonical Coefficients
Satisfaction	.585
Repurchases intent	.529
Product Quality	
Durability	.389
Reliability	.004
Appearance	.065
Structural design	.107
Technical quality	.056
Service Quality	
Complaint resolution	.262
Telephone response	.065
Information accuracy	.126
Inquiry responsiveness	.242
Shipment timeliness	.080
Other Attributes	
Market price	.265
Productivity benefits	.036
Corporate image	.146
Canonical correlation	.787
F ratio	7.715*

*$p < .0001$

dictor of satisfaction than repurchase intent although the difference is rather small.

Of the attributes, durability is the best predictor of the set of dependent variables as indicated by its coefficient of .389. Following durability in importance are market price (.265), complaint resolution (.262), inquiry responsiveness (.242), corporate image (.146), information accuracy (.126), and structural design (.107). This type of data allows a variable list to be ranked ordered very quickly.

For a researcher interested in finding out how the relationship between each dependent variable is related to the set of independent variables, canonical correlation is useful. Typically this type of analysis would be followed up with separate multiple regression models for each dependent variable. This would provide more detail into the nature of the relationships in the data.

Multivariate Summary

The three multivariate techniques of factor analysis, multiple regression, and canonical correlation are the most appropriate techniques to use in the construction of a CSM model. These techniques are very powerful and will identify variables that need to be dropped from the model. Further, they indicate the strength of the relationship between individual attributes and overall satisfaction measures. These techniques are so important that constructing a CSM model without them is very dangerous.

Once a model has been identified and ongoing relationships are being tracked periodically, the statistical analysis becomes less complex and more straightforward.

TRACKING ANALYSIS

Once a model is statistically derived, the primary data analysis techniques are cross tabulations, frequency distributions, and means and standard deviations. If a researcher prefers to statistically calculate importance, or derive it from the data, then regression analysis will need to be done each time data are gathered.

The primary purpose of tracking data is to identify the sequential changes in customer responses from one time period to the next. In most cases, this means tracking and posting the key metrics so the results can be used to drive process improvement. As a result, much of the tracking analysis is quite similar to the statistical process control techniques used in production situations.

Unlike the multivariate techniques that attempted to explain or predict variation in a dependent variable, tracking analysis involves the use of techniques that describe patterns in the data. Thus, these techniques are referred to as descriptive statistics. Descriptive statistics do simply that—describe patterns in the data.

Cross-Tabulations

Cross tabulations, or cross tabs, are simply comparisons of responses or demographics against other questions. For example, you may wish to review a particular question to see how one region's customer responses compare with another region's. In CSM, cross tabs are often used to see how customers who indicated that you have excellent or very good value compare with those customers who rate you lower. You will find that those customers who rate you high in value, overall quality, willingness to recommend, and future reliance also rate other attributes higher than the norm.

A paper manufacturer surveyed its customers including some interdivisional office products customers who purchased its white business papers for an office products distribution business. The results of all surveyed customers were broken out in cross-tab form into two separate segments: interdivisional customers and external customers. The comparison showed that the interdivisional customers rated performance higher in all areas except corporate image. These were interesting findings given that both customers and suppliers work for the same company! Several other studies that had both interdivisional and external customers had similar findings. This finding provided information for organizational discussion and provides further insight into image internal and external to the company.

Cross tabulations are a good way to get managers involved in the CSM process. They identify patterns of relationships in the variables. It is then up to the managers to identify why the patterns exist. Because of the simplicity and clarity of cross tabs, few managers are intimidated by this or other descriptive techniques.

Frequency Distribution

If the questions have been scaled using categories, normally from three to five, then the responses are categorical, not interval. Therefore, data analysis must use frequency distributions, not means and standard deviations as is sometimes done.

Frequency distributions indicate the frequency of responses in each category. The results of frequency distributions are usually presented as percentages of respondents falling into various categories. These percentages then become the key metric that is tracked from one period to the next.

Often, the percentages are presented as a pie chart showing the percentage of responses in each category. Or the percentages in the Satisfied category or categories can be displayed. Some firms may prefer to produce bar charts or line graphs that portray longitudinal trends. With frequency distributions, a good dose of managerial judgment comes into play.

Xerox Corp. uses a five-category scale to measure overall customer satisfaction. Any respondent indicating a 4 or 5 is considered to be satisfied. AT&T, on the other hand, also uses a four-category scale but feels that only a score of 4, which represents excellent, is enough to retain a customer. AT&T considers a customer who selects a 3 or lower to be vulnerable to competitive alternatives. The decision to select two or even three categories as indicating a satisfied customer often results in an aggregation bias as valuable data can be lost.

Some firms use cross tabs between categorical independent and/or dependent variables to better understand responses. For example, a firm may believe that a customer who is very satisfied (a 5 on a 5-point scale) is four times as likely to remain a loyal customer. This type of statement is made by comparing the response patterns of those selecting a 5 with the patterns of those selecting a 4 or lower. AT&T provides a good example of this.

Ray Kordupleski, director of customer service at AT&T, states that between 92 and 97% of customers who select excellent on a relative value measure will buy again. This compares to between 62 and 67% of those would select good. But even more striking is the fact that only between 15 and 17% of those who select fair will buy again, and only 0 to 2% of those who select poor will buy again. Being rated good, fair, or poor carries a heavy burden of customer turnover. Incidentally, AT&T uses a variety of measurement scales in addition to this one.

Using five or fewer response alternatives certainly results in categorical data. Technically, a scale with six or seven response alternatives is also categorical. However, studies have shown that the seven-category response structure closely resembles true interval data. Thus, the data generated by six or seven response categories can be analyzed using both categorical and interval techniques. And the results will generally be about the same.

Means and Standard Deviations

Calculating means for tracking analysis is pretty straightforward, and numerous examples of this have been provided previously. Unfortunately, the analysis of means is often abused. The most common error is to not consider the standard deviation when comparing means. The result is that erroneous conclusions are drawn from the data. This is particularly true in the analysis of importance data.

Asking customers what is important intuitively makes sense; your customers are the judges of your products and services and should know what is important to them. The problem with this approach though is that you will find that everything is deemed important. The responses are often skewed and the researcher is left with a list of important attributes that is often as long as the original questionnaire. Research has also shown that, when asked to identify what is important, customers tend to identify tangibles more often than intangibles. It is more difficult to identify and clarify the importance of intangibles.

Let's say that a firm is trying to evaluate the relative importance of fifteen attributes by using a 10-point scale, with 1 being Very unimportant and 10 being Very important. It would not be at all unusual to have ten of the fifteen attributes have a mean rating of greater than 9.0 on this scale.

Very often, a firm simply rank orders the means from highest to lowest and concludes that this is the order of importance to the customer. That conclusion, however, is fundamentally incorrect.

There is a statistical procedure referred to as a paired t-test, which should be used to determine if the means are significantly different from one another. The test is relatively simple and considers the mean, standard deviation, and sample size.

In our example, if the means of the attributes were in the range of 9.05 to 9.48, hypothetically, then the means are probably not statistically different from one another. The differences could be due simply to sampling variability and not real differences in customers' perceptions. Hence the proper conclusion would be that the ten attributes are all equally important to customers.

The implication is that, when calculating means, the researcher should not attempt to split hairs by implying the data are more refined and precise than they really are. Often this implies that the researcher must educate the users of the data regarding how to interpret the data. This requires that means, standard deviations, and significant differences be calculated and explained fully to the users of the data.

After all of this, mean responses to interval data can be presented as numerical means, bar charts, line graphs, or process charts. The decision about how to present the data is based on the preferences of the user groups.

Derived Importance

Because of the tendency of customers to rate almost everything as important, some researchers are wary of self-explicated, or self-report, importance data. Researchers often prefer to supplement self-report data with derived importance.

Derived importance uses statistical analysis to determine which attributes are most important in affecting, in either a positive or a negative manner, the overall satisfaction index or value. This is usually determined through the use of multiple regression analysis. The specific attributes are the independent variables that affect the overall satisfaction measure or dependent variable. Depending on the specific technique used, a calculated statistic such as a regression coefficient, a t statistic, or an F statistic is used to determine importance. The larger the statistic, the greater the importance. Regression analysis or a variation is used by nearly all CSM researchers to determine importance or impact. Interestingly, self-reported importance and derived importance are seldom the same. Derived importance data are generally more reliable.

One way to explore the relationship is to graph stated importance versus derived importance as shown in Figure 11.8. In this example the delivery had both high stated and derived importance. Customer service had the lowest stated importance but highest derived importance. This indicates that the customer service area should be investigated further.

American Express embarked upon a CSM process with customers who use its American Express card. Customers stated that the most important attribute to them was that an immediate replacement card would be available if their American Express card were lost or stolen. But the reality is that only 2–3% of customers ever lose a card, and customers who had lost a card were very satisfied with the replacement procedure. In order to determine what else might be driving satisfaction, American Express ran a regression analysis to derive importance. The company found that three key elements affect satisfaction: that the card is accepted at a business, that the billing is correct, and that the card is perceived as a prestige item. Because of the study, American Express was able to focus process improvement efforts on the elements of derived importance and focus marketing efforts on the replacement card issue.

AT&T's Universal Card (UC) had very similar CSM findings. The three most important attributes for UC were the number of businesses accepting it, accurate billing, and multiple uses. The wide acceptance and multiple use features have been stressed in the UC's advertising campaign.

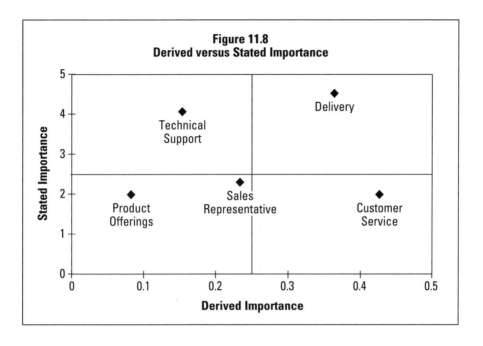

Figure 11.8
Derived versus Stated Importance

Verbatim Comments

Verbatim comments are comments either made by customers in response to open-ended questions or, in some instances, offered spontaneously. The comments could be written on a mail survey or given verbally by phone or in personal interviews. These comments can be quite valuable and should be captured completely, or verbatim, whenever possible. Unfortunately, there is a tendency on the part of interviewers to filter such responses and to capture only the essence of what was said. When filtering occurs there is almost always a loss of information of some type.

Although verbatim responses can be valuable, care should be taken in developing a managerial response. If negative responses get all of the attention (as in management by exception), it could be a case of the squeaky wheel getting the grease at the expense of other more important issues.

The chief executive officer of a Fortune 200 company, when told that the company did not meet the expectations of 6% of customers, asked the CSM director what the main reason was for not meeting expectations. The main issue, voiced by four customers, was that the sales reps were not well trained. As the chief executive was about to ask the divisional vice president what the problem was, the CSM director quickly pointed out that among the 94% of customers whose needs were being

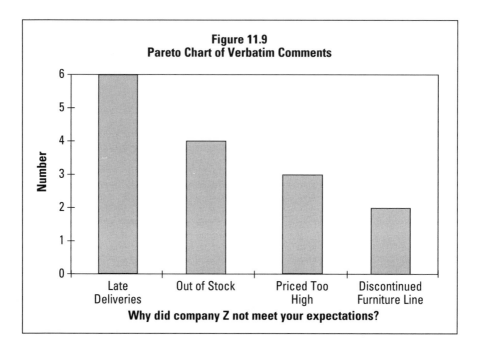

Figure 11.9
Pareto Chart of Verbatim Comments

either met or exceeded, fifty had cited great sales reps as the reason! Obviously, the division overall has a good sales team, which was also substantiated in the quantitative data. Focusing on only the few negative responses could have made for a very costly solution. This is not to say comments are unimportant, but they do need to be interpreted cautiously.

The best way to deal with verbatim comments is to aggregate them into categories through content analysis and then use a Pareto chart to show the findings. Content analysis requires that several individuals independently allocate comments into categories. The results of each allocation are then compared for consistency, and inconsistent allocations are discussed and jointly allocated. The comments that are most common will have the largest bar and should also enhance the quantitative findings. An example of a Pareto chart used for collecting comments from an open-ended question is shown in Figure 11.9.

Verbatims can be a particularly good source of information regarding emerging attributes considered important by your customers. For example, in a survey of 600 office products customers, two customers requested in verbatim comments the identification of office products that are manufactured from recycled materials. Further marketing research after the CSM process found that this issue was indeed emerging in the marketplace. The office products distributor thus changed its ordering catalog so that products containing recycled materials were indicated by the international recycling logo. This has proven to be a success for that distributor.

Verbatim comments should be used to supplement and enrich the quantitative analysis. Depending upon the objectives of the CSM program, verbatim comments may provide the best data about where your customers are moving in terms of expectations and preferences. Quantitative analysis yields a good profile of current trends.

Motivational Issues

Data analysis should be conducted with the intent of making the results as user-friendly as possible. Overly complex and technical analysis tends to intimidate users who are unfamiliar with statistical analysis. And that intimidation represents a large part of the reluctance to accept CSM results. A regional manager, when waiting for the results of a rather expensive CSM process, said, "We're not interested in the numbers. Just give us the verbatims." That same person had had a negative experience with a market researcher in the past and has since never trusted the results of surveys. This lack of trust was simply due to a lack of understanding of very basic statistical concepts, as well as the market researcher's inability to educate the manager through simple graphs and charts.

It is also important to have credibility within the organization regarding the integrity of the data and the data analysis. Data must be kept confidential and anonymous unless the customer requests otherwise. Although CSM data should be widely dispersed throughout an organization, the database should be locked to prevent the accidental alteration of the data by a user. Computer terminals should be secure if there is a serious trust issue in the organization.

Credibility issues can also arise with either a consultant-assisted or an in-house process. It is important for the individuals conducting to the research to understand all the specific details of each type of analysis, and, most important, the researcher must be able to articulate the statistical analysis in layperson terms and metaphors that are user-friendly. The inability to do this results in the filing of the data on the shelf and therefore forgotten.

On the positive side, the emerging power and user-friendliness of personal-computer-based data analysis software is making in-house data analysis more practical and understandable. What was once on a mainframe system and accessible only by way of a unique language is now available easily to any personal computer user through graphical icons and pull-down menus. Training in the use of software and data analysis techniques is also provided by many of the software manufacturers. Some of the basic spreadsheet packages now include statistical analytical capabilities. That technological capability allows many managers to access a database and explore the results, thus increasing managerial buy-in.

The next step will be the use of artificial intelligence that will perform our analyses for us and determine managerial actions or re-evaluations based upon defined parameters. Imagine having all of your analysis and reporting done by the push of a button. The time is not far off, as innovative statistical firms work toward this goal.

CHAPTER SUMMARY

Data analysis is essential in order to determine the attributes driving customer satisfaction. Identifying these attributes also drives two critical business objectives: continuous process improvement and business performance. Data analysis and subsequent understanding of customer satisfaction determinants is the driving force behind quality improvement efforts. Customer measurements help organizations move from conformance quality measures, or those that conform to internal specifications, to perceived quality measures, or those that conform to customer expectations. The use of a model framework can assist in the transition.

Customer satisfaction is linked to both business performance in terms of market share and profitability and internally driven critical processes. Business performance is driven by the willingness of customers to continue to do business with you and to recommend you to others based on their satisfaction; customer satisfaction is determined by the perceived value—determined by quality, price, and image—that customers receive from you; quality is determined by perception of specific quality and service attributes; and the attributes driving customer satisfaction point to the activities that underscore the critical processes in your organization. A focus on customer satisfaction allows you to improve not only in the eyes of your customer but also yourself as a business and employer.

Each CSM model is unique, and a number of techniques can be used to develop yours. Factor analysis, multiple regression, and canonical correlation are the most sophisticated analyses used. Simple yet powerful techniques for data analysis include cross-tabulation comparisons, frequency distributions, means and standard deviations, and verbatim comments. All of these techniques can be used to glean information from your data.

Finally, motivational issues are an important criterion in data analysis. Your peers, senior managers, frontline employees, customers, and perhaps prospective customers may see the results of your study for different reasons. Ensuring that the data are credible, easily understood, and illustrative of the integrity of the process will help your CSM process to progress at all levels.

SPSS

"Real Stats. Real Easy."

SPSS is a software products company that creates statistical product and service solutions. SPSS products and services are used worldwide in marketing, quality improvement, scientific research, reporting, education, and CSM studies. SPSS software delivers data management, statistical analysis, reporting, and presentation capabilities. SPSS's mission is "to creatively deliver world-class, easy-to-use products and services that drive the widespread use of statistics." The expressions *creatively*, *world-class*, and *easy-to-use* are ones that aptly describe SPSS's achievements, particularly in the past two years.

The SPSS software system was developed in the late 1960s, and the business was incorporated in Chicago in 1975. Initially, the SPSS system operated on large computing systems for large institutions and corporations. In 1984, SPSS shifted the statistical analysis paradigm by introducing the first statistical software product for the personal computer. Statistical analysis could now be done on the desktop. SPSS introduced a desktop system for a variety of operating environments. In late 1992, SPSS was the first major statistical software vendor to offer a product for Microsoft Windows. This is the program that many corporations and consultants now use for CSM data analysis and reporting.

SPSS for Windows employs an easy-to-use graphical user interface and offers complete data management in the form of a spreadsheetlike data editor, extensive statistical functionality, and integrated graphics. Due to the demand for its products and services, SPSS versions are available in French, German, Kanji, and Spanish.

In essence, SPSS has made statistical analysis more available. No longer do you have to wade alone through a mainframe system to undertake data analysis. SPSS technical representatives are available by phone to help you with problems or special issues. SPSS manuals and specialized training classes put the process within a layperson's vocabulary.

One major area remains to be unraveled, however; that is the area of judgment and the art of analysis. The person running the SPSS software still needs to know when to accept or reject an analysis, when to try running the analysis another way, or what the analysis actually means. Leave it to SPSS to already be thinking about these issues. The future is closer than we think.

And finally, SPSS practices what it helps facilitate. The company undertakes a customer satisfaction process every year. You can probably guess what software program it uses to analyze and report the results!

12

Using the Data for Process Improvement

Now that the gathering and analyzing of the data are done, the hard work of organizational change comes in. It is not enough to know what affects customer satisfaction and what strengths an organization currently has in the marketplace. It is essential to improve the critical processes that affect customer satisfaction and to further leverage the organization's strengths. With commitment and planning, use of the data can provide a focus and a direction for continuous improvement throughout the entire organization. Some organizations have also been successful in directly linking customer satisfaction with financial performance. This chapter explores the domain of process improvement and the spreading of the voice of the customer throughout the firm, with customers, and directly into the marketplace.

COMMUNICATING YOUR CSM RESULTS

The first step in using CSM data consists of communicating the CSM results in a timely and effective manner to the various internal and external audiences. However, effective communication of CSM results is both an art and a science. Each audience is interested in different aspects of the research. Senior management and divisional management are usually extremely curious about the results, particularly as the results pertain to overall business performance and the competitive profile. In addition, if variable compensation is tied into

241

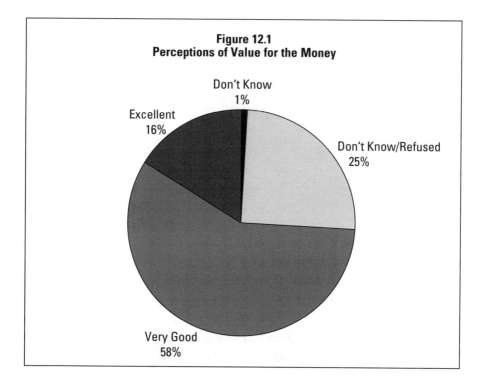

Figure 12.1
Perceptions of Value for the Money

the results, it's not difficult to gain their attention. It is often much more difficult to inform middle-level managers, who are the messengers bringing the data and the details about subsequent process improvement efforts to the frontline employees.

It is important to include frontline employees in the communication process because the more that employees know about customers, the better the employees can serve them. After all, it is customers who really provide the paycheck on payday.

As discussed in the previous chapter, CSM results need to be explained in a consistent manner. The purpose of communicating results is not only to give recognition for excellent performance but also to help in the critical activities for process improvement efforts. Consistent communication over time promotes understanding and a customer focus within the organization.

A good way to communicate results is in a graphic format. For global questions, a pie chart is an appropriate format (Figure 12.1). A pie chart shows the percentage of customers in each response category. They are easily interpreted and need little explanation. They are also useful to show employees the customer's perceptions of competitive performance

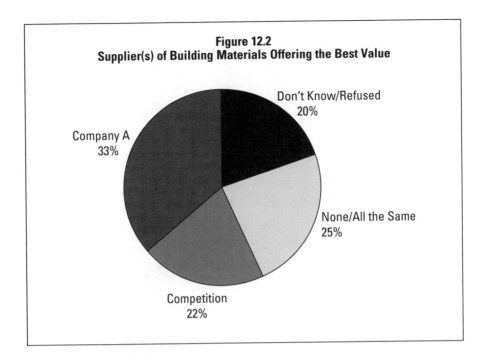

Figure 12.2
Supplier(s) of Building Materials Offering the Best Value

Don't Know/Refused
20%

Company A
33%

None/All the Same
25%

Competition
22%

in the market for your customers (Figure 12.2). Any type of general performance or demographic information that can be expressed as a percentage is well suited to be shown in this way.

For using CSM data as the driver of process improvement, a mirrored bar chart is a very effective format to present the data (Figure 12.3). In this type of format, the top two response categories of Excellent and Very Good are shown in the graph on the right side to describe performance. Most CSM consultants believe that only top-two responses contribute to customer satisfaction; being labeled good or fair in today's competitive environment doesn't count and may even detract as the AT&T example in the previous chapter indicated. On the left side of the figure in a mirrored bar chart are the same attribute's impact, or relative importance, scores—from a regression analysis in this case. For the purpose of a general audience, the larger the number, the greater the impact on customer satisfaction. If one impact score is .4 and the next is .2, the first attribute has twice the impact on customer satisfaction as the second. In this example, only the attributes Understands Product Needs, Timely Response to Product Inquiries, and Knowledge of Products and Services impact the perceptions of overall quality of customer service support.

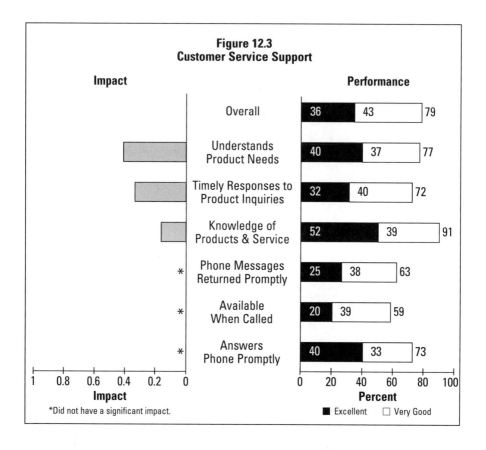

Figure 12.3
Customer Service Support

Probably the most powerful component of the mirrored bar chart is that it clearly illustrates an important point: lowest performance scores do not necessarily indicate the attribute on which to focus process improvement efforts. In the example shown, the worst performance is customer service's Availability When Called, with only 59% of customers indicating excellent or very good performance. However, derived importance shows that this attribute doesn't significantly impact overall perception of the quality of customer service. The attribute with the most impact on overall quality perception is Understands Product Needs, which received a performance score of 77%. And, even though the highest performance at 91% is Knowledge of Products & Service, this attribute is the third most important attribute with about only 20% of total influence. CSM programs that do not derive importance usually focus on the attributes with the lowest scores, but the customer may not really even care about that attribute! By ranking the attributes by impact

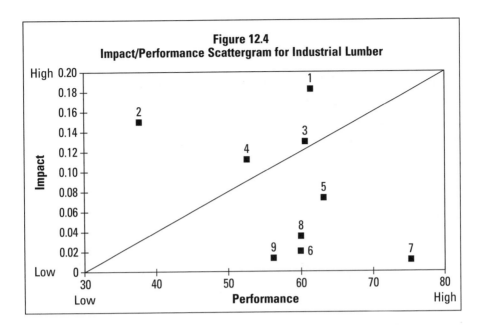

Figure 12.4
Impact/Performance Scattergram for Industrial Lumber

scores, the company is educated to look for process improvement efforts that will improve performance of these attributes.

Another tool for presenting data is the scattergram (Figure 12.4). A scattergram is a matrix that is used to facilitate the prioritization of attributes for process improvement. The horizontal axis represents performance (the percentage of respondents selecting the top two categories), and the vertical axis is the impact or importance score from the multiple regression. In this matrix, only the attributes that had significant impact are displayed, and they are numbered one through nine. To prioritize attributes, start in the top left corner of the matrix (high impact, low performance). Using a line parallel to the central 45 degree angle guide, move the line down and across the matrix. As the line passes through a plotted attribute point, that attribute is listed as a priority. Continue prioritization until the bottom right corner is reached. This type of prioritization uses a balanced approach that considers both impact and performance. In this example, the priority order of improvement is 2, 1, 4, 3, 5, 8, 9, 6, and 7. Attribute #2 is extremely important, since it is very important to customers but performance is very low. Attributes 5, 8, 9, 6, and 7 should receive little attention, since performance is relatively high on relatively low importance attributes. In the chapter on benchmarking, an example is provided showing how this type of data can be combined with competitive position to develop a more refined prioritization.

Critical Processes Ultimately Drive Customer Satisfaction

Once the attributes that impact customer satisfaction are identified, the company and its employees need to identify which activities create or affect that attribute. Many CSM programs end before this point is tackled, because inward focus presents a very difficult task, especially after the first CSM process. A company culture must be ready for change and encourage input from cross-functional teams to provide input to the improvement process.

An example of process improvement can be found in Marriott Corporation. Marriott International's Lodging Group is composed of four hotel and suite divisions as well as a service group that provides food and facilities management, distribution, and retirement center management. As a part of its total quality efforts, Marriott embarked on a comprehensive customer satisfaction process to determine what attributes impact a guest's satisfaction most. The research identified the five key attributes for customer satisfaction in terms of hotel guests: check-in speed, friendliness, cleanliness, value, and breakfast.

With the exception of breakfast, the other attributes all occur or are evaluated during the guest's first ten minutes at the hotel. Marriott initiated a "1st 10" program, which focuses on the Marriott processes that impact those first ten minutes of a stay. By making all necessary arrangements when the reservation is made for the room (e.g., room preference, credit card, etc.), guests can go almost immediately to their room and essentially bypass the traditional check-in process. Phones are being removed from the front desk so that front desk Marriott employees can concentrate uninterrupted on guest needs. These employees can create and maintain a more friendly attitude as well. (The phones, incidentally, will be placed in a customer service center.) Value is also an area where Marriott has some differentiating advantage, as Marriott has a separate target market for each of its hotel groupings; Marriott Resorts, Hotels and Suites (full-service hotels), Courtyard (moderate price), Residence Inn (extended stay or relocation), and Fairfield Inn (economy lodging).

Defining a Corporate Metric

A few corporations have defined an overall corporate metric for customer satisfaction. This is a somewhat controversial area. Several com-

---

Figure 12.5

"We will meet or exceed the expectations of 97% of our customers by 1997."
Boise Cascade Corporation

"By 1995, the company aims to build a 10-percent lead over its nearest
competitor for each indicator of customer satisfaction."
Graniterock Company

"To be the world's preferred chemical supplier and to rated number one by
75% of our customers."
Eastman Chemical Company

---

panies have tried to achieve 100% customer satisfaction and have been discouraged by not reaching that number. Achieving and maintaining 100% customer satisfaction is extremely difficult because the 100% goalpost is constantly moving farther away because of increasing customer expectations. What would have been 100% last year could now be 90%. That is not to say that a company can't anticipate the changes and move at the same speed as the goalpost, but reality dictates that this is very difficult.

A very small number of companies have identified specific corporate CSM objectives that are not a form of 100% satisfaction. Three such metrics are shown in Figure 12.5. As you can see, they are all different from each other. Graniterock's metric (By 1995, the company aims to build a 10-percent lead over its nearest competitor for each indicator of customer satisfaction) focuses on the positive gap between the company's performance and the performance of its nearest competitor in a certain time period. Eastman Chemical's metric (To be the world's preferred chemical supplier and to be rated number one by 75% of our customers) focuses on the quantitative identification of preferred supplier. Boise Cascade's metric (We will meet or exceed the expectations of 97% of our customers by 1997) focuses on attaining world-class status in meeting or exceeding customer expectations in a certain time period. These metrics are obviously customized and linked to the unique approaches to CSM used in these corporations.

The development of a corporate metric is best done through a task force. A number of parameters help set the stage for a useful metric. The first is that the metric be simple. Complex calculations and formulas

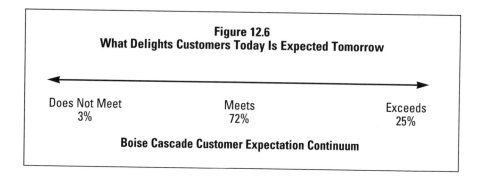

Figure 12.6
What Delights Customers Today Is Expected Tomorrow

Does Not Meet   Meets   Exceeds
3%   72%   25%

Boise Cascade Customer Expectation Continuum

should be avoided. The metric should also be easily understood and easily communicated throughout the organization. To the extent possible, the metric should reinforce corporate vision, mission statement, and strategy. It should be easily extracted from the data and be singular. Boise Cascade's metric was chosen because it was easily measured, had been measured companywide for several years, and met all of the criteria above. As indicated in Figure 12.6, the Boise Cascade metric was also decomposed into the categories Does Not Meet, Meets, and Exceeds Expectations.

Another area to consider is the time frame. Should the metric be a long-term or short-term objective? For long-term goals, should the company establish intermediate, incremental mileposts? At Boise Cascade, the task force investigating the corporate metric issue decided that the metric goal should be no more than three years out and that the current divisional baseline data established the starting point. The time line for the Boise Cascade metric goal is presented in Figure 12.7.

LINKING CSM TO CORPORATE FINANCIAL PERFORMANCE

All chief executive officers would like to have a direct linkage between their customer satisfaction scores and overall corporate financial performance. If one could easily determine that the ramifications of a certain percentage increase in overall customer satisfaction would be a percentage gain in revenues, margin, or market share, CSM would be fully implemented in every company. However, even though the linkage between CSM and financial performance is understood intuitively and through deduction, there is no generic quantitative formula. But several companies have developed a company or business-unit-specific model

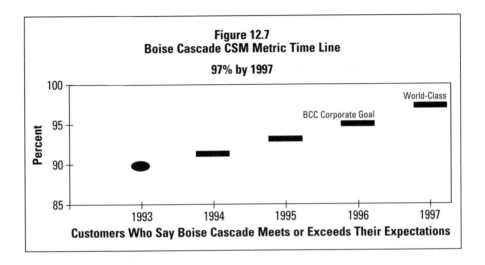

Figure 12.7
Boise Cascade CSM Metric Time Line

97% by 1997

Customers Who Say Boise Cascade Meets or Exceeds Their Expectations

for this linkage and have been successful in linking customer satisfaction measures and resulting financial performance.

AT&T business service has been able to directly link overall customer value with an increase in revenues. To do this, AT&T measured customer satisfaction quarterly over a four-year period. Using a model similar to those described in the previous chapter, AT&T derived the specific attributes that impacted overall perception of quality and, ultimately, customer satisfaction. AT&T also knew from the data how specific performance scores in customer value affected a customer's willingness to recommend and continue to rely upon AT&T. By measuring over time, AT&T used financial data from these customers to assign a dollar amount to the value of the increase in customer satisfaction and retention. As shown in Figure 12.8, AT&T found that overall quality is a function of five business processes in varying levels of importance; product carried the most weight, at 30%; sales was next, at 20%; and installation, repair, and billing were next, at 15% each.

The next step was to look at the customer needs that were identified as impacting their perceptions of the business process. In the product area, reliability and features/functions account for 40% each; in the sales area, knowledge has the greatest impact, at 30%. AT&T then identified the internal metrics for these attributes and began to measure and track their internal performance. In most cases AT&T discovered that financial or human resources were necessary to improve the stability and capability of the internal processes. How could AT&T determine which in-

Figure 12.8
AT&T Model

Business Process	Customer Need		Internal Metric
30% Product	Reliability	40%	# of repair call
	Easy to Use	20%	# of call for help
	Features/Functions	40%	Functional performance test
20% Sales	Knowledge	30%	Supervisor observations
	Responsive	25%	% prosposal made on time
	Follow-Up	10%	% follow-up made
15% Installation	Delivery Internal Meets Needs	30%	Average order interval
	Does Not Break	25%	% repair reports
	Installed When Promised	10%	% installed on due date
15% Repair	No Repeat Trouble	30%	% repeat reports
	Fixed Fast	25%	Average speed of repair
	Kept Informed	10%	% customers informed
15% Billing	Accuracy, No Surprise	45%	% billing inquiries
	Resolved on First Call	35%	% resolved first call
	Easy to Understand	10%	% billing inquiries

(Business Process column grouped under **Overall Quality**)

Percentages may not total 100% due to the minor influence of other variables.

vestments to make in order to increase customer satisfaction and get the biggest bang for the buck?

AT&T went back to the model. Would it be better to make a capital expenditure to improve the reliability of the product or should the company invest in a sales training program to increase the knowledge of the sales reps? Many managers traditionally look only at the highest-impact number for the business process and decide to put all of their money and efforts into that process. AT&T, however, looks at all of the processes and the cost to make the process stable and capable. For example, let's say that it takes a $500,000 capital expenditure to increase customer satisfaction one percentage point and that that point will account for a 0.5% market share increase. For sales rep training, it will take $50,000 to improve the process, and that will increase customer satisfaction 0.9

of a percentage point; that in turn translates to a 0.45% market share increase. Now we know that a 0.5% market share in some industries is worth the extra expenditure, but clearly AT&T is getting the largest return from the sales training. By going through all of the key attributes and associated improvement costs, AT&T can probably use the $500,000 over several projects and increase market share more than 0.5%. This model has been so effective that AT&T uses it as the major component of the strategic planning process.

Another example of linking financial performance with customer satisfaction and process improvement is illustrated by a pharmaceutical company. Again, using a similar model to the one described in the previous chapter as well as extensive market data on pharmaceutical products were used. The company was able to determine the market share increase in a particular pharmaceutical product if customer satisfaction improved one percentage point. This allowed management to prioritize both improvement efforts and marketing efforts for its brand-name drugs. Because the company is under increasing pressure from the generic drug market, the CSM survey that included measurement against the competition helped determine which generic markets were serious threats. Incidentally, because of the nature of the industry, the firm paid respondents to their twenty-minute phone survey on the following scale: patients, $35; pharmacists, $75; and physicians, $125! The company's CSM budget thus had included a large line item for incentives.

COMMUNICATING CSM RESULTS TO CUSTOMERS

A powerful use for CSM data is communicating results to the customers. By sharing information with customers, a firm is creating an opportunity to learn more about individual customers. This new knowledge will help a firm to customize an approach that meets the customer's needs more effectively.

Communicating CSM results with customers usually works in the following manner. The account sales team usually takes the CSM report or presentation to the customer. It can be done during a routine sales call or perhaps used in a meeting with several individuals from the customer company. The sales team shares the results of the CSM survey with the customer. In a preface to the information sharing, members of the sales team explain that because of the confidentiality and anonymity agreement, they don't know whether the customer was included in the study.

At this point, the customer may offer that information. In any event, the sales team says that the information represents the entire customer base and explains the overall findings. After reviewing all of the material, the team asks the customer for agreement with the findings. In other words, are the performance highlights and impact attributes in agreement with the customer? The feedback can help the sales team to better understand the customer and thus customize its approach to that specific account. It also gives the customer some recognition and appreciation for the customer's time spent providing input that is being used to improve product and service offerings. This type of communication of CSM results has been enthusiastically endorsed by both sales teams and customers, and it has opened dialogue between companies.

Prospective customers may also be interested in your CSM process and findings. The information demonstrates your company's commitment to customers and improvement efforts. The goodwill and potential to impact corporate image attributes make sharing the information with prospective customers valuable. For example, Solectron invites prospective customers to its weekly customer satisfaction meetings.

KEY CORPORATE PERFORMANCE MEASURES

To put CSM into perspective, a number of corporations have identified the linkage between CSM and key corporate performance measures. These measures always include customer satisfaction, employee satisfaction, and business performance; some companies include a metric for process stability and capability or process improvement. Northern Telecom's five key corporate measures are shown in Figure 12.9. Northern Telecom believes that employee satisfaction drives quality and quality drives customer satisfaction. The measure of customer satisfaction is exhibited by market share, and market share drives financial performance.

Another example illustrated by the key measures used by Boise Cascade Corporation and shown in Figure 12.10. The key measure logo—very similar to the Boise Cascade corporate logo—illustrates the underlying philosophy. Employee Satisfaction is the foundation of the business. Satisfied employees will be committed to their work such that operational and organizational processes will be improving in order to be stable and capable of meeting customers' needs. Stable and capable processes will drive customer satisfaction. Customer satisfaction leads to

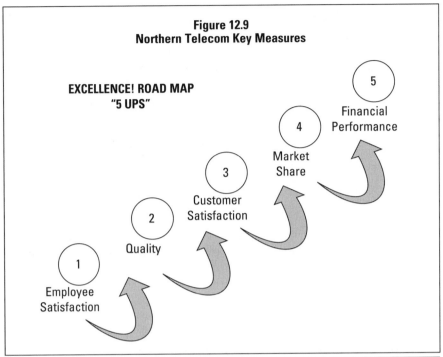

**Figure 12.9
Northern Telecom Key Measures**

EXCELLENCE! ROAD MAP
"5 UPS"

1 Employee Satisfaction

2 Quality

3 Customer Satisfaction

4 Market Share

5 Financial Performance

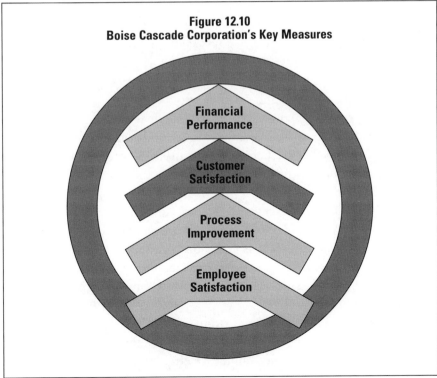

**Figure 12.10
Boise Cascade Corporation's Key Measures**

Financial Performance

Customer Satisfaction

Process Improvement

Employee Satisfaction

more loyal customers which in turn enhances Boise Cascade's financial performance.

A very exciting part of the key measure process has been implemented in the Executive Review of Operations at Boise Cascade. Every year in January, operational managers review their previous year with the chief executive officer, the president, the chief operating officer, and others. Prior to 1992, the focus of the review was always the bottom line; the discussion rarely veered from the financial or strategic topics. In 1992, however, former chief executive officer John Fery asked that operational managers prepare for their executive review in a very specific format: the key measures. He expected the divisions to first discuss employee satisfaction. Following that was a discussion of current activities and progress in the process improvement area. The next topic was customer satisfaction, which included CSM as well as other sources of customer information. Finally, financial performance was discussed. This change in procedure was a radical shift, but it reinforced the commitment to the key measures by those at the highest level.

GETTING EMPLOYEES TO USE THE DATA

Employee attitudes and customer attitudes are positively related to one another, as suggested in the previous examples of Northern Telecom, Boise Cascade, and others. That relationship has also been supported by research in a wide variety of industries and settings: in consumer goods, industrial goods, services, and tangible products.

As employee satisfaction increases, customer satisfaction also increases. When customer satisfaction is low, employee satisfaction is also low. When employees have high perceptions of product and service quality, customers also have high perceptions. But the relationship extends beyond attitudes and perceptions—to behavior.

When employee turnover is high, customer turnover is also high. When employee turnover is low, customer turnover is also low. From the research, the causal direction is from the employees to the customers. When employees are dissatisfied, disgruntled, and angry and they intend to quit, their attitudes and behavior spill over, causing similar attitudes among customers.

Dissatisfied employees treat customers in a rude, abrupt, uncaring fashion. Dissatisfied employees may even complain to customers about the way things are done. The cumulative effect is that customers develop negative perceptions of the organization's products, service, or overall corporate image.

The challenge for management, then, is to foster an organizational environment that contributes to positive employee attitudes and low employee turnover. The solution to that challenge is a complex one that has been the subject of many books and a great deal of research. Synthesizing that large body of literature is far beyond the scope of this book. However, providing a very brief description of what that organizational environment looks like may be helpful. For it is within that environment that the rest of this chapter is cast. The broader context and must be carefully and comprehensively integrated.

Clearly, organizations have become flatter with fewer layers of management. The various units are operating with more local autonomy than in the past as power and authority are being dispersed. The wider distribution of power at all levels results in worker empowerment and involvement and the emergence of teams of various types. The manager's role becomes one of coach—asking questions, offering challenges, and assessing training needs. Managers seek to remove the obstacles constraining employees.

It is within such an environment that CSM data can be linked most effectively to individual employees. In this environment, linking CSM data to each person's job is part of an integrated corporate culture.

INTRINSIC REWARDS

Highly satisfied employees tend to accrue a good deal of intrinsic satisfaction from actually performing the job itself. Most studies suggest that intrinsic satisfaction is more important than the extrinsic rewards such as money and recognition that an organization bestows on individuals.

Since intrinsic satisfaction flows from the job itself, increasing these rewards requires some degree of job redesign in most organizations. The techniques for redesigning jobs have evolved over the years, but in some cases, only the name has changed. In the 1960s and 1970s, the popular techniques were job enrichment and participatory management. In the 1990s, those techniques are now called empowerment and involvement. The quality circles of the 1970s and 1980s evolved into cross-functional, empowered teams. But regardless of exactly what term is chosen, the underlying theme remains the same.

The more that employees are involved in the planning, decision making, and continuous improvement of their jobs, or of the organization as a whole, the greater the intrinsic satisfaction employees derive from their jobs. The justification for this flows from early theories of motivation such as Maslow's Hierarchy of Needs. Maslow contended that satisfying higher-order needs such as self-esteem and self-actualization was necessary for workers in industrial societies. Worker involvement enhances an individual's self-image through participation in more challenging and intellectually stimulating activities. And over the years, a variety of techniques have emerged that effectively increase employee involvement in one way or the other.

These techniques range from relatively simple add-ons that can be superimposed over a traditional organizational structure to the radical redesign of jobs that requires a major organizational commitment. Normally, an organization makes some type of progression from simple to complex techniques as both the workers and the managers adjust to their changing roles and responsibilities. The appropriateness of a particular technique depends on where an organization is in the evolutionary process. And these techniques are not mutually exclusive of one another; many organizations may simultaneously use four or five.

Although extrinsic rewards are addressed later in the next chapter, extrinsic rewards can, and should, reinforce and enhance intrinsic satisfaction. The relationship between intrinsic satisfaction and extrinsic rewards is certainly synergistic. Using both jointly has a far greater impact on employee attitudes than either type has individually.

With that in mind, let's now examine some of the more commonly used involvement techniques that can be used with CSM data. All of these techniques can increase intrinsic satisfaction and improve employee attitudes.

Information Sharing
The first and most basic technique to enhance intrinsic satisfaction is to share the CSM results with *all* employees. Someone once said that the three most important things for a manager are communication, communication, and communication. While that is a bit simplistic, it does underscore the importance of sharing all CSM data with employees.

The mechanism for doing this will vary from company to company. In some, the data can be loaded onto the local area computer network for individual access. In others, CSM data could be shared in regular meetings. Or the data could be either individually distributed in hard copy to each employee or featured in an employee newsletter. Earlier sections of this chapter provided some ideas on how to present the data in an easily understood format.

Regardless of the method by which CSM data are shared, a powerful signal is sent to all employees that customer satisfaction is important. It shows that management is walking the talk. On the other hand, if management says customer satisfaction is important but never measures or shares the CSM data, an equally powerful, contradictory message is also sent.

As you may recall from other discussions in this book, quality, particularly service quality, emanates from the corporate culture. Thus, a wider cross section of employees is usually involved in delivering good service than in delivering product quality. Sharing the CSM data provides those employees with feedback on their performance from a highly credible evaluator—the customer.

When *all* CSM data, not just a few overall, aggregate measures, are provided for employees, the employees are able to see more clearly how a particular job or process fits with the other attributes to create customer satisfaction. This awareness of the importance of each job normally allows the employee to identify more closely with the broader organizational goals and feel more a part of the team. In other words, the commitment of each employee is improved.

If a firm is beginning organizational change initiatives, sharing CSM data is often a good place to start. It can unfreeze old behavior patterns and break traditional practices. In these instances, sharing competitive CSM profiles is particularly useful. The competitive profiles not only identify who the competitors are but also highlight the firm's competitive strengths and weaknesses. When large weaknesses exist, employees can quickly internalize the need for improvement.

When CSM data are shared broadly, the first-line supervisors are typically the individuals who experience increased communication the most. Normally, employees will want more information or explanation of the data. Thus, the supervisors themselves should be thoroughly debriefed about the details of the research design.

Employees in many organizations experience the old mushroom treatment: they are kept in the dark and fed garbage. The best initial step to improve the intrinsic satisfaction that employees derive from their jobs is to bring employees into the light. In many cases, this requires both sharing CSM data and a broad range of other organizational performance information.

Sharing CSM data is a one-way communication process. The assumption is often made by management that the employees will see the relevance of the data and take it upon themselves to improve. Although this may happen, it is much more effective when a formal system for soliciting ideas *from* employees is in place and when all of the remaining involvement techniques explicitly solicit an upward flow of communication.

Suggestion Programs

Suggestion programs vary a great deal in complexity and detail, but all are intended to solicit and capture employees' ideas for improvement. Many suggestion programs are abysmal failures because they lack one of three essential elements. First, since most suggestion programs are oriented toward the lowest levels in the organization—the workers who actually perform the work—the role of the first-line supervisor is critical. Many, if not most, suggestions are directly related to the way employees perform their own individual job. Therefore, the supervisor has a good deal of influence in establishing a climate receptive to new ideas. Also, a supervisor often helps employees to polish and refine suggestions, acting as a sounding board and a source of information. Negative comments, attitudes, and feedback from the supervisor can quickly kill the interest and enthusiasm of employees. Therefore, strong supervisor support must be an essential prerequisite to a good suggestion program.

The second characteristic is prompt feedback. An employee's enthusiasm is highest when a suggestion is first submitted. Gradually, the air of enthusiasm turns to skepticism and even resentment if nothing is done. This is particularly true if the suggestion system is accompanied by financial rewards of some type. Milliken, a Baldrige award winner, provides personal feedback for its employees, thanking them within 24 hours for the idea. And Milliken will implement the suggestion, if at all possible, within 72 hours. By promptly acknowledging and implementing suggestions, Milliken shows employees that their ideas are important and valued. Milliken, like other firms with highly successful suggestion programs, such as Toyota and Honeywell, implement about 90% of all suggestions.

The third element of a good suggestion program consists of recognition and financial rewards. Although recognition and financial rewards are extrinsic rewards, both can serve to reinforce the employee's involvement in suggestions. Recognition can range from a supervisor's or executive's thank-you, to features in newsletters, a picture on the bulletin board, or an award dinner, for example. Financial awards can range from a $10 bill to a percentage of the cost savings. Regardless of either how minor or how lavish, some type of recognition or reward should accompany a suggestion system. This clearly communicates to employees that their suggestions, ideas, and involvement are noticed and appreciated. And it has the obvious impact of increasing an employee's intrinsic rewards. Many firms have found that customer-contact employees who engage in many moments of truth each day with customers are an excellent source of ideas for improvement. Again, this is especially the case for improvements in service quality.

The suggestion program at Honeywell is particularly good. To ensure supervisor support, the number and quality of suggestions submitted by subordinates constitute a significant part of the supervisor performance evaluation process. The suggestor is contacted several times personally: at submission, during evaluation, and at time of final disposition. The suggestor is rewarded with gift certificates and a percentage of the savings. Each employee averages two or three suggestions annually, reflecting a high level of employee involvement.

Group Discussions

A relatively simple way to solicit employee feedback on CSM data is to use some sort of group discussion. This can range from an open, free-flowing meeting to a highly structured approach, such as nominal group technique. If a firm's CSM model has, say, twenty attributes, a group discusses ways to improve one or more value-added processes. Some firms have taken this idea further, conducting group discussions that focus on each attribute. The goal, then, is to identify several specific steps that can be taken and to get organizational buy-in to the implementation of those ideas.

The biggest obstacle with group discussions is often the supervisor or the manager. There is no precise way to predict the recommendations that emerge from a discussion. If a manager doesn't like a particular idea that results from a group discussion and exercises veto power, employee involvement thereafter may be reduced or eliminated. The employees would feel that their ideas are valuable only if those ideas coincided with those of management. Thus, employees would lose faith in the process.

Therefore, the use of group discussions to involve employees in the generation and implementation of ideas carries with it a strong implied commitment to honor the group's wishes. The brainstorming nature of group discussions can often generate some very creative ideas for improving customer satisfaction. The energizing atmosphere of such discussions can contribute to each individual's intrinsic satisfaction.

Task Forces

Somewhat more formal than group discussions, a task force is an ad hoc cross section of managers and employees brought together to analyze a particular problem or challenge. In this case, the focus of the task force would be on how to improve customer satisfaction. Given a set of CSM data, the task force would evaluate the data, conduct additional information gathering, and develop a set of specific recommendations. The recommendations would then be passed along to management for the appropriate action. And then the members of the task force would disband, returning to their normal jobs.

Because the task force is a temporary mechanism with a limited life expectancy, it is a low-risk involvement technique. Although task force members may solicit ideas from other employees and meld them into a coherent set of recommendations, management is not always compelled to implement the recommendations. Unfortunately, sometimes task force recommendations disappear into a black hole, never to be seen again.

Because task forces are small, normally comprising fewer than a dozen employees, they generate less involvement by a broad range of employees. Intrinsic satisfaction tends to accrue only to the task force members, and even those rewards disappear if the recommendations are not implemented. Another problem with using task forces is that the narrow range of participation does not elicit the strong buy-in by employees that typically results from more comprehensive involvement techniques.

Cross-Functional Teams

The use of teams of various types is probably the best way to use CSM data to increase an individual's intrinsic satisfaction. By being actively involved in the problem solving and implementation of the solutions, employees normally experience a high degree of organizational commitment. They also tend to internalize the corporate goals so that satisfying the customer becomes part of their own personal agenda.

A very widespread and popular of the teaming techniques is the quality circle (QC). QCs are permanent committees that have a rotating voluntary membership of some type. Because QCs identify their own priorities, CSM data are useful in highlighting the most critical issues that need to be addressed. The goal of the QC is to improve customer satisfaction through the improvement of various activities.

Two problems typically accompanied QCs, at least in their early form. Most QCs were restricted to a specific activity or group of workers; they were not process oriented. Therefore, QCs were useful in making an existing process better as it related to their work area. They were not particularly effective in radical process redesign that cut across functional boundaries.

A second common problem was that QCs were usually not empowered to implement their recommendations. Typically, they made their recommendations to a management team that would ultimately decide what should be done. Thus, many QCs acted as a fact-finding and idea generation process rather than a problem-solving and decision-making unit. As a result, some employees remained skeptical of the real value of QCs.

The remedy to those two shortcomings is in the form of empowered cross-functional teams. These teams are usually process oriented, cut across functional boundaries, and are empowered to implement their recommendations within some budgetary constraints. Although cross-functional teams do not ensure acceptance of the recommendations by all functional areas, the probability of such certainly increases.

Feeding CSM data into these cross-functional teams not only facilitates significant process improvement but also makes the voice of the customer far more tangible and relevant to employees. This linkage to the customer is a significant contributor to intrinsic rewards for many employees.

Autonomous Work Groups

While cross-functional teams can operate within the existing structure of most organizations, autonomous work groups require a very significant job redesign. And whereas cross-functional teams require a strong managerial commitment to be successful, the use of autonomous work groups requires even more managerial commitment.

Autonomous work groups are responsible for some natural work unit or process. Instead of each worker specializing at a given task, all workers are cross-trained to perform several tasks well. The more task knowledge and skill that an individual possesses, the more valuable that person is to the group.

In many cases, the group has complete control over how the process is performed. This requires the group to plan, schedule, redesign, and measure the process. The group also has control over hiring new members to optimize the fit of the individual into the group. The group is responsible for performance evaluations, identifying training needs, and compensation. In general, these groups are almost totally self-managed and align work group goals with organizational goals and those of other work groups.

The role of the manager changes dramatically with autonomous work groups. The manager's goal is to make the group self-sustaining by providing information and training. The manager acts as a liaison between groups, improving coordination. Because of the self-managed nature of the groups, fewer managers are needed. This reduction is normally at the middle management level, resulting in a flatter organizational structure.

CSM data constitute a valuable input into autonomous work groups, for such data provide an objective, external evaluation of group outputs. The work groups can quickly respond to customer feedback, often changing processes within a few days with the intent of improving customer satisfaction.

Because of the very high involvement nature of these self-managed teams, members of autonomous work groups usually experience high levels of intrinsic reward. Rather than being merely a cog in the machine or a small part of a large organization, work group members feel they are more of a cohesive part of the organizational team.

Ciba Geigy, the Swiss-based chemicals and pharmaceuticals multinational, has cascaded the philosophy of autonomous work groups from its Basle, Switzerland, headquarters to all parts of the company. While the philosophy of high employee empowerment and involvement starts at headquarters, each business unit is allowed to adapt the actual implementation to fit its situation. To be consistent with this philosophy, the company reorganized in 1990 into fourteen autonomous, product-related business units.

The process of employee involvement varies considerably between those business units and also varies considerably within a business unit. The nature of work group involvement can be quite different for production versus marketing, for example. In marketing, the secretaries are involved in the work group, participating in decisions ranging from budgeting to developing proactive strategies to improve customer satisfaction.

The only unifying theme among *all* the various work groups is the continuous improvement of customer satisfaction. The specific approach depends on the judgment of a particular group.

Virtually every organization should be utilizing CSM data in some form of employee involvement. Those that are not are at a significant disadvantage, particularly in the increasingly competitive environment that demands continuous improvement. The customer is by far the best judge of which processes need to be improved. Organizations that are engaging in involvement techniques are attempting to harness the knowledge of employees to constantly improve customer satisfaction. Those that are not involving employees are implicitly sending the message that management knows everything it takes to be successful. And that is a very dangerous assumption.

CHAPTER SUMMARY

Using the voice of the customer to improve your business, both financially and operationally, is the goal of CSM. By deploying data throughout your organization, everyone gains a greater understanding of customer expectations. Management and frontline employees gain a broader appreciation of involvement in the workplace. Part of that appreciation comprises the changed work expectations of staff. Strategic and business decisions are based on data-driven customer concerns. Morale generally increases, and all individuals feel a heightened ownership of customer problems and successes. The companies that have deployed customer data throughout their organization are the ones that are extremely successful and tend to be on the list of the best companies for which to work.

Additionally, with an adequate amount of CSM data from multiple survey processes and market information, linkage of CSM with financial measures is possible. With CSM data, one can make well educated decisions about process improvement efforts after learning the ultimate impact on the bottom line.

Using CSM data is also critical for employee satisfaction. Customer and employee satisfaction are strongly correlated and should be recognized in your organization. There are a number of methods that you can use to intrinsically reward your employees for responding to customers. Ultimately these intrinsic rewards motivate an even stronger link to customer focus, satisfaction, and business performance.

L-S ELECTRO-GALVANIZING COMPANY

LTV and Sumitomo Metal Industries formed a joint venture in 1986 called L-S Electro-Galvanizing Company (LSE). From its conception, LSE was designed with the intent of using high-involvement techniques to achieve customer satisfaction. To coordinate the activities of other committees and maximize customer satisfaction, the customer concern team (CCT) was developed in 1990. Rather than have a variety of teams individually contacting customers, LSE felt there needed to be some coordinating effort so that customers wouldn't become annoyed by redundancies.

The CCT was composed of volunteer members from many areas within the firm. The first task was to develop a new CSM program to replace the old system that was based primarily on customer complaints. LSE realized that responding to complaints was only a firefighting, reactive approach to customers.

The CCT has responsibility for administering surveys, compiling data, and analyzing the results. The new survey covers many attributes that contribute to customer satisfaction, including a wide range of both product quality and service attributes. All LSE employees get a copy of the aggregate satisfaction score and the data relevant to their specific job or activity.

The CCT meets monthly—the frequency of survey administration—to discuss the results. The employees meet in weekly three-hour quality meetings on Friday to discuss the results and develop appropriate strategies.

The CCT appointed LSE union workers as product-quality coordinators assigned to a particular customer. The coordinators visit the customer site once or twice a month to solicit feedback from customer employees who would never see the CSM survey. The coordinators feed their findings back into the weekly meetings of departmental and cross-functional teams. In some cases, the coordinators also serve on the interorganizational cross-functional teams.

The coordinator of the CCT also arranges customer visits for LSE teams. These site visits spread the direct customer contact over a wider array of LSE employees. The visits enable employees to engage in joint problem solving, identify opportunities for improvement, and directly witness competitive profiles.

The CCT also assigned a customer service engineer to each customer. The customer service engineer maintains records and charts profiling LSE performance with a particular customer. SPC control charts and Pareto diagrams are most commonly used for this.

In addition to direct involvement of employees in various committees, the CCT shares data of all types in newsletters and on local area computer networks.

To reinforce these various types of employee involvement, LSE has implemented a gain-sharing program, a topic to be discussed in the next chapter. The program rewards team efforts with bonuses of up to 25% of the base compensation. And as you might expect, the whole gain-sharing program was designed and implemented by a voluntary team of employees.

13

Linking CSM Data and Compensation

In order for comprehensive organizational change and continuous improvement to occur, all aspects of the organization must reinforce and support the change efforts. The previous chapter dealt with a variety of ways that CSM data can be used to drive change, predominantly through communication, involvement efforts, and intrinsic rewards.

For those efforts to be effective, there must also be changes in the management style, as previously discussed, as well as in other dimensions of corporate culture. A firm must expand training and development so that the highly involved employees have the proper skills to make good decisions. The performance evaluation systems must shift from purely individual based criteria to broader criteria such as a variety of teaming skills. Information systems must change so that all employees have better access to a wide variety of data, thus enhancing decision making.

This chapter addresses an extremely important change that reinforces a shift to customer-driven continuous improvement. This is very new for virtually all businesses. The changes involve modifying an organization's reward systems to include customer-driven elements. By linking rewards to CSM data, an organization sends a powerful message to all employees. That message is that customer satisfaction is so important that it must involve *everyone*. By rewarding employees for improvements in customer satisfaction, an organization is reinforcing all of the other change efforts.

These rewards can take the form of recognition or financial rewards. While some of those in personnel, human resources, and compensation areas do not consider recognition as a significant issue, some recent studies show that recognition is highly valued by employees. In some cases, employees view recognition as *more* important than some financial rewards. Therefore, a variety of recognition programs will be described prior to a discussion of gain sharing, the predominant mechanism for linking CSM data to financial rewards.

RECOGNITION PROGRAMS

Recognition programs are important because of the powerful message that they send about what is important to the company. The actual cost of the reward is not critical to the success of a recognition program. But *what* is rewarded provides an implicit message about the company values. Therefore, a recognition program must be carefully designed to be consistent with the corporate culture, intrinsic rewards, and other extrinsic rewards.

Recognition programs typically refer to all "nonfinancial rewards." However, in some firms, recognition programs have been accompanied by a very significant cash bonus. Recognition programs for salespeople are often of this variety, and to many salespeople, the so-called bonus is actually as part of their salary.

For purposes of this discussion, recognition rewards include intangibles, tangibles, or small token-cash awards. Large cash awards often lose their motivational power when they become an expected part of the compensation package. Large cash awards are probably better viewed as individual financial incentives, which is what they really are.

Recognition is a means of explicitly rewarding employees for their effort or success in improving processes, dealing with customers, or contributing to the organization's goals. For a recognition program to be successful, it must satisfy four requirements.

First, the recognition must be consistent with corporate values. For example, if an organization with a corporate goal of 100% customer satisfaction recognizes salespeople only on sales volume, a conflicting message will be sent. The recognition criteria should include some dimensions of customer satisfaction along with the sales volume goal.

If a firm is trying to cultivate a high-involvement team environment and most recognition is for individual performance, a conflicting message will be sent to employees. In a team environment, most awards should be based on group performance. Some recognition should still remain to acknowledge above-and-beyond efforts by individual employees however.

If an organization is striving for continuous improvement but it rewards only meeting existing quality standards, a conflicting signal will be sent. Therefore, the recognition program must be consistent with the organization's value system, goals, objectives, job design, and other reward systems.

Second, the recognition criteria should be objective and measurable. If employees think that winning recognition is based on luck, they will quickly become skeptical and distrustful. When employees can observe and measure the criteria, they will easily identify the linkage between performance and rewards.

If an organization is going to reward employees based on improvement in customer satisfaction, the employees should have a clear idea of how customer satisfaction will be measured. Using customer complaint data would not be a very good surrogate measure for satisfaction, for example.

Recognition criteria can be the same criteria used in gain sharing or incentive programs. The gain sharing may be paid out quarterly or semiannually by using a composite of productivity increases, cost reduction, and customer satisfaction improvement. On a monthly basis, a firm could recognize the top groups or units in *each* area, the top overall performers, the most improved groups, or maybe the top three groups. Regardless of *which* criteria are used to drive the recognition, however, the criteria should be objective and measurable.

The third requirement is that the recognition be timely and meaningful. The recognition should come as close to the performance as reasonably possible while the behavior is still top of mind to both the employee and peers. When one of IBM's divisions did an analysis of the recognition program in that division, it found that almost two-thirds of all employees thought that recognition was slightly or significantly delayed. This was one of the reasons that a new recognition system was designed for that unit.

ICL, the British computer firm, gives out about 2,500 recognition awards annually, primarily for excellence in customer care. Most of the awards are given out within days of the actual performance.

If recognition is given out based on CSM data or indexed criteria, the awards should be made as soon as possible after the data are gathered.

If recognition for June performance is not made until September, the awards lose their luster.

A large delay between the performance and the recognition implicitly sends the message that management has other, more important things to do and will give recognition when it has time. This has the effect of negating many involvement efforts.

The recognition must be meaningful to the employee. ICL used to give out gold, silver, and bronze medallions until it found these awards weren't very meaningful to the employees. It replaced the medallion with an Excellence Collection of merchandise in the form of a gift catalog. Other firms such as British Aerospace have found gold pens, watches, ties, or scarves more meaningful. The chief executive officer of Hewlett-Packard, Lew Platt, has phoned employees to congratulate them for excellent performance on their completion of a graduate degree.

The fourth requirement is that the recognition program create winners and winners, not winners and losers. This means that the broader range of employees should be recognized for both individual and group contributions. Rather than recognize just the top-performing groups, perhaps the top three groups should be recognized. Rather than recognizing just overall performance, perhaps percentage improvement should also be recognized.

If too many awards are given, the recognition program may lose its meaningfulness and be viewed as superficial. So the fine line is between giving as much recognition as possible without diluting it too much. But the danger of dilution applies primarily to symbolic or token awards.

When recognition is in the form of a personalized thank-you from a manager or executive, dilution is seldom a worry. Lew Platt's phoning an employee to say "Congratulations for a good job" will rarely lose its effect. So managerial recognition is certainly a way to supplement a recognition program and create more winners.

These four requirements are all essential to creating a successful recognition system. In many organizations, recognition programs are designed by managers or consultants. However, the best way to design a recognition program is to allow employees to develop it themselves. When employees, normally in the form of a voluntary committee, design the recognition program, they must clarify the values to be reinforced, the evaluative criteria, the mechanics of the program, and the supplementary elements. This has the net effect of greatly increasing employee buy-in and support.

An IBM Example

One of IBM's marketing offices in the Midwestern United States had a recognition program that wasn't working particularly well. The cash bonuses had come to be viewed as another form of compensation.

IBM hired a consulting firm to conduct an unbiased, third-party assessment of the existing recognition program by surveying employees. The results indicated that there was general dissatisfaction with the program. Employees felt that contributions to customer satisfaction weren't adequately recognized, the cash awards had come to be viewed by sales representatives as expected compensation, teamwork was not recognized, recognition was not timely, and the program was primarily top down and not well organized.

All of this information was fed into an employee committee that designed major changes. Since the cash awards were expected compensation, their removal would constitute a pay cut. So the committee decided to leave the cash bonuses in place and supplement them with other forms of recognition.

A gift such as flowers or steaks was sent to the employee's home as a surprise. The recipient also received another, event-type recognition to supplement the cash award such as a dinner, or tickets to a play or sports event. The intent was to move the reward past simply depositing a check into a bank account.

To encourage more group cohesiveness, a peer-level recognition was created called ETHYL (Encourage the Heart with Your Leadership.) This award is based on the goal of exceeding customer expectations. When an employee exceeds the customer expectations, another employee fills out an ETHYL form and gives it to the program administrator. The administrator hands that employee an envelope containing a thank-you card and $20. That employee then uses the $20 to buy a personalized gift that recognizes the original employee for the outstanding performance. This peer-to-peer award is very effective in creating group cohesiveness.

Recognition Summary

Recognition programs are simply an explicit means to recognize employees for high-involvement behavior. There are many types of customer-related recognition programs ranging from those tied to CSM data for groups or work units to those rewarding individual effort. Recognition is only a supplement, a means of reinforcing behavior encouraged by employee involvement.

Therefore, an organization must first address the issue of job redesign, implementing structures and practices that encourage employees to become psychologically involved in their jobs. A firm's core values such as customer satisfaction or continuous improvement must be ingrained into the involvement effort as well.

It is over this foundation that a recognition program is laid. It is hard to think of any type of group recognition effort that could be successful without high-involvement job design in place that reflects a firm's core values. To be successful, it is also over this same foundation that a financial reward system must be laid. And that is the topic of the next section.

FINANCIAL REWARDS

Financial rewards are fundamental to the labor exchange between an employee and a firm. Financial rewards can take many forms such as salary, benefits, retirement programs, base wage, individual incentives, group incentives, and employee stock ownership plans. It is beyond the scope of this book to discuss how each of these types of rewards could be linked to CSM data. Therefore, this discussion will be limited to group incentives, primarily gain sharing, for that is the predominant linkage between CSM and compensation. There are certainly inferences in this chapter for the overall design of a compensation system, however.

In the simplistic form, a firm uses financial rewards to buy an employee's ability and willingness to perform a task of some type. For executives, the details of that labor contract can be quite complex. For middle managers, the labor contract is usually simpler. For lower-level workers, particularly if unionized, the details of the labor contract are very specific. Traditionally, what was expected of a worker by the organization was clearly spelled out, often in the form of a job description. In addition to these formal aspects of the explicit or implicit labor contract, a variety of informal group norms influence the labor exchange.

These norms in one way or another indicate to an individual what the appropriate willingness to perform means in that organization. Perhaps the executive should be in the office working until 6 p.m. every evening and until noon on Saturday. Perhaps middle managers should show up at 7:30 or 8 a.m. even when they don't officially start until 8:30 a.m. Perhaps the norms dictate the appropriate volume of output for a blue-collar worker.

There has been an increasing realization that the traditional compensation systems don't do a very good job of reinforcing high-level performance or continuous improvement, thus breaking those traditional norms. As a result, there has been a rapid spread of nontraditional compensation methods that *do* reinforce high performance. These nontraditional techniques are only one element in the broader organizational change effort, and the other elements will be discussed shortly. However, all of these efforts are based on one broad assumption that is probably quite valid.

That assumption is that the firm's human resources hold a large, untapped potential for productivity increases, creativity and innovation, and quality improvements. By redesigning jobs through job involvement and then providing extrinsic rewards to reinforce the desired behavior, a firm can harness some of that untapped potential. In other words, the old norms can be effectively shattered.

The assumption holds that traditional job design and traditional compensation elicit only traditional performance levels, both individually and collectively, for the organization. The high-involvement work environment will improve employees' *intrinsic* satisfaction through involvement in problem solving and decision making. But employees must also partake of the financial rewards that accrue from their additional abilities and effort. Sharing in the increased financial rewards is the intent of virtually all nontraditional compensation systems.

In essence, this represents an attempt to link an individual's rewards to the organization's performance. While some benefits may result from employees working harder and putting out additional effort, most of the benefits come from employees working smarter, developing new ways of doing something. And this is at the heart of what continuous improvement is all about.

Most of the nontraditional reward systems focus on group behavior. Work outcomes are the result of interdependent work flows, of complex organizational process. Although one individual may influence an outcome, a product, or a service, the individual seldom has total control. Rewarding individual performance in this situation is not only difficult because of measurement problems; it is also inappropriate. If work is performed by groups or teams, then singling out one person for financial reward can destroy group cohesiveness and perceptions of equity.

Also, when an organization is changing and evolving rapidly, traditional performance standards become less important and meaningful.

The installation of a new piece of equipment may dramatically change the technological base, altering the individual, or even group, performance standards. In these cases, overall organization performance is the most appropriate level of analysis.

Since customer satisfaction is a broad, organizational outcome, no one individual has complete or even predominant control. Therefore, linking CSM to compensation should be done only at the overall, aggregate level. The mechanics of how to do this will be discussed later, but for now the fact that CSM is a group performance indicator makes CSM very compatible with nontraditional group incentives.

There are two types of nontraditional group incentive systems: One is profit sharing, and the other is gain sharing. Profit sharing has been around for quite some time and is used by as many as 400,000 firms. Profit sharing will be discussed only as a basis for comparison with gain sharing, which is becoming increasingly popular and widespread.

Profit Sharing

Profit sharing is a reward system whereby employees are paid a portion of overall corporate profits in addition to a base wage. Some profit-sharing programs pay employees a lump sum cash bonus annually or semiannually. But the vast majority—more than 75%—of profit-sharing programs pay on a deferred basis. A portion of profits is regularly paid into an individual's account, but the individual can't draw on the funds until retirement, disability, or death. Thus, most profit-sharing programs represent more of a pension or retirement account. This limits the motivational impact of profit sharing for several reasons.

First, profit sharing is usually done on an aggregate, corporatewide basis. If the firm has 20,000 or 30,000 or 40,000 or more employees, it is pretty difficult for individuals to see how they personally can influence profitability. They simply become one of the masses. Individuals cannot identify how their work behavior is directly related to profits; the relationship is simply too tenuous and complex.

Second, the profit-sharing trust fund is usually managed by managers, consultants, or outside experts. The performance of the fund is beyond the control of the individual. The employee therefore does not identify personally with the fund except, of course, when the statements on fund performance are sent out. But this has very little to do with the individual's work behavior.

Finally, because most profit-sharing programs are deferred, the employee cannot access the funds. So, even though an employee may have a substantial individual account balance, the asset is rather abstract. It is far enough removed from day-to-day financial issues that it really has very little motivational impact for most people.

This discussion does not mean to imply that profit-sharing programs are bad. Indeed, profit-sharing programs are an important element of the compensation system, and, arguably, every company should have one. But a profit-sharing program is not a sterling motivational tool. It is simply one element of an overall compensation system.

A profit-sharing program can be a potentially divisive tool as well, a sore point for employees. In some firms, profit sharing applies only to the executives, creating a have-and-have-nots, or us-versus-them, organizational environment. If the employees perceive that most of the benefits of improved performance, namely higher profits, go to the managers, resentment will occur. So if a firm is going to use a profit-sharing program, it should do it right and include all employees.

An example of a very good profit-sharing program is Hewlett-Packard's. Though the basis of payment is overall corporate profitability, the bonuses are paid out in cash semiannually. Meetings are held companywide to explain in detail why profits were at a certain level. Such information sharing helps individual employees to see their role in profitability and organizational effectiveness. During tough financial periods, H-P employees have actually voluntarily given the company a "free workday." During more prosperous times, profit-sharing bonuses can exceed 25% of employees' actual wages.

In Japan, especially among larger corporations, profit-sharing bonuses are often in the range of 30–40% of annual compensation. In the United States, 10–20% is more common. In both cases, profit-sharing bonuses can act as a wage-reduction buffer. As profits fall in hard times, the profit-sharing bonus is the first compensation element to decrease.

Because of their generally poor ability to serve as a motivator, profit-sharing programs are not a good group incentive to reinforce the behavioral change of employees. Conversely, the effectiveness of gain-sharing programs as a group incentive is the reason for their rapid spread.

GAIN SHARING

Gain sharing is not a new technique; it has been around at least since the 1930s, when the Scanlon plan was introduced. But recently it has been used in new ways to reinforce product quality and service quality improvements and customer satisfaction. Before we can apply gain sharing to CSM data, we must first clearly define it, examine how it differs from profit sharing, and describe the organizational context in which it is most effective.

Gain sharing is a group incentive system in which employees are paid a portion of the gains or improvements in organizational performance. The payment is a cash bonus paid frequently—monthly or quarterly in most cases. The employees, in the form of a voluntary committee, are usually involved in the design, implementation, and maintenance of the gain-sharing program.

Gain-sharing programs were initially applied in production situations that were fairly structured. Employees were paid for their labor savings and cost reductions, based on some historical cost figure. The three most popular plans are the Scanlon, Rucker, and Improshare plans, and each has a slightly different twist on program design. There is extensive business literature on how these plans can be implemented in a production environment. The list of firms that have reported significant results from their gain-sharing efforts in manufacturing is quite impressive: Motorola, Herman Miller, Donnelly Mirrors, General Electric, TRW, Dana Corporation, 3M, Firestone, Rockwell, Amoco, and Mead, to name just a few. Many of these firms began gain sharing in the manufacturing environment and then extended the concept to all employees. Holiday Inn, Taco Bell, Xerox, and Lincoln National Life have successfully applied gain sharing in service environments.

Gain sharing differs from profit sharing in several ways, and these differences appear to account for some of the success and popularity of gain sharing. In a gain-sharing program, individuals are rewarded for performance that is more or less under their control, something the individual or group can influence. Bonus payments are frequent events; thus, they serve as a visible, behavioral reinforcement. Because those bonus payments are in the form of cash, they are far more tangible than abstract, deferred retirement accounts. Profit-sharing programs are global, broad systems for sharing organization success. Gain sharing operates much more closely to the individual, linking individual and group behavior to specific rewards.

Gain sharing promotes collective, group success. The group reinforces a new norm of behavior, one directed toward continuous improvement. This typically increases cooperation, collaboration, and joint effort, both within and between groups, suggesting that the context of the organization influences the success of a gain-sharing program.

Every gain-sharing program should be custom designed for a specific firm or unit. Some firms have a slightly different program for each division or unit. The contextual factors require that modification be made in order to optimize the organizational fit. The situations in which gain sharing has failed typically occurred when a firm, specifically management, attempted to install a program off the shelf, with no modifications. Therefore, a brief discussion of the major contextual dimensions will be helpful.

The context within which gain sharing is most successful is typified by high levels of organizational trust, both horizontally and vertically; open communication and sharing of information; and a willingness to change and adapt the gain-sharing plan as the need arises. There must also be a good deal of cooperation between management, employees, and unions. Collectively, this environment has implications for specific dimensions of the organization context.

Involvement

The most important single factor is high employee involvement. This involvement must take two forms: One is employee involvement in the improvement process, and the other is employee involvement in the gain-sharing process.

The various types of employee involvement such as information sharing, suggestion systems, and committees and teams were discussed earlier in this chapter. However, the earliest gain-sharing plans, particularly the Scanlon plan, used information sharing, a somewhat restrictive suggestion program, and joint management-employee committees. Now, a gain-sharing program encourages the use of almost all types of involvement at a much higher level.

The rationale behind the high involvement is that employees must be given wide latitude to implement their ideas for improvement. If employees must jump over an array of bureaucratic hurdles to make changes, enthusiasm for the gain-sharing program will quickly fade. So a high-involvement work environment must be in place *before* a gain-sharing program is implemented.

The other extremely important aspect of involvement is employee involvement in the design, implementation, and maintenance of the gain-sharing program. Since the details of a gain-sharing program directly affect the rewards, the employees should have some influence in the design of the program. Employees can identify relevant criteria and measurement methods and can provide insight into perceived equity. Collectively, employee involvement in the design stage leads to a higher level of trust, communication, and understanding.

Employee involvement in the implementation stage increases employee buy-in and ownership of the plan. Often, this requires the committee designing the program to "sell" their ideas to other employees by explaining how and why various decisions were reached. This is most often done in group discussions of some type.

No plan is perfect, for virtually every gain-sharing plan needs to be changed and modified as technology changes and as the business environment gradually evolves. If management arbitrarily adjusts the gain-sharing formula, then employees may question the fairness and equity of those changes. But if employees are actively involved in the maintenance of the plan, changes are much more palatable and widely accepted.

Organization Strategy and Culture

The overall strategy and corporate culture set the framework within which gain sharing operates. If the overall strategy is oriented toward innovation, creativity, continuous improvement, change, and flexibility, then gain sharing is very compatible and appropriate. If, on the other hand, the strategy tends to be bureaucratic, reinforcing the status quo traditional way of doing things, then gain sharing is not likely to be successful.

Firms operating in a dynamic environment tend to pay based on individual, group, and organizational performance. Thus, a higher proportion of the total compensation package tends to be in the form of individual or group incentives. Gain sharing is obviously quite in alignment with that tendency.

Gain sharing without supporting mechanisms and culture is seldom successful. Therefore, a firm's strategic orientation should filter down through all aspects of the company, such as hiring, training, personnel practices, and other aspects of the reward system. If all of these types of areas reflect a strategic consistency, gain sharing is more likely to be successful.

In particular, management skills and attitudes are critically important. Managers must be receptive and supportive of a higher degree of employee involvement. For some managers with poor interpersonal skills and traditional bureaucratic views, this may be a tough pill to swallow. The increase in employee involvement is typically accompanied by an erosion of the managerial power base. This shift in power requires that new skills be used.

The manager must seek out and facilitate employee suggestions. Some of those suggestions may challenge a manager's assumptions, beliefs, and behaviors. And that questioning process may make managers feel threatened by the gain-sharing program.

Technology

Initial arguments held that gain sharing worked well only in an environment that was stable and fairly static. This may have been true when gain sharing focused only on labor and material inputs. A rapidly changing technological base made historical baseline comparisons of little value or totally meaningless. Now, however, gain sharing may actually encourage technological improvement.

As firms have moved from narrow measures such as labor or material costs per unit to broader index measures such as CSM levels, gain-sharing programs can encourage employees to search out and rapidly implement technological improvements. Employees realize that individual and group rewards will increase due to better technology, process redesign, and labor savings. Thus, resistance to change is greatly reduced.

Although specific gain-sharing criteria will be discussed in detail shortly, index measures are composite or aggregate measures that indicate overall performance. The three most common are productivity, quality, and customer satisfaction indexes. These can be used individually or jointly in the gain-sharing formula.

Competition

Highly competitive industries place a heavy burden on firms to continually improve. Competitors will always attempt to erode or neutralize a firm's competitive advantage. To maintain or improve market share, a firm must continually improve its products and processes.

Because gain sharing is a program that elicits and rewards improvements, it is particularly well suited for a highly competitive environment. Applying gain sharing in an electric utility would be difficult, because in most cases there are no direct competitors to steal market share although this is changing. And because the rate-setting process generally does not reward improvements, the external mandate is missing. There are a few exceptions in California and Mississippi that tie CSM results into rate-making proposals, so change is occurring. However, in general, it is the competitive impetus that provides strong support for gain sharing.

Size

When gain sharing is applied on a broad, corporatewide basis, it often suffers from the same weaknesses as profit sharing. The individual still has only a tenuous linkage or contribution to overall organizational performance. Therefore, a gain-sharing program should be designed for the smallest organizational unit that is practicably feasible.

Generally, this means that a gain-sharing program should have between 500 to 1,000 participants at the upper limit. For a bank or hotel, gain sharing in an individual unit is easily done. For a manufacturing facility with 5,000 or more employees, the challenge becomes one of identifying discrete organizational units that have some degree of internal cohesiveness.

Although big is not always bad, smaller is usually better as a rule for gain sharing. The smaller the work group unit, the more each individual can personally identify with and contribute to the improvement process.

Unions

Traditionally and for various reasons, unions have opposed pay-for-performance mechanisms such as gain sharing. As a result, incentive systems of any type are much less frequently used when a workforce is unionized. The resistance was generally due to the fact that two workers performing the same task could have quite different compensation levels. The disparity in compensation would break down work group cohesiveness and lessen the collective support for the union. This same argument also applied to many types of work groups.

During the 1980s and 1990s, there has been less union opposition to group incentive programs, primarily profit sharing and gain sharing. The unions have come to realize that they have a vested interest in contributing to the success of a firm. The increasingly competitive environment has increased the possibility that any firm could go out of business, and all union jobs would be lost.

Therefore, union support for gain sharing appears to be increasing because the program can increase employee compensation and also improve the work situation. However, the presence of constraining work rules may present an obstacle to major improvements.

Benefits of Gain Sharing

Because the organization context varies from firm to firm, each of the preceding factors should be considered in the design of a gain-sharing program. The most certain aspect of gain-sharing programs is that they are usually successful. More than 75% of firms using gain sharing feel that the programs are successful and have a variety of benefits. Although it is often difficult to distinguish the benefits due to changed management attitudes, increased employee involvement, and the gain-sharing plan itself, collective benefits do result.

Organizational efficiency as measured by cost or productivity usually improves. Social cohesion improves as indicated by cooperation, teamwork, and communication. Group norms reinforce improvement, high individual and group performance, and process improvement. Employees are much more receptive to new ideas, new technologies, and more flexible work behaviors. Organizational, managerial, and individual goals become more closely aligned and mutually supporting.

These widespread benefits are the primary reason for the rapid increase in gain-sharing programs. Although many of the benefits would accrue without gain sharing if all the other enabling factors were in place, gain sharing certainly serves as a reinforcing reward system.

IMPLEMENTING GAIN SHARING

One of the dominant considerations with all aspects of a compensation package is fairness, or equity. There are two types of such fairness that must form the backdrop for a gain-sharing program. If a program lacks either type, success is unlikely.

The first type of fairness deals with the overall *level of compensation* and is sometimes referred to as distributive justice. This fairness deals with whether employees are paid adequately for their contributions to the organization, and it must include all facets of compensation. This fairness issue deals with external equity: How does the employee's compensation compare with the perceived job market? And this fairness deals with internal equity within a firm: How does the employee's compensation compare with other workers or managers?

For example, the increasingly wide pay gap between "workers" and "executives" has led to the executive pay controversy. Pragmatically, this indicates a breakdown in internal fairness in some organizations.

If employees do not feel that their overall compensation package is fair, they will probably not be supportive of gain sharing. Gain sharing is not effective as a strategy to correct a compensation flaw, such as unfairly low wages. Gain sharing is an effective strategy to elicit and reinforce behavioral change if fairness already exists.

The issue of fairness has two implications for compensation strategy. The affected employee must be reasonably satisfied with pay *before* the gain sharing is implemented. And second, the employee must be satisfied with the *amount* of savings that are distributed by the gain sharing formula. There will be more on how to do this shortly.

The second type of fairness, in addition to distributive justice, is procedural justice. Procedural justice deals with the *system of distribution* of the compensation. If managers are fair and consistent in allocating financial rewards, employees tend to be much more satisfied with pay. This implies that the whole performance evaluation and reward system should be efficient and clearly understood. With respect to gain sharing, the design of the plan must be based on factors that are largely controllable by employees, especially with CSM.

If employees feel that the evaluative criteria are beyond their control, that they can't significantly influence outcomes, then the gain-sharing program will lack procedural fairness. Therefore, it is important to identify the controllable and uncontrollable factors that influence the gain-sharing criteria.

During implementation of a gain-sharing program, the best way to ensure that both distributive and procedural justice exist is to use a committee, normally a task force, to design and implement the program. Simply adopting a gain-sharing program from another firm and implementing it is a dangerous policy because of the contextual factors and fairness issues. A consultant is often helpful to the process and can speed the work of the task force by serving as a sounding board, raising overlooked issues, and educating the committee members.

There are ten elements to consider in the design of a gain-sharing program (Table 13.1). The assumption is made here that the first element is already in place: namely, there must be specific mechanisms that encourage employee involvement. Without involvement, gain sharing has no chance for success.

The second assumption is that the primary concern lies with how to link CSM data with gain sharing. So other gain-sharing applications, such as cost reduction or labor savings formulas, will not be addressed in detail. With these issues in mind, we can now get down to the nuts and bolts of how to design a gain-sharing program.

Table 13.1 Critical Elements of a Gain-sharing Program

 1. Employee-involvement environment
 2. Gain-sharing task force
 3. Designing of the appropriate group
 4. Development of a formula
 5. Development of the baseline
 6. Identification of the share
 7. Identification of payout frequency
 8. Identification of payout method
 9. Determination of deficit reserve
10. Adjustment of deficit reserve

Gain-sharing Task Force

The gain-sharing task force is really just an extension of the previous element, employee involvement. The goal of the task force is to design and implement the gain-sharing program. Because customer satisfaction is a broad organizational outcome, the task force should be composed of ten to twelve employees from the areas represented in the firm's CSM model. A consultant, if used, should also be a regular member of the task force.

The task force should include managers and workers. The workers' involvement should be voluntary and consist of influential, respected employees. This will typically increase broader employee buy-in and support from the different functional areas. The task force members should communicate with and solicit input from other employees during the development process. This is normally most effectively done by using formal meetings, rather than ad hoc, random employee input.

The task force should be fully empowered to design and implement the gain-sharing program. Therefore, managerial concerns and constraints should be stated at the beginning and during the design process. If management reserves veto power or tosses the recommendations back to the task force for further work and modification, then trust and enthusiasm for the program can be destroyed. The managers on the task force must act as the conduit for input from management.

Designation of the Group

The group refers to those who will be covered under a gain-sharing program, and there are three considerations: The first is what levels of employees will be participating. Some organizations include only hourly or unionized personnel. Other organizations include first-line supervisors because of their enabling role. Still others include some or all of the managers to provide managerial incentives for training.

If only hourly employees are included, an us (workers)-versus-them (managers) environment may be created. The issue of distributive justice comes into play here. If the worker-manager pay gap is large or if managers already have an attractive profit-sharing program in place, then including managers in the gain-sharing program may be viewed as unfair since managers are already rewarded handsomely in other ways.

On the other hand, if the worker/manager pay gap is not large, managerial inclusion may be very acceptable. Including managers has the effect of fostering a more cohesive, team culture. This is particularly true when bonuses are paid out as a flat amount per employee rather than as a percentage of base income.

The second consideration is what geographical group is most appropriate. In many cases, the group may consist of all employees at a particular site or location such as a bank, hotel, hospital, or branch office. This works well when all value-added processes are handled on site.

But when there are high levels of interorganizational interdependency, geographical distinctions may break down. A manufacturing facility, a customer service department, and a marketing office may be at three different locations, but all certainly contribute to customer satisfaction. The appropriate group in this case would be a combination of the three locations. The sampling design of the CSM must be able to pick up these types of geographical distinctions and combinations.

The third consideration in defining the group is the issue of multiple products and processes. A particular production facility may produce a variety of products destined for quite different customer segments. In this situation the most appropriate CSM data would be some type of composite index for the different products.

In some firms, separate gain-sharing programs may need to be developed for different value-added processes. This is often the case in very large organizations whose total employment base is too large for one program. Perhaps production would be covered by a gain-sharing program concentrating on productivity and quality, and customer contact personnel would be covered by a gain-sharing program focusing on controllable aspects of service quality.

The key challenge consists in defining a group that is small enough for individual meaningfulness and discrete enough to identify with CSM data. The grouping, whatever it may be, will typically lead to greater intragroup cohesiveness, cooperation, and problem solving. Identifying the appropriate group is, for many firms, the most difficult element of gain sharing.

An example can be found in the Sears, Roebuck and Co. Sears is revamping its variable pay schedule to include customer satisfaction results at its auto repair locations. Since 1992, service consultants have been paid commissions for sales of tires, batteries, and shock absorbers. Prior to 1992, service advisers also received commissions for brake and tire-alignment jobs; you may remember the case against Sears for falsely diagnosing problems and padding bills in the auto service area. That case resulted in the removal of services from the commission sales plan.

In 1995, Sears will implement a variable pay schedule for service consultants at its auto repair centers with a customer focus. Two options were under consideration. The first option based a consultant's pay on 60% salary, 21% commission, and 19% customer satisfaction results. The second option based pay on 60% salary and 40% customer satisfaction results. Customer satisfaction results are determined from report cards filled out by customers. Sears also planned to include a customer satisfaction component in variable pay for mechanics.

Developing the Formula

In traditional manufacturing applications, the formula stated what criteria would be evaluated and how those criteria would be measured. For example, Nucor Steel uses the measurement of tons per operating hour, other firms use labor as a percentage of the total cost structure, and still others evaluate labor and materials factors in combination. These measures obviously do not consider the customer.

Internal cost reductions have a direct linkage to profitability. As costs go down, other things being constant, profitability goes up. The linkage between customer satisfaction and profitability is more circuitous but no less important.

Customer satisfaction leads to higher customer retention, which leads to increased profitability. But since twenty or so attributes may each contribute to customer satisfaction, measurement becomes a problem. Linking only sales performance to customer satisfaction is of little value because many other issues also influence satisfaction.

Because of these difficulties, gain sharing normally uses only aggregate, overall measures in its formulas. Performance on each attribute can be recognized in the firm's recognition program. Indeed, CSM data for processes should be a part of the recognition program. But the appropriate level of analysis for CSM data consists of aggregate indexes for gain-sharing purposes.

The aggregate CSM measure should be a composite index. It should include at least three different overall questions. For example, one question might be, "Overall, how satisfied are you with the product/service?" Another might be, "Would you recommend this product/service to a friend?" Another might be, "Would you use this product/service again?" By aggregating three or four of these types of questions, the index becomes more reliable.

Since reliability and validity are key concerns in the development of an index, the sample size should be reasonably large. The use of a composite index and a large sample size increases the precision of the data, as you may recall from the chapter on sampling. When financial rewards are linked to CSM data, precision is an important issue.

Because of inherent sample variability, it is often wise to use a two- or three-period rolling average. If CSM data are gathered monthly, the composite index would be averaged for the current and two previous months. This rolling-average method reduces most of the variation due to sampling.

A firm can use the CSM composite index either individually or in combination with other measures. Using the composite CSM index is quite appropriate in firms that have a stated corporate goal of 100% customer satisfaction. Experience has shown, however, that in firms with a single criterion, other important factors may be neglected.

As a result, some firms combine the CSM index with one or two other measures to create more balance. In particular, a three-way composite of customer satisfaction, productivity, and quality appears quite valuable. The CSM index ensures a customer focus, the productivity index rewards process improvements, and the quality index rewards product and service quality improvements. In a diverse group, this type of measure would have something for virtually every employee.

Rather than use broad index measures, some firms prefer to use very specific criteria. Eggers Industries, a wood products manufacturer, uses about thirty cost measures. Mobay Corporation uses ten indicators. Motorola uses five categories with multiple measures in each: production cost, quality, delivery, inventory, and safety.

When CSM data are used in combination with other indicators, the relative weighting of each indicator becomes an issue. There is no single answer to this. The relative importance of each indicator is a reflection of the firm's strategic initiatives. If customer satisfaction is an explicit strategic goal, then customer satisfaction should receive relatively more weighting.

The formula then addresses how customer satisfaction will be measured and used either individually or jointly. The specific way that movements in the index influence the payout will be discussed shortly.

Baseline

Once the components of the formula have been identified, the basis of subsequent comparison or baseline must be calculated. There are two types of baselines: one is historical and the other is targeted.

The most commonly used baseline is either a fixed or rolling baseline. A fixed baseline would occur when all subsequent calculations are compared with a specific, unchanging baseline. Perhaps in 1990 a firm had 88% of all customers satisfied. That 88% level could be used as the baseline indefinitely.

The problem with this is that some degree of improvement is normal and expected. A slight gradual improvement may not really be worthy of a reward. Also, if a firm used a fixed 1990 baseline, the firm in 1995 would be paying for increases that occurred four or five years previously. Again, this may not be a particularly good basis for rewards since many contextual factors may have changed. Because of these problems, more firms are using a rolling baseline.

A rolling baseline would average the CSM data over several years. A firm using a three-year rolling baseline might use 1990, 1991, and 1992 data as the comparison for 1993. Either at the end of the year or on a monthly basis, the earliest time period would drop out, being replaced by the most recent time period.

This has the net effect of rewarding employees for gains in customer satisfaction during three years. After that, the rewards accrue 100% to the company. This type of rolling average is consistent with the fact that customer expectations are always going up and that the firm must continually improve. This type of average is consistent with a firm pursuing continuous improvement as a strategic goal.

Another type of baseline consists of setting a targeted goal—a certain satisfaction level a firm must meet to trigger payment. For example, customer satisfaction may be 90% for an industry. A firm currently at 85%

may not want to reward employees for improving on below-average performance. So the gain-sharing rewards would kick in after the 90% customer satisfaction level has been attained.

For firms operating in dynamic industries, the rolling baseline is probably most appropriate. In stable industries or in firms that are already at a high satisfaction level, the fixed baseline is probably most appropriate. For some firms that are below average or those at a very high satisfaction level, a targeted baseline might be appropriate. A high target, say 96%, could be a trigger for payment, thus rewarding employees for keeping up the good work.

In most cases, there should be some process designed into the plan for periodic recalibration if a fixed baseline is used. That recalibration should be the responsibility of a committee charged with maintaining and fine-tuning the gain-sharing program. When management arbitrarily adjusts the baseline without input from employees—and such has been done—employee enthusiasm for the plan can be quickly destroyed.

If CSM deteriorates, there should not be a penalty. One must be aware of the margin of error in the CSM numbers as well as the negative tone that a salary decrease can generate. If CSM cannot be measured for all employees, it is critical that CSM results be a significant component (25–35%) of variable pay for senior management.

Share

In manufacturing applications, share refers to the percentage of total savings that are paid out to employees. The most common range of savings payout is 25–50%. For gain-sharing plans covering only labor savings, a payout of 70% is not unusual. For some plans with a rolling baseline, 100% of first-year savings is paid out. This obviously gives employees a very strong incentive to improve each year.

For a customer satisfaction index, the value of the gain is less clear. A firm must equate improvements in customer satisfaction to a payout figure. This is normally done by linking a one-point change in the CSM index to either an absolute amount or a percentage of profits. A 1-point shift, say, from 89 to 90%, might be worth $1 million. Or the 1-point shift might be worth 1% or 2% of pretax profits. The logic behind these linkages is that higher customer satisfaction will lead to more profits.

IBM–Rochester has linked customer satisfaction levels to profitability for the AS-400 computer. A 1% improvement in overall customer satisfaction yields $257 million in sales over a four-year period on a base of $4.5 billion in sales. From the sales figure, profit contribution could be calculated, a portion of which goes back to employees. These incentives used to be in the form of individual awards, but they are now team based. In 1993, the variable pay payout for CSM results was 6.5% of salary to teams.

Linking a CSM index to a percentage of profitability makes the gain-sharing plan look suspiciously like a profit-sharing plan. But the customer satisfaction index is more controllable by employees due to the impact of service quality. And the gain-sharing payout is more frequent, providing more reinforcement for behavioral change.

Normally, profit-sharing programs have an upper limit of about 20% payout to employees. Assuming that is the case, 10% of profits could be allocated to the traditional deferred-profit-sharing program. The other 10% could be pegged for current cash payout based on the CSM index.

Since a rolling baseline is pretty common for a CSM gain-sharing index, relatively large rewards are offered to employees for current performance. The logic behind this is that firms accrue all of the residual benefits after the baseline period expires. Let's assume that an average customer has a ten-year life expectancy as a customer. The gains from the increased satisfaction and retention would flow largely to the employees for the first three years (assuming a three-year rolling baseline) and to the firm for the next seven years.

Payout Frequency

The frequency of payout should be consistent with the frequency of data gathering. CSM programs that are implemented annually are not a very good basis for a gain-sharing index. The feedback periods are too far apart to provide meaningful reinforcement to behavioral change.

Ideally, a CSM index would provide monthly or quarterly payout of gains. If the share is based on a percentage of profits, the payout period must be compatible with a firm's quarterly financial reporting schedule. If a firm is using a continuous survey of customers, the data should be aggregated for the appropriate period.

The danger in too frequent a payout is that the bonus may be viewed as insignificant. A payout of $50 a month may be meaningless, but a payout of $150 may be more significant and useful as a motivator.

Payout Method

The payout method dictates how much of the total payout will go to each employee. One approach is to calculate the payout as a percentage of base pay. The total payout pool would be compared with total wages to provide an overall percentage. Then everyone would get the percentage of base pay as a bonus. Higher-paid workers would get a larger bonus check, but their percentage would be the same. This method has the potential to create some work group divisiveness because the size of the bonus check may not reflect contributions to improvement in the index. Unions tend to favor a bonus expressed as a percentage of base pay because it favors more-senior employees.

Another method is to use a flat rate per employee. The total payout pool is divided by the number of participants, and everyone gets an equal share. This method treats all employees, both managers and workers, equally, and it tends to build group cohesiveness.

With both the flat-rate and percentage-of-pay plans, eligibility issues arise. Employees on leave of absence, sick leave, or vacation and new employees present special situations that must be considered in the plan design.

To overcome this, some firms pay based on an individual's total hours worked. The payout pool is divided by the total number of labor hours. Then the product is multiplied by the hours each individual worked. This approach is based on the assumption that the people working the most probably contribute the most ideas for improvement and should get the largest gains or rewards.

Deficit Reserve

A deficit reserve is a common feature of many gain-sharing programs. Rather than distribute the full payout pool, the company holds back a percentage as a hedge against downturns in the index. The deficit reserve normally amounts to about 20–30% of the payout pool.

If the CSM composite rose from 89 to 90%, a payout pool of, say, $1 million might be generated; $700,000 would be distributed to employees and $300,000 would be held back. As long as performance improved, the deficit reserve would gradually increase. But if performance deteriorated by dropping below the baseline figure, then the gain-sharing program would repay the firm from the deficit reserve. The amount repaid would be proportional to the gains created on the way up. A 1% drop in this case would require a $1-million repayment to the firm.

The deficit reserve could carry a negative balance if performance lagged below the baseline for a period of time and the total reserve had to be used to repay the firm. Subsequent gains would normally pay fully into the deficit reserve account to eliminate the negative balance before resuming distribution to employees.

When a deficit reserve has not been drawn down, the reserve pool can become quite large. Periodically, normally once a year, the deficit reserve is reduced to zero through a payout. The payout can be in the form of an additional cash bonus, which could be paid in December or at the end of the fiscal year. Or the bonus could be paid on a deferred basis as an additional deposit into an employee's retirement account.

If the formula specifies a three-month rolling average as the index or plan criterion, a deficit balance is less important. The three-month rolling average acts as a buffer so that a one-period downturn may be offset by two positive months. The three-month average would have to be negative to trigger a deficit reserve withdrawal. For most firms, a consistent three-month decline is relatively unusual.

Adjustment Mechanism

Over time, gain-sharing programs must be modified. The two most common features needing adjustment are the baseline and the formula. A fixed baseline must be adjusted periodically as the context changes. New capital investment may change the technological base underlying the productive system. This often renders the old baseline obsolete. With a rolling baseline, the aggregation period may be too long or too short, so the period must be readjusted.

The specific way that a formula is calculated may have to be adjusted as the firm and the employees gain better insight into the appropriateness of various criteria. An evolving technological base also causes the assumptions underlying the composite index to change.

Less frequently, the share, the payout procedures, or the deficit reserve may need to be modified. The share may prove insufficient, or it may prove to be an unexpected financial burden to the firm. Payout frequency may be in need of adjustment to enhance reinforcement of behavioral change.

There needs to be a formal mechanism in place for making these kinds of changes, and it is best accomplished by a committee charged with that purpose. The maintenance committee can benefit from the membership of individuals involved in the original design task force when feasible. This adds some organizational memory to explain the initial rationale behind the decisions.

Regardless of how it is technically accomplished, a gain-sharing program should have some inherent flexibility built into the design. If this is done at the start, subsequent modifications will be faster and easier to make and have more widespread support.

Payout Cap

An additional factor that is an optional element and not included in Table 13.1 is a payout cap. Normally, gain-sharing payouts are limited to 25–30% of an employee's base wage. This usually provides a large enough motivational reinforcement without becoming too large.

There are cases in which payouts approached 100% of base salary. In some instances, employees came to depend on the bonus as an expected part of their compensation. When bonuses shrank, employees experienced financial difficulty, for their budgets had expanded to use the added income. To reduce the risk of bonuses being perceived as wages, caps were installed.

If gain sharing generates a bonus larger than the cap, the excess bonus can go into a deferred account. The deferred account can be used to pay a maximum bonus when the calculated bonus is less than the cap. Or the deferred bonus can be paid out in a lump sum annually or paid into a retirement account, depending, of course, on federal and IRS limitations.

CHAPTER SUMMARY

Customer satisfaction is linked to all of the processes and activities in an organization. Process improvements are led and made by teams of employees who value both the customer and the recognition and rewards they receive from their employer. In order to reinforce the gains that a company makes, it is necessary to link rewards and compensation to customer satisfaction measures.

Recognition programs are beneficial in that they communicate the organizational commitment to customer satisfaction. Recognition programs, to be effective, must be aligned with corporate values, timely, and objective. The recognition must be in the form of a win-win situation; there should be no downside potential, for that it has a very negative impact on the process.

Gain-sharing programs are also becoming an increasingly popular way to reinforce the importance of quality improvements, productivity gains, development of a customer focus, and the stressing of customer satisfaction. A CSM composite index that includes key measures should be developed for the gain-sharing program. Although a CSM composite index is a bit more complicated to apply than traditional gain-sharing programs, it is a fair and comprehensive way to drive the importance of the customer into the organization and share in the benefits.

HARRIS CORP.

Linking CSM Data and Gain Sharing

Most firms would like to know the expected value of an increase in customer satisfaction. This would allow the firm to do several things. The first would be to conduct a cost/benefit analysis to see if the marginal benefits are worth the marginal costs. Because the benefits usually do exceed the costs, this also allows a firm to determine the size of the profit pool allocated to gain sharing. A firm that has attempted to resolve these difficult issues is Harris Corp. (HC).

Harris Corp. is a Melbourne, Florida, electronics firm with annual sales of more than $3 billion and a workforce of more than 30,000 employees. The company has four major divisions: Electronics, Semiconductors, Communications, and Lanier Worldwide. The importance of customer satisfaction cuts across all four.

The fundamental assumption that underlies HC's CSM program is that customer satisfaction and customer loyalty are positively related. That is, an increase in customer satisfaction will lead to an increase in customer loyalty, and as customer loyalty increases there is a direct impact on sales and profits. Harris developed its analytical approach in concert with Prognostics, Inc., a consulting firm in California.

HC gathers customer perceptions of importance, performance, and overall satisfaction measures. The importance and performance issues are measured using a 10-point scale. One of the overall measures pertinent to this discussion is a loyalty-intent question, which is categorical. The three categories are will continue, will not continue, and undecided.

Rather than use just a four-quadrant, importance/performance grid as most firms do, HC segments the grid into five cells as depicted in Figure 13.1. This grid could be used for each attribute, or all attributes could be aggregated for a composite score.

HC assumes that performance on unimportant issues is usually insufficient to cause a customer to switch, within reason. Thus, cell 5 equates to those fundamental customer expectations that are simply expected to be there.

Cells 3 and 4 represent generally secure customers who are very unlikely to switch. Cells 1 and 2, however, consist of vulnerable customers waiting for or actively seeking an alternative supplier. The number of customers in each of these cells has important financial implications for HC.

To better understand who the customers in cells 1 and 2 are, HC compares satisfaction with purchase intent. An example of HC performance on the service support attribute is provided in Figure 13.2. The solid line represents the percentage of customers selecting the will-continue purchase intent category. The dotted line represents both the percentage of customers selecting the will-not-continue or undecided categories. Of all respondents who selected a 9 or 10 on the satisfaction scale, more than 90% also selected the will-continue category, and less than 10% selected will not continue or undecided. If a 5 or 6 satisfaction score was selected, just over 60% selected will continue and just under 40% selected will not continue or are undecided.

The data allowed HC to develop a graph relating the impact of a 1-point change in the satisfaction rating on customer loyalty. As indicated in Figure 13.3, a 1-point change in satisfaction had a 7.5% impact on repurchase intent.

The assumption is made that all of those expressing "Will not continue" or "Undecided" will eventually leave. In highly competitive industries with continually increasing customer expectations, this is probably a pretty valid assumption.

For a firm with annual sales of $100 million, a 1-point satisfaction improvement is worth $7.5 million in sales. For a firm with a 40% gross margin on sales, the annual value of the 1-point shift is worth $3 million in gross profit.

This is a fairly conservative estimate. Highly satisfied customers tend to *increase* their purchases from preferred suppliers, so sales usually increase. Highly satisfied customers require less peripheral support, are the source of ideas for innovation and improvement, and generate new customers through referrals. So, the $3-million economic value represents only the easily identifiable benefits.

To tie this back to cost/benefit analysis, the firm could invest $1 million in new investment or training to yield higher satisfaction, contribute $1 million to a gain-sharing pool, and still have a $1 million increase in profitability.

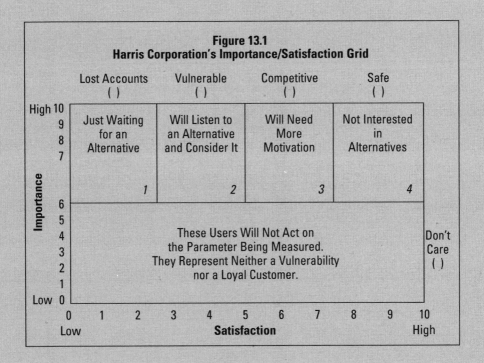

Figure 13.1
Harris Corporation's Importance/Satisfaction Grid

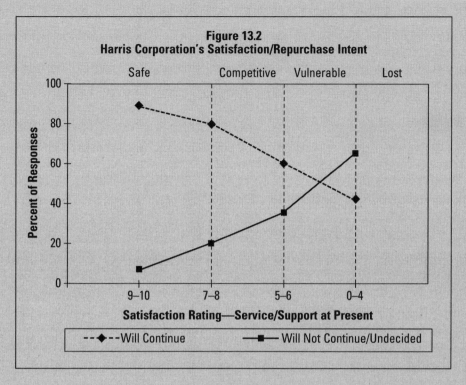

Figure 13.2
Harris Corporation's Satisfaction/Repurchase Intent

Safe   Competitive   Vulnerable   Lost

Percent of Responses

Satisfaction Rating—Service/Support at Present

- - ◆ - - Will Continue   ━━■━━ Will Not Continue/Undecided

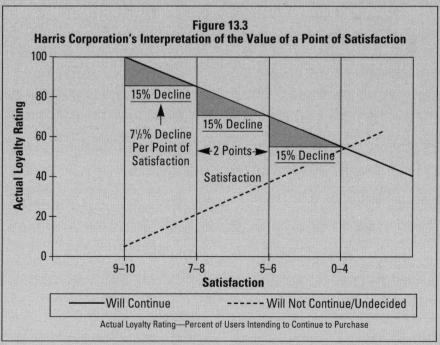

Figure 13.3
Harris Corporation's Interpretation of the Value of a Point of Satisfaction

Actual Loyalty Rating

15% Decline

7½% Decline
Per Point of
Satisfaction

15% Decline

◄—2 Points—►

15% Decline

Satisfaction

Satisfaction

———— Will Continue   - - - - - Will Not Continue/Undecided

Actual Loyalty Rating—Percent of Users Intending to Continue to Purchase

FIRST INTERSTATE BANK

Linking CSM to Recognition Systems

First Interstate Bank in California has stressed high-quality customer service. Because customer service is a reflection of millions of moments of truth—those daily customer-employee interactions—each employee must support and buy into the effort.

Therefore, customer satisfaction is a part of performance appraisals and incentive compensation systems. One type of reward is the Five Star recognition system.

Five Star awards are given to both individual employees and bank branches. Individuals who consistently provide outstanding customer service are awarded a white name badge with five stars. Only about 10% of the employee base receives the award badges, so awardees are viewed with special recognition by peers. From the pool of Five Star award winners, employees get additional recognition. Some may be featured in television or radio commercials, some have their photo appear in internal newsletters, and some may have lunch or dinner with senior executives.

The Five Star program also extends to branches. Based on CSM data, the branches that exceed customer expectations are given an award. One part of the branch program is the awarding of a five-star decal that is put on the entrance doors. Branches are reevaluated every six months. If performance drops below the minimum Five Star standard, the bank manager must remove the decal.

The recognition program at First Interstate helped it move from having one of the worst customer satisfaction levels of all California banks to having one of the very best. And that increase in customer satisfaction has a concomitant major impact on profitability at First Interstate as well.

MOTOROLA'S TEAM COMPETITION

Linking CSM Data to Recognition

Motorola's commitment to Six-Sigma quality levels and 100% customer satisfaction is well-known. Being selected an inaugural winner of the Malcolm Baldrige National Quality Award simply served to reinforce Motorola's internal focus on the customer.

To encourage company-wide adherence to the 100% customer satisfaction goal, Motorola conducts an annual Total Customer Satisfaction (TCS) competition. The TCS competition consists of a team-based recognition program culminating in an awards presentation affair with all the hoopla of the Emmy or Grammy awards.

The TCS competition is entered into by problem-solving teams that achieve high levels of customer satisfaction. The teams can come from any area of the firm and consist of any combination of employees. When possible, the three- to ten-member teams should include customers and suppliers, either internal or external. The duration of the team's efforts is usually three to six months.

The only major constraint is that the team must focus on one or more of Motorola's five key initiatives: Six-Sigma quality, cycle time reduction, product and manufacturing leadership, profit improvement, and participative leadership.

All TCS teams are scored using the following criteria: teamwork (10%), project selection (10%), analysis techniques (20%), remedies (20%), results (20%), institutionalization (10%), and presentation (10%). Throughout all seven criteria, improving customer satisfaction is a dominant theme.

To be successful, a team must demonstrate a high level of commitment and involvement. Tough, reach-out goals must be set and supported by a measurement system. Best-in-class practices must be benchmarked, and training needs identified.

The successes of the teams are widely publicized throughout Motorola. And the recognition given at the award ceremony is the major motivator for the competition.

14

Benchmarking

Benchmarking is clearly one of the most important business concepts to emerge in the later part of the 1980s. The concept is diametrically opposed to the mentality that believes, "If it's not invented here, it can't be any good." The concept of benchmarking is a part of and a supplement to continuous improvement efforts. Thus, benchmarking is fundamental to quality improvement efforts of all types. But despite its popularity, benchmarking is still shrouded in ambiguity.

Benchmarking is different things to different people. The ambiguity exists because there are three types of benchmarking: internal, competitive, and best in class. Each type is conceptually different from the others, and each requires a different methodology to implement.

The choice of which type of benchmarking to pursue is not an either-or proposition. Each is essential to continuous improvement in a different way, so firms would be prudent to simultaneously pursue all three. The purpose of this chapter is to clear away the foggy ambiguity that surrounds benchmarking and show how each type can be successfully implemented.

INTERNAL BENCHMARKING

The very concept of continuous improvement implies that a firm improves its value-adding processes and products continually. This suggests that firms periodically compare their current performance level with a previous performance level.

The initial baseline standard is often referred to as an internal benchmark. This benchmark is the performance level with which subsequent performance levels are compared. Hence the internal benchmark is the key base of comparison. When Motorola reduces its cycle time by 30:1, the comparison is with some initial measurement level. When a firm initially measures its customer satisfaction, it may have 84% satisfied customers; the 84% becomes the internal benchmark with which subsequent levels are compared. When a firm initially measures customer retention, it may have an 86% retention rate, which becomes the benchmark.

Since the initial benchmark serves as an important base of comparison, it should be as accurate as possible. In statistical terms this means it should have both a high level of precision and a high confidence level. Pragmatically, this means that the initial CSM survey, if it is to be applied as a benchmark, should comprise a relatively large sample size. As you will recall from the chapter on sampling, increasing the sample size can simultaneously improve the precision and confidence levels.

The use of an initial CSM benchmark has caused some firms to freeze their CSM programs, using the same sampling procedure or questionnaire over and over again, even though problems may exist. Their mistaken belief is that the longitudinal consistency in the questionnaire, for example, makes benchmark comparisons more meaningful. If problems exist in the questionnaire, or any other part of the research design, the primary effect is to reduce reliability. If reliability is low, benchmark comparisons are of little value.

Because no CSM program is perfect, modifications, slight tweaking, or, in rarer cases, a major overhaul may be needed. To facilitate benchmark comparisons, a firm has two choices. The easiest is to simply discard the old benchmark and establish a new one. Unfortunately, this presents serious managerial problems, especially when CSM data are used in performance evaluation or incentive compensation systems. In these cases, the changeover from the old to the new program can be timed to coincide with the end of an evaluation or compensation period.

In some cases, this may also require a split sample. Half the sample would use the old approach so that beginning and ending data are comparable for evaluation and compensation purposes. The other half of the sample would use the new approach and establish a beginning point for the next observation period. This makes subsequent observations a year or two in the future inappropriate to compare with the original benchmark.

To maintain comparability, a firm can calibrate some of the more important measures. Let's say a firm initially used a 7-point Likert-type scale with end points of Very Satisfied and Very Dissatisfied to evaluate some aspect of service quality and that its last survey resulted in a mean response of 5.7. Perhaps the firm decided to replace this rather unsophisticated scale with a five-category expectations scale like the following one.

Greatly Below Expectations	Moderately Below Expectations	Met Expectations	Moderately Exceeded Expectations	Greatly Exceeded Expectations

Directly comparing the old mean figure with the new data is like comparing apples and oranges.

To overcome that lack of directly comparable scales, the firm could again run a split-sample test. Half would get the old scale, and the other half the new scale. For reliability purposes, the split sample should normally run for two observation periods. Then a mathematical conversion factor could be calculated so that a certain figure on the old scale is equivalent to a certain figure on the new scale.

As long as the underlying attribute remains the same—a specific service characteristic in this example—then calibrating one scale against another allows comparisons to be made back to the original benchmark. The process is rather simple, but if the wording of the question is changed so that the underlying meaning of the question changes, no amount of calibration will make comparisons meaningful. Then we'd be back to comparing apples and oranges again.

Internal benchmarks are essential to determine both the rate and magnitude of improvement. Joe Parkinson, former chairman of Micron Technology, a Boise, Idaho, dynamic-random-access-memory-chip manufacturer stated Micron had to get 20% better on a variety of dimensions every year. Parkinson was concerned with the *rate* of annual improvement. When Xerox conducted its initial benchmarks in cost structure, it found the Japanese were selling copiers at prices lower even than Xerox's manufacturing costs. David Kearns, chief executive at the time, was concerned with the *magnitude* of improvement necessary.

Although internal benchmarks are very important to assessing the improvement of various processes, they carry an inherent danger. Comparing current performance against past performance ignores what is happening in the rest of the industry. For instance, during the mid-1980s, Cadillac's internal benchmarks were showing a steady increase in quality and customer satisfaction. But at the same time, Cadillac's market position was eroding. Although Cadillac was improving, the competition was improving faster, so the competitive gap between Cadillac and its competitors was growing.

The next type of benchmarking is intended to ensure that firms don't develop a myopic view of competitive reality.

COMPETITIVE BENCHMARKING

Internal benchmarking yields an internally focused self-assessment. Conversely, competitive benchmarking yields an external, customer-driven view of how a firm stacks up against the competition. There are two types of competitive benchmarks. The first type develops a competitive profile against a particular competitor or small set of competitors. The other type develops a competitive profile against an industry average. The use of each requires a different research approach.

Key Competitor Benchmark

Developing a competitive profile against key competitors means a firm conducts a CSM program using competitors' customers as the sample frame. To maintain objectivity, competitive benchmarking should be anonymous so that respondents don't know who is actually conducting the study.

To maintain comparability of the results, the questionnaire and other aspects of the research design should remain as stable as possible. For example, questionnaires may need to be modified slightly to remove sponsor identity. Screening questions may need to be added to identify which competitor a particular respondent actually does business with. But the underlying attributes—measurement and scaling, sampling procedure, and so forth—should remain constant.

There are two ways of identifying the sampling frame. For many industrial products, the competitors' customers are known or easily identified. In many cases, a firm's own customers may also buy from a competitor. Thus, existing customers may actually be a good source of competitive data. Former customers that a firm has lost are particularly good at identifying competitive strengths and weaknesses. In all of these cases, the sample frame is identified either from company data and records or from managerial judgment.

When a competitor's customer base is not easily identified, a random sample of customers is often possible. For instance, a bank might randomly survey 1,000 households in a particular town or region. The respondents could be expected to roughly approximate the market share of different banks. This random approach works well for an industry with a high household-penetration rate. For example, most households have bank accounts and own cars, televisions, and stereos. A smaller percentage would have personal computers, answering machines, and power tools. A smaller percentage yet would have CD-ROM hardware, certain types of investments, or custom-tailored clothing. The lower the overall household-penetration rate, the less appropriate the use of a random-sampling, because many potential customers may have to contacted for each usable response.

Regardless of how the sample frame is generated, a sample in the range of 100–200 customers for each competitor should be drawn unless there is a very restricted customer base. Normally, a sample of that size is fairly reliable but not necessarily extremely precise. However, because the objective of competitive benchmarking is to find out how a firm compares with its competitors, 100–200 is normally adequate to yield actionable data.

Once the sample frame and sample size are determined, the next step is to decide whether perceptions or actual experiences are to be measured. If perceptions are desired, a researcher can ask respondents to evaluate two or three or four actual firms, whether they have actually dealt with those firms or not. The subject firm would normally be included in this type of study, as would a small set of competitors. The customer's perceptions can identify very quickly how a firm's image, either overall or based on a set of attributes, compares with the competitors.

If actual experiences are to be evaluated, respondents could rate their current supplier or, if the study desired, rate any suppliers with whom they have experience. By screening of respondents for actual experience, the responses are often more accurate and detailed, but more contacts may have to be made to generate a minimum sample size for each competitor. For this type of study, it is often worthwhile for a firm to include an anonymous sample of its own customers for the sake of consistency. It can also allow a firm to measure the sponsorship effects of its broader CSM program.

Once the data have been gathered, they can be analyzed by any of several statistical techniques to determine whether the differences between competitors are significant. When combined with importance data, areas of competitive strength and weakness quickly emerge. Doing poorly (being rated worse than competitors) in an important area is a competitive weakness that must be corrected quickly. Being rated better than competitors in an important area is a competitive strength that must be maintained. To show how this can be done, the following example has been developed.

The (fictitious) Wonder Corp. operates in an industry that has been dominated by a key competitor, the (fictitious) ABC Co. Because ABC has almost 50% market share compared with Wonder's 20%, the management of Wonder decides to develop a competitive CSM profile. Wonder's management believes that ABC's success has made the latter firm's management a little complacent, and the result has been a slow but gradual increase in market share for Wonder. Wonder is now planning a more aggressive assault on ABC and wants to use the customer's view of competitive strengths and weaknesses to craft a broader strategy.

Wonder's CSM program has been in place for several years now. After several revisions Wonder had developed a pretty reliable CSM model for its key product and customer base (Figure 14.1). Although customers were concerned with many attributes, the specific eighteen in the model were those that had the strongest impact on customer satisfaction. This conclusion had been reached both in focus groups and through statistical analysis using multiple regression.

To link the attributes to Wonder's value-added processes, the twenty-one attributes were grouped into seven categories. These categories roughly approximated key internal processes.

By periodically surveying its own customers, Wonder had developed a clear understanding of what customers thought of Wonder's performance on individual attributes and on the overall categories. Wonder had also determined the customer's view of the relative importance of each attribute and of the overall categories. The results of its last survey are presented in Figure 14.2.

While Wonder had similar data for each attribute, for purposes of simplicity Figure 14.2 includes only the broader categories for simplicity. The vertical axis represents the relative importance of each category to the customer. The horizontal axis represents the customer's view of Wonder's performance in the broader categories. By simultaneously plotting

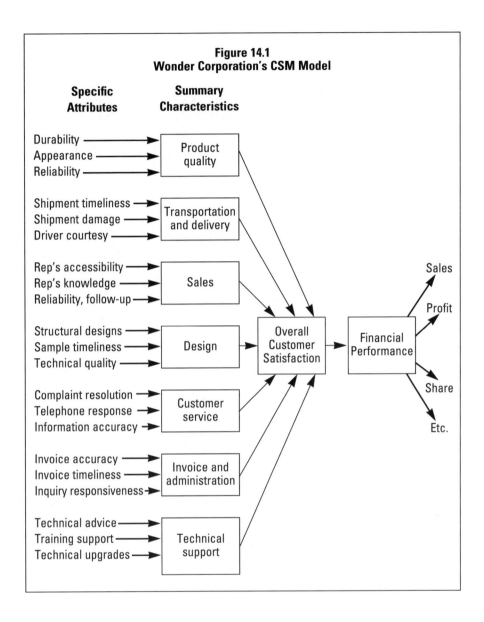

Figure 14.1
Wonder Corporation's CSM Model

importance against performance, each category was positioned on the grid.

The upper right quadrant indicates that the issue was important and Wonder was doing reasonably well. The upper left quadrant indicates that the issue was important to customers but Wonder's performance was lacking. The bottom right quadrant indicates that the issue was of low importance to customers, but Wonder's performance was high. And

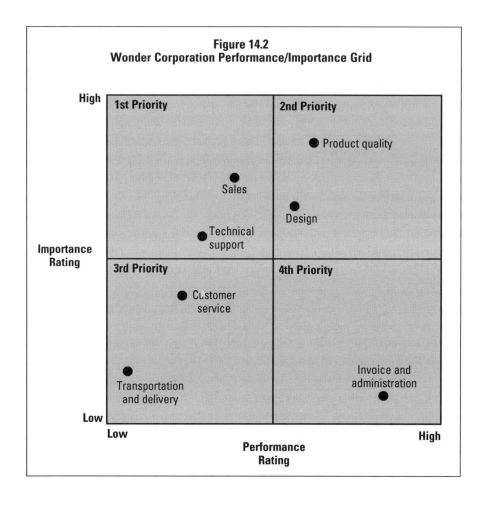

Figure 14.2
Wonder Corporation Performance/Importance Grid

the bottom left quadrant indicates that the issue was of low importance to customers and Wonder's performance was also low.

Wonder had used this grid to identify priorities for improvement. The top left quadrant was the obvious first priority, for the attributes were important to customers, but Wonder's performance in both Sales and Technical Support was rated moderately low. The second priority was given to the categories in the top right, Product Quality and Design, since both had room for improvement. The third-priority issues were Customer Service and Transportation and Delivery. Although these issues weren't terribly pertinent at the time of this analysis, they may be more important in the future and Wonder's performance was certainly not good. For the time being, Invoice and Administration was left alone because this category was the least important and Wonder's performance was relatively good.

While this type of analysis had been very helpful in opening the eyes of many managers and shaking them out of their view that everything was great, something was lacking. Wonder did not know whether it was better or worse than ABC on any of the attributes or categories. Indirectly, ABC's performance would influence customers' perceptions of acceptable performance. But Wonder did not know how ABC was rated by customers on any of the attributes, and it decided to correct that shortcoming.

Since ABC was the market share leader, identifying a sample frame of ABC customers was pretty easy. Wonder identified 600 ABC customers and decided to randomly draw from that pool until a sample of 200 usable responses was attained. To ensure comparability, Wonder also randomly surveyed its own customers until a similar sample size of 200 was reached.

The survey was conducted by telephone and anonymously, so neither Wonder nor ABC customers knew who was conducting the study. The respondents were asked to rate first the importance of the seven categories. This was done by using a 100-point forced allocation approach. Respondents were asked to rate the relative importance of each category by allocating the 100 points among categories based on their perceptions of relative importance. The more important a category, the more points it would get. This process was repeated for each category so that 100 points were allocated among each group of the three or four attributes.

Performance was measured using a 7-point Likert-type scale with the end points labeled Very Poor and Very Good. The higher the score, the better the performance. Respondents were first asked to rate the overall performance of their respective supplier, either ABC or Wonder, on each category. Each respondent then evaluated each attribute individually.

The results of the competitive profile are presented in Table 14.1. The first column lists the seven categories from Wonder's CSM model. The second column gives the mean portion of the 100 points that was allocated based on the relative importance of the seven categories. Product Quality, with a mean of 25, was the most important category followed by Sales, Design, Technical Support, and so forth. Invoice and Administration, with a mean of only 4, was the least important category.

The third column shows the mean competitive difference in performance between Wonder and ABC. A positive-difference figure indicates that Wonder was better than ABC by that magnitude. A negative-difference figure indicates that Wonder was worse than ABC. For example, ABC's mean rating was 4.5 for Product Quality while Wonder's

Table 14.1   Competitive Benchmarking Profile

Category	Mean Importance Weight	Mean Competitive Difference	Strategic Weight	Priority
1. Product Quality	25	+1.0	+25.0	7
2. Transporation and Delivery	6	−1.4	−8.4	4
3. Sales	19	−0.5	−9.5	3
4. Design	18	+1.2	+21.6	6
5. Customer Service	12	−1.2	−14.4	2
6. Invoice and Administration	4	+2.3	+9.2	5
7. Technical Support	16	−1.0	−16.0	1

mean rating was 5.5, resulting in a positive 1.0 difference. This obviously represents a competitive advantage for Wonder. In three of the seven categories, Wonder was rated as better than ABC, but in the remaining four categories Wonder was rated as worse than ABC.

The fourth column is referred to by Wonder as the strategic weight. Wonder management realizes it must somehow integrate the concepts of importance and performance to develop actionable data. Therefore, Wonder multiplies the relative importance figure times the mean competitive difference. This simultaneously integrates the two concepts. The larger the product is, the more it represents a competitive strength. The smaller, or more negative, the product, the more it is a competitive weakness. Wonder's most negative numbers are for Technical Support, Customer Service, and Sales, in that order. This indicates that these three areas must become the first priorities for managerial action (column five).

From the Performance/Importance Grid (Figure 14.2), the order of priority would probably have been Sales, Technical Support, and Customer Service. But when competitive position is considered, the order of priority changes. This logic is based on the old strategic advice that a firm must correct its weaknesses and then build on its strengths.

Wonder repeated this same evaluative process for each attribute. Because the firm did not want to rest on its laurels in those areas where it had a competitive strength, management decided to create a cross-functional, empowered team to improve each attribute. Therefore, the

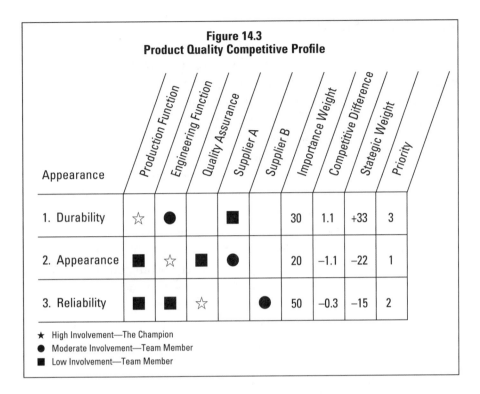

Figure 14.3
Product Quality Competitive Profile

Appearance	Production Function	Engineering Function	Quality Assurance	Supplier A	Supplier B	Importance Weight	Competitive Difference	Stategic Weight	Priority
1. Durability	☆	●		■		30	1.1	+33	3
2. Appearance	■	☆	■	●		20	−1.1	−22	1
3. Reliability	■	■	☆		●	50	−0.3	−15	2

★ High Involvement—The Champion
● Moderate Involvement—Team Member
■ Low Involvement—Team Member

competitive profile data were fed into these teams so the voice of the customer was sure to be heard.

The way Wonder decomposed the broader categories into individual attributes in the area of product quality is shown in Figure 14.3. The attributes of durability, appearance, and reliability contribute to product quality. Reliability is most important followed by durability and appearance in that order. But when competitive position is introduced, appearance becomes the number one priority for the improvement of product quality. Cross-functional teams composed of individuals from production, engineering, quality assurance, and several suppliers jointly worked to develop improvement strategies for each attribute.

Overall, Wonder's management felt that its competitive analysis had been quite useful in pinpointing exactly what needed to be improved and in which order. Unfortunately, this type of competitive profile is relatively costly to produce. In essence a firm is conducting a small CSM program for each competitor, but keeps the data for strategic purposes. An easier and potentially less costly competitive profile consists in comparing a firm's performance with an industry average.

Industry Average Benchmark

There are several ways that an industry average can be generated. In some industries, the major competitors agree to share the cost of one large CSM study, usually conducted by an independent research firm. Each participating firm gets its own data plus an aggregate profile of the entire industry. In some industries an independent firm gathers data and sells various types of output to firms. The J. D. Power survey of customer satisfaction in the automobile industry is an example of this. Another form is the industry group or trade association coordination of a CSM study for an entire industry. This occurs in the pharmaceutical industry. Still another form occurs when a marketing research firm gathers CSM data in several, somewhat similar industries and then sells the results and reports to individual firms. Elrick and Lavidge Marketing Research does this for gas and electric utilities, cable television companies, long-distance telephone carriers, and local telephone companies.

All of these types of industry averages yield an objective, third-party profile of the competitive strengths and weaknesses within an industry. Most of the overall and individual attribute measures are carefully designed and pretested, so the validity and reliability are good. Because of the very large sample sizes, the aggregate measures are usually very precise and have a high confidence level. But there are some problems with these industry average benchmarks.

By their very nature, industry averages tend to focus on broad, general issues that extend across an entire industry. The unique differences that may exist between unique market segments may be lost through aggregation bias, and the broader, general measures may not be as actionable and relevant to a specific firm's value-added processes.

Industry average benchmarks, even when data are provided for a specific firm, are seldom as useful as a firm's own custom-designed CSM program. However, when used as a supplement to a more detailed CSM program, industry average benchmarks do provide a good overall competitive profile. To better understand how these industry average benchmarks work, the Elrick and Lavidge ServQuest II program will be described.

The ServQuest II program consists of a national customer panel of 27,000 households dispersed across the United States. The panel is surveyed once a year to develop a set of service standards for electric and gas utilities, local and long-distance telephone companies, and cable television companies. The specific issues addressed are expectations, importance ratings, performance ratings, satisfaction levels, attitudes and opinions, complaint handling, and lifestyles. The data can be profiled for national, regional, or demographic segments. The ServQuest II program is intended to supplement, not replace, local customer CSM efforts.

To illustrate how the data are developed for utilities, more than 14,000 customers evaluate a nationally dispersed sample of 160 electric utilities. More than 8,000 customers evaluate a sample of more than 100 natural gas utilities. Customers evaluate their own utility on an array of issues such as overall satisfaction, satisfaction with the last transaction, and satisfaction with complaint handling. Customer expectations about installation, transmission quality, repair service, billing, and overall performance are measured.

Customers evaluate the importance and performance levels of fourteen attributes such as no service interruptions, billing accuracy, convenient office locations, friendly employees, and trustworthiness. Therefore, an individual utility could compare how its performance compares with the national average on attributes such as trustworthiness, billing accuracy, or problem solving. It could also compare overall satisfaction levels.

The ServQuest II program also gathers attitudes and opinions on an assortment of broader issues affecting the overall industry. One recent survey had about thirty-five questions dealing with issues such as solar energy, nuclear power, the role of public utility commissions, industry advertising, environmental and health concerns, and union relations. This would allow an individual firm to buy into a broader database than would normally be possible with an individual CSM program.

From that large database, Elrick and Lavidge is able to generate a wide variety of cross tabulations, analyses, and reports depending on the interests of a particular firm. When used as a supplement to a CSM program to compare broad issues, the program is excellent. But the sample sizes for any particular company are small, often fewer than 100, and the demographic criteria may not exactly describe a specific firm's customer base or segments. So a program like this is not a substitute for an individual CSM program.

Although developing a competitive benchmark against key competitors often elicits a more visceral reaction among employees, industry average data are also useful. In both cases, a firm's strategic strengths and weaknesses become more visible, allowing managers to focus more tangibly on improving value-added processes. Developing a specific strategy for process improvement can be greatly enhanced by pursuing the third type of benchmarking, best-in-class.

BEST-IN-CLASS BENCHMARKING

Internal benchmarking is concerned with consistent improvement over some time period, and the primary focus is internal: "How much have we improved?" Competitive benchmarking is an equal blend of internal and external focus: "How are we doing compared with the competition?" Best-in-class (BIC) benchmarking adopts a predominantly external focus by trying to identify the best business practices that exist anywhere: within the same industry, in a different industry, in the United States, or elsewhere in the world.

Ideally, BIC benchmarking is a firm's ongoing process that analyzes the best processes in other organizations with the intent of improving its own processes. BIC is not a one-shot, occasional effort. It is a continuous, ongoing process that attempts to bring new ideas, information, and innovations into the company.

BIC was applied successfully by such firms as Xerox and Motorola in the early 1980s. During the mid-to-late 1980s many other firms such as AT&T, DuPont, Boeing, 3M, IBM–Rochester, and Hewlett-Packard applied the concept. Robert Camp, a Xerox engineer, wrote *Benchmarking: The Search for Industry Best Practices That Lead to Superior Performance* in 1989. Camp described Xerox's benchmarking experiences, and his book has become the standard reference on the subject.

An example of an application for BIC benchmarking occurred in Boise Cascade Corp.'s building products division. In the division's CSM process, customers identified the claims settlement process as having impact on their overall perception of value with Boise Cascade products. The management of the timber group was perplexed for two reasons: The time required to process a claim had overall been reduced two days since the previous survey (internal benchmark), and Boise Cascade had the best claims processing system in the industry (competitive benchmark). What was missing was the final piece. Yes, Boise Cascade had reduced its average claims settlement period from twenty days to eighteen and that is the fastest in the industry. Purchasers, however, are also doing business as consumers in other products and services. We all know how Nordstrom's department stores credit your account immediately when there is a problem. This type of experience on the part of a consumer who is also an industrial purchaser makes an internal or an industry benchmark irrelevant.

More recently, such consulting firms as Price Waterhouse have created benchmarking networks. The most popular networking organization appears to be the International Benchmarking Clearinghouse (IBC), a division of the American Productivity and Quality Center in Houston, Texas. The IBC serves as a sort of repository for best practices by virtue of coordinating networking contacts among members and producing a variety of materials on benchmarking. Before a discussion of the current role of organizations such as IBC, it would be useful to develop some common foundations of BIC benchmarking.

Since best-in-class benchmarking often requires radical organizational change involving the redeployment or reallocation of resources, top management commitment is essential. Some BIC teams waste their time by visiting an operation unless a chief executive officer, president, chief operating officer, or vice president is part of the team. Other organizations assess the benchmarking maturity of the visiting team to see if enough skill is present to make the benchmarking visit worthwhile.

Because benchmarking is oriented toward process improvement, the individuals involved in the implementation of process improvement are usually part of the benchmarking team. One of the measures of benchmarking maturity, in addition to top management commitment, is employee involvement in the change process. The presence of cross-functional, empowered work teams is a common benchmarking characteristic.

A third indication of benchmarking maturity is the presence of a coordinating point or mechanism in an organization. Rather than have three or four different people all attempting to contact the same firm with a request to benchmark, there should be a centralized conduit for both inbound and outbound requests. When a benchmarking visit is completed, a brief summary report over the names of members of the benchmarking team should be collected. Kodak and IBM have all their benchmarking data fed into a database that can be indexed by the firm visited, the practice benchmarked, or the individuals involved.

Another indication of benchmarking maturity is the presence of training and materials. There are a variety of background, internal analyses that should be done before a benchmarking site visit. There are a variety of materials, questions, and questionnaires that should be developed before a site visit. After the site visit there are issues of data analysis, implementation, and communication of the results that need to be addressed. All of these can be improved by training the benchmarking team.

BIC benchmarking should, therefore, have top management commitment, involve an empowered cross-functional team, and be a coordinated organizational effort involving explicit training. Without achieving some degree of benchmarking maturity, the whole effort may be of little value. If that degree of benchmarking maturity does exist, however, then embarking on the benchmarking process can be very fruitful.

Camp described Xerox's benchmarking effort as a ten-step process (see Figure 14.4). The real purpose of the process is to establish goals and objectives consistent with those of world-class firms. Since this method is quite different from the incremental, X% improvement from year to year that most firms use, attaining the goals may require significant organizational stretch, leading to a major reengineering of processes. Motorola, for example, instead of a 10 to 20% reduction in defects, established a 100 times quality improvement goal. This obviously meant rethinking the whole approach to quality.

The ten steps were grouped into the four phases of planning, analysis, integration, and action. Once those initial goals are achieved, a fifth phase, maturity, is also evident.

Planning Phase

The first step is deciding what to benchmark. Virtually any process can be the subject of a benchmarking effort. Some organizations prefer to start with an easily attainable goal that will demonstrate the success of BIC benchmarking. They often select a relatively discrete process, such as order processing or billing, for their initial focus, gradually expanding into more complex, challenging processes. This strategy is sometimes referred to as grabbing the low-hanging fruit.

Some firms, particularly those who were asleep at the wheel and now facing intense competition, start benchmarking the most important, critical processes. These processes are often the most difficult to radically redesign, but because of their importance, usually hold the greatest payoff potential.

Regardless of the specific processes to be benchmarked, some logical coherence and priority should exist in phasing in benchmarking. Suddenly benchmarking forty different processes can lead to utter chaos and frustration in an organization.

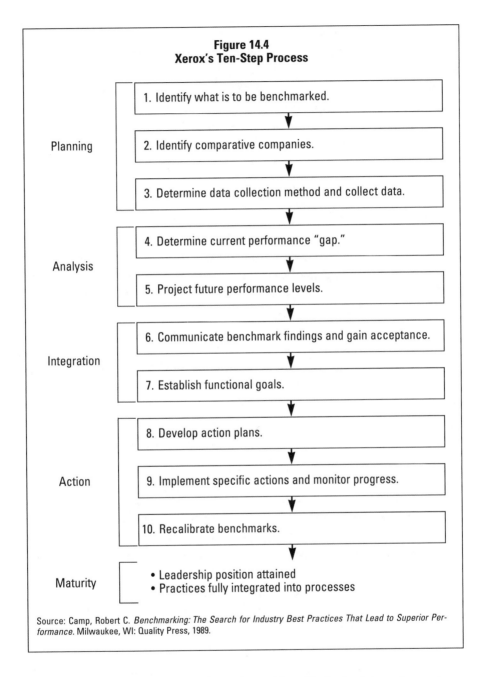

Figure 14.4
Xerox's Ten-Step Process

Planning
1. Identify what is to be benchmarked.
2. Identify comparative companies.
3. Determine data collection method and collect data.

Analysis
4. Determine current performance "gap."
5. Project future performance levels.

Integration
6. Communicate benchmark findings and gain acceptance.
7. Establish functional goals.

Action
8. Develop action plans.
9. Implement specific actions and monitor progress.
10. Recalibrate benchmarks.

Maturity
• Leadership position attained
• Practices fully integrated into processes

Source: Camp, Robert C. *Benchmarking: The Search for Industry Best Practices That Lead to Superior Performance.* Milwaukee, WI: Quality Press, 1989.

Once the target processes have been identified, the second step is to identify which firms are best in class. This is not as hard as it might appear. The business literature is full of firms telling their story. Consulting firms such as Andersen Consulting, A. T. Kearney, Price Waterhouse, and

Arthur Young continually compile databases on who is doing an out-standing job at a particular activity. For firms that are serious about widespread benchmarking, the International Benchmarking Clearing-house gives access to more than 400 innovative firms. In addition, trade associations often compile profiles of the industry leaders.

Individuals in other firms may have studied a particular process. Suppliers and customers can often suggest who is particularly good. Professional organizations such as the Purchasing Management Association or Sales and Marketing Executives can act as coordinating mechanisms.

It is important that a firm look beyond its own industry or even its own country. Studies on sources of innovation show that the best ideas for innovation often come from outside an industry. The motorcycle industry provides an excellent example of this.

The Daytona motorcycle race has traditionally been dominated by multimillion-dollar racing teams from Ducati, Honda, and Suzuki. But the 1994 race was won by John Britten, a New Zealander. Britten built a carbon-fiber frame and body and designed and built a new, more powerful engine in his workshop. He did this mostly in the evenings with the help of a few friends. His idea to use carbon-fiber construction came from New Zealand's Americas Cup competitor, the *Endeavour*. His ideas for engine redesign came from aircraft engines. His motorcycle, a one-of-a-kind prototype, completely outclassed all of the big factory racing teams that tried to get a little better each year. Benchmarking only in the motorcycle industry would never have produced such radical breakthroughs.

The third step is to decide how the data will be collected and then to carry that out. A surprisingly large amount of data can be gathered through secondary, published sources. All of the Malcolm Baldrige award winners have packets of materials available describing how key processes are designed. The award winners are also the subject of numerous videos, conference presentations, articles, and books. All of these can be obtained very quickly and inexpensively.

When such secondary data are lacking, site visits are necessary. Because of the increasing popularity of benchmarking, some best-in-class companies allow visits only on certain days—perhaps once a month and by reservation. Some BIC firms want a reciprocal arrangement with the visiting firms—sort of an I'll-scratch-your-back-and-you-scratch-mine approach. The previously discussed training should take place before a site visit so that the benchmarking team knows what to look for, what kind of questions to ask, and what data to gather.

Analysis Phase

The fourth step is to determine the size of the performance gap. The gap is the difference between the BIC firm and the benchmarking organization. In order to directly compare the two firms, common metrics must be developed. To compare order processing cycle time, for example, a common definition of when an order begins and ends is necessary. Some firms may define the order cycle as beginning with receipt of an order; others as beginning with the customer's communicating or sending it. Some firms may define the end of the order cycle as the shipment of the order; others as the delivery to the customer; still others as ending with the customer's satisfied acceptance. Developing a common metric means ensuring that all data be in comparable form. The size of the current gap indicates how good, or how poor, a firm's processes are.

Once performance gaps have been identified, then next task is to learn why they exist. This means critically evaluating the BIC firm's processes to identify the superior practices. This can often require a very detailed discussion of how and why certain activities are performed in a certain way. Identifying the causes behind the performance gap is one of the most critical steps of the process. The fifth step is the projection of future performance levels, for both the BIC firm and the benchmarking firm. If the goal is to reach a current target and the BIC firm is rapidly improving, a performance gap will always exist. This is especially true if two or three years are necessary to reach the target. Therefore, many firms set a target based on future performance, not current BIC levels. Many find it very enlightening to decompose the factors causing a change in the BIC firm's performance so that the impact of those underlying trends can be examined in the benchmarking firm's industry.

Integration Phase

The integration phase does just what the name implies: the benchmarking findings are integrated into the firm's decision processes. The newly acquired knowledge must be communicated to employees in some fashion. And that new knowledge must be melded into the goal-setting process.

The sixth step is to communicate benchmark findings throughout the organization. This means much more than generating a memo to all employees or writing an article for the company newsletter. Since good communication is always a two-way process, this is best done through face-to-face discussions. Depending upon the process, the discussions should involve all affected organizational functions, so some issues will be communicated widely, and others more narrowly. For the firm to achieve effective buy-in of the results, the presentation of benchmark findings should "sell" why a BIC firm was selected, how its performance compares with others', and how it has designed its processes. It is from this interactive communication that the seventh step flows.

Step seven requires the formulation of functional goals for a process based on the newly acquired knowledge. The most ineffective way to do this is for management to formulate the goals and pass them down to lower levels. The most effective way to do this is to clearly communicate the benchmarking findings and involve employees in the development of the goals.

Because a process can seldom be cloned exactly as it comes from the BIC firm, this step requires the sifting and evaluation of ideas and practices. BIC practices are usually modified to fit the benchmarking firm's corporate culture and underlying technology, but in some cases even BIC practices can be improved. The process of modification often requires that additional, more detailed information be gathered, so a second site visit sometimes occurs at this point.

The key issue at this step is to get high involvement in the goal development process so that employee buy-in and support will be attained. This involvement is enhanced by having influential individuals from a functional area be members of the benchmarking team that gathers the data. This will improve the credibility of the process.

Action Phase

Whereas many of the previous steps certainly required specific actions, the remaining steps are concerned with actually changing the processes. When done properly, these actions flow smoothly from the functional goals. When bungled, this is where resistance to the process emerges.

Step eight requires the translation of functional goals into action plans. Functional goals are concerned with what you are trying to do, identifying a specific target. Action plans are concerned with how the target will be reached. As suggested in the previous step, action plans benefit from active involvement of the affected individuals. The individuals who actually perform the work are usually most capable of determining the how-to aspects of action plans, and harnessing those individuals' creative energy is essential.

Whereas many of the process changes concern how a process is done, some changes may require new technology or capital investment. Because of the financial constraint, formulating action plans is very much an iterative process. If management is serious about making large changes in processes, there should be an equal commitment to making a financial investment.

One important part of this step is to identify and develop the metrics that will be used to assess progress toward the goals. All must be apprised of the way they, individually, and the overall process will be evaluated. In some cases, the metrics can be the same as those used to identify performance gaps; in other cases, new metrics must be developed.

Step nine calls for the actual implementation of action plans. A common first measure takes the form of a training seminar or workshop so that everyone starts from a common platform or understanding of the issues. Then the implementation normally follows the phased-in timetable specified in the action plans. From a managerial standpoint, the problems at this stage are predominantly behavioral.

Employees may have to discard the old way of doing things. The experience and knowledge they have acquired over the years at significant cost and effort may suddenly be of little value. Most people can accept the concept of technological or functional obsolescence of a computer system, a car, or equipment such as a lathe. Much more difficult to accept is the idea that a knowledge base, including that of management, becomes gradually out of data. The implication is that any significant change effort must be accompanied by a heavy dose of training that develops new knowledge and skills.

Progress toward the intermediate goals in the action plan should be monitored at periodic intervals that are far enough apart to allow progress but close enough together to provide good feedback. When possible, the performance evaluation should be done by the employees actually doing the work. For Globe Metallurgical, a Baldrige award winner, this meant putting computer terminals on the shop floor so the employees could have continuous access to production data and perform quality inspections themselves.

The tenth, and last step, covers the periodic recalibration of the benchmark targets. It simply recognizes that in a highly dynamic, competitive environment, continuous improvement is certain. And even the best-in-class practices of today will become obsolete.

If world-class performance has been achieved, then minor tweaking and gradual improvement may be adequate. But if an innovator comes along and builds a revolutionary new motorcycle in his garage, completely outclassing previous state-of-the-art design, a new standard emerges. And in that case, all other firms must start the benchmarking process all over, for John Britten, the New Zealander, will not be satisfied with current design, and he, like any industry leader, will strive to improve and do better next year.

INTERNATIONAL BENCHMARKING CLEARINGHOUSE

A number of consulting firms have specialty areas in benchmarking, and your firm or corporation may be or may already have been asked to participate in a study, usually for a fee. Although such firms do provide resources, probably the best source of information, networking, and resources is the International Benchmarking Clearinghouse.

The vision of the IBC is as follows: "The International Benchmarking Clearinghouse will be the world leader in promoting, facilitating, and improving benchmarking. As a catalyst of national and international benchmarking, the Clearinghouse will help stimulate a significant improvement in the productivity and quality of organizations." The IBC's mission is "to work with members, resource partners, and other organizations to provide benchmarking services as well as continuously improve benchmarking technology."

The IBC is essentially a networking organization that promotes benchmarking. It has a resource library on benchmarking and other quality topics. In addition, as a result of member interest, the IBC formed a special interest group for customer satisfaction measurement; the members meet every quarter for a day of presentations and discussions.

As of January 1995, nearly 400 organizations were members of the IBC. Organizations of all sizes—from 1 to more than 100,000 employees—are members. There are an initiation fee and annual fees. In addition, members can participate in studies and other training activities offered by the American Productivity and Quality Center. The IBC also offers training on benchmarking to assist firms in obtaining information.

BENCHMARKING ETIQUETTE

Regardless of how you obtain information, there is an etiquette to the process. Such companies as Hewlett-Packard and Xerox have had so many requests for benchmarking that they now require written requests giving specific details of the reasons for the benchmarking (Figure 14.5). Also, legal issues, especially with respect to pricing and antitrust, can innocently arise in these sessions.

Because of this, the IBC developed a Code of Conduct (Figure 14.6) that outlines the guiding principles of benchmarking. The code is a good summary of the protocol, expectations, and courtesies in this area.

CHAPTER SUMMARY

Benchmarking is the process of investigating the best practices within a company as a standard of comparison for your own organization. These practices all directly or indirectly affect customer satisfaction. Benchmarking forces you to understand your own internal and external processes and then to compare those process practices and results within your own functional or operational areas in your company, with your competitors, within your entire industry, and, finally, in the global business context. Benchmarking's importance is underscored by its inclusion in the application of the Malcolm Baldrige National Quality Award.

Benchmarking is undertaken for a number of reasons. Probably the two most common ones are to accelerate process improvement efforts and to achieve world-class status. Organizational goals for benchmarking can also include overcoming complacency or promoting breakthroughs. By studying best-in-class or world-class companies and processes, your own company can acquire learning that has the potential to be a catalyst for improving the processes that impact customer satisfaction and ultimately impact business performance.

Benchmarking is a critical component of the customer satisfaction measurement process. Benchmarking allows you to understand where you stand with reference to your firm's previous performance, to the competition, and to best-in-class companies. Benchmarking allows you to identify best practices and continue to improve—all critical for survival in our times. Resources such as the International Benchmarking Clearinghouse can help you in the process.

Figure 14.5
Benchmarking Request

To enhance the effectiveness of your benchmarking exchange, please attach a detailed response to the following categories and questions. The more information you provide, the more likely the organization will be able to respond positively to your request.

1. Goals/purpose/intended use of information or data obtained from benchmarking study.

2. Process/function/area to be benchmarked.

3. Time frame for benchmarking study.

4. Current status or stage of benchmarking study.

5. Targeted industries and/or companies to be benchmarked.

6. What are the key performance metrics associated with this benchmarking study?

7. Other companies/organizations agreeing to participate in benchmarking study.

8. At what stage is the internal analysis of the process being benchmarked?

9. Has the internal process been documented? If so, how? Please attach any process flow diagrams.

10. Has the benchmarking questionnaire been developed? How extensive is it? (copy optional)

11. Please indicate any limits/restrictions on the exchange of information.
    Questionnaire
    Process documentation
    Telephone interview
    Site visit
    • Desired duration of visit
    • Number of participants
    • Preliminary list of names, titles

13. Have all participants signed or are they willing to sign the IBC Code of Conduct and a nondisclosure agreement?

14. Do you require a nondisclosure agreement?

15. The final report/analysis of this benchmarking study will be shared by and with which benchmarking partners?

16. Describe other areas or processes that offer an opportunity for a reciprocal benchmarking study.

17. Do you have a consultant acting as your agent?

For further legal and ethical guidelines regarding benchmarking studies, please refer to the International Benchmarking Clearinghouse Code of Conduct.

Other comments:

Figure 14.6
International Benchmarking Clearinghouse Code of Conduct

Benchmarking—the process of identifying and learning from best practices anywhere in the world—is a powerful tool in the quest for continuous improvement.

To contribute to efficient, effective, and ethical Benchmarking, individuals agree for themselves and their organization to abide by the following principles for Benchmarking with other organizations.

1. Principles of Legality. Avoid discussions or actions that might lead to or imply an interest in restraint of trade: market or customer allocation schemes, price fixing, dealing arrangements, bid rigging, bribery, or misappropriation. Do not discuss costs with competitors if costs are an element of pricing.

2. Principles of Exchange. Be willing to provide the same level of information that you request, in any Benchmarking exchange.

3. Principles of Confidentiality. Treat Benchmarking interchange as something confidential to the individuals and organizations involved. Information obtained must not be communicated outside the partnering organizations without prior consent of participating Benchmarking partners. An organization's participation in a study should not be communicated externally without its permission.

4. Principle of Use. Use information obtained through Benchmarking partnering only for the purpose of improvement of operations within the partnering companies themselves. External use or communication of a Benchmarking partner's name with its data or observed practices requires permission of that partner. Do not, as a consultant or a client, extend one company's Benchmarking study findings to another without the first company's permission.

5. Principle of First Party Contact. Initiate contacts, whenever possible, through a Benchmarking contact designated by the partner company. Obtain mutual agreement with the contact on any hand off of communication or responsibility to other parties.

6. Principle of Third Party Contact. Obtain an individual's permission before providing his or her name in a response to a contact request.

7. Principle of Preparation. Demonstrates commitment to the efficiency and effectiveness of the Benchmarking process with adequate preparation at each process step; particularly at initial partnering contact.

TORONTO STOCK EXCHANGE

Competitive Benchmarking

Competitive benchmarking requires clear identification of the competitors. However, in many cases that is easier said than done. The difficulty is well illustrated by the challenges facing the Toronto Stock Exchange (TSE).

World financial markets have become far more integrated through advances in telecommunications and computer technology. Foreign direct investment, mergers, acquisitions, and alliances by multinational corporations have also increased rapidly. In that turbulent financial environment, TSE had to define its competitors.

First, TSE considered other Canadian exchanges. TSE is the major player in Canada, followed by the Montreal and Vancouver exchanges. But with its big neighbor to the south, TSE thought a broader definition of the competition might be more appropriate.

Therefore, TSE defined the competitive set as all North American exchanges. TSE's market share dropped from 76% to 3.4% by changing the market definition.

But TSE was well aware of the increasingly integrated global investment environment. TSE's market share dropped to 0.9% by using that global competitive set.

The definition of competitors as Canadian or North American or global didn't seem particularly appropriate to the management at TSE. Therefore, TSE redefined its market as Canadian securities. It then determined the volume of Canadian securities being traded on each exchange. By using this definition of the market, four key competitors emerged, which were used in conducting subsequent competitive benchmarking studies.

For some firms, conducting the competitive benchmarking of traditional competitors may not be appropriate. TSE found much more actionable data by redefining its competitive set.

15
Soft CSM

The preceding chapters have concentrated on issues related to the design and implementation of customer satisfaction measurement programs. The primary focus has been on how to measure, gather, and use empirical data in an objective, accurate manner. This chapter examines a somewhat different approach to using the voice of the customer to drive organizational improvement.

A CSM program should generate hard, empirical data that can be used for tracking. The tracking variables are normally those that are linked directly to the firm's value-creating processes. A good CSM program also solicits some verbal or unstructured feedback from customers that can provide additional insights and ideas for improvements and innovations. However, there is a good deal of value to be derived from using a soft approach to CSM as well.

A soft approach is typically a nonquantitative, proactive way to solicit input from customers. It must be proactive, that is, initiated by the supplier, to be a meaningful tool. Responding to a customer's complaint is simply fire fighting. Personal contact can be made through either telephone or personal interviews. However, since phone surveys were covered earlier, this discussion is restricted to personal, face-to-face methods.

OBJECTIVES OF PERSONAL CONTACT

There are many forms of personal contact with customers, but the objectives of the contact are much the same. The general objective is for a firm to get closer to customers. Unfortunately, getting close to customers is an ambiguous concept. By being a bit more specific, a variety of objectives become more apparent.

One consistent objective of personal customer contact is to establish and maintain better long-term supplier-customer relationships. By going through the trouble of making customer contact, the firm sends the implicit, and hopefully explicit, message that the customer is an important, valued asset. If a customer can associate a face with a name or voice, then creating rapport between the supplier and customer is far more likely. Direct interpersonal communication is necessary to establish and maintain this relationship.

Another objective of personal customer contact is to gain a better understanding of the customer's production processes and/or use of the product or service. By better understanding how their products or services are used, suppliers can interpret and respond to customers' needs more effectively. Evaluating a customer's equipment, production processes, quality control systems, training programs, and workforce skills is possible in the context of personal interviews, but is extremely difficult to evaluate by way of survey.

Another objective of personal contact is to determine the customer's future plans, goals, and direction. Although a CSM program will determine current and past performance, such efforts seldom, if ever, give insight into the customer's future needs, including potential uses of substitute products and services. A future change in the customer's products could lead a supplier to invest in new equipment, training of workers in new skills, or even recruiting and hiring new employees. The only way to proactively anticipate a customer's needs is to conduct personal interviews regularly.

Regardless of the exact type of customer contact, these three objectives should be kept in mind: Establishing interpersonal relationships, harmonizing supplier and customer processes, and proactively anticipating customer needs are important to the long-term success of any firm in almost any type of industry. Table 15.1 outlines methods for obtaining customer feedback in three forms: reactive, proactive, and both.

This chapter is divided into three parts. The first part is a discussion of the different types of personal contact. The second is a discussion of issues that must be addressed before initiating the contact. The third part is a discussion of issues to be considered during and immediately after the customer contact.

Table 15.1   Some Methods of Obtaining Data for Customer Satisfaction Measurement

Reactive	Proactive	Other/Both
• 800 number/ customer hot line	• Customer interviews	• Surveys
• Customer service center	• Competitive customer interviews	• Public affairs/ customer service department
• Comment cards	• User labs	• Customer/supplier audits (of company)
• Monitoring return rates	• Partnering meetings	• Benchmarking
• Complaint handling	• Focus groups	• Consortium studies
	• Mystery shoppers	
	• Customer visits	
	• After-installation follow-up	
	• Image research	
	• Adopt-a-customer	

TYPES OF CUSTOMER CONTACT

There are many types of proactive customer contact, and the following list is not intended to be exhaustive. However, it does provide a good sampling of the things that can be done.

Proactive Customer Contact

A proactive approach means that the organization initiates contact with the customer for the purpose of getting advice and input that may not show up on customer satisfaction surveys. A proactive approach means that a firm contacts some of the 90–95% of customers who will never voice complaints or initiate contact. It means that the human touch of customer contact must be integrated throughout a firm's decision-making processes.

The term *customer* is used broadly here and means much more than just the consumers or end users of a product. The term *customer* also includes channel intermediaries such as wholesalers, distributors, and retailers. In many cases, facilitating organizations such as marketing research firms or shipping companies or advertising organizations need to be integrated into the firm's decision-making processes. The philosophy that underlies every aspect of customer integration is that all types of customers are valuable assets or portions of the value-added chain, and they need to be treated accordingly. Customers are not targets; they are assets that must be nurtured and developed.

Some of the types of proactive customer contact are listed in Table 15.1. The type of contact is limited only by the creativity of a particular organization, but these provide a good sample of proactive activities.

Executive Contact

The president of Pepsi-Cola North America, Craig Weatherup, runs a corporation with more than $5 billion in sales annually. Yet he takes time to talk to at least four customers each day. Executives at Procter and Gamble conduct consumer intercepts in grocery stores to interview customers and get their opinions about Procter and Gamble products. Procter and Gamble executives also personally answer customer service phone lines periodically. At Hewlett-Packard, executives are assigned to key clients to maintain regular, open, high-level contact.

The message cascading through these organizations is that the customer is vitally important. If the top management is concerned enough to contact customers, it is probably in the best interest of other managers to do so as well.

Customer Visits

At Motorola and 3M, managers from the chief executive officer (CEO) on down make visits to customers' facilities. Such visits are often conducted by a team of managers who meet not only with executives of the customer firm but also with the actual users of their company's products. These visits often result in written reports that are broadly shared throughout Motorola or 3M. The primary reason for the visits is to get direct feedback about products and ideas for improvement from customers who would never see a customer satisfaction survey or initiate direct contact.

Other companies have pioneered the customer visit concept at the senior levels of the company. The CEO of Porsche spends 25% of his work time with customers—both end users and dealers; you can probably bet that much of the time is spent driving around! At Xerox, senior executives are assigned one or two major account customers, and they serve as champions of those accounts. One day per month, the CEO takes customer calls. Motorola CEO Bob Galvin rediscovered customers during the Baldrige award application process. Galvin visited one customer a month, spending the day on its production floor and in the customer service and accounting departments and talking with all levels of employees. He then wrote extensive trip reports that were communicated throughout the company.

When Diners Club of Argentina saw market share eroding due to increased competition and customer satisfaction, 130 executives were assigned to call 10,000 randomly selected customers to search for delight elements. The result was 50% greater loyalty and a 30% increase in card usage.

Staff managers and vice presidents can often get left out of the customer visit process because such personnel don't usually have direct contact with customer processes. In fact, having the vice president or general counsel of the firm visiting a customer could be perceived as intimidating! What innovative firms are doing in order to include staff officers in customer contact is to have the managers meet with their peers at customer firms. In this way, discussions about practices and issues that concern those managers form the common ground. The vice president of human resources meets with the customer's vice president of human resources, and the two can discuss employee or labor relations; the general counsels from both firms can discuss upcoming legislation and how it will affect their relationship; and the directors of corporate communications can discuss upcoming communication campaigns and get firsthand feedback from each other on positioning. Staff manager visits to customers can therefore provide an unexpected source of both information and organizational strengthening of the customer relationship.

New-Product Development
When Boeing was considering the development of a more fuel efficient aircraft, representatives of eight major customer airlines were involved in the initial-concept discussions. Areas of common concern and unique differences were identified early in the design process. Major suppliers also were involved in the initial-concept discussions to provide ideas and suggestions as well as to learn about the ultimate customer's evolving needs.

When Hewlett-Packard begins development of a new laser printer, key customers are involved from the start. Hewlett-Packard views early customer integration as an important part of cycle-time reduction and improving speed to market. By obtaining customer feedback early in the product design stage, the firm needs less time for test marketing. Design changes are made early in the development process, not after the production begins.

The line between customers and suppliers often becomes very hazy in new product development. General Motors and General Electric often have researchers working at each other's facilities in a joint commitment to continuous improvement.

Beta Sites
For some firms, prototypes are furnished to key customers for trial and feedback. Those beta sites constitute a type of user lab that allows early customer input. Xerox uses this technique to test new products and identify necessary changes before full production begins.

A beta site doesn't have to be highly technical. Some computer firms have customers simply go through the process of uncrating and installing a computer just to find out if the directions are actually read.

Customer Panels
Both Bank of America and Weyerhaeuser have customer panels that meet regularly at corporate headquarters to advise the company how to improve. At Bank of America, the customer group sits onstage in an auditorium, and the managers in the audience ask the customers questions. After these lengthy sessions, the managers develop action plans based on customer preferences.

At Weyerhaeuser, customers and executives meet for four days. The results of the discussions help identify customer needs as well as facilitate the formation of partnerships by identifying common opportunities.

Some firms have found that data from customer satisfaction measurement programs provide an excellent starting point for these discussions. The empirical data often identify issues that need more detailed analysis and discussion. Both Humana Corporation and Marriot Hotels-Resorts use survey data as a starting point for more detailed root-cause-analysis discussions with customers.

Customer Representatives on Internal Teams
IBM invited customers from around the world to join in a top-level strategic-planning conference. The customers were asked to tell what IBM was doing right, wrong, or not at all. Such top-level, face-to-face contact with customers was designed to ensure that the voice of the customer made it to the top level of IBM.

Adopt-a-Customer Programs

Customers should not be restricted to only executive-level contact. Customers could be involved in a variety of cross-functional teams at all organizational levels. Boise Cascade Corp. has a unique program that was initiated at one of its paper mills. Cross-functional teams have adopted specific customers. The teams include individuals from the manufacturing floor, customer service, technical support, sales, and accounting. The team personally addresses any problems or complaints that arise with their adoptee. The team also visits its customer at least once every two years. The customer visits by the team are powerful for both Boise Cascade and the customer. Boise Cascade provides an opportunity for employees at any level of the organization to understand, interact, and satisfy the customer, and the customer sees the commitment that Boise Cascade has made.

PLANNING FOR CUSTOMER CONTACT

Making personal contact with customers is not like phoning an old friend to chat for a while or dropping in on a relative for a visit. Those contacts are highly informal and made on the spur of the moment. Making customer contact should be part of a planned, organized program with clear objectives.

Customer Selection

For industrial customers and channel intermediaries, internal company records should provide a good sample frame. Once the sample frame has been identified, some logical approach to sample selection must be developed. One approach is to randomly select any customer from the sample frame. Random selection has some problems, however.

All customers are not equally profitable. Therefore, a completely random approach may result in a sample that includes overrepresentation of small customers. Such an approach may be acceptable if one person is making contact or if the customers are close geographically. However, if customers are scattered across the country and a team-based contact is used, the resulting costs could be quite high.

Another, and probably a preferable, approach is to segment customers through the use of ABC analysis into three groups. A customers are those that are extremely important to your company's success; B customers are of moderate importance; and C customers are of lesser importance. Depending on the number of customers in each category, a different customer contact program may be developed for each group.

Group A customers may be visited twice a year by a cross-functional team, with more frequent contact made by other individuals, such as the CEO or COO. B-level customers may be visited once a year by a cross-functional team, with additional individual contact made by midlevel managers. C customers may be contacted twice a year by midlevel managers.

Regardless of the importance of each customer, all customers are valuable and should be contacted several times a year. This contact is obviously in addition to sales calls and normal interaction.

When dealing with ultimate consumers rather than organizations, sample selection becomes much more difficult. If your firm deals directly with consumers, as in the banking or insurance industries, company records again provide a sample frame. If you have only indirect contact and a tangible product, then warranty or guarantee registrations make a good sample frame. Otherwise, you may have to use a more random approach such as store intercepts with customers or a large-scale screening survey.

Customer Analysis

Once the sample frame and some logical system to select individual customers have been developed, customer analysis is necessary. This essentially constitutes doing your homework before making actual contact. Again, internal records of customer purchases, complaints, and any interaction must be compiled and then shared by all personnel actually making customer contact.

Customer analysis should include relevant external sources as well. Dun & Bradstreet reports, financial statements, and credit reports can provide insight into the financial stability and strength of customers. The business literature such as *The Wall Street Journal*, *Forbes*, *Business Week*, and *Fortune* may yield data about a firm's strategies, structure, or managerial transitions. These sources can be accessed through the Business Periodicals Index (BPI) in most libraries. In addition, nearly all industries have trade associations that publish material about industry trends or specific firms.

The purpose of the customer analysis, both internal and external, is to learn as much about the customer as possible before the contact. Very often, this analysis raises important questions that can be addressed in personal interviews.

Table 15.2   Possible Agenda Items for Customer Contact

1. Goals of the customer's company in terms of growth, market changes, product modifications, new product introductions
2. Plans for quality improvement, quality goals, supplier alliances
3. Manufacturing process, anticipated process improvement, product and process control systems
4. Cost-control systems and goals, use of activity-based costing
5. Purchasing processes, materials storage and flows, inventory control procedures
6. Education, training, and development programs
7. Finished-product quality control, consumers' expectations, trends
8. Current downstream channels, anticipated changes, distributors, wholesalers, retailers
9. Role of your company's products in the customers' value-added processes
10. The most acute problems and challenges facing your customer due to industry, technology, workforce, or competitive changes

Setting the Agenda

The agenda for personal contact should be a reflection of your program objectives. Your customer contact should not be just an informal discussion of how your products are perceived. A list of possible agenda items are included in Table 15.2. The details depend on the particular situation, however.

The specific agenda should reflect a genuine desire to develop a more thorough understanding of your customers and their individual situation. Everyone who makes customer contact, particularly in the case of a team site visit, should be working from the same agenda and share a common understanding of the goals. A customer contact should not be an attempt to sell products. In fact, any sales effort is likely to destroy the credibility of the customer visit.

Issues Affecting the Customer Interview

Each form of customer contact requires a somewhat different procedure. However, there are a few issues that pertain to all forms of contact and that should be considered. These issues result either from behavioral dimensions of interpersonal interaction or from the potential access to confidential information.

Flexibility

Personal interviews are easily the most flexible way to gather information from customers. However, that flexibility is actually the source of error. If we assume that a detailed agenda has been developed, the interviewer must translate the agenda into a series of questions appropriate to the customer. Since the specific wording of each question influences the customer's response, it is generally advisable to develop specific questions before contacting the customer, particularly when a team approach is used.

A site visit represents a common means of personal contact with business customers and often involves a team. Each team member must know not only the specific wording of each question but also who will ask it and who the preferred respondent will be. The same question asked of a purchasing manager, a production manager, a worker on the assembly line, and a COO could result in four distinctly different answers. Therefore, the actual customer interview should be planned as carefully as possible to elicit unbiased, accurate information.

Respondent Motivation

The mere fact that customer contact is taking place can influence responses. On one end of the continuum, a customer or customer organization may grudgingly agree to a visit, even though it would prefer not to do so. The customer may see the visit as an imposition and a waste of time and simply pay lip service to the interviewer.

On the other end of the continuum is the customer who welcomes the contact enthusiastically and wants to establish supplier partnerships or alliances. In these two extreme situations, vastly different responses from the customer could be expected.

On a more personal level, respondents may filter their responses so that contact personnel hear what the respondent thinks they want to hear. The customer in face-to-face interviews may feel motivated to tell a supplier that the products are OK when in fact they are not.

The implication is that interviewers must be sensitive to the customer's motivation and try to determine the impact on responses. Normally, responses are improved when customers are fully informed that the primary purpose of the contact is to identify areas for supplier improvement.

Time Considerations

Scheduling and interview length are the primary time considerations that must be addressed, particularly when dealing with business customers. Most customers feel that time is a very valuable, scarce commodity, and they are unwilling to waste it. Therefore, each customer contact, or contribution of time, must be viewed as a valuable asset and used wisely.

Since most businesses have significant variations in production levels throughout a year, a month, or even a week, customer contact should be scheduled for slack periods. Otherwise, managers may be hesitant to cooperate. On one customer site visit, the interviewers were warned not to talk to employees and to watch out for forklifts because everyone was pushing to catch up on a severe back-order situation. This customer site visit should probably have been rescheduled for a more convenient and appropriate time so that more meaningful results could be obtained.

The duration of the customer interview obviously depends on the specific situation. In a store intercept of consumers, anything beyond five minutes will probably result in customer impatience. In a customer site visit, an hour-long interview with a manager may be acceptable, but you might get only five minutes with assembly line workers while they are performing their regular tasks.

A significant advantage of personal interviews is that customer impatience can be visually observed, and the interviewer can reassure the respondent of the importance of the information or move quickly to the most important agenda items.

Ethical Issues

If customers are willing to share confidential information about their current operations or future plans, a variety of ethical and legal issues arise. As a general rule, all information gathered in personal contact with customers should be treated as strictly confidential and not shared with any other businesses. In large firms, this can be a significant problem.

Hewlett-Packard's laser-jet printers have been extremely successful, and sales volume has been much greater than predicted by initial forecasts, in fact into the billions of dollars. HP is heavily dependent upon Canon—a major supplier *and* a competitor—for component parts. Because of the heavy dependency, HP as a customer had to share information with Canon regarding technological breakthroughs in successive generations of the printers. Canon needed the information so that the architecture of components would be compatible with HP's new designs.

Unfortunately, the technological advances originated by HP gradually made their way to the R&D efforts in Canon's printer division. HP's new competitive advantages were soon being designed into Canon's laser printers before the HP products were on the market. When HP found out and complained to Canon's CEO, the CEO immediately stopped the use of the HP breakthroughs. Although Canon's CEO acted appropriately, controlling the use of proprietary information in a large organization can be a significant ethical issue.

CONDUCTING THE CUSTOMER INTERVIEW

With all of the preceding information as background, preparation for the actual visit must be done. Obtaining background information from your company's database or record file can facilitate the actual meeting. A customer profile sheet as shown in Figure 15.1 is a useful tool. This customer profile sheet has spaces for information to be completed prior to the interview, which provides the interviewer with an overview of the customer's business, decision influencers, locations, competitive influence, strategic selling plans, product mix, and account strengths and weaknesses. It also has a place for directions to the customer's facility from the nearest airport! This form is invaluable for managers or company visitors at any level, and it sets the stage for a beneficial, professional meeting. In some companies, all of this information is in a database that is kept up-to-date and can be printed out immediately before a customer visit is made.

Summary Report

When each customer contact is completed, whether by an individual or by a team, a summary of the interviews should be completed that captures all relevant information. The report should be produced as soon as possible after the interview, preferably within an hour. If a team contact, all team members should meet and discuss their impression and ideas and capture those ideas in writing. If your company uses a computer system, the information should be put directly into the computer. If you have e-mail within your company, copies of the summary report or a brief overview can be shared with others.

Figure 15.1
Customer Profile

_____
Revision Date

Customer Name   Ownership

Address   Business Focus

Phone   Fax

Decision Influencers

Name and Title	Motivation				Critical Concerns			
	Security	Affiliation	Power	Actualization	Performance	Price	New Ideas	Relationships

Other Customer Locations

Location	Main Contacts		Location	Main Contacts
1)		6)		
2)		7)		
3)		8)		
4)		9)		
5)		10)		

Sales Rep   Customer Service Rep

Location   Phone   Location   Phone

National Account Reponsibilities

Point Person   Specific Responsibilities

Directions from the Airport

_____

_____

_____

Approximate Driving Time _____

Figure 15.1 *continued*
Customer Profile

Competitive Influence

Company	Share	Volume per Month	Warehouse Service Program	Activities/Reputation

Strategic Selling Outline

Stage of Buyer/Seller Relationship _____

Description of that Relationship _____

Assessment of Current Situation _____

Problems	Opportunities
1)	1)
2)	2)
3)	3)

What, if any, significant changes have taken place recently? _____

Overall Objective of Executive Visit _____

It is particularly important to identify all the action points that came up in the interview. These are usually requests by customers for additional information. Swift response to such requests creates a positive image.

The summary report should become part of that customer's data file so that subsequent contacts can build upon earlier conclusions. When appropriate, the reports can be shared with cross-functional improvement teams in the same manner as the empirical customer satisfaction data are shared

CHAPTER SUMMARY

The soft side of customer satisfaction is an important component of the overall customer satisfaction management process. Quantitative data resulting from the measurement phase can be used as an entrée into the emerging issues that tend to be more qualitative. Soft methods such as personal contact create the opportunity to personally know the customer and obtain information that is otherwise difficult to elicit. For most companies, more organizational ownership of CSM can be obtained by recognizing the softer side.

Clearly, a proactive approach to customer contact is the best. Reactive approaches, however, aren't necessarily bad. A reactive approach can at least help you get back on track. It is important that individuals from all levels in your organization, from CEO to frontline, make customer visits to learn how to empathize with the customer. Customers are the ones who usually create the catalyst for new product development, and they are often more than willing to be involved with beta testing of your products, to become a member of customer panels, or to act as a representative on your internal teams. Sometimes all you have to do is ask!

Planning for customer contact is important. It is necessary that the meeting be professional and beneficial for both parties. By taking the time to plan, you will efficiently utilize both your time and your customer's, and you will also impress the customer with your knowledge and abilities. With all of the recent downsizing in all industries, workloads have increased so time has become an especially precious element.

Summarizing and communicating the findings of the visit are critical. The information you obtain will ultimately help prepare for the next visit. If you develop a database or communication process, the shared information becomes a valuable tool for your entire organization.

INTUIT, INC.

Soft CSM in Software

Intuit, Inc., is the financial software company that produces Quicken, the incredibly successful personal and small business financial software program. Intuit was started from a home desktop in 1983 and is now a $228-million company that sells six times the number of programs that its nearest competitor sells.

CEO Scott Cook has used a number of soft CSM techniques in his business. For example, he focuses not on the activities of his competition but on the needs of his current customers and prospective customers. A number of years ago, Intuit implemented its Follow Me Home program. The program worked as follows: When a customer purchased the Quicken program in the San Francisco Bay area (which is where Intuit is headquartered), the outside of the package had a card that asked whether the customer would be willing to let an Intuit engineer witness the initial use of the software. An incentive was offered to the participant. If the participant wanted to take advantage of the offer, an appointment was scheduled for a product engineer to go to the customer's home or place of business and witness the entire process, from opening the package, loading the software, setting up accounts, and filling in financial data. The process engineer was trained to watch and take notes only and not advise or offer to drive the computer. This actual customer contact was a turning point for the organization. The feedback that sales and marketing had given to the product engineers was usually substantiated when engineers saw how average folks dealt with the product and the directions.

After the success of the Follow Me Home program, other programs were developed in the company. Intuit has an individual who categorizes comments and concerns gleaned by the help desk. A computer program is used to analyze for recurring themes. Soft CSM techniques have allowed a small, entrepreneurial business to reap the rewards of being what could be called a customer fanatic.

16
Multinational Issues

A new firm, excited about research opportunities in the former Soviet Union, decided to undertake a marketing research study. The firm's two entrepreneurs developed a mail questionnaire with an attractive incentive. They spent a lot of time and money in the development of their instrument and then proceeded to have the envelopes printed. Of course, they followed the standard U.S. practice of placing the addressee's name and address in the middle of the front of the envelope and the return address of their firm in the upper left corner of the envelope. They took the thousands of envelopes to the post office, paid the postage, and then waited. One week. Two weeks. Three weeks. They began to wonder what had happened. They started checking and found that no one had received the survey. At the beginning of week six, the post office delivered to the entrepreneurs four boxes of their unopened surveys. The two couldn't understand why all of the envelopes were returned. Upon investigation they found out that in the former Soviet Union, the mailing address is placed in the upper left corner of the envelope. So, when the surveys got to Moscow, they were sorted and sent right back (but not by airmail!).

Like marketing research, a CSM program developed for use in the United States cannot simply be administered in other countries. While CSM programs with industrial customers are more transferable than CSM programs that focus on consumers, all programs require some modifications. The primary reasons for this are cultural divergence and differences in infrastructure.

339

Cultural differences influence most aspects of the research design in some way. The attributes of importance to customers in parts of Asia may be different from attributes important in the United States or Europe. Data-gathering techniques in Africa are significantly different from those used in Europe. Due to the importance of interpersonal relationships in Japan, phone and mail surveys have much lower response rates and lower levels of reliability than in the United States. Question wording and scaling techniques are frequently culturally bound, and what is appropriate in the United States may not be appropriate elsewhere in the world. Many households outside the United States are composed of extended families, so identifying the correct respondent is more difficult.

In addition to cultural issues, infrastructure variances require modification of CSM programs. Mail and telephone systems in particular are divergent in many countries. Secondary lists for mail surveys are difficult to obtain, and telephone surveys often result in more sample bias.

Generally, cross-cultural CSM requires that separate programs be developed for each country. This chapter explores the primary issues that relate to multinational CSM research based on personal experiences conducted with numerous large international research projects and cross-cultural comparisons of marketing research in six different countries.

GENERAL ISSUES

Approximately 70% of the world's gross domestic product (GDP) is produced by the ten largest economies. Collectively, the forty largest economies control well over 80% of the world's GDP. The result is that most foreign direct investment (productive assets located in other countries) and over 70% of all world trade takes place among industrialized economies.

The implication is that most international CSM research takes place within an industrialized economy of some type. As of this point in time, very little CSM research is done in Africa, the Middle East, South America, Latin America, or large portions of Asia. But even within industrialized countries, a tremendous amount of cross-cultural variation exists.

There are a variety of general issues that are relevant regardless of where the CSM research is conducted. These issues are research quality, cultural diversity, the appropriate unit of analysis, who conducts the research, the infrastructure, and costs.

Research Quality

A researcher must decide on the appropriate quality of international CSM data. This is normally referred to as equivalence. Complete equivalence means that the results of domestic and international research are exactly comparable. To achieve a high degree of equivalence, the concepts underlying the questions, the accuracy of measurement and scaling, sampling procedures, and many other activities or assumptions must be cross-culturally transferable. Since this is seldom the case, the researcher must decide on how comparable the CSM results must be.

If a multinational firm implements a CSM program within a country and the results are used only within that country, equivalence is not an issue. But if a firm wishes to compare customer satisfaction data across several countries, equivalence becomes the predominant consideration.

American Express conducts three types of cross-cultural CSM research projects. One of the three is a cross-border study, which measures cardholder satisfaction when the American Express card is used outside the home country in one of twelve destination markets. The home, or origin, countries surveyed are the United States, Canada, the United Kingdom, Germany, Japan, and Australia. The study requires 3,000 respondents to complete a twenty-minute phone interview and is conducted once a year. To ensure a high degree of equivalence, each interviewer uses virtually identical questions, adjusted for linguistic differences in Germany and Japan. By stressing high equivalence, the database serves as a base of comparison for individual studies that may be conducted periodically in other countries. Because this study serves as a benchmark, a good deal of care must be taken to ensure cross-cultural equivalence and high research quality.

Cultural Diversity

Greater diversity exists internationally in most aspects of the business environment. Foreign operations may be joint ventures rather than wholly owned subsidiaries. Foreign workforces may be ethnically and demographically more diverse than U.S. operations. Some products may be slightly (or significantly in some cases) modified to adapt to the foreign market. Each of these issues could require changes in the design of a CSM program.

The external environment is even more diverse. A wider array of political economic, and sociocultural variables must be considered. Income levels vary from country to country, and dramatic differences even exist within countries. The average per capita income in China's Guandong

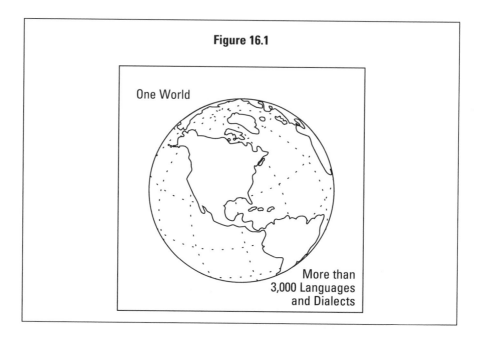

Figure 16.1

One World

More than
3,000 Languages
and Dialects

province, near Hong Kong, is several times the per capita income in other provinces. Although literacy rates are high in most industrial countries, linguistic homogeneity is not. Many European countries have two, three, or four official languages. In China, there are six major versions of Mandarin Chinese and many more local dialects, some so different they are incomprehensible to those from another area. In India, there is one official language, Hindi, but nearly 200 regional or local languages loosely derived from Hindi. Within Russia, there are more than thirty different languages spoken as first languages in the home. Deciding the appropriate language or dialect to use for CSM research can be quite challenging. Figure 16.1 illustrates the complexity of multiple languages in one global environment.

Within countries there are often very large geographic differences in culture. In Spain, the Basques' culture is quite different from the Spaniards'. In Canada, French Canadians are quite different culturally from western Canadians. Even within a relatively small country such as Switzerland, there are significant differences between the French, German, Italian, and Swiss subcultures. In Malaysia, the Malay, Chinese, and Indians each have different subcultures.

Although economic, demographic, and cultural differences may not be a problem for some CSM studies, such diversity certainly presents some challenges for research design. It may be necessary to have several questionnaires and multilingual interviewers to carry out a CSM study in just one country. In many cases nine or ten questionnaires and languages may be necessary to survey three adjoining countries. It is simply not a case of one questionnaire per country.

Unit of Analysis

In some situations, the appropriate unit of analysis may be regional such as the European Community, or North America, or Latin America. Or the appropriate unit of analysis may be a market segment that cuts across an entire region. A nation is the most common unit of analysis, but different subcultures or geographic areas are also used as units of analysis.

The smaller and more discrete the unit of analysis selected, the more expensive a CSM program becomes. The more specialized CSM programs are often more accurate because they are customized to fit a particular group of respondents, but the process of customization is costly. The same steps of the research design process must be repeated for each unit.

Who Conducts the Research?

A cross-cultural CSM study could be either conducted internally or contracted out to a research firm as shown in Figure 16.2. Both alternatives present some thorny research issues.

A CSM program conducted internally could be centrally facilitated from corporate headquarters. The assumption here is that corporate CSM experts are aware of all the possible cross-cultural nuances and are capable of making the necessary adaptations. A centralized program typically ensures greater consistency in methodology. A centralized approach also greatly increases the potential for cross-cultural equivalence. A highly centralized CSM program reduces the likelihood of local (foreign) buy-in to the results because locals weren't involved in design issues.

A CSM program could be decentralized to the local foreign operating level. The range of control could allow a local foreign unit to develop its own unique CSM program. Or the local program could be standardized against specific corporate guidelines. Highly decentralized programs allow for extensive adaptation to fit local needs. But as the adaptation increases, the compatibility, or cross-cultural equivalence, with CSM data from other countries decreases. This obviously reduces the organi-

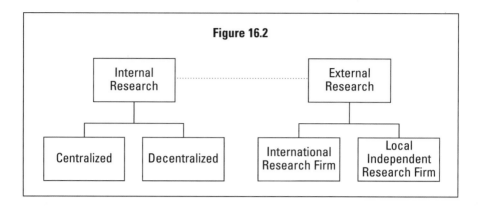

zation's ability to compare various international units. Some firms that pursue this approach send a CSM expert from headquarters around to the different operating units as a coach or internal consultant to provide conceptual and methodological consistency.

When the CSM program is contracted to an outside firm, there are again two major alternatives. One option is to contract with an international research firm that has offices in all countries of interest. The research firm could then standardize the program as much as possible, allowing for local differences. Or the research firm could have each country office develop a separate CSM program based on certain guidelines. An international research firm should possess much more detailed knowledge of unique research differences in each country than corporate staff can. Hiring such specialized expertise is often quite costly, however.

The other option is to allow each local operation to hire a local independent research firm. This allows a good deal of adaptation and also creates goodwill, since a local supplier is being used. Firms pursuing this strategy often have a headquarters CSM expert involved as a liaison, again to increase conceptual and methodological consistency. The problems that arise with this approach are that the overall costs tend to be higher, cross-cultural equivalence is lower, and high variability in the quality of research firms is common from country to country.

Probably the most common approach is for a corporate headquarters to develop some specific guidelines that ensure reasonable cross-cultural equivalence and then to allow local operations to adapt by adding customized questions. This typically requires the use of corporate CSM experts who travel periodically to each local operation to assist in research design and implementation.

Research Infrastructure

Research infrastructure refers to such issues as availability of research firms, interviewers, or telephone and mail systems. Although the research infrastructure is fairly consistent in the advanced industrialized economics, it is partially or completely lacking in many newly industrialized and most of the less-developed countries.

In Seoul, South Korea, recently there were only three marketing research firms listed in the phone book. And all were small management consulting firms that lacked skill in conducting high-quality primary research. In most of the East European countries, the postal system is slow and unreliable when it exists at all and the phone system isn't much better. Even in Mexico, couriers are often used in lieu of a postal system.

When conducting CSM research in foreign countries, a firm must often recruit, hire, and train the interviewers to do the fieldwork. This obviously lengthens the time to complete a project as well as increases the costs.

The research infrastructure is generally consistent and reliable in the twenty to twenty-five most advanced industrial economies. Beyond that, rapid decline in infrastructure quality normally results in significant modifications to the research design. Therefore, cross-cultural equivalence is much more difficult to achieve in nonindustrialized economies.

Costs

Although research infrastructure is fairly consistent across industrialized countries, the cost of research is not. Total research costs are usually 70–100% higher in Japan than in the United States. Research costs in Europe are normally 30–50% higher than in the United States, depending on the country. Research costs in Australia and New Zealand are usually 10–20% lower. Research costs in Mexico, Brazil, and Argentina are only about 30–40% of U.S. costs. So the total costs to conduct a sample of 1,000 could easily vary by 200–400% depending on the countries involved.

Fluctuations in foreign exchange rates can cause changes in research costs, also. As the Korean won has strengthened against the U.S. dollar, research costs have gone up considerably, much as they have in Japan and Germany. The same, or even a slightly larger, research budget may result in a progressively smaller sample size each year.

Because sample size has little to do with the size of a country, CSM costs, as a percentage of sales, can fluctuate considerably from country to country. A small market, such as Switzerland, with its several distinct linguistic and subcultural groupings, could have a high cost per respondent, often many times that of U.S. levels.

The general issues of desired research quality, greater international diversity, who conducts the research, research infrastructure, and costs influence the overall design of an international CSM program. Dealing with these broad issues can present quite a managerial challenge. But there is also a wide array of more specific issues that must be considered at each stage of the research process, from clarifying the objectives to data analysis.

SPECIFIC CONSIDERATIONS

The more specific issues that must be considered are discussed in roughly the order that they would be encountered. But, as noted earlier in this book, designing a CSM program remains very much an iterative process. Issues often emerge at a later sequential stage that cause the researcher to go back and modify an earlier decision.

Objectives

The first, and possibly most important, issue is modification of the firm's CSM research objectives. If the objectives of international CSM research are oriented primarily toward continuous improvement of local operations, then research design can be more flexible and adaptable. The whole CSM program can be customized to fit the needs of the local managers. Cross-cultural equivalence becomes only a minor consideration.

But if the objective of the international CSM program is to facilitate comparison of various local operations or to compare foreign and domestic operations, then a highly standardized CSM program becomes essential. And cross-cultural equivalence becomes the dominant consideration.

So the first issue that management must wrestle with is why the international research is being conducted. If management wants to compare customer attitudes across countries to determine what product and service characteristics can be standardized, then cross-cultural equivalence is important. If management wants to compare customer satisfaction levels across countries to determine the relative effectiveness of various operations, then cross-cultural equivalence is important. Since most corporate headquarters want to be able to make cross-cultural comparisons of some type, achieving a moderate to high level of equivalence is necessary. For the remainder of this section, therefore, the assumption is made that such equivalence is an important issue.

Identification of the Attributes

Firms operating in or selling their products in various countries often assume that all customers value the same product attributes equally. The implicit assumption underlying an American Express cross-border study was that the same attributes contributed to customer satisfaction regardless of whether the customer was American, British, Canadian, Australian, German, or Japanese. Such an assumption may or may not be valid.

Renault, the French auto manufacturer, found that it had to stress different attributes in different countries due to cultural differences. Italians were concerned most with road handling. Germans were concerned with performance, technical features, engine power, braking ability, and, as anyone who has driven in Germany would guess, speed capability. In Sweden, safety attributes such as braking, seat belts, passenger safety, crash test results, and strength of windshield glass were important. So for each of those three countries, customers placed predominant importance on different product attributes for the same model of car.

Although Coke is a highly standardized product around the world, it is consumed differently in various countries. In many parts of Asia Coke is consumed warm or, at best, slightly cooled. Thus, finding a cold Coke in China is difficult. The differences in temperature may change the attribute mix for customers, for warm Coke tends to "fizz" in the mouth.

Because it is common for attributes to vary in importance across countries, a firm must use qualitative research techniques in each individual country to confirm that the attributes are cross-culturally transferable. This means conducting both depth interviews and focus groups.

Skilled interviewers are critical to the success of both depth interviews and focus groups. Generally, interviewers should be from the local culture so that they have a high degree of cultural awareness. But experienced interviewers are often scarce in developing and less developed countries, so they may need special training.

Internationally, the focus group moderator must be sensitive to both verbal cues and nonverbal cues such as gestures, tone, and expressions. In some countries respondents may be hesitant to discuss personal motives and attitudes or to voice an opinion divergent from the group. This is the case especially in Japan, for example, among older respondents, who tend to acquiesce to group norms. Even something like eye contact can have an impact. In the United States, eye contact indicates assertiveness; in some Asian and Hispanic groups, it indicates aggression. In some Middle Eastern cultures, averting the eyes indicates deception. In some countries ethnic composition can become a significant concern in setting up a focus group. In some countries, such as Indonesia, the person moderating the focus group or conducting the interview must be of the same social level or caste as the interviewee.

Once the attributes are cross-culturally transferable, then the questions must be translated to the new language. If new attributes are identified, then new questions must be developed. In either case, the next step, questionnaire design, introduces many cross-cultural issues.

Questionnaire Design

All aspects of a questionnaire must be reconsidered in an international context. Too often the cover letter, introduction, directions, and routings are neglected. Also neglected occasionally is the fact that measurement scales are not uniformly transferable. And, of course, the questions themselves must be scrutinized.

One of the first issues normally addressed in cross-cultural CSM is the formal equivalence of the questionnaire; other materials are addressed when appropriate. A U.S.-based questionnaire written in English must be translated into the appropriate foreign language. Correctly translating an English word to the same word in, say, French or German is formal equivalence. The technique for checking formal equivalence is back translation, which uses different bilingual individuals to translate that French or German questionnaire back into English. If the translated questionnaire ends up the same as the original, formal equivalence has been achieved.

But formal equivalence is quite different from functional equivalence. Functional equivalence is achieved when the concept underlying a question, phrase, or scale is accurately transferred to another language. In some cases it may be necessary to lose formal equivalence in order to achieve functional equivalence. For example, even in English, some words do not travel well, as shown in Figure 16.3. An American airline passenger may be concerned with a "clean bathroom" or a "clean rest room." The functional equivalence may be a "tidy loo" in England, or a "tidy toilet" in New Zealand or Australia, or a "sanitary water closet" in some Asian countries. The words for home, house, household, and family often don't transfer well.

Figure 16.3
Which Is Correct?

American English	British English	Antipodean English	Asian English
Rest room	Loo	Toilet	Water closet

An American carmaker may be concerned whether customers want more trunk space. But the trunk is called the boot in most other English-speaking countries. The car hood is called the bonnet, the windshield is a wind screen, a flashlight is a torch, and sometimes car headlights are also torches in other English-speaking countries.

It just wouldn't occur to most U.S. CSM researchers to translate their questionnaire from American English to Australian or British English. The assumption is made that formal equivalence is the same as functional equivalence. This assumption is obviously not always accurate.

Now, when we add the idea of *linguistic* functional equivalence, we are trying to determine whether questions are conceptually equivalent from one language to another. Conceptual equivalence requires that the meaning of a question be the same for all respondents across all cultures. In the United States, the concept of reliability may mean a long-lasting product. In Mexico, reliability may mean the seller is available if the product breaks down. In France, reliability may be generalized into a corporate image of trustworthiness. In this case, *reliability* lacks conceptual equivalence. Therefore, the responses are not comparable in any way because in each country a different concept is being measured.

Even if a question is conceptually equivalent across several cultures, the salience, or importance, of each attribute is not. As we saw with the earlier Renault example, the relative importance of product attributes varied considerably. The implication is that the overall CSM model will vary not only in the composition of attributes but in the relative importance of each attribute as well.

The measurement and scaling of responses also raises issue of conceptual equivalence. Respondents from different countries may consistently respond differently, even when their underlying attitudes are essentially the same. Americans and Germans are far more likely to mark extreme points on a scale than are Koreans, Chinese, Japanese, or Eng-

Figure 16.4
Scaling Differences

	Poor				Excellent
United States	1	2	3	4	5

	Poor				Excellent
Germany	5	4	3	2	1

lish. Additionally, scaling differences in terms of order are striking between Americans and Germans, as shown in Figure 16.4. The Chinese in Malaysia tend to offer more positive responses than Malays or Indians. The French tend to respond more positively than the British. The proportion of respondents checking a don't-know response category often varies considerably from one country to another.

These differences in responses can be caused by respondent acquiescence and social desirability bias. Asian cultures are far more likely to exhibit acquiescence than Western cultures. In Asian countries, respondents tend to respond in a manner intended to please the researcher. This tends to greatly reduce the incidence of negative responses. When this idea combines with the tendency to not mark extreme points, responses may cluster on the positive end of the scale and be very consistent.

Social desirability bias occurs when respondents respond the way cultural values suggest people should respond. Individuals in Western societies *should* respond that environmental concerns are important. Fuel efficient cars *should* be important. Recyclable products *should* be good. Toys *should* be safe and encourage the "right" values. But the behavior of individuals may be significantly different from the attitudes expressed. Customers may consider only price and a few product characteristics and forget all about environmental issues when buying a product. Customers told Heinz that dolphin safe was an important product attribute, but few customers considered the issue when actually buying a can of tuna.

The effect of a lack of equivalence in measurement and scaling means that the mean responses will be distorted or biased in some way. The same mean response will mean different things in different countries, making accurate cross-cultural comparisons impossible. Perhaps 90% of

Japanese respondents responded as satisfied or very satisfied and 85% of U.S. respondents checked the same categories. The U.S. respondents could very possibly be more satisfied than Japanese respondents, but an acquiescence tendency skewed the responses of Japanese. Thus, the Japanese results mean something different from the U.S. results.

Making the assumption that conceptual equivalence exists for all aspects of a CSM questionnaire is quite risky. Therefore, firms are urged to exercise care in making detailed cross-cultural comparisons until equivalence has been established.

The safest approach to questionnaire design is to assume that functional and conceptual equivalence are lacking. Then in focus group discussions, each aspect of the cover letter, introduction, question wording, scaling, and so forth should be checked for functional equivalence. From those focus group discussions should emerge a questionnaire that is ready for pretesting.

Pretesting

Whereas pretesting is essential in domestic CSM studies, it is even more important in cross-cultural studies. The pretest should follow the guidelines suggested in a previous chapter. As you might guess, however, the pretest should also address the equivalence problem.

This is normally addressed by debriefing the respondent in detail. An interviewer would ask a respondent the meaning of each question, why the respondent responded in the particular way, what a specific response category meant, and so forth. The key issue is to try to establish whether the respondent's interpretation of meaning is the same as that of respondents in other countries or even in the same country. This debriefing should begin with the cover letter or introduction and address every aspect of the questionnaire.

For large multinational corporations, it is often helpful to have persons from various countries meet and individually go over the pretest results. This normally highlights very quickly the commonalities and differences that must be addressed to establish equivalence.

Sampling

As in domestic studies, the sample used in the CSM research should be representative of the entire customer base. If the target markets are the same from one country to another, then drawing a random sample should yield roughly comparable results. But if the markets are systematically or randomly different from country to country, the CSM results will not be comparable. Hence, a researcher must be concerned only with all those issues influencing representativeness, but must also be concerned with the degree of comparability in the sample.

American Express conducts its cross-border study in six countries. If the average customer is hypothetically 45 years old, and college educated, with a mean income of $47,000 in the United States, and 52 years old, with some college education and a mean income of $35,000 in Australia, the comparability of the sample would have to be questioned based on variation in age, education, and income. The sample in each country may be very representative of the customer base in that country but lack comparability to other countries.

Additionally, in many cases the foreign target market may be quite different. In some cultures, most food and household items are purchased by a maid rather than a family member. Likewise, the actual user of products could be a maid, housekeeper, or gardener instead of the purchaser of the products. Organizationally, purchasing, engineering, and quality assurance may be centrally involved in the purchase and postpurchase evaluation of products in the United States. In Europe or Japan, a different mix of individuals may perform the same role. Since each person brings a unique set of attitudes based on individual background and experiences, the different composition of the buying center would likely produce different results. These issues would present comparability problems and reduce cross-cultural equivalence.

The sample size issue is a problem internationally as well. Because of the greater diversity of customers in foreign markets, the variance within a population is often greater for various satisfaction measures. If a firm chooses equal samples sizes in four countries and the variance is different in each country, then the confidence level and precision will also vary. For results to be truly cross-culturally equivalent, precision and confidence levels must be very close to the same in each country. Therefore, making cross-cultural comparisons when large differences exist in variance, precision, and confidence level is questionable at best.

The solution to this problem is to increase sample size based on the variance found in the customer base. The more variable the underlying customer attitudes, the larger the sample size. However, since research costs are usually higher in other industrialized countries such as Japan and in Europe, this often requires a significant budget increase. The 40–50% higher cost per respondent coupled with a larger sample size could make the foreign CSM budget twice as large as the domestic budget.

Thus, greater variance in foreign CSM research may be due to the actual variance in customer attitudes. Or the greater variance may actually be introduced by the sampling methodology.

To achieve comparability, a firm may choose to conduct a telephone survey in, say, Japan, England, Spain, and Italy. Although the rate of telephone ownership is high in all these countries, social acceptance of telephone surveys may vary. For example, the use of telephone surveys is much less frequent in Japan than in the United States due to lower social acceptability. Even when telephone surveys are used in Japan, the response rates among both consumers and businesses are about 20% lower than in the United States (about 60% in the United States compared with 40% in Japan). When Japanese customers do respond, they are often less willing to share their perceptions of attitudes and performance. Since differences like this exist in many countries, some of the variance may be a result of the customer's acceptance of research methodology.

Another sampling procedure issue is equivalence of the research expertise. While variable expertise can influence all aspects of the research, a telephone survey example will again be used to illustrate a potential problem. Let's again assume that the four countries of interest are Japan, England, Spain, and Italy. To adapt to cultural variation that may exist locally, let's also assume that four independent telephone interview firms are hired to gather the data.

Then let's assume that the average interviewer in Japan is a college-educated male; in England the interviewers are male and female college students; in Spain the interviewers are full-time employees but with average education levels; and in Italy the interviewers are housewives working part-time. In telephone interviews, the experience and skill of the interviewer directly affect data quality. Differences can exist in asking questions, in the use of follow-up probes, in interpreting and recording responses, and in motivating the respondent. The big differences between the interviewers from country to country could also induce a big variation in data quality. Having a data collection firm that accounts for and trains to eliminate problems is critical. Hence making detailed cross-cultural comparisons would again be questionable. And this example could be created for every aspect of research design. Even if sampling procedures produce directly comparable data, the CSM program must be modified to account for another change in the foreign environment: competitors.

Benchmarking

One of the important aspects of a CSM program is the identification of competitive strengths and weaknesses. This implies that a firm must compare its performance to that of its competitors, from the customer's perspective. Although the competition within industries is becoming globally more uniform, it still varies from country to country. Also, competitive intensity often varies from country to country, and this certainly influences customer expectations.

The implication of this is that a firm should periodically, probably at least once a year, conduct some sort of competitive analysis to identify the similarities and differences that a particular competitor uses in different countries. Since the marketing strategies of most firms must be adapted internationally, competitive benchmarking clearly identifies the areas of necessary modification.

Data Analysis

To improve or enhance cross-cultural equivalence, firms must exercise a good deal of care in the analysis of data. This adds another layer of complexity that does not exist in purely domestic data. The initial concern is with handling data consistently from one country to another.

To improve consistency a firm should have standardized procedures from one country to the next for editing and coding of data. When a respondent displays inconsistencies in responses, refuses to answer questions, answers only part of the interview, or when interviewers make errors, these situations should be handled in the same manner in all countries. In particular, one of the difficulties in telephone and personal interviews is how to handle open-ended questions and probes. Because subjective responses can be handled quite differently if left to local operations, the guidelines and response categories should be developed by headquarters that are used uniformly in all countries. Assuming that the raw data are cleaned up and entered in some consistent fashion, the next issue is the actual data analysis.

In most cases, data analysis is centralized for an entire study. Most commonly this is done at corporate headquarters by using many of the same techniques used in domestic studies. The initial statistical analysis is usually concerned with the reliability of the data.

As you may recall from the discussion in an earlier chapter, reliability indicates whether the same results would be generated if the survey were repeated. If comparable results are generated, then a high degree of reliability exists. The issue of reliability can be applied to either an entire questionnaire or a specific question.

To determine whether a questionnaire is reliable, a researcher would need to perform a test-retest procedure with at least a portion of the sample. The retest would occur soon after the original survey, normally within a week, so that underlying attitudes probably would not have changed significantly. If the responses were the same for both surveys, a high reliability coefficient could be calculated.

A researcher would expect a high degree of reliability for objective measures such as the demographic variables of age, education, and so forth. But one cross-cultural analysis of reliability found that only 91% of American and 98% of British respondents were consistent in stating age in a test-retest procedure. The consistency for education was only 74% for Americans and 66% for British. Logically a researcher would expect almost total, 100%, consistency from respondents for such questions. Either respondents were making only rough estimates each time or they lied and couldn't remember their previous response. Test-retest reliability studies have shown that attitudinal measures usually have even greater variability from one survey to the next.

Rather than use test-retest measures, researchers use statistical tests that show the reliability of a question within a survey. One such test is the Cronbach Alpha test, which examines the variability that exists from respondent to respondent in answering each question. A high degree of divergence among responses indicates a lack of item reliability. Because the test-retest procedure is a stronger test of reliability, when a test such as the Cronbach Alpha indicates a reliability problem within a survey, a follow-up test-retest should be done.

When a questionnaire, or a specific question, lacks conceptual, functional, or scale equivalence, the result is a low level of reliability. In pragmatic terms, it means that each respondent is reading a somewhat different meaning into the question. If the results of a CSM survey are also cross-culturally equivalent (and this is sometimes a very big "if"), then further data analysis is justified.

To facilitate cross-cultural comparisons when mean values vary significantly from country to country, the data can be standardized in some fashion. The mean in each country could be set at zero and individual observations could be analyzed based on their deviation above or below the mean. This would theoretically adjust for mean differences, but unfortunately, the dispersion of the responses can vary from country to country just as the mean does. This can be corrected somewhat by normalizing data based on percentile distributions.

The difficult issue of determining whether the means are, in fact, different still remains, however. If the mean response is an accurate representation of the customer's true attitudes, the data should not be standardized or normalized. But if the mean and deviation are partially or totally caused by the research methodology or a unique aspect of culture instead of by the customer's true attitudes, then the data should be standardized or normalized.

The first type of data analysis is, typically, within-country analysis. Although data analysis is often conducted at headquarters by CSM experts or quantitative specialists, the techniques are those that were described previously in the chapter on data analysis. Basic descriptive statistics such as means and standard deviations are determined, and levels of precision and confidence are calculated. The data are often crafted into a CSM model through the use of factor analysis, multiple regression of some type, or analysis of variance. Developing a CSM model for each country is therefore really straightforward. The more difficult comparisons are cross-cultural. Making cross-cultural comparisons has the effect of adding another variable to all statistical tests. Sometimes this is referred to as adding another treatment or partition to the study, for the effects of country differences must be isolated.

Two relatively simple tests are chi-square cross-tabs and paired t-tests. A chi-square test indicates the probability that the observed differences in variables are significant. That is, the observed differences are greater than would be expected by chance occurrence. As in all other statistical tests, sample size and the standard deviation of the sample influence the significance level. The smaller the sample or the greater the standard deviation, the less likely the chi-square test will be able to detect significant differences. Chi-square cross-tabs are most commonly used to examine the relationship between two variables such as country and overall satisfaction or country and a particular attribute. The value of a cross-tab is to give the researcher a quick, easy glimpse of what the data are saying, although a cross-tab is relatively unsophisticated statistically. The cross-tab approach is used when all the data are aggregated into one sample, hence one sample size and standard deviation for each question.

When samples are drawn independently from two or more countries and each sample is treated as distinct, the differences in mean values for each question can be compared through the use of a paired t-test. The t-test statistic indicates the significance level of the differences. As a general rule, if cross-tabs or paired t-tests don't show that significant differences exist, then more powerful techniques won't display a conclusive pattern of results. However, when these simple tests do show differences are significant, the more powerful tests often provide a much richer understanding of what is actually going on.

A more powerful technique used in cross-cultural CSM is analysis of variance, or ANOVA. With a one-way ANOVA, the satisfaction level of customers in several countries could be simultaneously compared. The country would be one treatment that is used to explain the variation in satisfaction, either on an overall level or for an individual attribute.

With a two-way ANOVA, the impact of two treatments on satisfaction level could be simultaneously examined. For example, a researcher may want to analyze the impact of country and purchase volume on satisfaction. If in the study five countries and four purchase volume levels were included, a 5×4 factorial design with twenty cells would result. Based on the table in the sampling chapter, about fifty observations per cell would be necessary resulting in a minimum sample size of 1,000 usable responses. The advantage of a two-way ANOVA is that several variables can be simultaneously evaluated. This provides a more realistic understanding of how different variables may influence customer satisfaction either jointly or singly. However, when conducting both domestic and cross-cultural CSM, a researcher may want to examine the impact of many variables on customer satisfaction. This requires the use of multivariate techniques.

The array of multivariate statistical techniques is really quite broad. The most commonly used approaches are analysis of covariance (ANCOVA), multiple regression (several kinds), multivariate analysis of variance (MANOVA), and factor analysis. While a technical discussion is not presented on each of these, the country issue is a dominant treatment for each technique. Basically, the impact of country on customer satisfaction must be factored out in some way. Although each technique is somewhat different in its approach, each tries to explain how country issues, individually and jointly with other variables, influence customer satisfaction. Collectively, these techniques can be very usefully applied to cross-cultural CSM studies.

A final word of caution is necessary. All statistical analyses are based on the idea that the data are valid measuring what is supposed to be measured, reliable (stable over time), and equivalent (conceptually the same cross-culturally). If the data are lacking in these areas, then all the great analysis in the world won't make the results managerially meaningful. The statistical output may look good but it will lack meaning. This again is the old garbage-in, garbage-out situation. Serious conceptual flaws cannot be corrected even by powerful statistical analysis.

Soft CSM

Most of the issues in this chapter thus far have been concerned with establishing a reliable cross-cultural database that is comparable and equivalent from country to country. Although hard data allow quantitative comparisons, the primary prerequisite to establishing equivalence is the factoring out of the impact of cultural differences. In contrast, the purpose of soft, nonempirical CSM is to capture the more intangible, often culture bound, dimensions of attitudes.

A previous chapter addressed the specific ways that a firm can create a program that generates nonquantitative responses from customers, so those approaches won't be restated here. However, there are two general objectives of soft CSM that are possibly even more important internationally than domestically. One is to solicit customer input on issues that would never appear on a survey, and the other is to foster stronger bonding relationships with customers.

In domestic markets, managers often have a better feel for what customers desire. This is usually due to a cultural understanding that is acquired gradually over a long period of time. Often it takes many years to gain cultural awareness of customers in other countries. This problem, which faces outsiders, has been well documented in Chinese and Japanese cultures but it also exists to a lesser degree in many, if not most, cultures.

Developing proactive approaches to customer contact helps to educate managers, both domestic and foreign, about what customers feel. Such improved understanding could be developed by interviewing a wider range of customers than those who complete a survey in a site visit. The improved understanding could come from discussion of the problems, challenges, and constraints encountered by a particular customer or firm. The improved understanding could come from a discussion of the customer's future needs, say, one, two, or three years ahead. These types of issues could never be effectively addressed in a CSM survey, but such information about customers can be extremely valuable and useful in staying close to the customer.

Another objective of proactive customer contact is the development of bonding relationships. Customers are valuable, cherished assets and they like to be treated as such in all countries. A proactive approach to customer contact has the effect of personalizing a firm to its customers in virtually all countries and cultures. The personalization shatters erroneous stereotypes for both managers and customers.

In other countries, Americans are often viewed as insensitive, aggressive, and ostentatious. The French are often viewed as arrogant and rude. The British are often viewed as aloof and reserved. Mexicans are often viewed as jovial and unenergetic. In reality, none of these stereotypes are accurate, particularly when applied to an individual. Probably the best way to destroy such stereotypes is through personal, face-to-face contact with customers. Then customers very quickly cease being a target market and become living, breathing people.

CHAPTER SUMMARY

Conducting cross-cultural CSM research presents a whole new set of potential problems, pitfalls, and challenges. The process of developing and implementing a CSM program can be replicated internationally. The specific issues discussed in previous chapters pertaining to clarifying objectives, identifying the attributes, and developing a questionnaire are all processes that remain important but potentially have significant differences. However, in an international context, a whole new set of cross-cultural factors must also be considered.

For most CSM programs, these additional cross-cultural factors make it impossible to simply replicate a domestic effort in another country. Although replication may be possible in rare cases, some adaptation is usually necessary. The degree of adaptation is determined by a wide array of factors, including research quality, cultural diversity, unit of analysis, who conducts the research, research infrastructure, and costs.

MOORE CORP.

"As We Lead the Way to Total Customer Satisfaction"

When customers talk, Moore Corp. listens. The firm monitors its performance in the eyes of customers and then provides solutions to meet those customers' information handling needs. As an integral part of its quality management initiatives, Moore asks customers for their feedback, and then it links the feedback to a strategic planning process. That linkage enables Moore to identify any gaps that may exist between its strategic goals and the expectations of its customers.

In 1992, the U.S. Business Forms & Systems Division of Moore further exemplified that customer focus when it embarked on an ambitious and comprehensive customer survey process called customer satisfaction measurement (CSM). This two-way communication between Moore and its customers confirmed the organization's strengths and opportunities, and it uncovered some areas in need of improvement.

Moore began the CSM process by conducting focus groups with a representative sample of its customer base. The focus groups revealed what customers look for when selecting a supplier. Moore found that product quality, service quality, price/value, perception of sales representatives, and billing were key drivers of customer satisfaction. As a result, these qualities were used to design Moore's model and were incorporated into the firm's actual telephone survey, the second part of the CSM process.

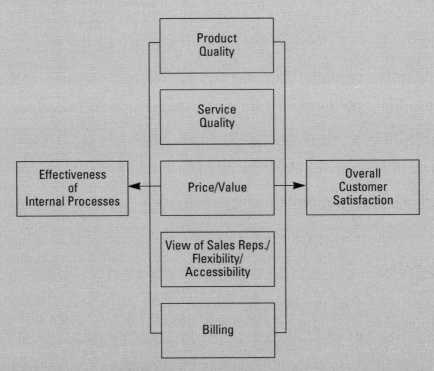

The telephone survey focused on three areas. First, it tried to gain a better understanding of customers' needs and priorities. Second, it tried to get a sense of how customers perceive the quality of Moore's products and services. Last, the survey identified actionable items. The results of the survey were communicated to internal employees in the rollout of the strategic business plan, and they were communicated to customers during the fourth quarter of 1993.

Moore Corp. again surveyed its customers in May and June of 1994 under the direction of Robert Goss, vice president of quality management at Moore North America. Moore embarked on its World-Wide Customer Satisfaction Measurement Survey to solicit feedback from customers around the globe.

Using the World-Wide Customer Satisfaction Measurement Survey, Moore conducted ten worldwide focus groups prior to telephone surveys in countries such as Mexico, Brazil, France, Japan, the Netherlands, Britain, the United States, Australia, and Canada. Sales associates from across the organization provided the names of current, former, and prospective customers worldwide, who were surveyed via telephone over the course of a three-month period. Approximately 9,000 telephone surveys were conducted, and the same survey was translated accordingly and used in each country.

The World-Wide Customer Satisfaction Measurement Survey provided three pieces of information. First, it provided Moore Corp. with a standard, world-wide measure of customer satisfaction. Second, it provided the data the Moore units needed to understand and meet the needs of their own customers. Third, it tracked the impact of the entire corporation's actions on customer satisfaction.

Jackie Pauls, project manager, worked on the company's first Customer Satisfaction Measurement survey and then represented the U.S. Business Forms & Systems Division of Moore in the World-Wide Survey. Pauls has had contact with many organizations that have undertaken similar projects to measure customer satisfaction. "A world-wide measurement gets at such valuable information, especially when the organization uses the same survey for all units and divisions across the globe," said Pauls. "Many times large organizations survey their customers, but their surveys tend to vary in scope from division to division. As a result, comparisons cannot be made from one unit to the next."

Knowing the organization's performance in the eyes of customers has enabled Moore to reengineer processes and develop strategic business plans in alignment with customer needs. The information received from both surveys continues to dictate the direction of the organization and enables Moore to better meet the information handling needs of its customers.

17

CSM for Internal Customers

Just as your external customers rely on your company's employees to meet and exceed their needs, internal customers are simply employees that rely on each other for products, services, and support in order to meet or exceed their needs. Some internal customers, such as the payroll department, interact with each and every employee at least once a month, whereas other internal customers, such as the legal department, have much more limited contact. There are differences and similarities between internal and external customers; it is important to know and understand them.

When we think of the internal workings of an organization, we often think of an extended process of inputs and outputs. Figure 17.1 illustrates the extended process. A supplier provides inputs for the system in the form of products or services. A supplier who determines and understands the needs of the system through quantitative measurement is better able to supply superior inputs in the forms of products and services. The system then adds value to the input through raw materials, processing, or employee labor and produces an output. Again, adding the correct components to produce the output results in superior value; the appropriate components are determined by quantitative data and feedback. In most cases, we think of an external customer as the recipient of the output, and our CSM process tells us whether or not we are meeting or exceeding needs and expectations through quantitative data, so we can rest on our laurels—or can we? You'll notice that the extended process iden-

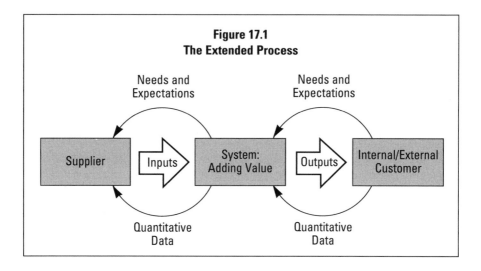

Figure 17.1
The Extended Process

tifies the final output going to external and internal customers. Both internal and external customers therefore need a CSM process to tell your company whether or not you are creating customer value and satisfaction.

UNIQUE CHARACTERISTICS OF INTERNAL CUSTOMERS

In theory, we should be customer driven for both internal and external customers. In practice, such is rarely the case. There are some unique characteristics of employees versus internal customers.

Internal customers are, by default, captive customers. Those in marketing department usually have very little input about those hired into accounting or printing services, and vice versa. You usually aren't allowed to choose to outsource a product or service unless you are the manager of that particular product or service. Even if you have good reasons for outsourcing, such as better service or product quality or price, peer pressure is often severe enough to obscure the rational choice. You, as an employee, are therefore stuck with products and services that can be far substandard and company driven rather than customer driven. Have you ever been the regular recipient of a confusing payroll summary form every payday, or a burdensome expense-reporting system, or summary printouts of your 401(k) savings plan that arrive two months after the statement date? I'm certain that you have. And the usual response to complaints is either that you are lucky to get a paycheck/expense check/

statement or that it has always been done this way. Because of the captivity issue, there is no pressure to change.

Aligned with the captive internal customer setup is the outdated theory that whatever worked in the past will continue to work in the future unless a cataclysmic event occurs. If your company has somehow managed to avoid all of the changes taking place in the world and in business, this book will serve as a cataclysmic event! Typical cataclysmic events are customer departures and the resulting decline in profits and share, alarming employee turnover, safety violations and accidents, and regulatory or social backlash. The discovery that employee satisfaction is linked to customer satisfaction will hopefully be enough of an event to encourage discussion of and research into the internal customer arena.

In companies managed by fear and blame, feedback from other people within the organization is not only discouraged but also a source of nightmares. No one wants to get any feedback because it is always negative, and everyone is reluctant to provide any feedback because there will be retribution. Not unlike a dysfunctional family, dysfunctional organizations continue to destroy themselves from within by not taking an honest look at the imperfections of the world and developing a philosophy of respect for the uniqueness and value of other people. A change in its philosophy usually takes place when a company truly embraces total quality management.

Employee seniority within corporations also contributes to the uniqueness of internal customers. The longer we work for a corporation, the more we think we know what our internal customers need—based on our own prejudices and anecdotal information. With all of the reengineering and downsizing taking place nowadays, futurists suggest that individuals will work at five to ten different companies in their lifetime. The changing nature of business requires that we be able to accept and adapt to new situations.

Finally, recognition and reward programs are traditionally more department-based rather than cross-functional. In this situation, teamwork across functions is not emphasized. A poignant example of this occurred with internal customers in a public utility. Through a CSM process, external customers said that when they needed connection service at their home, they wanted it within forty-eight hours. The customer service department, upon learning this, began to book the service technicians in the forty-eight-hour window and assumed that now the customers would be satisfied. It turned out, however, that the service technicians ended up having no travel time built into their schedule and they were often double-booked. As you can guess, the service technicians received the bulk of the customers' frustration and anger. The service technicians were also frustrated because they wanted to do a good job. Because this utility had in place a total quality management system with the subsequent evolving cultural change, both departments sat down and discussed the issues. The result was the formation of a cross-functional team of customer service representatives and service technicians that worked on the scheduling process to meet customer needs. Part of the result was that a more flexible schedule was devised whereby technicians could go to customers' homes in the early morning or the evening so that customers did not have to take time off from work to be available. In this case, everyone won.

INTERNAL CUSTOMER SATISFACTION MEASUREMENT

We have discussed the strong correlation between employee satisfaction and customer satisfaction. The extended system of employees (internal customers) needs to know what the external customer requirements are in order to drive continuous improvement and financial performance. Internal customers need to be surveyed so that internal suppliers understand how they are doing (performance) and what counts (importance). Doesn't this sound familiar?

A rigorous CSM process as outlined in this book is usually not necessary for the internal customer process. If the corporate culture has trust and respect and is committed to a total quality management approach, then a simplified method of obtaining feedback can be used. Just making the commitment to recognize and include internal customer feedback in planning and evaluation processes will change the corporate culture for the better.

A Process for Soliciting Internal Customer Satisfaction

The process for soliciting internal customer satisfaction is straightforward. Figure 17.2 is a flowchart outlining the process that Boise Cascade Corp. uses for internal CSM. It was developed by a quality team at Boise Cascade Corp. so that internal departments and teams had a basis for understanding the process of internal CSM. The flowchart of the process was distributed widely so that duplication of effort was minimized as the internal CSM focus was championed throughout the organization.

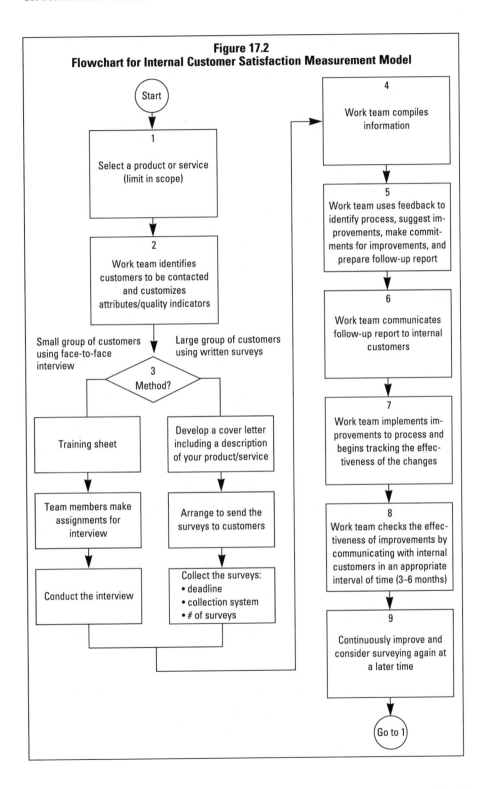

Figure 17.2
Flowchart for Internal Customer Satisfaction Measurement Model

Start

1
Select a product or service
(limit in scope)

2
Work team identifies
customers to be contacted
and customizes
attributes/quality indicators

3
Method?

Small group of customers
using face-to-face
interview

Large group of customers
using written surveys

Training sheet

Develop a cover letter
including a description
of your product/service

Team members make
assignments for
interview

Arrange to send the
surveys to customers

Conduct the interview

Collect the surveys:
• deadline
• collection system
• # of surveys

4
Work team compiles
information

5
Work team uses feedback to
identify process, suggest improvements, make commit-
ments for improvements, and
prepare follow-up report

6
Work team communicates
follow-up report to internal
customers

7
Work team implements im-
provements to process and
begins tracking the effectiveness of the changes

8
Work team checks the effectiveness of improvements by
communicating with internal
customers in an appropriate
interval of time (3–6 months)

9
Continuously improve and
consider surveying again at
a later time

Go to 1

The starting point for internal CSM is to select a product or service that is limited in scope but recognizable to your customers. For example, if you are part of the corporate communications department and produce a company magazine, videos, consulting services, advertising strategies, and company bulletins, you will want to measure each of these products, services, or processes separately. You may want to take a presurvey to determine which products and services are most important to your customers and then get the specific details about the attributes of the product or service that have the most importance for these products, services, or processes. Either way, limiting the scope of the research allows you to ultimately focus on the activities that drive the critical process that contribute to an efficient and effective workplace.

The next step is to identify the customers and the customer-defined attributes that contribute to satisfaction. Customer identification can be done through your work team. For some departments, distribution lists are available and are a good source of information. The attributes can be determined through customer interviews or feedback that you may already have. Just as with consultants who explore issues with external customers, employees need to develop listening skills.

The next step in the flowchart is a main decision point. You must decide the appropriate format for the surveys: face-to-face, telephone, e-mail, or written. As previously discussed, the response rate will vary by the media. Face-to-face and written surveys are the most commonly used; many high-tech and computerized businesses have used the e-mail format with great success. It is important to understand a critical difference between external and internal CSM for the data collection. In the case of internal CSM, external consultants should not be used for the surveying. Using your own team or an internal group such as marketing research to act as a third party reinforces the culture change to becoming internally driven. If you think that your internal customers need a third party, ask the CSM director or the marketing research department to act as the third party for survey receipt and data tabulation.

The key concerns of mail and e-mail surveys for both internal and external customers are the same. It is still important to consider prenotifying internal customers of upcoming surveys, ensuring the acceptance of the instrument, and pretesting the survey. Treating the internal CSM process with the same professionalism and attention to detail as you use with your external CSM process will ensure participation.

If the number of customers is small or if customer needs are not well-known, a personal interview is the more appropriate format. Unfortunately, not all individuals are natural interviewers, particularly when the information collected may not be what the interviewer expected to hear! It is helpful to have a short training session giving guidelines for the personal interviews. An outline of key points for the interview are listed in Table 17.1. The overall focus must be on listening and taking good notes. When the temptation arises to defend, one must probe. Ask why five times or until the issue is clear. With internal customers, the internal supplier and internal customer are best served by talking together rather than using a third party to conduct the interview.

Whether you plan to use mail, e-mail, phone, or personal interviews, a survey instrument is necessary for data collection. Figure 17.3 is an instrument/template developed for use within the entire Boise Cascade Corp. The standardized format can be customized with specific attributes, and a training session is used to discuss tabulation, analysis, reporting, and communication of the results. In this way, departments don't have to spend a lot of time re-creating the instrument. By using the same format, individuals receiving surveys from their internal suppliers also become familiar with the same format of the instrument, which makes responding easier and also improves the response rate. Additionally, most of us are overwhelmed by the number of surveys we receive at work and at home, so standardization creates recognition and understanding of how to complete the survey with minimal instructions. The instrument measures both performance and importance, which helps a department determine what products or services are important to the customer and on which areas or attributes to focus process improvement efforts. This prevents you from focusing on the attribute that receives the lowest performance score, because it may not be important to customers.

By using the format of the Boise Cascade instrument, one can easily analyze the data by using the mean scores for performance and importance. Assign Excellent a 5, Very Good a 4, Good a 3, Fair a 2, and Poor a 1. Likewise, rate Extremely Important to Not at All Important" with the same 5-to-1 scale. Take care not to assign a 0 (zero) to Don't Know, Not Observed, or blanks. When conducting the statistical analysis, the zero scores can be excluded and evaluated separately. It is important to keep track of the Don't Know, Not Observed, and blanks and check for

Table 17.1   Internal CSM Training Sheet for Personal Interviewing

Prior to interviewing

- Familiarize yourself with the survey instrument. Pay close attention to questions that permit more than one response. Make sure answers to open-ended or probing questions are recorded precisely.

- Practice administering the questionnaire with other team members before using it with customers. Rehearse with someone not associated with the study. Interview should not last longer than 30 minutes.

Introduction

- Deliver introduction sincerely. Be careful not to introduce bias into the interviewing process. Don't express your own opinions or comments in any responses received from the respondent.

Interview

- Interviews should be conducted in an atmosphere that avoids distraction.

- Explain:
  - What the survey is about
  - How the respondent will benefit
  - How the respondent was selected and that responses are important

- Stay on topic, and focus on the objective of your survey. Be brief and to the point so that your respondent does not lose interest.

- Read all questions verbatim.

- Be easy to understand. Speak clearly and concisely using simple grammar. Don't use terminology or acronyms that the respondent might not understand.

Closure

- Thank the respondent.

- Let the respondent know that survey results will be acted upon and results will be reported back to participants in the survey.

---

attributes that have high numbers for these. It could indicate a problem with the survey or internal processes.

   The next step is to analyze the data. Analyzing the data for internal customers should be kept simple. The prioritization of process improvements is done by reviewing two key measures: the ranking of importance

Figure 17.3
Internal Customer Satisfaction Survey

Product/Service Being Measured Is:

E=Excellent VG=Very Good G=Good F=Fair P=Poor
5=Extremely Important 4=Important
3=Somewhat Important 2=Neutral 1=Not at all Important

Attribute/Quality Indicator	Not Observed	Performance	Importance	Comments
A. Overall Service/Product Quality How do you rate the overall quality of our product service?	N/O	E VG G F P	5 4 3 2 1	
B. Value How do you rate the value of our service, product, and cost-effectiveness?	N/O	E VG G F P	5 4 3 2 1	
C. Satisfaction How do you rate your overall satisfaction with our product and/or service?	N/O	E VG G F P	5 4 3 2 1	
D. Accessibility How do you rate our accessibility when you need us (in person, by fax, by e-mail, by phone)?	N/O	E VG G F P	5 4 3 2 1	
E. Responsiveness How do you rate our timely responsiveness to your requests and/or needs?	N/O	E VG G F P	5 4 3 2 1	
F. Problem Solving How do you rate our ability to provide effective solutions to your problems and/or complaints?	N/O	E VG G F P	5 4 3 2 1	
G. Delivery Timeliness How do you rate our ability to deliver damage-free goods within the time frame that you require?	N/O	E VG G F P	5 4 3 2 1	
H. Attitude of Personnel How do you rate the courteous, helpful, and "can-do" attitude of our personnel?	N/O	E VG G F P	5 4 3 2 1	
I. Collaborative Approach How do you rate our ability to work with you as partners by understanding your needs and working together with you towards common goals?	N/O	E VG G F P	5 4 3 2 1	
J. Accuracy How do you rate the ability of our product/service to fulfill your requirements by being dependable, reliable, and error free?	N/O	E VG G F P	5 4 3 2 1	
K. Innovative How do you rate your perception of our being aware of best-in-class, creative, and aware of trends/technology?	N/O	E VG G F P	5 4 3 2 1	
L.	N/O	E VG G F P	5 4 3 2 1	
M.	N/O	E VG G F P	5 4 3 2 1	
N.	N/O	E VG G F P	5 4 3 2 1	
O.	N/O	E VG G F P	5 4 3 2 1	

Additional comments:

and the gap between importance and performance. Process improvement efforts should focus on those activities that are important to internal customers and currently have the greatest gap between performance and importance. Items that have a higher performance score are ones that can be used for recognition in departments.

One of the easiest ways to do this is to show the data in bar charts as illustrated in Figure 17.4. In this example, the results of the survey for three attributes—accessibility, responsiveness, and accuracy—are shown. In the case of accessibility, the importance score is higher than the performance. In the case of responsiveness, both the importance and performance scores are the same. In the case of accuracy, performance exceeds importance. Therefore, this internal supplier should focus on those activities that contribute to the attribute accessibility as top priority. The next round of measurement will determine whether these conclusions were appropriate.

At this point it may be tempting to compare your results with another department's or work team's. There is a word for this: Don't! Results of the surveys are specific to a team and product/service and should not be compared with others. The relevant comparison takes place over time to determine how much the processes have improved. Top management, if truly committed to total quality management, will be concerned about what the customer's needs and expectations are and will determine how the organization can be fine-tuned to meet those needs.

Once you have decided upon priorities and an action plan, you need to communicate your improvement plans to your internal customers. You can do this in a memo or by e-mail or in person. One innovative practice used at Boise Cascade is to produce eye-catching greeting cards that thank the respondent and explain which areas will be the focus of process improvement efforts.

Within the department or the natural work team, process improvements are implemented and/or measurement systems are put in place. If, based on the internal customer feedback, there has been a radical change to the process, touching base with your customers in a month or two just to get a sense of the impact of the changes is often valuable. If all is going well, continue with the efforts and make plans to survey again.

Products can also be thought of in terms of routine and nonroutine outputs. Process products and services are routine outputs that have a consistent customer base. An example of a routine output is a monthly report from a controller. Internal surveys for routine outputs should

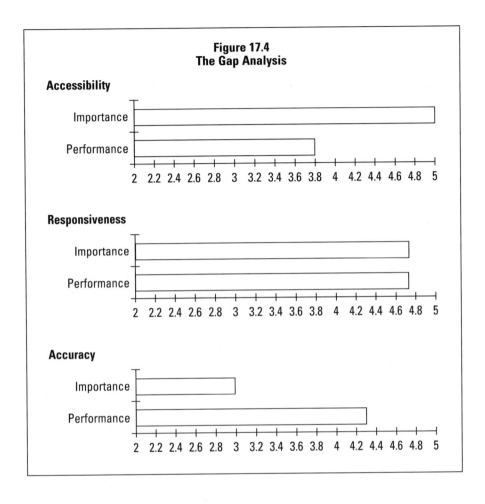

focus on either seven to ten key customers with periodic sampling, surveying of all customers, or a random sample of customers once a year. Nonroutine outputs are projects and services that have a varying customer base such as corporate engineering or marketing research. Internal surveys for nonroutine outputs are tied to the specific project or phase, and feedback is collected at completion of the project. Transaction services have spot demand and can have a wide, unpredictable customer base. Internal surveys for transaction services are best done at the time of delivery.

Employee Satisfaction versus Internal Customer Satisfaction

There is a distinction between employee satisfaction and internal customer satisfaction. Employee satisfaction consists of employee attitudes about the overall satisfaction with the workplace, the type of work that is done, how the work is done, and how the compensation and benefits systems treats the employee. Conversely, internal customer satisfaction consists of a more narrow focus on the outcome of the company's internal processes. Therefore, internal customer satisfaction is a reasonably accurate measure of the company's systems. As might be expected, these two types of satisfaction are closely linked; a satisfied employee is probably also an employee who is cognizant of internal customer needs and is a reliable supplier. World-class internal suppliers and customers make everyone's job easier!

As discussed earlier, employee satisfaction is also strongly linked to external customer satisfaction. Employees have tremendous influence over the quality and delivery of products and services that reach the external customer. Xerox has found that the correlation between customer satisfaction and employee satisfaction is 0.57. Another study of the linkage of employee perceptions of service quality and actual customer perceptions of service quality in a bank found a correlation of .67. Numerous proprietary studies have been done since then, all with similar findings. The yearly list of the Best Companies to Work for in America considers primarily the human resources component of the corporation for the list. A look at the list will reveal that all of these companies are extremely successful and profitable. Customer relations mirror employee relations, and vice versa.

LaSalle Partners, a building management company, asks all employees to complete a customer survey as if the customer were completing it. The firm has found that employee perceptions about customer perceptions become more accurate as employees' customer contact increases. Frontline employees have the most accurate perceptions of the customer. Senior management can use that information both to leverage the findings of frontline workers and to demonstrate its commitment to and concern for employees at all levels in the company.

An interesting study was completed in Canada in 1993. Since Canada has a substantial amount of information on quality improvement in organizations, an analysis was completed on quality and performance in Canada. When attempting to improve labor productivity or to increase value added per employee, firms that had high usage of leadership, empowerment, and process improvement and a customer focus realized a 90% higher increase in value added per employee than the average. In addition, in terms of market share, firms that had high or moderate use of process improvement and customer focus tools enjoyed a 9% greater increase in market share than the average company using some quality tools. Therefore, a customer focus can provide a firm with increases in both market share and productivity.

An example of a successful internal customer satisfaction measurement process comes from a petroleum company. Phillips Petroleum implemented its Internal Customer Satisfaction Process for all corporate staffs in 1993. The purpose of the Internal Customer Satisfaction Process was to align staff services with the needs and requirements of internal customers. For Phillips corporate staffs, internal customer satisfaction is defined as meeting the agreed customer requirements at the lowest possible price. Five measures of service quality are currently used: alignment, reliability, responsiveness, competence, and value/price. Internal customer satisfaction is a factor in determining the variable component of the staff's pay. Phillips is only one of a handful of companies that tie internal customer satisfaction measures with incentive pay. Part of the Phillips report is a visual display of results as shown in Figure 17.5.

The farther out the line, the higher the rating is. So competence, responsiveness, and value/price are the highest ratings, but all three have room for improvement because each has a mean of 3.0 on the 5-point scale. Reliability and alignment are both in significant need of improvement.

As with external CSM at Phillips, the customer defines requirements, priorities, and performance. Phillips divides its services into three types—transactional, process, and project—and divides its customers among the services. It collects data and then rolls up the baseline measures for incentive awards. The results of the internal measurement process are communicated to both employees and customers. Plans are also made for the next year that include process improvements, targets, and communication.

CHAPTER SUMMARY

Internal CSM is a necessary component of an integrated customer focus. Internal customers in all parts of your organization contribute to or detract from external customer value. Everyone in the organization is a customer of many departments and team efforts. By understanding the

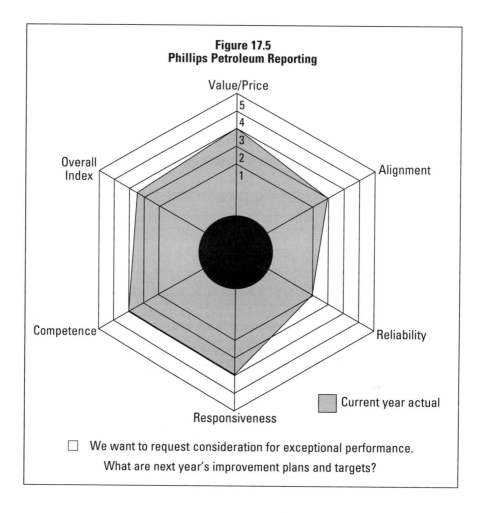

Figure 17.5
Phillips Petroleum Reporting

performance and importance of the various attributes of products, services, and processes, the goal of process improvement can be achieved. And the ultimate result is delighted customers in the form of employees!

There are some unique characteristics of being an internal customer. Most of these characteristics emanate from two components. The first is that such customers are truly captive. Internal customers traditionally don't have the option to outsource, though that option is becoming more viable in the changing business environment. The second is that management culture promotes or demotes the concept of internal customers. Successful organizations with a total quality culture are ones that promote the application of internal CSM.

Internal CSM has the same process flow and objectives as external CSM, with few exceptions. Generally, external consultants are not used for internal CSM. The cultural change required for an internal customer focus is modeled by the use of internal resources through organizational learning. Employees gain new abilities and respect for others in the organization. Also, the skills developed internally will also be useful in the process of bringing the external CSM process in-house if appropriate. Some standardization of the process and instrument design allows for easy implementation and understanding, which in turn will drive the voice of both the internal and external customer into the organization.

CORNING

Corning, the Fortune 500 company with 32,000 employees on 5 continents, specializes in specialty materials, information display, opto-electronics, consumer housewares, and laboratory services. Corning developed a list of ingredients in order to integrate internal customer satisfaction in their organization through a program called Goal$haring.

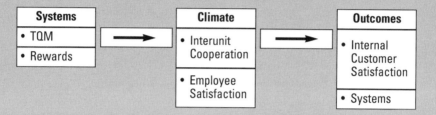

Goal$haring was developed in the late 1980s in the manufacturing operations and expanded throughout the entire corporation in 1992. Goal$haring is a combination of profit sharing and gain sharing. It is a unit bonus plan based on long-term business goals, continuous improvement, and corporate ROE. Goal$haring supports greater employee involvement and meeting quality goals. Key considerations of Goal$haring are shown below:

- Are the goals understood? (line of sight)
- Do people know what they can do to influence the goals? (line of impact)
- Does the plan capture attention and generate excitement? (employee involvement)
- Are the goals fair? ("stretch")
- Are the business priorities reflected in the weights? (priority balancing)

The following is an example in the information services department of the company. Information Services (IS) measures internal customer satisfaction in four key areas: partnership satisfaction (for senior-level customers), project management satisfaction, direct support, and HelpLine. Twenty-five percent of the Goal$haring payout is determined by these measures. Key elements measured in partnership satisfaction are leadership, proactivity, responsiveness, communication, and value. Corning's IS group has been doing this for four years. The group has found that there is confidence in its indicators, it has trend data, top management has reviewed the group's progress, and the group is fully deployed and accepted by business managers. What isn't working so well is that there are problems in interpreting measures consistently, and trend performance is flat.

In order to foster intergroup cooperation, Corning has developed a program called Valentines. In this program, individuals write messages to other groups with the following introduction: "In order for me to meet my customer needs, I need you to do the following . . ." These individual messages are posted and read by the whole receiving group. Functional groups sort and discuss messages and prepare a nondefensive response that includes an action plan.

18

Complaint Handling

The flight from Sydney, Australia, to Bangkok, Thailand, on the Lauda Airline's new 747 had been smooth and uneventful, with the exception of a few toilets becoming inoperable. For some reason, the new vacuum toilet system, which saved space and weight, had been prone to occasional failures, so having a few toilets out of service was not particularly alarming. However, about an hour after reaching a cruising altitude of 43,000 feet on the fourteen-hour flight from Bangkok to Vienna, Austria, things got worse. The flight attendant, in a cheerful voice, announced to the 300 or so passengers, "We regret to inform you that all of the toilets have become inoperable. However, for your flying convenience, we have buckets at the rear of the aircraft if mother nature calls. Please feel free to ring your flight attendant button if we can be of assistance. Have an enjoyable flight!" The passengers squirmed nervously in their seats, wondering if they were going to need to use the buckets or if they could hold out until the landing.

Imagine the reaction of Lauda Airlines CEO Nikki Lauda, former Formula 1 world champion driver. Whether negotiating the hairpin turns of Monaco or roaring down the straightaway in Brazil at over 200 miles per hour, Nikki Lauda expected precision engineering and meticulous maintenance, an expectation that carried over to his airline. To have something as mundane as a toilet system fail was almost unthinkable.

Assume that you are the customer service manager for Lauda Airlines. What would you do? If you were the customer service manager for Boeing or the customer service manager for Boeing's supplier that had designed and manufactured the toilet system, what would you do? If the response to this situation is too straightforward, let's try a few more typical customer complaints.

A father took his son, an aspiring tennis player on his junior high team, shopping for a new tennis racquet. The son finally selected a rather expensive model. He had used the new high-technology graphite racquet for just three days when the shaft broke while he was serving (at 105 pounds, the tennis player was no Arnold Schwarzenegger). When the parents attempted to return the broken racquet to the local outlet of a national sporting goods chain, both the salesclerk and the store manager told them that "junior high kids are real hard on racquets." Therefore, the store wouldn't exchange the racquet because they assumed it had been abused. The store, however, was willing to return the racquet to the manufacturer on the slight possibility it was actually defective. Meanwhile, Dad had to buy a new racquet—at a different store, naturally.

Five weeks later, the local retailer phoned the parents to say that the original racquet was indeed defective and they could pick up a new one. After much negotiating, the store manager agreed to offer a credit slip that could be used on other merchandise, for the racquet had already been replaced. However, the store manager made it clear that he didn't really like the solution. What should have happened in this situation?

A customer had just had his jet boat serviced at Sears Marina in Anchorage, Alaska, and was looking forward to a day of salmon fishing in the Alaskan wilderness. After a few hours' drive north of Anchorage, the boat was launched in the Susitna River, known locally as the Big Su. The Big Su is a large glacial river with many channels, islands, and log jams, and all parts of the river are fast and icy cold.

After our boater had traveled only a few miles downstream from the launch site, a bearing in the jet unit froze up. Apparently, as it turned out, a careless service technician forgot to grease the new bearing after installation. When a bearing seizes, the boat becomes basically powerless, just an awkward raft. The boat drifted sideways down the river and into a log jam, almost capsizing as it became entangled in the logs, with the water within inches of overflowing the upstream side. After the owner spent a few harrowing minutes and did some frantic chopping with an ax, the boat was freed from the logs.

The customer had to flag down a passing boat and hitch a ride back to the landing site. Then he had to drive 100 miles to Anchorage, get the necessary parts, drive the 100 miles back, and hitch another boat ride. Then he had to disassemble his jet unit and make the repairs on a sandbar. What would have been the appropriate response by Sears to mollify this customer?

As the Christmas buying season began, a regional bank decided to increase automatically the credit limit of all of its credit card holders by 15%. Surely, this would increase customers' ability to purchase and would create higher levels of customer satisfaction (as well as interest income for the bank). Unfortunately, a computer programmer at the bank made an error that resulted in all credit limits being automatically *lowered* to 15% of the credit limit.

Customers including some of the bank's own executives were stranded around the world. And nearly all customers suffered the embarrassment of having their credit card purchases declined. All of this was accomplished by a few mere strokes on the keyboard. How should this situation have been handled?

Situations such as these are commonplace. Millions probably occur every day, though possibly not as memorable or severe as these. With no formal systems or guidelines for responding to customer complaints, organizations respond to such situations on an ad hoc and inconsistent basis. And in today's highly competitive business environment, customers experiencing ad hoc and inconsistent complaint handling are very much at risk. Odds are that most such customers will vote with their buying power and fire the business.

ENCOURAGE COMPLAINTS!

Many firms dread hearing complaints from customers, trying to avoid any type of negative feedback. These firms are operating on the assumption that if there are no customer complaints, everything must be great. This is the epitome of the speak-no-evil, hear-no-evil, see-no-evil mentality. Unfortunately, such an assumption can be a fatal mistake.

Depending on the industry, studies show that between 11 and 53% of customers report they have experienced problems recently, as illustrated in Figure 18.1. Thus, in virtually every industry, customers experience problems of some type. Customers who experience problems with a firm are two or three times as likely to quit doing business with that firm as customers who experience no problems, as shown in Figure 18.2. These

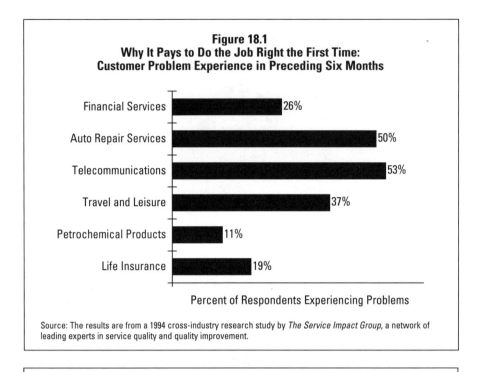

Figure 18.1
Why It Pays to Do the Job Right the First Time:
Customer Problem Experience in Preceding Six Months

Financial Services — 26%
Auto Repair Services — 50%
Telecommunications — 53%
Travel and Leisure — 37%
Petrochemical Products — 11%
Life Insurance — 19%

Percent of Respondents Experiencing Problems

Source: The results are from a 1994 cross-industry research study by *The Service Impact Group*, a network of leading experts in service quality and quality improvement.

Figure 18.2
Intent to Repurchase is Strongly Influenced by Problems

Industry	Repurchase Intention Problem	Repurchase Intention No Problem
Financial services	40%	73%
Auto repair services	44%	87%
Telecommunications	60%	93%
Travel and leisure	70%	93%
Petrochemical products	70%	91%
Life insurance	69%	89%

Source: The results are from a 1994 cross-industry research study by *The Service Impact Group*, a network of leading experts in service quality and quality improvement.

studies do not differentiate between whether the customer perceives that the problem was major or minor, or the frequency of having a problem.

By combining the frequency of problems occurring with repeat purchases, a customer could easily experience several problems. For ex-

---

Figure 18.3
Why Have Satisfied Customers?

- In the packaged goods industry, a satisfied customer tells **4 to 5** people about the experience. A dissatisfied customer tells **8 to 10** people about the experience.

- In the automobile industry, a satisfied customer tells **8 to 10** people about the experience. A dissatisfied customer tells **16 to 18** people about the experience.

- **Thirty percent** of customers with problems complain to the direct provider of the product or service.

- **Two to five %** of customer complaints get voiced to the headquarters level.

- A satisfied customer tells **four or five** people about the experience.

- A dissatisfied customer tells **eight to ten** people about the problem.

- **70–90%** of complaining customers will do business with you again if they are *satisfied* with the way the complaint was handled.

- **20–70%** will not do business with you again if they are completely *dissatisfied* with the way their complaint was handled.

- Only **10–30%** of customers with problems who not complain or request assistance will do business with you again.

- The average business spends **2 to 25** times more, on average, to attract new customers than it does to keep old ones.

Source: Technical Assistance Research Programs (TARP), Arlington, VA.

---

ample, it is very common for a customer to have experienced two or three problems with a firm. And the greater the number of problems encountered, the more likely customers are to take their business elsewhere unless the problem is satisfactorily resolved. Figure 18.3 illustrates some intriguing findings. Obviously, firms will lose more customers when there is a major problem, but minor problems also cause customers to leave.

Now, one additional fact needs to be introduced. Most customers experiencing problems do not complain (Figure 18.4). Depending on the industry and the severity of the problem, most studies show that only between 4 and 80% of customers go to the trouble of actually complaining. Instead, the silent majority simply take their business elsewhere.

An example may illustrate the severity of this situation. Let's assume that 40% of a firm's customers have experienced some type of problem during the past three months and that the average number of problems

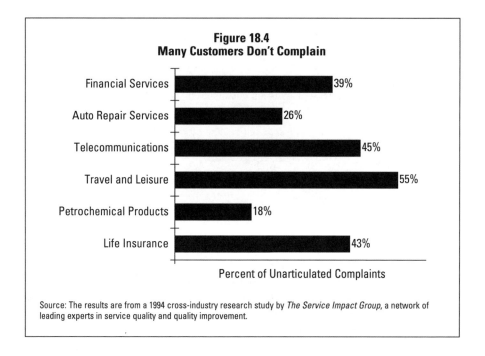

Figure 18.4
Many Customers Don't Complain

Financial Services	39%
Auto Repair Services	26%
Telecommunications	45%
Travel and Leisure	55%
Petrochemical Products	18%
Life Insurance	43%

Percent of Unarticulated Complaints

Source: The results are from a 1994 cross-industry research study by *The Service Impact Group*, a network of leading experts in service quality and quality improvement.

experienced is three. Let's further assume that 50% of customers experiencing problems formulate an intention to switch suppliers (and 50% is a conservative figure). This means that 20% of a firm's customers are ready to switch suppliers and may be actively searching for an alternative.

But if 10% of customers with problems actually complain, this is only 4% (.10 × .40 = .04) of the total customer base. Most firms would make the assumption that the remaining 96% must therefore be satisfied. Unfortunately, nothing could be further from the truth.

So the sad fact is that actual customer complaints are really only the tip of a very large iceberg. For most firms, the size and shape of the iceberg of customer discontent lies hidden beneath a sea of relative tranquility. The magnitude of customer discontent will be exposed only after the firm's ship strikes the iceberg and begins to hemorrhage not blood but market share. But trying to make repairs after the collision with the iceberg is like trying to repair a sinking ship. Such efforts are often too little and come far too late.

So, the overall goal of a customer complaint system does not consist in effectively responding to that vocal minority of 5 to 10% of the cus-

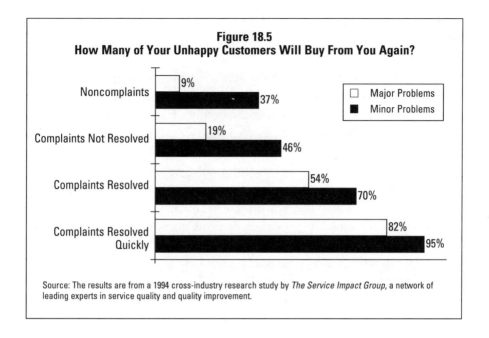

Figure 18.5
How Many of Your Unhappy Customers Will Buy From You Again?

Noncomplaints: 9% (Major Problems), 37% (Minor Problems)

Complaints Not Resolved: 19% (Major Problems), 46% (Minor Problems)

Complaints Resolved: 54% (Major Problems), 70% (Minor Problems)

Complaints Resolved Quickly: 82% (Major Problems), 95% (Minor Problems)

☐ Major Problems
■ Minor Problems

Source: The results are from a 1994 cross-industry research study by *The Service Impact Group*, a network of leading experts in service quality and quality improvement.

tomer base. The overall goal of a customer complaint system is to determine the shape, size, and cause of the iceberg. Quite simply, this requires a proactive system, not a reactive system to ensure that customers will continue to do business with you. Figure 18.5 illustrates the repurchase intent of customers experiencing both major and minor problems with a firm. Obviously, the more rapidly a complaint is resolved, the greater the repurchase intent. In fact, repurchase intent is *higher* for those customers who experience a minor problem that is resolved quickly. That's not to say that one should go out and deliberately create and resolve a problem to increase repurchase intent, but that a good complaint handling system is worth the money.

In order to be proactive, a firm must understand who does or does not complain and why those customers do or do not complain. The first issue is probably a little easier to address than the second. Customers who complain are seldom representative of a total customer base. Consumers who complain tend to have a higher income and be better educated, younger, and part of a larger household than non-complainers. With regard to personality, complainers tend to be independent, assertive, imaginative, self-sufficient, politically committed, and self-confident.

Organizationally, very little data exist about complaint behavior. But it appears that customers who are more innovative, creative, and demanding tend to complain more frequently.

Whether the complainer is a consumer or an organizational customer, both groups share a common characteristic. Complainers have an expectation that the supplier firm will actually do something as a result of the complaint. This expectation often has two parts. First, the customer usually has an expectation regarding what should be done to correct the immediate problem. This also includes an expectation of how the complaint should be handled. Second, customers generally have ideas about what should be done to prevent similar problems in the future. They may expect to see a change in processes or procedures as a result of their efforts. In effect, these customers are saying, "Look, here is something you can do to improve your business!"

The reason most customers with problems do not complain is another story. The most common reason for customers is that it's just too much trouble. This is especially the case for firms that require customers to put the complaint in writing. For many firms, the requirement to put complaints in writing is just a way to discourage customers from voicing any complaint at all.

Another reason for customers to remain silent is the expectation that complaining wouldn't do any good. The customer may feel that the firm just doesn't care and wouldn't make any changes. Or customers may not know where to file a complaint. Or customers may fear that complaints would cause worse service in the future.

Interestingly, virtually all of the reasons for reducing customer complaints can be overcome relatively easily. A firm must let customers know that complaints are encouraged. And a system of easy access must be set up.

Maine Savings Bank pays customers one dollar for each complaint letter. The bank publicizes the program extensively so that customers know that complaints are encouraged and welcome. The one-dollar reward is purely symbolic, letting customers know every input is important.

The Chevrolet Division of General Motors provides a good example of a customer complaint system. There are 36 million Chevrolet vehicles on the road, sold by a dealer network of over 5,000 dealers.

In the past, when a customer had a complaint, it was handled by the local dealer. If the local dealer was unable to resolve the complaint, the customer was referred to one of Chevrolet's forty-four branch offices. Each branch office maintained a small customer service staff. This decentralized approach resulted, however, in a fragmented, inconsistent response to customer complaints. And Chevrolet had no systematic way to collect and analyze the customer feedback.

As a result, Chevrolet centralized its customer service into a single Customer Assistance Center. Chevrolet found that about 40% of customers with problems would actually complain. But 80% of those customers expressed an intent to repurchase if the complaint were handled in a professional, efficient, concerned manner. Interestingly, the complaint did not even have to be fully resolved for a repurchase intent to exist. Essentially, the customer really simply wanted someone to listen and do what could be done to help.

Of the 60% of customers with problems who don't complain, only 10% of those will repurchase. So, for every 100 customers experiencing problems, 60 remain silent. Of those, 6 will repurchase, but the other 54 will buy a competitor's product. Thirty-two of the 40 customers who actually complained were willing to repurchase. The message to Chevrolet was clear: The division needed to get all customers with problems to complain!

To provide easy customer access, Chevrolet installed a toll-free 800 number to the Customer Assistance Center. The number is printed in owner's manuals, sales literature, posters in the sales area, and most phone books in the United States. The number is available through 800 information, and it has been publicized in newspapers and magazines.

The Chevrolet Customer Assistance Center now gets 5,000 calls daily, handled by a staff of more than 200 service representatives. The normal waiting time for customers is only five seconds, and 80% of the calls are answered on the first ring.

Chevrolet's predominant goal was to get *all* customers with problems to break the silence and open a dialogue with the company. The second goal was to then handle the customer complaints in a professional, efficient manner.

The experience of Chevrolet is not unique. In the first two years of Mazda Motor Company's 800 number for customer service, 437,000 customers contacted the company. Although not all of those calls were complaints, the number represents almost 14% of the 3.2 million Mazda owners in the United States. And the majority of these calls were from owners of cars less than two years old. So Mazda was able to open a dialogue with a significant portion of its recent buyers.

The implication from all of this is that a firm must develop a system of easy access for customers and publicize it extensively. It must not sit back and wait for customers to complain. A firm must proactively *encourage* complaints. And once a customer does complain, the firm must close the loop and say, "Thank you for letting us know where we need improvement!"

CHARACTERISTICS OF A GOOD COMPLAINT SYSTEM

Regardless of the industry, the nature of the complaints, or the volume of complaints handled, all good customer complaint systems share some common characteristics. These characteristics are presented in Table 18.1. However, since customer complaint systems must be adapted to fit a corporate culture, there is no one best approach for each characteristic, but the following discussions illustrate the approaches used by innovative firms.

Easy Access

Despite the benefits of toll-free customer complaint numbers, a complaint system must be far more comprehensive. Customer complaints can be made to customer contact personnel, through channel members, through the mail, or directly to executives. In extreme situations, complaints could come through Better Business Bureaus or government agencies. Or the complaints could be expressed on a customer satisfaction survey or a payment invoice. A good customer complaint system allows customer input to quickly enter the system, regardless of where it originates.

For Mazda, customer complaints most commonly come through phone calls, letters, and comments on customer satisfaction surveys. Customer complaints are also made in person by customers both at corporate offices and at dealers. If the Mazda system accommodated only phone calls to the service center, the complaint database would be incomplete.

British Airways has video booths in London's Heathrow Airport so that passengers can express their attitudes immediately after completing

Table 18.1 Key Characteristics of a Customer Complaint System

1. Easy Access—Customers should have many ways to express complaints.

2. Fast Response—Customers should receive fast, personalized acknowledgment and resolution.

3. No Hassle—The complaint system should be free to the customer.

4. Empowered Employees—Employees must be empowered to resolve customer problems.

5. Employee Staff and Training—Employees, particularly customer service employees, must receive both technical product training and interpersonal skills training.

6. Customer Database—The firm should have a computerized, accessible database on all customers.

7. Organization Commitment—Top management must commit resources and attention to complaint resolution.

their flight. Marriott has a twenty-four-hour customer service hot line designed to solicit immediate feedback from customers while they are still in the hotel. Many firms have installed suggestion boxes to solicit ideas for improvement from customers. In all of these examples of easy access, customers generally identify areas where they've experienced problems of some type.

To this point, we've seen that businesses need to actively *encourage* customers to complain if they experience problems. And businesses must make it easy for customers to lodge a complaint through whatever means is convenient. The remainder of this discussion focuses on what should be done *after* the complaint is received.

Fast Responses

A good complaint system provides fast, personalized response. When Solectron, a Baldrige award winner, receives a complaint, the customer is contacted within twenty-four hours. The contact is normally made by phone, or by fax if a phone call fails. Solectron acknowledges complaints, thanks customers for expressing themselves, and seeks any necessary clarification. Within one week, Solectron gets back to the customer and says, "Here's what caused the problem and here's how we changed our processes to prevent the same problem from happening again." Solectron also has a no-hassle return policy so customers can easily return any defective merchandise.

Solectron's system illustrates the two components of fast response. The first component consists of simply acknowledging that the complaint was received and that the firm is investigating the problem; the acknowledgment should be personalized to the customer if at all possible. But even the dreaded form letter to the generic "Dear Customer" is better than nothing. And doing nothing is the option many firms choose when handling complaints.

Firms that don't respond to customer complaints are creating a negative corporate image. Customers with problems will share their negative experiences with other existing or potential customers. Bad news travels faster by three to four times than good news. The act of not responding to complaints has an immediate financial impact due to the behavior of existing customers.

In a recent study of large consumer products firms, nearly 25% of customers received no response to their complaints. The perceptions of corporate image held by those customers plummeted across all six dimensions measured (fairness, satisfaction, reputation, interest, courtesy, and quality). About 25% of customers received only a letter responding to their complaint. Those customers perceived the corporate image to be far better, 20 to 30 percentage points higher, than customers receiving no response. About half of the customers received a letter and a free item such as a product replacement, some type of coupon, or a refund check. These customers held a corporate image that was better, by a margin of about 10 percentage points, than customers receiving only a letter.

For customers receiving a response of any type, a quick response resulted in a better image, by a margin of 2 to 10 percentage points, than a slow response. The implication of all this is that a firm should quickly respond to *all* complaints, if only to acknowledge receipt of the complaint.

This brings us to the second aspect of fast response. A firm must resolve the complaint quickly in some way. The complaint resolution could take many forms, from acknowledgment ("Sorry, there's nothing we can do") to refund ("Here's a refund check") to replacement ("Here's a new product"). Complaint resolutions that offer something of value to the customer, in whatever form, create a more positive image.

When deciding the appropriate resolution, a firm should weigh the cost of satisfying the customer versus the cost of losing the customer.

Normally, the lifetime value of a customer is far greater than the resolution cost. But whatever option a firm chooses, the choice should be made quickly.

No Hassles

The complaint system should not be an endurance course, rewarding only those customers who persevere. One of the larger U.S.-based airlines advertised that it had partnership arrangements with several foreign airlines so fliers could get credit for mileage flown on those airlines. Therefore, one of their customers planned a trip from the United States to New Zealand and Australia. At ticketing, he gave his frequent flier card to the ticket agent, who said the airline could give credit only for the U.S. miles. At the ticket counter in Los Angeles, he attempted to give his frequent flier card to the ticket agent for the foreign airline. The agent had no idea what to do and so called a supervisor. The supervisor provided a form that needed to be completed for each leg of the flight. The form was to be given to the person who takes the tickets at the gate. But the person at the gate had never seen the form before and told the passenger to hang on to it. No one at any of the foreign cities would take the form either.

After returning to the United States, the customer complained to the ticketing personnel, who said that he was welcome to complain to the company if he wanted. The customer then complained that he'd just spent the past ten minutes explaining the situation to them, for after all, they represent the airline. But the employees simply said, "We don't handle complaints; that's home office."

So the customer asked for the toll-free customer service number. The person at the desk said, "We don't have one. We want complaints in writing." The customer was instructed to write a letter, explaining everything and including all boarding pass stubs for documentation, and then send it to the home office. The customer growled, "You've already got my itinerary on your computer." The person at the desk responded that that was the airline's policy.

After complying with the request for documentation, the customer sent everything to the "customer service" department but never heard back from the airline. When the customer made his next trip a month later to the South Pacific, he flew on a different airline.

Unfortunately, situations such as these are not terribly unusual. These types of situations are what makes Walmart's no-hassle return policy or

Quill Corp.'s "100 percent Satisfaction Guarantee" so effective with customers. When customers have bad experiences with one firm, those customers are more appreciative of good service at another firm.

For firms utilizing a channel of distribution with several intermediaries, a reverse channel should be designed. Most channels are designed for the outbound flow of products to the ultimate customer or consumer. The channel should also be designed for the return flow of defective or returned merchandise. For most consumers, it is easier to simply return merchandise to the retailer where the item was purchased rather than ship the item to a customer service center. But for such a no-hassle system to work, the entire channel must be coordinated.

Research shows that unconditional, no-hassle return policies are seldom abused by customers. Many firms have found that by advertising such policies, their corporate images have been significantly enhanced.

Empowered Employees

In order for fast, no-hassle response to occur, employees must be empowered to make decisions on the spot. Installing bureaucratic hurdles and approval processes slows responses and typically increases the burden of proof on customers.

Empowering employees is more a corporate attitude than a set of actions. Empowerment requires that "managers" have faith in the ability of "employees" to make the right decisions. At one end of the continuum is McDonald's Corp., which empowers employees to make sure customers are satisfied, providing a free meal if necessary. At the other end of the continuum is Lexus, empowering dealers to do "whatever it takes" to satisfy a Lexus owner. In both cases, no approval from "higher-ups" is necessary. Ritz-Carlton Hotel employees can spend up to $2500 to resolve a customer complaint.

So one aspect of empowerment is behavioral. It's a firm's recognizing that it has good employees capable of making good decisions. The firm not only *allows* employees to make decisions, but *encourages* employees to proactively respond to customers, and the firm then *recognizes* outstanding customer care.

In addition to empowering employees to act, a firm must give employees guidelines and parameters to assist their decision making. For some firms, this may mean a certain dollar limit for authority, giving employees flexibility within that range. For other firms, like Marriott, employees are told that their job is "to ensure that guests experience excellent service and hospitality." Marriott employees are given wide latitude in achieving that goal.

The issue of empowerment is not restricted to customer service employees. Certainly, empowering customer service employees is important. But all employees who have customer contact need to be aware of the firm's customer complaint system, guidelines, and procedures. All of these employees must be empowered to make decisions quickly to resolve customer complaints.

Employee Staffing and Training

Employee staffing and training are critical aspects of any corporate activity, and customer complaint handling is no exception. A customer service department requires good, well-trained employees, not low-skilled, part-time workers. Many companies make customer service an initial career track starting point.

Hewlett-Packard (H-P), like many other firms, staffs its customer service with college graduates. Within H-P, customer service positions lead to careers in marketing, product development, sales, quality, and human resources. After two years in customer service, employees have a thorough understanding of how important satisfying the customer is. By making customer service a career starting point, H-P also sends the message to the entire organization that customer service is important.

Training in customer complaint handling should not be restricted to customer service employees. All customer-contact employees need to understand the company's policies and procedures. Therefore, the complaint system needs to be well marketed within the firm to all employees. For most firms, this means a formal training effort that explains the how, what, and why of the customer-complaint-handling system.

The more difficult training challenge lies with comprehensive training of the customer service staff. The first challenge is deciding how much training is appropriate. Federal Express requires five weeks, General Motors requires four weeks, and H-P requires four weeks. For these firms, this represents only the initial training for new hires. These firms also have an extensive array of ongoing group and individual training.

Group training addresses issues common to all customer service personnel such as product characteristics and system changes. Individualized training is based on each employee's strengths, weaknesses, and career aspirations. Firms like Dow Chemical and H-P develop catalogs of courses from which customer service employees and other employees can choose. While most such courses are delivered internally, external courses and seminars are also available. But the training is not restricted to courses alone.

Customer service personnel can be included on site visit teams so they may gain firsthand understanding of the problems facing customers. They can also be involved in cross-training in such areas as production, new product development, and quality improvement so they can see how customer input can be used in those areas.

A strong argument could be made that customer service personnel need more extensive training than most employees, because their job is inherently more diverse, requiring a broader range of skills. For good resolution of customer problems, an organization must develop a strong, well-trained customer service function. The question that logically emerges is, What type of training is best?

Most customer service training falls into one of two broad categories: behavioral and technical. Behavioral training deals with communication and interpersonal skills. Behavioral training at General Motors includes topics such as defusing angry customers, stress management, time management, negotiation, and interpersonal communication. The training is delivered through a combination of classroom instruction, role-playing, and experimental exercises. The goal of the behavioral training is to improve the service representative's interpersonal skills so that interaction with customers moves toward a win-win situation instead of the initial adversarial position where most complaints begin. The six basics of customer behavioral training are listed in Figure 18.6.

Many of the phone calls to customer service centers are not complaints. At General Motors, about 40% of calls are complaints, and the rest are inquiries about company products or policies. The implication is that customer service personnel need to know much more than how to resolve a customer complaint. This leads to the need for service reps to be well versed in technical areas as well.

At the Hewlett-Packard Network Printer Customer Support Center, over 600 employees receive extensive technical training in the installation and operation of new products before the new products are released. Each new introduction brings a flood of customer inquiries. H-P employees also receive extensive training in various software packages such as word processing, graphics, and spreadsheets because each such program has unique peculiarities in terms of its interaction with printers. Knowing a great deal about only printers would be woefully inade-

---

Figure 18.6
Six Basics of Customer Service

Recognize and Appreciate Customer
Listen and Reiterate Issue
Empathize
Meet or Exceed Customer Expectation
Verify Resolution of Issue
Thank Them for Their Business!

---

quate. Therefore, an employee must be well trained in technical product features in addition to being trained about other types of products as well.

Since many customer contacts made to service centers are not complaints, Monsanto found that sales training was very beneficial. Therefore Monsanto's customer service personnel receive training in competitive strengths and weaknesses, sales promotion, pricing structures, and delivery schedules. The customer service people have been very successful at sales efforts and now work closely with marketing and distribution.

Technical training can include company policies, procedures, computer system training, and product knowledge. Customer service personnel need to know much more than just product features to be effective.

Extensive training of many types must be provided for employees handling customer complaints. And all employees must be trained in the handling of customer complaints. Computer applications, the next characteristic to be discussed, are closely related to the training issue.

Customer Databases

The trend in organizational handling of customer complaints is to centralize the operation to one location. This has occurred primarily through technological advances in computer hardware, software, and communication systems.

Virtually every firm should have a computerized customer database accessible to customer service personnel. Such a database should contain all of the traditional demographic and sales histories. But the account should also have a section for all customer service contacts. For example, at Cellular One, all customer service contacts are recorded. The service rep knows when the last contact was, what the problem was, and when and how the problem was resolved. Each new contact is added to the customer's database.

The complaints do not go only to the customer database, however. Complaint data go to engineering and new product development too. There, engineers can get daily and weekly reports on the problems being experienced by customers. This type of feedback clearly identifies areas of needed product or service improvements for Cellular One. H-P has a similar system, called Spirit, which feeds current customer data into new product development terms.

A key feature of many complaint systems is the exception report by which the computer automatically identifies complaints that have not been resolved in a certain time period such as twenty-four hours or seven days. For example, Texas Instruments' standard is that 95% of inquiries get a response within two hours.

Related to the computerized database is the call management system. At Quill Corp., with a volume of over 7,000 calls daily, the goal is to have a delay period of less than fifteen seconds. At General Motors, the normal delay is five seconds, with 80% of calls answered in the first ring. At H-P, employees know how many calls are in the queue, the average hold time, and the longest hold time.

Some companies design their phone system so that calls are routed directly to line managers. In other companies, customers on hold for thirty or forty-five seconds can leave their name and number and be phoned back within thirty minutes or an hour. The technological capability exists for firms to design their direct-dial systems any way they wish.

Polaroid has implemented a toll-free line for the hearing impaired. Many firms have added bilingual or multilingual service staff to respond to speakers of Spanish, Chinese, or Korean. This is a particular concern for multinational corporations, for many countries have a high degree of linguistic diversity.

Technological advances in hardware, software, and telecommunications have enabled firms to develop integrated customer databases that facilitate high levels of personalized service. Any firm that does not have such a database will soon be at a competitive disadvantage.

Organization Commitment

As is evident from the preceding discussions, high-quality customer complaint handling will not result from superficial, ad hoc support. An organization must be strongly committed to allocate enough resources for staffing, training, and support systems. The more innovative firms approach complaint handling as an investment rather than an expense.

L. L. Bean has found that customers who complain are more loyal, after the complaint is resolved, than the average customer. As a result, employees are told to do whatever the customer asks. Only higher levels of management have the authority to say no to a customer. L. L. Bean has made a significant investment in and commitment to its system of encouraging and resolving customer complaints.

CHAPTER SUMMARY

Customer complaints do more damage to a firm's reputation and image when the complaint is not registered with the firm. Bad news spreads fast, and disgruntled customers are usually eager to tell others about their misfortune and bad experiences. Therefore, a firm should approach customer complaints proactively, extinguishing the spark of customer discontent before it becomes a raging inferno that consumes the firm's market share.

Customer complaints are opportunities—opportunities to identify overlooked problems, opportunities to drive continuous improvement, opportunities to retain dissatisfied customers. Customer complaints are not something to be dreaded and avoided at all costs. That was the 1970s and 1980s way of looking at the problem: Bury your head in the sand, and maybe the problem will go away.

Companies must proactively seek out, solicit, and *encourage* customers to complain. Thus, complaint handling systems must be inherently proactive, not reactive, in nature. The complaint system must be easily accessible, designed for no-hassle, fast response. Employees must be fully empowered to resolve problems, supported by comprehensive training and computerized support systems. And the whole organization must be committed to customer satisfaction and customer retention. Such a commitment means significant allocation of resources so as to effectively handle complaints and enhance customer loyalty. But the alternative—ignoring customer complaints—carries an even greater cost. That cost is called survival.

DIAMOND SHAMROCK

Complaint Handling

Diamond Shamrock (DS) is a San Antonio, Texas, oil company. It operates two refineries in Texas, supplying over 2,000 gasoline stores in eight states. DS owns about 800 of the stores, and the rest are operated by franchised jobbers. The firm has embraced a commitment to total quality management for many years, as reflected by its vision statement: "We will be the best, emphasizing outstanding customer service, quality products at competitive prices, a safe and productive work environment, corporate responsibility, and superior returns to our stockholders."

The company's commitment to customer service quality is reflected in its complaint management system. The flowchart in Figure 18.7 depicts the major elements of complaint handling. This system is designed for easy access, accommodating complaints from a wide variety of sources. Once a complaint is received, it is quickly acknowledged either by phone or letter depending upon the urgency. The complaint system is a closed loop, providing the customer with feedback about what happened as a result of the complaint. Since the system is computerized, exceptions are automatically kicked out. For example, a particular complaint may justify a follow-up phone call thirty days after initial resolution. The computer automatically pulls the file for the customer service representative to handle.

To facilitate data analysis and use of the data for continuous improvement, DS developed a flowchart and file (Figure 18.8). Each of the items can be tracked on a weekly or monthly basis. This quickly highlights the major causes of customer complaints. Then the continuous improvement teams can focus their attention on the most critical items. To encourage employee buy-in, this type of data is distributed widely throughout the organization. Each employee can quickly identify individual contribution to the company's improvement effort.

The system tracks not only complaints but suggestions, compliments, and customer requests as well. By including positive feedback, along with complaints, employees tend to be more supportive and accepting of the program.

Developing a flowchart that tracks customer complaints can be quite enlightening. Many firms find that they have several dead ends that become black holes, allowing complaints to fall through the cracks. Firms also benefit from developing a flowchart showing how customer input is actually used.

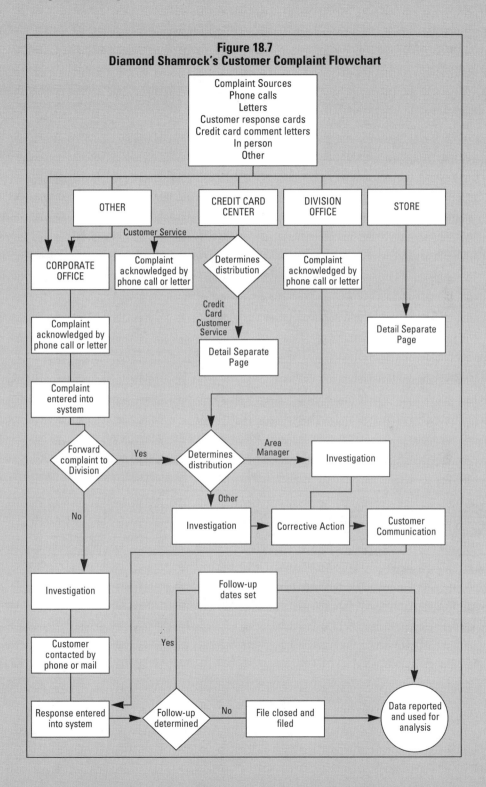

Figure 18.7
Diamond Shamrock's Customer Complaint Flowchart

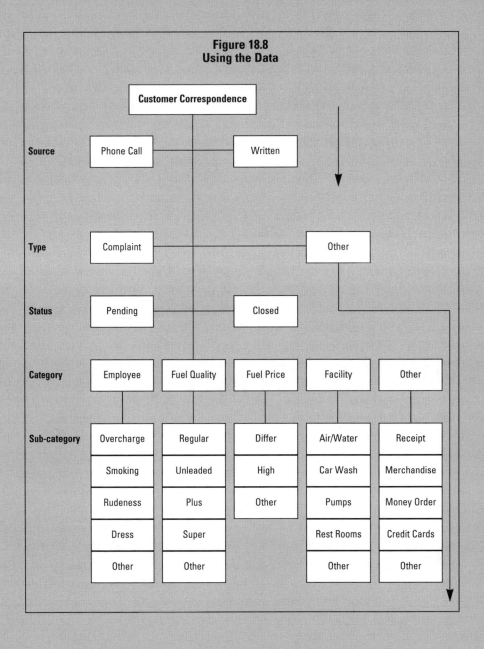

Figure 18.8
Using the Data

19

CSM for the Small Business

All of the discussions throughout this book are pertinent to businesses of all sizes, large and small. Unfortunately, the fact is that most CSM programs are in place at large businesses. Very few small businesses have a formal program to solicit customer input. Instead, most entrepreneurs or small business owners *assume* that they know what the customer wants and needs. And many entrepreneurs are even more certain that their own product or service is clearly superior to all the competitive offerings.

There is actually some credence attached to the first assumption. Entrepreneurs usually do have a better understanding of the customer's wants and needs than do managers in large firms. That understanding often grows out of being closer to the customer and having direct, personal interaction with customers on a daily basis. Entrepreneurial ideas often come from the ability to anticipate or cash in on an unmet need or want. This closeness to the customer is just a result of the soft, nonquantitative approaches to CSM discussed elsewhere in this book.

However, the second assumption, having an accurate competitive profile, is almost always inaccurate. Very few entrepreneurs have a good understanding of their competitive strengths and weaknesses relative to the competition—from the customer's perspective, that is. Obtaining an accurate, customer-driven competitive profile is, by itself, ample justification for designing, implementing, and maintaining a CSM program. But, of course, there are other benefits as well, such as capturing ideas for innovation, creating a clearer vision, and having better information for decision making.

Rather than try to sell the idea that CSM is important for small businesses, the authors make the assumption that anyone reading this has already accepted that CSM is important and the reader is now grappling with the difficult "how to" issue. Therefore, the remainder of this chapter presents a sequential flow of the steps a small business should take to implement a CSM program.

Step One: Get Help!

Most owners or managers of a small business lack the time, expertise, and/or money to do everything suggested in this book. Those three constraints, however, are the dominant considerations that lead to modifications for small businesses. So each modification from the earlier suggestions is spawned by one or more of these issues, including the first: get help!

Getting help does not mean immediately hiring a consultant, particularly for a small firm. In fact, you are holding one of the best ways to get help—this book. All of the key issues pertaining to CSM programs are contained here. After a thorough read of this book, you will have greater knowledge of CSM than at least 95% of all managers. So, the expertise constraint can be resolved by studying this book. But the time and resource constraints are not resolved by this book. Instead, there are some free or low-cost outside sources of help for many small businesses.

Most colleges or universities offer marketing degrees or at least marketing courses. In some of those courses, faculty often use real-world projects, usually in the form of local small businesses. The courses that would be appropriate for CSM projects are customer satisfaction, marketing research, and marketing for small business. At some colleges, consumer behavior or marketing strategy courses would also use real firms for projects. The initial step in this situation is to phone the department chair in marketing and describe your firm. The department chair can quickly apprise you of the likelihood of the school's using your firm as a project. There is normally no cost to your firm except for the out-of-pocket expenses necessary for the research, such as photocopying or computer time for data analysis.

Instead of having a CSM program implemented in your firm as a college class project, the use of student internships is also a possibility. To tighten the linkage between academic and real-world applications, many business schools are now requiring an internship of all students. Internships are usually topically focused toward a specific major such as marketing, accounting, or finance. With the help of this book, most marketing students should be able to design a CSM program. Most business schools have an internship director who coordinates the program, and that is whom you should contact.

Another source of help is the Small Business Administration (SBA). The SBA has a Small Business Institute program that compensates business schools for conducting small-business projects. The compensation is about $400 per project and is intended to offset incidental expenses. The SBA maintains contact with many colleges and universities and acts as a liaison. The SBA also has a variety of other services that may be beneficial to a small business implementing a CSM program.

When using business schools as a source of help, you must keep two things in mind: First, projects are normally a part of a course; thus, the project will usually start at the beginning of a semester (August or January) or quarter (September, January, or April) and be completed at the end of the semester (December or May) or quarter (December, March, or June). Very few projects are started at other times, so you can't expect more rapid completion of the project. The second issue is that the quality and motivation of college students are highly variable. Some students will do truly outstanding work; others will barely get by. So you should confer with the instructor about the strengths and weaknesses in your project. Don't assume that the project is perfect.

If a small-business owner or manager is going to have someone else either partially or totally design the CSM program, the entrepreneur must, at minimum, be familiar with the key issues in this book. The reason for this is that no CSM program is perfect; every program can be improved in some way. And CSM programs must change and evolve just as customers' wants and needs change and evolve. In a small business, the ultimate responsibility for this expertise rests with the entrepreneur or owner.

Step Two: Define the Objectives
Of the five CSM objectives discussed earlier in this book, two emerge as most critical for small businesses; the other three are less important. The two least important attributes are *closer to the customer* and *identify customer-driven innovations*. Feedback on these issues results largely from the entrepreneur's frequent customer interaction and possible mo-

tivation for starting the business in the first place. Hence, a formal program to capture customer input about these really isn't necessary. The third, less important, objective is linking CSM to performance evaluations and reward systems. This use of the data is simply less necessary for small businesses due to a more pervasive customer orientation. It is relatively easy for all employees to identify with the customer due to their more direct contact.

That leaves the two remaining objectives identified in Figure 19.1: identifying competitive strengths and weaknesses and measuring continuous improvement. With the identification of competitive strengths and weaknesses as an objective, the CSM program becomes more complex. Questions must make a comparative assessment of performance, and, if possible, competitors' customers should be surveyed.

The other objective, measuring continuous improvement, requires that a database be developed that allows longitudinal tracking of CSM measures. This is normally done on an aggregate or overall basis, but could also be done for specific attributes. Fulfilling this objective means that there needs to be a fair amount of consistency from period to period.

As we shall see, these two objectives will influence many of the subsequent activities and design issues. Therefore, the assumption is made that all small businesses should adopt these last two objectives.

Step Three: Identify the Customers

If a firm's customer base is very homogeneous, this is a pretty easy step to accomplish. With a high degree of homogeneity, all customers are more or less the same. Therefore, it doesn't make too much difference which customers are surveyed or contacted. The results will be roughly the same, regardless.

If a firm's customer base is very heterogeneous, with a variety of distinctly different segments, each major segment must be identified. The reason that this must be done is that different segments may have distinctly different decision criteria. In the extreme case, the divergent criteria may require a different questionnaire for each major segment. But at the least, a questionnaire must address the attributes relevant to each segment.

For example, a small business may sell to individual consumers, other small businesses, and large businesses. Each of these three segments would probably be concerned with quite different criteria. Unless the

---

Figure 19.1
Two Key CSM Objectives for Small Businesses

1. Identify competitive strengths and weaknesses.

2. Measure continuous improvement.

---

same criteria were important to all three segments, three different CSM questionnaires may be needed.

For firms whose customers are other businesses, the familiar problem reemerges of identifying which individual or individuals are the appropriate "customers." The customer in these instances should be defined as a cross section of individuals who are involved in the purchase and use of the product. Except for very small organizations, two or three individuals should be identified in each firm so that a representative profile can be developed. Relying on only one respondent per firm can result in biased data, depending on the respondent's area of responsibility.

If it is at all possible, competitors' customers should also be identified. Many of a firm's current customers may have bought from competitors, so the existing customer base is often capable of providing a competitive profile. Otherwise, an attempt should be made to identify the competitors' customers. This is normally difficult for a retail business but is quite easy for a firm selling to other businesses. Competitors' customers often provide a very enlightening perception of a business, and those competitive perceptions are necessary to identify both strengths and weaknesses.

Once the customers have been identified, with as many segments as appropriate, the next step is to identify the issues that are important to them—those key attributes.

Step Four: Identify the Attributes

The entrepreneur should first make a list of all the attributes believed important to customers. The attributes should address the features of the core product or service. But additionally, the attributes should include that array of support services as well. This process, by itself, is an eye-opener for most entrepreneurs.

When an entrepreneur is asked, "Why do your customers buy from you?" the most common response is to list from three to five attributes. With a little prodding and further thought, entrepreneurs can get the list up to ten or twelve attributes. But even with fifteen attributes, the list is usually still incomplete, for customers are often able to identify twenty to thirty, and a focus group can sometimes identify more than forty.

It is important to note that a separate list of attributes should be developed for each major customer segment. With a homogeneous customer base, one list of attributes is adequate, but for now, trying to identify the differences and commonalities between all segments is necessary.

Once the entrepreneur has compiled the list of attributes, customers' input must be solicited. For each segment, about six customers should be contacted, preferably through the use of personal interviews, although telephone interviews may be adequate. Generally, the interviews should be built around the question "What factors influence your overall satisfaction as our customer?" This type of interview often benefits from some structured prods such as "What product factors . . . " or "What service factors . . ."

The primary danger is for the entrepreneur to lead the customer's responses. Therefore, care must be taken so the entrepreneur remains neutral during the interviews.

At this point, the entrepreneur should have six or seven attribute lists—one from each customer, for each segment. From these lists, a clear pattern of attributes should have emerged. There should be patterns both within and between different segments. If the different segments have very similar profiles, collapsing the lists into one composite list is possible at this point. However, if the lists are different for each segment, they should be kept separate.

The next task consists of reducing the lists to the ten or so most important attributes. Although large businesses may have more than twenty attributes in their CSM models, ten attributes are generally ample for most small businesses.

There are three ways to reduce the list to the ten most salient attributes. The best way is to have a customer focus group of six to ten customers identify the ten. The second-best way is to contact six or so customers individually and ask each to pick the ten; then pool the results. The least-preferred way is for the entrepreneur to arbitrarily pick the ten based on the previous interviews. These ten attributes form the heart of the CSM program, so accurate selection is critical.

Step Five: Develop the Questionnaire

The design of the questionnaire is determined by the overall research design and method of administration. The easiest and most commonly used method of administration for small businesses is transaction based. Customers in a retail establishment may be asked to complete a questionnaire upon entering or leaving a store or at the time of purchase. A coupon for a discount on the next purchase is often given as a reward for cooperation. A firm that sends out a billing statement could include a questionnaire in the mailing.

In both of these cases, the questionnaire should be short and simple, preferably about one page long, but certainly no longer than a double-sided page. As covered in detail in the appendixes, the questionnaire should have a good introduction and initial set of directions leading into a general first question.

There should be two or three global, overall measures. The most commonly used overall questions deal with satisfaction, referral, and repurchase intent. Although the scaling can vary based on the researcher's preferences, the following are typical:

Overall, how satisfied are you with (product, store, etc.)?

Very Satisfied						Very Dissatisfied
1	2	3	4	5	6	7

Would you recommend this (company, product, etc.) to a friend?

Definitely Would Recommend						Definitely Would Not Recommend
1	2	3	4	5	6	7

In the future, will you (shop here, buy this product, etc.) again?

Definitely Would						Definitely Would Not
1	2	3	4	5	6	7

The satisfaction question is a very common first question because of its global nature. The other questions would normally be spread out, one at the middle and one at the end of the questionnaire.

If a firm has a relatively small group of competitors who are clearly defined, each could be evaluated individually on each attribute. For example, a question like "How does XYZ company perform on delivery timeliness?" could be repeated for each competitor on each attribute. Because of the problems with questionnaire length, this approach works well only for three or four firms. This approach does yield a very accurate and detailed assessment of each competitor's strengths and weaknesses, however.

If a firm has a larger, less well defined group of competitors, more general questions are more appropriate. These questions refer to competitors as "other firms" as in the following example.

Compared with other firms, our delivery timeliness is:

Among the Worst	Worse Than Most	Slightly Below Average	About Average	Slightly Above Average	Better Than Most	Among the Best	Don't Know

The use of general, overall measures allows the firm to develop a simple, straightforward tracking index. All three general questions could be aggregated into a single score or could be kept separate. This type of data could then be easily distributed to employees.

The competitor profile questions for specific attributes allow competitive strengths and weaknesses to be quickly identified. This provides excellent input for defining needed process improvement.

In addition to the questions measuring a firm's absolute or comparative performance on the key attributes, there should also be questions measuring the relative importance of each attribute. If ten attributes are included in the questionnaire, it is unlikely that all of them are equally important to the customer. Instead, three or four may be critically important and the rest of lesser importance. The relative importance of each attribute, particularly when coupled with competitive profiles, allows priorities for improvement to be established.

The customer's perception of the relative importance among attributes normally changes slowly. Thus, relative importance can be measured periodically, such as once or twice a year. This allows the questionnaire to be a little shorter for most surveys, because only the firm's performance is being measured. For consistency, particularly when the overall questionnaire is short, some firms use the same questionnaire every time, measuring both performance and importance.

Step Six: Pretest the Questionnaire
Most questionnaires need to be revised many times during their development. Once the entrepreneur has developed a good questionnaire, it should be pretested on a group of good customers; about ten will suffice. The customers should be informed that their advice is desired on how the questionnaire can be improved.

With this feedback, a questionnaire will usually benefit from minor modifications. If major changes were necessary, a second pretest may be justified. It is important to remember that the data can be no better than the underlying questions, so don't skip the pretest!

Step Seven: Select Sampling Procedures

The sampling procedure should specify who will be surveyed, the frequency of administration, and the method of administration. The easiest sampling procedure for a small business is to simply survey customers at the time of a transaction. For retail businesses, this could be done at the point of sale, with a discount off the next purchase given as an incentive.

When a questionnaire is being administered in this manner, *all* customers should be included. There is a tendency on the part of people administering a survey to select customers who are more likely to respond. This type of subtle screening may yield a biased sample. For most small businesses, gathering CSM data once a month is adequate, as is a sample size of about 100. So a firm might gather 100 completed questionnaires during the first few days of the month.

In response to a personal request for completion of a questionnaire, customer participation is normally pretty high. Response rates of 60–70% are common. If response rates are low, say 20–30%, this indicates that there is a problem of some type. Perhaps the questionnaire is too long or the timing is inconvenient. Therefore, an entrepreneur should keep track of the participation rate, especially for the first few months. An incentive may increase response rates. A coupon for a discount on the customers' next purchase, a promotional item carrying your name or logo, or the chance to enter a drawing with other respondents for an expensive product or service are possibilities.

For firms that send CSM questionnaires enclosed with a billing statement, response rates of 25% are common. Thus, to obtain 100 completed questionnaires, 400 must be sent out. Again, the actual response rate needs to be calculated, particularly for the first few months of the program.

Samples such as these are sometimes referred to as convenience samples. The term comes from the idea that these samples are convenient and easy to reach. However, convenience samples are not necessarily exactly representative of a total customer base. The most common tendency is for convenience respondents to be more favorably disposed toward the firm unless their most recent experience was particularly negative. In this case, your customer may be testing you to determine your commitment to customer satisfaction and complaint handling. Customers with overall negative attitudes tend not to respond at all. So this type of sampling procedure produces results with a slightly positive bias.

The second problem with this sampling procedure is that it includes only the firm's current customer base. If customers also have experience with competitors, the competitor profile will be roughly accurate. But here again customers will tend to be more favorably disposed toward their current supplier, so the data will have a positive bias.

Because of that tendency toward positive bias, the sample plan should include a broader definition of the customer. The most accessible and often most discerning respondents are former customers. Former customers have experience with your business, as well as with competitors'. And since these individuals have made a conscious decision to switch, they can quickly and accurately identify competitive weaknesses.

Somewhat harder to identify are competitors' current customers. But if those customers can be identified and surveyed, they are able to provide the most accurate competitive profile. For most small businesses, it is well worth the trouble to extend the sampling plan beyond the current customer base.

Step Eight: Gather the Data

If the other aspects of the research design are well formulated, then gathering the data is relatively simple and straightforward. Most of the bugs, or program flaws, should have been identified in the pretest. However, problems may still emerge that require adjustments. Such problems are normally evident during the fieldwork.

For telephone surveys, such situations as no answers, unavailability, or answering machines require consistent procedures. If you plan to use your own employees to interview, basic training in interviewing techniques is important. Figure 19.2 outlines the critical areas of training for interviewing. For convenience samples, deciding which days and times to administer questionnaires must be resolved. For mailings with billing statements, the actual customer statements being stuffed must be determined. With all these types of decisions, the dominant objective must be to obtain unbiased, representative data.

One issue that almost always comes up is what to do with partially completed questionnaires. Generally, a questionnaire must be totally or substantially complete to be included. Questionnaires that are less than

---

Figure 19.2
Telephone Interviewing Tips for Employees

Prior to Interviewing

- Familiarize yourself with the survey instrument.

- Pay close attention to questions that permit more than one response.

- Make sure answers to open-ended or probing questions are recorded precisely.

- Practice administering the questionnaire with other team members before using it with customers. Preferably rehearse with someone not associated with the study. The survey should not last more than 10 minutes with a colleague because it will usually be longer with a customer.

During the Interview

- State your name, company, and purpose of the survey at the outset. State how the respondent will benefit from participation in the survey.

- Determine whether the time is convenient for the respondent; if not, reschedule at the respondent's request.

- Don't express your own opinions or comment on any responses received.

- Probe open-ended questions to find out all issues and details.

- Be easy to understand; speak clearly and concisely using simple grammar. Don't use terminology or acronyms that the respondent might not understand.

Closure

- Thank the respondent.

- Let the respondent know that the survey results will be acted upon and results will be reported back to participants in the survey.

80–90% complete would be discarded. It is also important to have different codes for categories on your questionnaire such as Not applicable and Don't know as well as a separate code for those questions left blank. Each of these three responses causes a different impact and therefore affects the conclusions of specific questions.

A significant number of partially completed questionnaires usually indicates one of two things: The first is that the questionnaire is too difficult for the respondent to complete easily. In those cases, the questionnaire may be too long, too complex, or ambiguous. Therefore, the questionnaire must be redesigned. The second cause of incompletions is uninterested respondents who may simply not care about the issues being addressed. This requires a change in the sampling of customers.

Given that your business and employee numbers are small, you may also want to survey your employees with the same instrument in order to predict how your customers will respond. Give your employees the same survey instrument; if it is a phone survey, you can easily translate it into a written survey. Ask employees to rate each area based on their perceptions of how your customers will rate them. Collect the data separately for analysis purposes.

Once the data have been gathered and screened for acceptability, the next step is to undertake some statistical analysis.

Step Nine: Analyze the Data

For most small-business CSM programs, calculation of means and standard deviations is adequate. Although more powerful analysis typically provides a better understanding of why certain perceptions exist, descriptive statistics such as means and standard deviations normally indicate the major trends.

The three global measures of overall satisfaction, referral, and repurchase intent can be aggregated into a composite satisfaction index. If all three are measured on a similar scale—7 points, for example—the three can be added together and the sum divided by three to get an index figure. This is usually more reliable and stable than relying on only one question such as overall satisfaction.

The mean scores on each attribute should be evaluated individually. The mean will be a pretty good indicator of customer perceptions of both performance and importance. Some firms simply rank the attributes by the size of the mean value to indicate performance or importance depending on how the questions were scaled.

The standard deviation for each question indicates the consistency among customers in their responses. A small standard deviation indicates that respondents were very similar in their attitudes. A large standard deviation indicates they weren't very consistent, that there was a good deal of diversity in attitudes. For CSM data, large standard deviations are more common with lower scores. Some customers may think your firm is doing pretty well, and other customers may think your performance is quite poor. From a practical standpoint, large standard deviations indicate that the data are less reliable. So, if large standard deviations exist, try to find out why. This can easily be done with basic spreadsheet software.

Data analysis is usually more complex when it comes to developing a competitive profile. If overall comparative questions, such as the among-the-best example provided earlier, are used, a mean and standard deviation will be adequate. But when each competitor is identified individually, mean scores must be calculated for each competitor. Then the mean scores must be compared with one another to determine who is "best."

The formal procedure for this is a paired t-test. This technique uses means, standard deviations, and sample size to calculate whether the differences are significantly different. Providing the formulas for that calculation is beyond the scope of this discussion. But the conclusion that should be drawn is this: If the mean differences among competitors are small, then customers don't see any significant differences. A mean difference of 0.5 or less on a 7-point scale is probably not significantly different. For example, a mean score of 6.1 for competitor A and a mean score of 6.6 for your firm could lead you to conclude that you and competitor A are about the same for that attribute. Mean scores with greater than a 0.5 difference are probably significant, and indicate a competitive strength or weakness. Comparatively large differences indicate competitive strengths and weaknesses. Any basic statistics book will provide a detailed discussion of this issue.

Finally, the data must be compiled into simple and understandable tables, graphs, or charts. Most people aren't really concerned about statistical techniques, but they are quite concerned about what the data are saying. At this point, it is also good to provide the comparisons of what customers actually said with what employees thought customers would say. Figure 19.3 is an example of the mean score of attributes on a 5-point scale for customers and employees. It is important to look for the gaps between the two: the larger the gap, the greater the issue.

Step Ten: Use the Data

CSM data that reside in one office, in one file cabinet, or on one computer do very little to improve the organization. Only when data are dispersed to virtually everyone are the benefits of a CSM program realized.

There is an old managerial adage that says that "knowledge is power." That school of thought held that the more knowledge a manager has, relative to other employees, the more powerful the manager. Managers pursuing this approach used the mushroom theory of communication, keeping employees in the dark and feeding them whatever. Information was given to others only on a need-to-know basis. After all, sharing knowledge would erode a manager's power base. Such thinking is now nonsense and fatalistic. Unfortunately, this was particularly

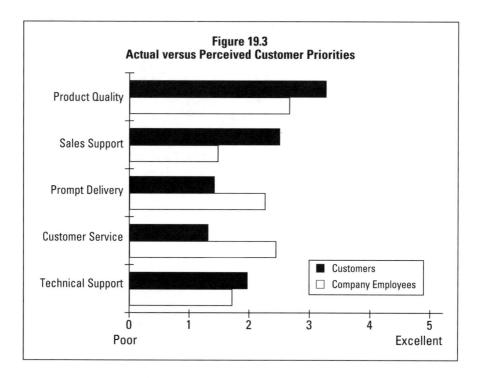

common in small businesses, especially those dominated by a founding entrepreneur.

The most effective organizations learn to harness the capabilities and expertise of all employees. This requires an open flow of communications in all directions: up, down, and horizontally. One of the most valuable types of information that can be shared with employees is CSM data. Hence, the authors recommend that CSM data be shared as widely as possible.

There are three choices available to small businesses dispersing CSM data. The choices are guided by the issues of how much to share and whom to share it with. In some firms, only the aggregate, overall measures are shared regularly with employees. Some firms post the satisfaction index prominently as a continued reminder that the customer is important. Others share the data via electronic mail, newsletters, or memos. Although it is good to let employees know, in general, what customers think of the firm, it is sometimes difficult for individual employees to identify their personal contribution to overall organizational performance. This leads some firms to use the second alternative.

The second alternative is to supplement the aggregate measure with specific attribute performance. Employees in the shipping department would receive the overall satisfaction data as well as data on shipment timeliness, accuracy, and damage, for example. Employees in accounting would receive data on billing accuracy and invoicing. Sales employees would receive data on sales representatives, knowledge, concern, and follow-up. Such uses of the data give each employee more direct, tangible feedback on how their job contributes to customer satisfaction. The weakness of this approach is that it doesn't allow employees to see the relative importance of their job to the customer. Nor does it allow employees to compare their performance with other areas within the firm. The next alternative corrects both of these problems.

The third alternative is to share all CSM data with all employees. All would receive comprehensive data so that employees understand the complexity involved in achieving high customer satisfaction levels. The first comparison for most employees is to compare their performance with other areas in the firm. This usually creates significant peer pressure for employees to improve.

Full sharing of the data is most useful when competitive profiles are available. For most employees, this is their first opportunity to see customer perceptions of competitive strengths and weaknesses. Because often employees' jobs are on the line, identification of weaknesses can serve as a powerful motivational tool. Employees very quickly buy in to the idea of continuous improvement. And the best use of CSM data is to drive process improvement.

Finally, if you had both customers and employees complete the survey and have identified the gaps, the next step is the best. Where customer perceptions are more positive than employee interpretations, give some recognition and praise to those who are doing such a great job. Where customer perceptions are less positive than employee interpretations, use the information in staff and employee meetings to determine why customer perception is less positive. Brainstorm ways that you can improve the service or product attribute to create a more positive perception. And if necessary, remind your employees of Stew Leonard's two rules of business: Rule #1: The customer is always right. Rule #2: If you think the customer is wrong, see Rule #1.

Step Eleven: Improve the CSM Program
Customer wants, needs, and expectations are dynamic, constantly evolving. Thus, the attributes and various aspects of your CSM research

design must also change and evolve. Entrepreneurs must be sensitive to customer changes and willing to seek improvement in the CSM program when needed.

Continual tweaking or slight improvements are fairly common. However, large changes are less common. When they do occur, large changes make historical comparisons meaningless. As a result, some firms overlap the old program with new program for a few time periods. This allows comparison of the old and new data, which in some firms is done with statistical analysis. Conversion factors can be determined in some cases so that historical data remain somewhat useful.

Regardless of whether changes consist of small modifications or major overhauls, changes in CSM programs should be made when justified by improved data quality. After all, the real goal of a CSM program for any size business is to make the voice of the customer tangible and visceral to the firm. If that requires a new question, scale, or sampling technique, so be it.

CHAPTER SUMMARY

The CSM issues for small and large business are conceptually the same. In some respects, small business has the advantages of being closer to the customer, employee involvement in the business, and potential financial rewards of the business. In other respects, smaller businesses generally have limited budgets and time for conducting CSM. Despite the latter, CSM is critical for the future success of any business.

An eleven-step process has been outlined to provide a guide to conducting CSM for a small business. Including employee estimations of customer perceptions in the data gathering and analysis process offers a unique and inexpensive way to reward and motivate employees.

DURHAM COLLEGE

Graduate to Customer Satisfaction

100% Customer Satisfaction guarantees are commonplace. L. L. Bean, Nordstrom's, and scores of other businesses have built their reputations on such claims. If the customer isn't completely satisfied, the products can be returned for a refund or exchange, no questions asked.

Durham College in Ontario, Canada, is taking a similar approach, except the "product" being returned is a human. Durham's approach can benefit both employers and students. Durham is providing a satisfaction guarantee to employers for their alumni in positions related to their major areas of study. It works this way: If a student becomes employed, and his or her employer feels that the student is not properly trained for that position, the college will provide additional training in the form of courses at no extra cost. This amounts to a "customer satisfaction guarantee."

Durham feels that higher education must prepare students for the "real" world. The college administrators believe that their students should have the ability to immediately add value to employers, and so they stand behind this belief with a guarantee. The guarantee was implemented in 1994.

Although the product (a former student) may object to being returned for "rework" to correct a "defect," the guarantee conveys a strong message to potential employers. And few faculty want to be the cause of a defective product.

20

Future Directions

The customer's level of satisfaction ultimately determines the success or failure of a business. If a firm's performance consistently falls short of customer expectations, customers will defect and the firm will ultimately fail. Many seemingly invincible firms have learned that lesson the hard way during the past fifty years. The casualties can be easily identified by the numbers of corporate bankruptcies, mergers, and acquisitions. The firms that have higher customer satisfaction levels are consistently stronger and more successful over the long run, as judged by almost any performance standard.

More than forty years ago Peter Drucker defined the purpose of a business as the creation and retention of satisfied customers. Yet, for more than thirty years, most businesses ignored his message, focusing instead on delivering what management wanted, not what the customer wanted. Only in the past five to ten years have innovative firms concentrated explicitly on becoming truly customer driven.

The initial effort to become customer driven consisted of the implementation of a CSM program. Typically, this involved conducting a simple survey of existing customers. However, as with most "programs," such an approach is woefully inadequate. Becoming customer driven requires both a major cultural shift in most organizations to a focus on process and a paradigm shift in management practice.

A CSM survey is only one part of that emerging management paradigm, although an important part. Various chapters in this book have addressed other essential elements such as direct customer contact and complaint handling. But a truly customer driven focus must be an explicit, dominant aspect of the company culture.

One of the primary reasons a customer-driven culture is now necessary is that the basics of competition are shifting. As the quality movement has matured and global competition has intensified, the differences between competitive products have eroded. When a new product of almost any type is introduced, competitors can clone the new features and build them into their own products, often in just a few weeks. When Hewlett-Packard introduces a new laser-jet printer, the window of uniqueness closes in four to six weeks. When Motorola introduces a new pager, the window of uniqueness is only two to four weeks. Competitors of both firms have learned how to respond and adapt very quickly.

As the customer's perceptions of competitive products have become more equalized, supporting services have become more important to the customer. The array of such services is extremely wide. But all of those services are influenced predominantly by the individual, or employee, delivering the service. And the behavior of all employees is intimately intertwined with corporate culture. Corporate culture strongly influences the shared beliefs and individual values of employees. If satisfying customers is a dominant cultural imperative, high service quality results. If the culture does not focus on the customer, then delivering high service quality and achieving high levels of customer satisfaction will be nearly impossible.

The implication of all this is that service quality is *more* important than product quality for most products. Although big improvements have been made in product quality during the past ten years, service quality has only recently begun to receive the strategic emphasis it deserves.

Competing on the basis of service quality means that we must harness the intellect of all employees. This means that each employee should search for and implement new ways of satisfying customers through improved service quality. It means that the intellectual capital of each employee must be cultivated, nourished, and harvested. And that is where we see the field of customer satisfaction measurement and management heading.

Customer satisfaction processes of all types will be linked to organizational competitiveness and continuous improvement efforts.

Customers will drive the identification and development of core competencies and organizational learning. Customer input will guide high-involvement teams in the reengineering of value-creating processes. Intermediaries of all types will be the subject of collaborative alliances and partnerships to improve value creation throughout the channel. And advanced information technology and electronic data interchange will enhance, enable, and support all of the other trends. Before examining the involvement of the customer in each of these areas, some discussion of a broader, emerging issue may be helpful.

AMERICAN CUSTOMER SATISFACTION INDEX

The American Customer Satisfaction Index (ACSI) is a new national index, similar to the U.S. Consumer Price Index. It is the result of a joint effort by the American Society for Quality Control and the University of Michigan. The purpose of the index is to provide a standardized measure across industries that can be used for comparative purposes. As such, the index will essentially serve as a broad-based benchmark that can be an unbiased reference point in each industry.

The ACSI comprises seven sectors of the U.S. economy: nondurable manufacturing, durable manufacturing, retail, finance and insurance, services, public administration and government, and the broad category of transportation, communication, and utilities. Each sector is divided into several industries, with more than 40 industries and 200 companies included. For example, in the durable manufacturing sector there are four industries: personal computers and printers, household appliances, consumer electronics, and automobiles and vans. In the personal computer and printer industry, there are four firms: IBM, Hewlett-Packard, Apple, and Compaq. In the automobile industry, 13 are included.

A key objective of the ACSI is to provide a quantitative measure of quality improvement that can be tracked over time. Accordingly, the ACSI is intended to be a complement to the traditional performance measures of return on investments, profits, and market share. In Sweden, where a similar index has been in place for several years, close linkages between customer satisfaction and financial performance have been found. Unfortunately, it will probably take four or five years to develop a domestic database. About ten other countries are in the process of developing their own national index.

The ACSI was first calculated in October 1994. Based on a telephone survey of 55,000 households, approximately 250 customers were surveyed for larger firms and from 100 to 225 customers for some smaller firms. Using a scale of 0 to 100, U.S. companies overall attained a satisfaction rating of 74.5. The ASCI founders believe that this satisfaction rating is an indication that U.S. business is not satisfying customers enough to thwart foreign competition. Ratings for major categories ranged from 55 to 81.6.

Because the ACSI is based on a large, national sample that cuts across industries, in aggregate it provides a rich database. However, with sample sizes for each firm ranging from 100 to 250 or so and with firms having a diverse array of business units and product lines, the data are not very actionable from a managerial standpoint. But the ACSI is an important step in identifying the value of an increase in quality—still an ambiguous concept for many. The following topics have more specific managerial implications.

CUSTOMER-DRIVEN CORE COMPETENCIES

The concept of core competencies is not new. The old adage of "build on your strengths and eliminate your weaknesses" certainly reflected the idea. Peters and Waterman in the early 1980s urged managers to "stick to the knitting" by focusing energy on the areas of distinct competence. The pattern of conglomerate mergers in the 1970s and early 1980s shifted to divestiture of peripheral businesses and acquisition of related businesses in the late 1980s and the 1990s. The major difference between the concept of core competencies and the earlier trends is the focus on the customer.

The true core competency of any business lies where the firm has the ability to create and own a market. Core competencies are demonstrated by products that are irresistible to the customer. In many cases, the firm does much more than satisfy customer needs. The firm satisfies needs that the customer didn't even realize existed.

When Akio Morita, then chairman at Sony Corp., promoted the Walkman despite negative market research conclusions, he created a market Sony still owns. When Hewlett-Packard pioneered the laser-jet, it created a market H-P still owns. Market ownership results from developing unique strengths and competencies and then translating those skills into products that yield high levels of customer satisfaction. The most important characteristic of a core competency is the ability to create benefits to the customer that are difficult for competitors to imitate.

Because of companies' decreasing ability to compete on product features, service quality must be developed as a core competency. Indeed, service quality in the future will hold the greatest potential for competitive advantage.

The implication of all of this is that the *customer* is the ultimate judge of core competencies. The increasing popularity of the concept of core competencies suggests that understanding of the customer will become even more important in the future. Customer satisfaction management will help a firm identify where core competencies exist and where they need to be developed. The most valuable of all core competencies are those that are closely linked to the customer, those that are the basis of long-term relationships.

CUSTOMER-DRIVEN LEARNING

The needs of the customer should be the predominant driver of all aspects of organizational learning. Earlier we discussed how intellect is the true basis of competition. The idea of intellect was also the foundation for the core competencies of a business. Thus organizational learning is fundamental to the development, maintenance, and expansion of both intellect and core competencies.

In the future, more firms will use the customer to identify training and development needs the way some innovative firms are now doing. Solectron, a Baldrige award winner, currently averages more than 150 hours of training annually per employee. The primary driver of Solectron's training lies in the future needs of the company's customers.

Solectron tries to anticipate the future needs of its customers six months or more in advance. It then designs training programs to develop employee skills, so the necessary skill base is ready when the customer needs it. If Solectron waited until a problem arose, it would always be in a reactive mode. Conceptually, Solectron's proactive approach of linking the customer to the learning of each employee gives a glimpse of the future.

Customer satisfaction management will drive organizational learning of all types. Boise Cascade Corp. had the fastest customer complaint resolution in the lumber industry. But customers complained the resolution process took too long. Their expectations were being shaped by complaint resolution in *other* industries, and then Boise Cascade was compared with those expectations. The result was that Boise Cascade had to "learn"—through best-in-class benchmarking—how to reengineer its complaint handling process. Customer feedback was the driver of Boise Cascade's learning process.

In the Boise Cascade example, customer feedback shattered the mental models for complaint handling. Without customer input Boise Cascade would have gradually tried to improve a system that management was convinced was already good. But customer feedback caused a fundamental rethinking of the whole process, instead of only marginal improvements.

For learning to be valuable, it must result in behavioral changes that improve organizational processes and products. When competitive benchmarking is used, customers are very capable of identifying where improvements are necessary. However, after the customer has spoken, the organization must determine what type of learning is necessary for improvement and must develop the appropriate learning systems. Organizational learning without customer input would be inherently ad hoc and incomplete. In the future, customer input will be linked explicitly to all aspects of organizational learning.

ALLIANCES AND PARTNERSHIPS

One of the major business trends of the 1990s is the formation of collaborative alliances and partnerships. Generally, such relationships are intended to link different core competencies to generate a symbiotic, mutually beneficial result. Probably the most common type is the supplier alliance.

Supplier alliances are most often initiated by a customer firm with key suppliers. The three major benefits are improved quality, reduction in cycle time, and reduced cost of ownership. The benefits accrue to both the customer and the supplier firms through harmonization of processes and activities. To facilitate the partnerships, firms must blur their boundaries via interorganizational teams, shared training, consistent standards, and open flow of information, normally through electronic data interchange.

Because of their success and their resulting benefits, these types of relationships are certain to spread during the next ten years. The trend has major implications for many businesses.

Alliance arrangements do not allow viewing the customer as a target market at which to fire the marketing campaign. The customer becomes an equal—someone the organization works with on a continual basis. The customer is often another integral link in a value-creating chain.

The view of the customer as a partner is an essential part of the emerging paradigm shift in management practice. And it requires a new, far more open way of dealing with alliance "customers." As this trend spreads, firms will be continually reinventing ways of getting closer to the customer, of solving the customer's problems, of creating better customer value, and of achieving even higher levels of customer satisfaction. Alliance relationships may epitomize the ultimate form of being customer driven.

CUSTOMER-DRIVEN REENGINEERING

The future will see the customer play a more prominent role in process reengineering. As just suggested, the ultimate in process reengineering may be found in supplier alliances. In some of these relationships, the boundaries between firms have largely disappeared, with the processes of two or more firms becoming integrated and harmonized. Those interorganizational process linkages demonstrate one of the key principles of reengineering: organizing around outcomes.

Because the ultimate outcome is a product or service of some type, which is being delivered to an external customer, the customer should be the initial starting point for reengineering. All processes should then be critically reevaluated starting *backward* from the customer.

Another reengineering principle is the use of information technology to supply customer input to those performing the process. It enables each individual to quickly change and respond to customer feedback. This will reduce cycle time, enhance continuous improvement, and improve responsiveness.

In the future, customer satisfaction management will be the dominant element of reengineering efforts. This means that we must strive to find new ways to make customer input managerially actionable. The metrics used for customer input must be consistent with internal processes. And CSM must offer timely customer feedback to those involved in the value-creating processes.

HIGH-INVOLVEMENT TEAMS

It is becoming obvious that high-involvement work teams are the most effective organizational change mechanism. The use of cross-functional, empowered work teams will become even more prevalent in the future. Customer satisfaction input into such teams will also continue to increase.

One of the key challenges in the future for CSM will be to make customer input user-friendly to teams. This may mean customizing data analysis to fit the needs of a particular team. Or it may mean adding customized questions to gather additional data.

A coordinating mechanism may need to be developed in order to centralize and disseminate customer data of all types. In many organizations customer input is fragmented. The CSM data are often kept separate and discrete from customer complaint data. And both of these areas may be kept separate from proactive contact such as customer panels, customer care teams, or site visits. When customer data are fragmented, each team will have to reinvent the wheel, pulling in bits of information from diverse sources. Therefore, customer databases that centralize all types of data will become more common in the future.

CHAPTER SUMMARY

Customer satisfaction measurement and management is increasing in importance to most businesses. But creative minds are continually finding new ways of becoming customer driven, getting closer to the customer. In general, such types of advances share certain common traits.

All of the advances are attempting *to get better customer input* of all types. For CSM surveys, this means better research techniques, better questionnaires, and better data analysis. It also means better customer complaint handling processes, better customer retention analysis, and better ways of initiating proactive, face-to-face customer contact.

Many advances are concerned with *how to better use customer input* for decision making. Customer input will be quickly dispersed to individuals and teams that can use such data to drive organizational learning, process reengineering, and high-involvement work teams. In short, most advances are concerned with how to make customer input of all types more actionable.

A third trait is the *increased use of technology* in all aspects of the CSM process. On-line computer terminals are being used to administer questionnaires, as well as tabulate and analyze the data. CSM data can be dispersed through electronic mail, and data analysis can be customized to fit a manager's needs. In the future, information technology will enhance the whole CSM process.

Our challenge, as these trends emerge and evolve, will be to stay abreast of the changes, continually learning and expanding our intellectual base. That challenge may at times seem daunting—even overwhelming. But if we keep up, we are certain to enhance our competitiveness both organizationally and individually.

THE ULTIMATE CASE STUDY—YOUR NAME HERE!!!

Another Unique CSM Case Study

Appendix

This Appendix has two actual questionnaires that are only slightly modified from their original form. They are examples of reasonably good quality questionnaire, but both were designed to fit very specific objectives, respondent profiles, and products. Therefore, neither should be simply replicated for a different firm, set of customers, or products.

The first questionnaire is for a telephone survey conducted by Intercept Research Incorporated in Portland, Oregon. The questionnaire has an initial screen for the correct respondent, a subsequent introduction, and an implied consent (i.e., "Is this a convenient time?" instead of "Will you participate?").

The questionnaire uses the same scaling for most of the questionnaire, a five point scale. This makes completion easier for the respondent. There are numerous follow-up, open-ended probes with notes to the interviewer. And there are rotations of questions that may have a sequential bias.

The first portions of the questionnaire are the same for all respondents. However, at the end of Section 2, Question 21, there is a direction to the interviewer: ***(GO TO ASSIGNED MODULE)***. This is then followed by three alternative modules.

To keep the overall length of the questionnaire in the 10–12-minute range, one of the three modules can be administered to the respondent. This is the split-sample technique referred to in an earlier chapter. This allows a larger number of attributes to be evaluated in one study. However, because of the larger sample size, the questions in the first portion have a higher confidence level and precision than those in the modules.

The second questionnaire is for a mail survey, and is fairly straightforward and easy to understand. This is one of the questionnaires used by Graniterock, a Baldrige award winner. This questionnaire could be the only one used, or it could be one of two or three in a split-sample research design. But since the questionnaire must contain all of the information, both wording and format are different and tighter than the telephone questionnaire. In the telephone survey, the interviewer serves as a reference in the event of questions by the respondent.

There are many ways to design a questionnaire. Ultimately, the true test of any questionnaire is whether the objectives are met with good quality, actionable data. Both of the questionnaires here easily passed that test.

CUSTOMER SATISFACTION MEASUREMENT SURVEY
INTERCEPT RESEARCH CORPORATION
(503) 635-5599

INTRVWR: _____   DATE: _____
EDITOR: _____   SEGMENT: _____(X)

SCREENERS

A. Hello, my name is Ms/Mr _____, with Intercept Research Corporation, a marketing research firm based in Portland, Oregon, calling
on behalf of _____. May I please speak with
(CONTACT)? (SCHEDULE CALL BACK APPOINTMENT IF APPROPRIATE)

CALL BACK AT: _____am/pm_____
          DAY/DATE/TIME   AREA CODE & PHONE NUMBER

_____
CONTACT NAME

_____
CONTACT NAME

B. TO QUALIFIED CONTACT: Hello, my name is Ms/Mr _____, with
Intercept Research Corporation, a marketing research firm based
in Portland, Oregon. Today we are talking with customers of
_____ and would like to include your opinions in our
survey.

You should have received a letter about this survey announcing that
your company has been selected as an important customer of
_____. The purpose of this survey is to help us better
serve you. All information you provide will be treated confidentially
and tabulated in combination with results from other companies.
The survey will take about XX minutes.

Is this a convenient time for you? (SCHEDULE CALL BACK APPOINTMENT IF
APPROPRIATE)

SECTION 1: QUALITY IMAGE
---

1. Based upon your experience, which supplier of _____
do you believe offers the best overall quality?

Supplier A	...1	Other (SPECIFY) _____	
Supplier B	...2	None/all the same	.5
Supplier C	...3	Don't know	.6
Supplier D	...4	Refused	.7

2. On a scale of one to five, with five—"excellent," and one—"poor," how would you rate the overall quality of _____ as a supplier of _____?

> One—poor . . . . .1 (X)
> Two 2
> Three 3
> Four .4
> Five—excellent 5
> Don't know 6

3. Why do you say (RESPONSE FROM Q2)? (MULTIPLE RESPONSE—CLARIFY FOR SPECIFIC REASONS)

> _____ (X)

> _____ (X)

> _____ (X)

4. Considering what other suppliers charge for similar products and services, would you describe _____ as low priced, competitively priced or high priced?

> Low priced . . . . .1 (X)
> Competitively priced 2
> High priced 3
> Don't know 4

5. I would like to ask you some questions about _____ pricing terms, volume discounts, and adjustments. On a scale of one to five, with five—"excellent," and one—"poor," how would you rate _____:

	POOR				EXCELLENT	DK	NA	
5. Pricing terms	1	2	3	4	5	6	7	(X)
6. Volume discounts	1	2	3	4	5	6	7	(X)
7. Adjustments	1	2	3	4	5	6	7	(X)

8. Now I'd like you to consider the overall value in relation to the cost and quality of products and services offered by _____ On a scale of one to five, with five—"an excellent value for the money," and one—" a poor value for the money," how would you rate the value for the money offered by _____?

> One—poor value for the money . . . . . . .1 (X)
> Two 2
> Three 3
> (SKIP TO Q10)   Four 4
> Five—excellent value for the money 5
> Don't know 6

9. Why do you say (RESPONSE FROM Q8)? (MULTIPLE RESPONSE)

_____ (X)

_____ (X)

_____ (X)

10. Compared to your expectations of other suppliers, would you say
    that _____ has exceeded your expectations, met
    your expectations or not met your expectations?

                    Exceeded your expectations . . .1   X)
                    Met your expectations 2
                    Not met your expectations 3
                    Don't know 4

11. What are your key expectations?

_____ (X)

_____ (X)

_____ (X)

IMAGE SECTION

12. Now I'd like to read you several statements that might be used to
    describe _____ as a supplier. Please use a scale of
    one to five, with five—"excellent", and one—"poor".
    REPEAT SCALE AS NEEDED Please rate _____'s:

(READ AND ROTATE)	POOR		EXCELLENT			DK	NA	
12. Credibility	1........2........3........4........5........6........7							(X)
13. Flexibility	1........2........3........4........5........6........7							(X)
14. Customer-orientation	1........2........3........4........5........6........7							(X)
15. Environmental responsibility	1........2........3........4........5........6........7							(X)
16. Support of minority and women owned suppliers	1........2........3........4........5........6........7							(X)
17. Ability to deal professionally with you	1........2........3........4........5........6........7							(X)

END OF IMAGE SECTION

18. Generally speaking, which do you consider most when selecting a supplier:

(READ AND ROTATE)

Product 1   (X)
Service 2
Price 3
Consider product, price and
   service equally 4
Don't know 5

SECTION 2: RELATIONAL OUTCOMES

---

19. On a scale of one to five, with five—"extremely likely," and one—"not likely at all," how likely would you be to recommend _____ as a supplier?

One—not likely at all 1   (X)
Two 2
Three 3
Four 4
Five—extremely likely 5
Don't know 6

20. When you think of the products and services you currently buy from _____, do you expect your future reliance on _____ will increase, decrease or remain the same?

INCREASE: Do you expect a moderate increase or a substantial increase?

DECREASE: Do you expect a moderate decrease or a substantial decrease?

Substantial decrease 1   (X)
Moderate decrease 2
Remain the same 3
Moderate increase 4
Substantial increase 5
Don't know 6

21. Why do you expect your future reliance to increase or decrease? (MULTIPLE RESPONSE—PROBE: Are there any other reasons?—CLARIFY FOR SPECIFIC REASONS)

_____   (X)

_____   (X)

* * *(GO TO ASSIGNED MODULE) * * *

MODULE 1

SECTION 3: ORDER FULFILLMENT

---

22. Among the suppliers of _____, which company do you think offers the best order fulfillment? By order fulfillment I mean from order placement through delivery.

Supplier A 1   Other (SPECIFY) _____
Supplier B 2   None/all the same 5
Supplier C 3   Don't know 6
Supplier D 4   Refused 7

23. Now I would like to ask you some questions about the quality of order fulfillment. On a scale of one to five, with five—"excellent," and one—"poor," how would you rate the overall service when placing orders with _____?

	POOR	EXCELLENT	DK	NA
Overall order fulfillment	1........2........3........4........5........6........7			(X)

24. Using the same scale, how would you rate the quality of order fulfillment with _____ in terms of:

(READ AND ROTATE)   POOR   EXCELLENT   DK   NA

24. Compatibility with your internal procedures   1........2........3........4........5........6........7   (X)

25. Flexibility such as FAX or EDI when you place orders
(IF NECESSARY, SAY: By flexibility I mean the options for placing orders by phone, fax, or electronically via computer terminal.)   1........2........3........4........5........6........7   (X)

26. Acknowledging receipt of your order, if required   1........2........3........4........5........6........7   (X)

27. Notifying you of incomplete order shipment   1........2........3........4........5........6........7   (X)

SECTION 4: INSIDE CUSTOMER SERVICE SUPPORT

---

28. Among the suppliers of _____, which company do you think offers the best inside customer service support?

Supplier A 1   Other (SPECIFY) _____
Supplier B 2   None/all the same 5
Supplier C 3   Don't know 6
Supplier D 4   Refused 7

29. Now I would like to ask you some questions about _____ inside customer service support. On a scale of one to five, with five—"excellent," and one—"poor," how would you rate the overall quality of the inside customer service support?

	POOR	EXCELLENT	DK	NA
Overall quality of the inside customer service support	1........2........3........4........5........6........7			(X)

30. Using the same scale, how would you rate the quality of _____ inside customer service support in terms of:

(READ AND ROTATE)	POOR	EXCELLENT	DK	NA
30. Answering your questions accurately	1........2........3........4........5........6........7			(X)
31. Understanding your needs	1........2........3........4........5........6........7			(X)
32. Timely response to your requests	1........2........3........4........5........6........7			(X)
33. Availability when you call	1........2........3........4........5........6........7			(X)
34. Courtesy and helpfulness	1........2........3........4........5........6........7			(X)
35. Assistance you receive when making special requests	1........2........3........4........5........6........7			(X)
36. Commitment to you and your business	1........2........3........4........5........6........7			(X)

SECTION 5: DELIVERY SERVICE

37. Among the suppliers of _____, which company do you think offers the best delivery service?

Supplier A 1   Other (SPECIFY) _____
Supplier B 2   None/all the same 5
Supplier C 3   Don't know 6
Supplier D 4   Refused 7

38. Now I would like to ask you some questions about _____ delivery service. On a scale of one to five, with five—"excellent," and one—"poor," how would you rate the overall quality of the delivery service?

	POOR	EXCELLENT	DK	NA
Overall delivery service	1........2........3........4........5........6........7			(X)

39. Using the same scale, how would you rate the quality of _____ delivery service in terms of:

(READ AND ROTATE)	POOR	EXCELLENT	DK	NA
39. On-time delivery	1........2........3........4........5........6........7			(X)
40. Order completeness	1........2........3........4........5........6........7			(X)
41. The accuracy of the order received	1........2........3........4........5........6........7			(X)
42. Compatibility of product packaging with your needs	1........2........3........4........5........6........7			(X)
43. Legibility of the address on delivered packages	1........2........3........4........5........6........7			(X)
44. Handling product returns	1........2........3........4........5........6........7			(X)
45. Being damage-free	1........2........3........4........5........6........7			(X)

SECTION 6: REPORTING AND BILLING

46. Among the suppliers of _____, which company do
    you think offers the best reporting and billing?

Supplier A	1	Other (SPECIFY) _____	
Supplier B	2	None/all the same	5
Supplier C	3	Don't know	6
Supplier D	4	Refused	7

47. Now I would like to ask you some questions about _____
    reporting and billing. On a scale of one to five, with five—
    "excellent," and one—"poor," how would you rate the overall
    quality of the reporting and billing?

	POOR	EXCELLENT	DK	NA
Overall reporting and billing	1........2........3........4........5........6........7			(X)

48. Using the same scale, how would you rate the quality of
    _____'s reporting and billing in terms of:

(READ AND ROTATE)	POOR	EXCELLENT	DK	NA
48. Packing slips that are easy to understand	1........2........3........4........5........6........7			(X)
49. Billing schedule flexibility	1........2........3........4........5........6........7			(X)
50. Invoice accuracy	1........2........3........4........5........6........7			(X)
51. Compatibility of invoicing with your needs	1........2........3........4........5........6........7			(X)
52. Timeliness of reports	1........2........3........4........5........6........7			(X)
53. Usefulness of report contents	1........2........3........4........5........6........7			(X)

MODULE 2

SECTION 7: OUTSIDE SALESPERSON SUPPORT
---

54. Among the suppliers of _____, which company do you think offers the best outside salesperson support?

Supplier A 1	Other (SPECIFY) _____	
Supplier B 2	None/all the same 5	
Supplier C 3	Don't know 6	
Supplier D 4	Refused ....·7	

55. Now I would like to ask you some questions about _____ outside salesperson support. On a scale of one to five, with five—"excellent," and one—"poor," how would you rate the overall quality of outside salesperson support?

	POOR	EXCELLENT	DK	NA
Overall quality of outside salesperson support	1.........2.........3.........4.........5.........6.........7			(X)

56. Using the same scale, how would you rate the quality of _____ outside salesperson support in terms of:

(READ AND ROTATE)	POOR	EXCELLENT	DK	NA
56. Frequency of contact	1.........2.........3.........4.........5.........6.........7			(X)
57. Ability to get things done	1.........2.........3.........4.........5.........6.........7			(X)
58. Availability when you need them	1.........2.........3.........4.........5.........6.........7			(X)
59. Assistance you receive when making special requests	1.........2.........3.........4.........5.........6.........7			(X)
60. Knowledge of products and services	1.........2.........3.........4.........5.........6.........7			(X)
61. Knowledge of _____'s systems and services	1.........2.........3.........4.........5.........6.........7			(X)
62. Understanding your business and your office supply needs	1.........2.........3.........4.........5.........6.........7			(X)

SECTION 8: RECOMMENDATIONS

63. What specific suggestions do you have that would help
    _____ section improve the quality and value of the
    products, services and support they provide to you? (MULTIPLE
    RESPONSE—PROBE: Do you have any other suggestions?—CLARIFY FOR
    SPECIFIC SUGGESTIONS)

    _____ (X)

    _____ (X)

    _____ (X)

64. Would you like _____ to know your specific
    responses to these questions so that the information can be used
    to better service your account?

                    Yes 1
                    No 2

VERIFY AND RECORD CONTACT INFORMATION ON FIRST PAGE.

Those are all of my questions. On behalf of _____,
thank you for your cooperation. Your comments will help
_____ as they make changes to better meet your
needs.

Dear Customer:

We, at Graniterock, thank you for your business. We are again looking for your input to help us learn how to serve you better. Your response is important to us and will remain strictly confidential.

This survey is for aggregate products and our transportation services. These products include fill material, sand, coarse aggregate, base rock and drain rock, and trucking done by Graniterock trucks. Your replies should refer to these products and services only.

When finished, please refold this survey, staple it, and drop it in the mail. It is already stamped and addressed to Graniterock. What you tell us will be used to improve the products and services supplied to you.

Please enjoy a cup of coffee or a soft drink on us while filling out the survey. Thank you very much for taking the time to give us your feedback.

Hal Poulin   Mike Marheineke

General Manager   General Manager
Aggregate Division   Transportation Division

Please rate the **customer service** you receive at **Wilson Quarry** *(check the appropriate box)*:

	No Contact	The Best	Better Than Competition	Average	Below Average	The Worst
Weighmaster/Scalehouse						
Dispatcher/Scheduler						
Loader Operator						
Sales Representative						
Plant Manager						

Comments: _____

_____

_____

_____

_____

Please rate the **customer service** you receive at **Southside Sand & Gravel** *(check the appropriate box)*:

	No Contact	The Best	Better Than Competition	Average	Below Average	The Worst
Weighmaster/Scalehouse						
Dispatcher/Scheduler						
Loader Operator						
Sales Representative						
Plant Manager						

Comments: _____

_____

_____

_____

_____

Please write in the names of the suppliers you use most often for **Aggregate Products**. *Then grade each company using this scale:*

A = The Best
B = Above Average
C = Same as Competition
D = Needs Improvement
F = Terrible

#1 Supplier (used most often)
#2 Supplier
#3 Supplier

Dependability			
Product Quality			
Product Availability			
Meets Job Specifications			
Plant Availability			
Pricing			
Resolves Problems Quickly			
Ordering Convenience			
Billing Accuracy			
Fast Loadout Time			
Product Knowledge			
Eager to Help			
Responsive to Special Needs			
Full Loads/No Overloads			
Credit, Payment Terms			

What would you like to see (products or services) from aggregate suppliers that is not currently offered?

_____

_____

_____

_____

_____

_____

If you do not use Graniterock's Transportation Division for trucking, skip this portion of the survey.

If you use **Graniterock's Transportation Division**, please rate the **service** you receive compared to the **average** supplier:

	No Contact	The Best	Better Than Competition	Average	Below Average	The Worst
Weighmaster/Scalehouse						
Dispatcher/Scheduler						
Loader Operator						
Sales Representative						
Plant Manager						

Comments: _____

_____

_____

_____

_____

Please write in the names of the **trucking companies** you use most often. *Then grade each company using this scale:*

A = The Best

B = Above Average

C = Same as Competition

D = Needs Improvement

F = Terrible

#1 Trucker (used most often)

#2 Trucker

#3 Trucker

Do your orders arrive on time?			
Are the dispatchers responsive to your needs?			
Is it easy to place orders or requests with them?			
Are their prices competitive?			
Are their dispatchers helpful?			
Are their drivers courteous?			
Do they address problems fairly and quickly?			

GENERAL COMMENTS

Here is what I like best about Graniterock:

_____

_____

_____

What aspects of Graniterock's service or quality of products need improvements?

_____

_____

_____

_____

Are you aware of Graniterock's Delivered Aggregate Program? ☐ Yes ☐ No
Comment:

_____

_____

Your Name (optional): _____

Company Name (optional): _____

Phone Number: _____

Please call me: ☐ Yes ☐ No

Regarding: _____

_____

_____

_____

Thank you! Please fold with stamp showing, staple, and mail.

INDEX

A

Adjustment mechanism for gain
  sharing, 289–290
Adopt-a-customer programs, 331
Alliances, 425–426
American Customer Satisfaction
  Index, 423
Anonymity, research alternatives and,
  48–49
Attitudes, questionnaire design and,
  96–97
Attribute identification, 69–92
  depth interviews for, 71–80
  external sources for, 71
  focus groups for, 80–86, 88
  at GTE Corporation, 91
  internal sources for, 69–70
  at Investors Diversified Services, 92
  for model building, 224
  for multinational CSM, 347–348
  reduction of attribute list and,
    86–90
  for small business CSM, 407–409
Awareness, questionnaire design and,
  105–109

B

Background research for depth
  interviews, 74–77
Baseline for gain sharing, 285–286
Benchmarking, 297–323. *See also*
  Best-in-class benchmarking;
  Competitive benchmarking
  etiquette of, 319, 320–321
  internal, 297–300
  International Benchmarking

Clearinghouse and, 318–319,
    321
  for multinational CSM, 354
Best-in-class benchmarking, 310–318
  action phase of, 316–318
  analysis phase of, 315
  integration phase of, 316
  planning phase of, 312–315
Beta sites, personal contact with
  customers and, 330
Bias
  questionnaire design and, 98–99
  research design and, 38
  Budgetary issues. *See* Costs

C

Canonical correlation, 228–230
Census, 192–195
  costs of, 193–194
  defining customers for, 192–194
  sample versus, 192
  time considerations and, 194–195
Ceridian Corporation, 32–33
Closed-ended questions, 168–172
Communication
  of CSM results, 241–248,
    251–252, 415–418
  two-way, need for, 30–31
Communication model, questionnaire
  design and, 93–95
Compensation, 265–296. *See also*
  Gain sharing
  financial, 270–279
  recognition programs, 266–270
  recognition programs and, 295
Competition

gain sharing and, 277–278
global, 2–3
Competitive benchmarking, 300–310
  industry average benchmark and,
    308–310
  key competitor benchmark and,
    300–308
  at Toronto Stock Exchange, 323
Competitive strengths/weaknesses,
  measurement of, as objective,
  25–26
Complaint handling, 381–402
  customer databases for, 387–398
  at Diamond Shamrock, 400–402
  easy access for, 390
  empowered employees for, 394
  encouraging complaints and,
    383–389
  fast responses for, 391–392
  lack of hassles in, 392–394
  organization commitment for,
    398–399
  staffing and training for, 395–397
Computer-assisted interviewing
  comparison with other research
    alternatives, 42
  by telephone, 174
Confidence level, sample size and,
  207–208
Confidentiality, research alternatives
  and, 48–49
Consultant(s), 53–67
  evaluating. See Consultant
    evaluation
  finding, 55
  reasons for using, 54–55
Consultant evaluation, 55–65
  commitment to total quality and
    CSM and, 63
  contract and payment schedule
    and, 59–62
  CSM expertise and, 56
  industry experience and, 56–57
  interpersonal skills and, 62–63
  project management skills and,
    57–59
  reference checks and, 64–65
  willingness to aid in transition to
    in-house processes and, 63–64

Continuous improvement,
  measurement of, as objective, 24
Contracts with consultants, 59–62
Convergent validity, 102–104
Core competencies, customer-driven,
  423–424
Corning, internal customer
  satisfaction at, 378–379
Corporate culture, 9–14
  CSM process and, 13–14
  embedding CSM program in,
    12–13
  gain sharing and, 276–277
  new, 10–11
Corporate metric, 246–248
Corporate performance measures,
  key, 252–254
CorporatePulse, 214
Corporate size, gain sharing and,
  278
Correlation, canonical, 228–230
Costs
  of census, 193–194
  of multinational CSM, 345–346
  of pretesting, 176–177
  of research alternatives, 40–41
  sample size and, 203
Cover letter for mail questionnaire,
  119–123
Cross-functional teams as intrinsic
  reward, 260–261
Cross-tabulations, 230–232
Cultural diversity, multinational
  CSM and, 341–343
Customer(s)
  access to complaint system, 390
  analysis for personal contact, 332
  changes in, 3–5
  communicating CSM results to,
    242–248, 251–252
  defining for census, 192–193
  defining for sample, 195–196
  getting close to, as objective,
    22–24
  internal. See Internal customer
    satisfaction
      presenting pretesting results
        to, 188
  on internal teams, 330

personal contact with. *See* Personal interviews
selection for personal contact, 331–332
of small businesses, identification of, 406–407
specific, identifying for sample, 209–210
variation in, sample size and, 205
Customer contact personnel as source for attribute identification, 70
Customer databases for complaint handling, 397–398
Customer-driven core competencies, 423–424
Customer-driven improvement as objective, 24
Customer-driven learning, 424–425
Customer-driven reengineering, 426
Customer list, 196–197
Customer panels, 330
Customer service records as source for attribute identification, 70
Customer value, 5
Customer visits, 328–329

D
Data, users of, 21–22
Data analysis, 215–239
for best-in-class benchmarking, 315
of depth interviews, 79–80
of focus groups, 86
of mail questionnaires, 135–136
model and. *See* Model building; Model components
for multinational CSM, 354–358
of pretesting data, 187–188
for small business CSM, 414–415
SPSS software and, 239
tracking analysis. *See* Tracking analysis
Data collection. *See also* specific data collection methods
at Deere & Company, 117–118
samples and, 210
for small business CSM, 412–414
Data errors, 212

Data quality, research alternatives and, 44–48
Declared pretests, 178–180
Deere & Company, data collection at, 117–118
Deficit reserve for gain sharing, 288–289
Depth interviews, 71–80
analysis and summary report of, 79–80
background research for, 74–77
conduct of, 78–79
design of, 76–77
interviewer and, 72–73
process for, 74
respondent and, 73–74
Diamond Shamrock, complaint handling at, 400–402
Directions
for mail questionnaire, 126–127
for telephone questionnaire, 160–161
Discriminant validity, 104
Diskette, surveys by, 145–146
Don't know option, 114–115
Durham College, 420

E
Eastman Chemical Company, 16–17
E-mail, comparison with other research alternatives, 42
Employees
communicating CSM results to, 242–248
compensation of. *See* Compensation; Financial rewards; Gain sharing
empowerment of, for complaint handling, 394
encouraging to use CSM data, 254–255
intrinsic rewards for. *See* Intrinsic rewards
involvement of, gain sharing and, 275–276
satisfaction of, internal customer satisfaction versus, 373–375
staffing and training for complaint

handling and, 395–397
Ethics, personal interviews and, 335–336
Etiquette, of benchmarking, 319, 320–321
Executives, customer contact by, 328
Expectations measures, 141–145
Expertise of consultants, 56

F
Facilities for focus groups, 84–85
Factor analysis, 224–225
Financial performance, linking CSM to, 248–251
Financial rewards, 270–279
    gain sharing and. *See* Gain sharing
    profit sharing and, 272–274
First Interstate Bank, recognition program at, 295
Fixed samples, 198–199
Focus groups, 80–86
    advantages of, 81
    analysis of, 86
    conducting, 85–86
    disadvantages of, 81–82
    facilities for, 84–85
    moderator for, 83–84
    objectives of, 82–83
    participants in, 84
    planning, 82
Forced allocation, 133–135
Frequency distributions, 232–233

G
Gain sharing, 274–290
    adjustment mechanism for, 289–290
    baseline for, 285–286
    benefits of, 279
    competition and, 277–278
    deficit reserve for, 288–289
    designation of group for, 282–283
    employee involvement and, 275–276
    formula for, 283–285
    at Harris Corp., 292–294
    implementation of, 279–280

organizational size and, 278
    organization strategy and culture and, 276–277
    payout cap for, 290
    payout frequency for, 287
    payout method for, 288
    share for, 286–287
    task force for, 281
    technology and, 277
    unions and, 278
Global competition, 2–3
Goals, objectives and, 20
Good-bad ratings, 137–140
Graniterock, mail questionnaire used by, 147–148
Group discussions as intrinsic reward, 259–260
Group for gain sharing, 282–283
Guarantees as source for attribute identification, 69

H
Harris Corp., gain sharing at, 292–294
Hypotheses. *See* Research hypotheses

I
Implementation time, research alternatives and, 44
Implicit hypotheses, 29–30
Importance, measuring, 128–135
Improvement
    continuous, measurement of, as objective, 24
    customer-driven, as objective, 24
Industry average benchmark, 308–310
Industry experience of consultants, 56–57
Information sharing as intrinsic reward, 256–258
Innovation, sources of, 8–9
Instructions. *See* Directions
Intercept Research, pretesting at, 190
Internal benchmarking, 297–300
Internal customers, presenting pretesting results to, 188

Internal customer satisfaction,
    363–379
  at Corning, 378–379
  employee satisfaction versus,
    373–375
  process for soliciting, 366–373
  unique characteristics of internal
    customers and, 364–366
Internal systems, linking CSM data
    to, 26–28
International Benchmarking
    Clearinghouse, 318–319, 321
Internet, comparison with other
    research alternatives, 42
Interpersonal skills of consultants,
    62–63
Interval scaling, 128–132
Interview(s). *See* Depth interviews;
    Personal interviews; Telephone
    questionnaires
Interviewers
  for depth interviews, 72–73
  inconsistent, 211
  for telephone questionnaire,
    152–153
Interview situation for telephone
    questionnaire, 153
Intrinsic rewards, 255–263
  autonomous work groups and,
    261–263
  cross-functional teams and,
    260–261
  group discussions and, 259–260
  information sharing and, 256–258
  suggestion programs and, 258–259
  task forces and, 260
Introduction
  to mail questionnaire, 123–126
  to telephone questionnaire,
    157–160
Intuit, Inc., soft CSM at, 338
Investors Diversified Services,
    attribute identification at, 92

K

Key competitor benchmark, 300–308
Key corporate performance measures,
    252–254

L

Learning, customer-driven, 424–425
L-S Electro-Galvanizing Company,
    264

M

Mail questionnaires, 119–148
  cover letter for, 119–123
  directions for, 126–127
  by diskette, 145–146
  expectations measures in, 141–145
  first questions in, 127
  at Graniterock, 147–148
  introduction to, 123–126
  measuring importance using,
    128–135
  open-ended questions in, 145
  overall ratings in, 137–141
  performance ratings in, 136–137
  statistical analysis of, 135–136
Management, 5–8
  communicating CSM results to,
    242–248
  determination of action to take
    and, 6–7
  determination of mechanism for
    improvement and, 7–8
  reduction of attribute list by,
    87–88, 88
  as source for attribute
    identification, 70
Mean(s), 233–234
Meaningfulness
  questionnaire design and,
    104–105
  research design and, 39
Measurement issues for pretesting,
    186–187
Model building, 223–230
  canonical correlation and,
    228–230
  factor analysis and, 224–225
  identifying key attributes and
    processes in, 224
  multiple regression and, 225–228
Model components
  business performance, 217
  critical activities, 222–223

overall customer satisfaction, 218–219
specific attributes, 221
summary characteristics, 220–221
Moderator of focus group, 83–84
Moore Corp., 360–361
Motivation
in personal interviews, 334
tracking analysis and, 236–237
Motorola, recognition program at, 296
Multinational CSM, 339–361
attribute identification in, 347–348
benchmarking for, 354
costs of, 345–346
cultural diversity and, 341–343
data analysis for, 354–358
at Moore Corp., 360–361
objectives of, 346–347
pretesting for, 351
questionnaire design for, 348–351
researcher for, 343–344
research infrastructure for, 345
research quality and, 341
sampling for, 351–354
sift, 358–359
unit of analysis for, 343
Multiple measures, sample size and, 208–209
Multiple regression, 225–228
Multiple segments, sample size and, 208
Multivariate techniques, model building and. See Model building

N
NCR Corporation, research design at, 50–51
New-product development, personal interviews and, 329–330
Noncoverage errors, 211
Nonprobability sampling, 200–202
Nonresponse errors, 212
Nonsampling error, 210–212
No opinion option, 114–115

O
Objectives, 19–28

clarifying, 19
customer-driven improvement as, 24–25
of focus group, 82–83
getting close to customer as, 22–24
goals and, 20
linking CSM data to internal systems as, 26–28
measuring competitive strengths and weaknesses as, 25–26
measuring continuous improvement as, 24
of multinational CSM, 346–347
of personal contact with customers, 325–326
research design and, 36
for small businesses, 405–406
users of data and, 21–22
Open-ended questions
for mail questionnaires, 145
for telephone questionnaire, 165–168
Organization commitment to complaint handling, 398–399
Organization culture. See Corporate culture
Overall ratings, 137–141

P
Participants in focus groups, 84
Partnerships, 425–426
Payment schedules for consultants, 61–62
Payout for gain sharing. See Gain sharing
Performance measures, key, 252–254
Performance ratings, mail questionnaires and, 136–137
Personal interviews, 325–338
adopt-a-customer programs for, 331
beta sites and, 330
conducting interviews for, 336–337
customer analysis for, 332
customer panels for, 330
customer representatives on teams and, 330

customer selection for, 331–332
customer visits for, 328–329
ethical issues related to, 335–336
by executives, 328
flexibility and, 334
at Intuit, Inc., 338
issues affecting interview and, 333
for multinational CSM, 358–359
new-product development and, 329–330
objectives of, 325–326
respondent motivation and, 334
setting agenda for, 333
summary report of, 336–337
time constraints and, 335
Planning
for best-in-class benchmarking, 312–315
for focus groups, 82
formation of personal contact with customers, 331–336
Praxis Institute, 214
Precision
research design and, 39–40
sample size and, 205–206
Pretesting, 175–190
costs of, 176–177
data analysis for, 187–188
declared versus undeclared, 178–180
at Intercept Research, 190
for multinational CSM, 351
presentation to internal customers and, 188
questionnaire-related issues in, 182–187
sample for, 180–182
for small business CSM, 410–411
time constraints and, 177
Probability sampling, 199–200
Process identification, 246
Process improvement, 241–264
communicating CSM results and, 241–248
communicating CSM results to customers and, 251–252
defining corporate metric and, 246–248

employee attitudes and satisfaction and, 254–255
identifying activities affecting critical attributes and, 246
intrinsic rewards and. See Intrinsic rewards
key corporate performance measures and, 252–254
linking CSM to financial performance and, 248–251
Profit sharing, 272–274
Project management skills, of consultants, 57–59

Q
Quality. See Continuous improvement; Total quality
Questionnaire design, 93–118
attitudes and, 96–97
awareness and, 105–109
bias and, 98–99
communication model and, 93–95
CSM model and, 115–116
for mail questionnaires. See Mail questionnaires
manageability of tasks and, 112–113
meaningfulness and, 104–105
for multinational CSM, 348–351
no opinion/don't know option and, 114–115
for pretesting, 182–187
questionnaire as funnel and, 113–114
reliability and, 110–111
salience and, 109–110
sample size and, 205
simplicity and, 111–112
for small business CSM, 409–410
specificity and, 112
of telephone questionnaires. See Telephone questionnaires
validity and, 99–104
volatility and, 97
Questionnaires, faulty, 211

R
Rank ordering, 132–133

Ratings
    overall, 137–141
    performance, 136–137
Recognition programs, 266–270
    at First Interstate Bank, 295
    at IBM, 269
    at Motorola, 296
Reengineering, customer-driven, 426
Reference checks for consultants,
    64–65
Reliability
    questionnaire design and, 110–111
    research design and, 36–37
Reports. See Summary report
Research design, 35–51
    alternatives for, 40–49
    anonymity and confidentiality and,
        48–49
    bias and, 38
    costs and, 40–41
    data quality and, 44–48
    implementation time and, 44
    meaningfulness and, 39
    at NCR Corporation, 50–51
    objectives and, 36
    precision and, 39–40
    reliability and, 36–37
    staffing characteristics and, 43–44
    validity and, 37–38
Research hypotheses, 28–30
Research infrastructure for
    multinational CSM, 345
Respondents
    for depth interviews, 73–74
    in personal interviews, 334
    to telephone questionnaire,
        150–152
Rewards. See Compensation;
    Financial rewards; Gain sharing;
    Intrinsic rewards

S
Salience, questionnaire design and,
    109–110
Sample/sampling, 195–214
    census versus, 192
    data collection and, 210
    defining customers for, 195–196

developing customer list for,
    196–197
fixed, 198–199
identifying customers to be
    contacted for, 209–210
for multinational CSM, 351–354
nonprobability, 200–202
nonsampling error and, 210–212
for pretesting, 180–182
probability, 199–200
sequential, 197–198
size of. See Sample size
for small business CSM, 411–412
Sample size, 203–209
    confidence level and, 207–208
    guidelines for, 209
    multiple segments and measures
        and, 208–209
    precision and, 205–206
    resources and, 203–204
    type of questionnaire and, 205
    type of sample and, 204
    variation in customer base and,
        205
Satisfied-dissatisfied ratings, 140–141
Scaling for pretesting, 186–187
Self-attribution bias in attribute
    identification, 71
Sequential samples, 197–198
Share, for gain sharing, 286–287
Simplicity, questionnaire design and,
    111–112
Small business CSM, 403–420
    assistance for, 404–405
    attribute identification for,
        407–409
    data analysis for, 414–415
    data collection for, 412–414
    at Durham College, 420
    identifying customers for, 406–407
    implementation of results and,
        415–418
    improving program for, 418
    objectives of, 405–406
    pretesting for, 410–411
    questionnaire design for, 409–410
    sampling for, 411–412
Soft CSM. See Personal interviews

Specificity, questionnaire design and, 112
SPSS software, 239
Staffing. *See also* Employees
  for complaint handling, 395
  research alternatives and, 43–44
  sample size and, 204
Standard deviations, 233–234
Statistics. *See also* Data analysis
  reduction of attribute list using, 88–90
Strengths, competitive, measurement of, as objective, 25–26
Suggestion programs as intrinsic reward, 258
Summary report
  of depth interviews, 79–80
  of personal interviews, 336–337
Task forces
  for gain sharing, 281
  as intrinsic reward, 260

T
Task manageability, questionnaire design and, 112–113
Technological change, 1–2
Technology, gain sharing and, 277
Telephone questionnaires, 149–174
  closed-ended questions in, 168–172
  computer-assisted, 174
  directions for, 160–161
  errors in, 154
  first questions in, 162
  general guidelines for, 154–156
  interview as social interaction and, 149–154
  interviewer for, 152–153
  interview situation and, 153
  introduction to, 157–160
  open-ended questions in, 165–166
  question structure for, 162–163
  question-writing guidelines for, 163–168
  respondent and, 150–152
  topic of, 153–154
Time constraints
  of census, 194–195

personal interviews and, 335
pretesting and, 177
Topic for telephone questionnaire, 153–154
Toronto Stock Exchange, competitive benchmarking at, 323
Total quality, consultants' commitment to, 63
Tracking analysis, 230–237
  cross-tabulations and, 230–232
  frequency distribution and, 232–233
  means and standard deviations and, 233–234
  motivational issues and, 236–237
  verbatim comments and, 235–236
Training for complaint handling, 395–397

U
Undeclared pretests, 178–180
Unions, gain sharing and, 278
Users of data, 21–22

V
Validity
  questionnaire design and, 99–104
  research design and, 37–38
Verbatim comments, tracking analysis and, 235–236
Volatility of attitudes, questionnaire design and, 97

W
Warranties as source for attribute identification, 69
Weaknesses, competitive, measurement of, as objective, 25–26
Work groups
  autonomous, as intrinsic reward, 261–263
  high-involvement, 426–427